HARDPRESS.NET
HOME OF HARD-TO-FIND BOOKS

Letters, Speeches, Charges, Advices, &C. of
Francis Bacon ...
by Francis Bacon

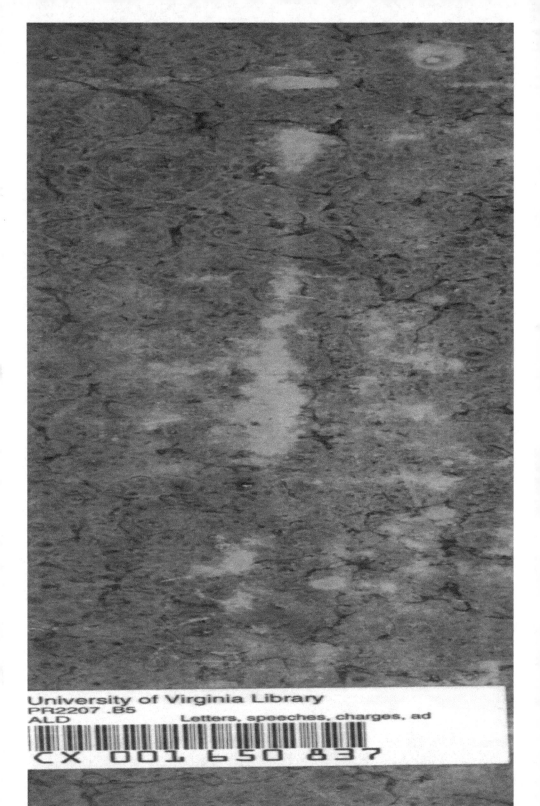

1706 176

Comps

LETTERS,

SPEECHES, CHARGES,

ADVICES, &c.

OF

FRANCIS BACON,

LORD VISCOUNT ST. ALBAN,

LORD CHANCELLOR OF ENGLAND;

Now first published

By THOMAS BIRCH, D.D.

Chaplain to her Royal Highness the Princess AMELIA,

AND

Secretary to the ROYAL SOCIETY.

LONDON,

Printed for ANDREW MILLAR in the Strand.
MDCCLXIII.

1763

To the Honourable

CHARLES YORKE,

Attorney General to his Majesty.

S I R,

THE gratitude, which I owe you for the honour, and other important advantages of your friendſhip, hath often made me wiſh for an opportunity of making you ſome return equal, in any degree, to your

A 2   merit,

merit, and my own obligations. It was therefore a very agreeable incident to me, when by means of your noble brother, the Lord Vifcount Royfton, always attentive to inlarge the fund of hiftory, as well as to encourage and reward every attempt in favour of literature in general, there was put into my hands a volume of original papers of the great Lord Bacon. This volume was, at his Lordfhip's requeft, readily intrufted with me by his Grace the Lord Archbifhop of Canterbury, whofe zeal for the advancement of ufeful learning of all kinds bears a juft proportion to that, which he has fhewn, in every ftation of the church filled by him, for the fupport of religion, and for, what is the moft perfect fyftem of its principles, laws, and fanctions, Chriftianity.

From

DEDICATION.

From the long acquaintance, with which I have been favoured by you, and the frequent converfations, which we have had upon fubjects, foreign to the profeffion, which you fo much adorn, I well knew your high veneration for the writings of Bacon, and your thorough knowledge of the moft abftrufe of them. Having therefore, with an application little lefs than that of decyphering, tranfcribed from the firft draughts, and digefted into order, a collection of his letters, little inferior in number, and much fuperior in contents, to what the world hath hitherto feen, intermixed with other papers of his of an important nature, I could not doubt, but that the publifhing of them would be no lefs acceptable to you, than, I perfuade my-felf, they will be to the public. For it is fcarce to be imagined, but that the bringing to light, from obfcurity and

A 3 obli-

oblivion, the remains of fo eminent a perfon, will be thought an acquifition not inferior to the difcovery (if the ruins of Herculanum fhould afford fuch a treafure) of a new fet of the epiftles of Cicero, whom our immortal country-man moft remarkably refembled as an orator, a philofopher, a writer, a law-yer, and a ftatefman. The commu-nication of them to the public ap-pearing to me a duty to it and the memory of the author, to whom could I, feparately from the confidera-tion of all perfonal connexions and in-ducements, fo juftly prefent them, as to him, whom every circumftance of propriety, and conformity of character, in the moft valuable part of it, pointed out to me for that purpofe? Similarity of genius; the fame extent of knowledge in the laws of our own and other coun-tries, inriched and adorned with all the

ftores

DEDICATION.

stores of ancient and modern learning; the same eloquence at the bar and in the senate; an equal force of writing, shewn in a single work indeed, and composed at a very early age, but decisive of a grand question of law and sanction of government, the grounds of which had never before been stated with due precision; and the most successful discharge of the same offices of King's Council and Solicitor and Attorney General.

These reasons, Sir, give your name an unquestionable right to be prefixed to these posthumous pieces. And I hope, while I am performing this act of justice, I may be excused the ambition of preserving my own name, by uniting it with those of Bacon and Yorke.

Your delicacy here restrains me from indulging myself farther in the language, which truth and esteem would dictate.

But

DEDICATION.

But I muſt be allowed to add a wiſh, in which every good man and lover of his country will join with me, that as there now remains but one ſtep for you to complete that courſe of public ſervice and glory, in which you have ſo cloſely followed your illuſtrious father, he, happy in the moſt important circumſtance of human life, the characters and fortunes of his children,

——*longo ordine Nati,*
Clari omnes patriá pariter Virtute ſuáque,

may live to ſee you poſſeſſed of that high ſtation, which himſelf filled for almoſt twenty years, with a reputation ſuperior to all the efforts of envy or party. Nor is it leſs to his honour, (and may it be your's at a very diſtant period) that, though he thought proper to retire from that ſtation in the full vigour of his abilities, he ſtill continues to exert them in

3   a more

DEDICATION.

a more private fituation, for the general benefit of his country; enjoying in it the nobleft reward of his fervices, an unequalled authority, founded on the acknowledged concurrence of the greateft capacity, experience, and integrity.

I am,

SIR,

Your moft obliged

and moft devoted

humble fervant,

London,
June 1, 1762.

Thomas Birch.

PREFACE.

AS the reader will undoubtedly have some curiosity about the history of the transmission of these papers, now presented to him at the distance of an hundred and forty years from the date of most of them, though the hand of the incomparable writer is too conspicuous in them to admit of any suspicion of their genuineness; it will be proper here to give him some information upon that subject. Dr. Thomas Tenison is known to have been the editor of the *Baconiana*, published at London 1679, though he added only the initial letters of his name *to the account of all the Lord Bacon's works* (a), subjoined to that collection. He had been an intimate friend of, and fellow of the same college (b) with, Mr. William Rawley, only son of Dr. William Rawley, chaplain to the Lord Chancellor Bacon, and employed, by his Lordship, as publisher of most of his works.

(a) This *account* is dated Nov. the 30th, 1678.
(b) Benet in the university of Cambridge.

Dr.

PREFACE.

Dr. Rawley dying in the 79th year of his age, June the 18th 1667, near a year after his son (c); his executor, Mr. John Rawley, put into the hands of his friend Dr. Tenifon thefe papers of Lord Bacon, which compofed the *Baconiana*; and, probably, at the fame time, prefented to him all the reft of his Lordfhip's manufcripts, which Dr. Rawley had been poffeffed of, but did not think proper to make public. The reafons of his referve appear from Dr. Tenifon's *account (d)* cited above, to have been, " that " he judged fome papers touching *matters of* " *ftate* to tread too near to the heels of truth, " and to the times of the perfons concerned : " and that he thought his Lordfhip's *letters* " concerning his fall might be injurious to " his honour, and caufe the old wounds of it " to bleed anew." But this is a delicacy, which, though fuitable to the age in which Dr. Rawley lived, and to the relation, under which he had ftood to his noble patron, ought to have no force in other times and circumftances, nor ever to be too much indulged to the prejudice of the rights of hiftorical truth.

Dr. Tenifon being, foon after the publication of the *Baconiana*, removed from the more private ftation of a country living to the vicarage of St. Martin's in the fields, Weftminfter, and,

(c) who was buried the 3d of July, 1666.
(d) p. 81.

after

PREFACE.

after the Revolution, advanced to the Bishopric
of Lincoln, and at last to the Archbishopric of
Canterbury, had scarce leisure, if he had been
inclined, to select more of the papers of his ad-
mired Bacon. These therefore, with the rest
of his manuscripts, not already deposited in the
library at Lambeth, were left by him in his
last will, dated the 11th of April 1715, to
his chaplain, Dr. Edmund Gibson, then Rector
of Lambeth, and afterwards successively Bishop
of Lincoln and London, and to Mr. (afterwards
Dr.) Benjam Ibbot, who had succeeded Dr.
Gibson as Library-Keeper to his Grace. Dr.
Ibbot dying (e) many years before Bishop Gibson, the whole collection of Archbishop Tenison's papers came under the disposition of that
Bishop, who directed his two executors, the
late Dr. Bettesworth, Dean of the Arches, and
his eldest son, George Gibson, Esq; to deposite
them, with the addition of many others of his
own collecting, in the manuscript library at
Lambeth : and accordingly, after his Lordship's
death, which happened on the 6th of Sept.
1748, all these manuscripts were delivered by
his said executors to Archbishop Herring, on
the 21st of October of that year, and placed in
the library on the 23d of February following.
But as they lay undigested in bundles, and in
that condition were neither convenient for use,

(e) the 11th of April, 1725.

nor

nor secure from damage, his Grace the present Archbishop directed them to be methodized and bound up in volumes with proper indexes, which was done by his learned librarian, Andrew Coltee Ducarel, LL. D. Fellow of the Royal and Antiquarian Societies, to whose knowledge, industry, and love of history and antiquities, the valuable library of manuscripts of the Archiepiscopal See of Canterbury is highly indebted for the order, in which it is now arranged; and by whose obliging and communicating temper it is rendered generally useful. Bishop Gibson's collection, including what is the chief part of it, that of Archbishop Tenison, fills fourteen large volumes in folio. The eighth of these consists merely of Lord Bacon's papers.

Of them principally, the work, which I now offer the public, is formed; nor has any paper been admitted into it that had been published before, except two of Lord Bacon's letters, which having been disguised and mutilated in all former impressions, were thought proper to be reprinted here, together with two other letters of his Lordship; one on the remarkable case of Peacham, the other accompanying his present to King James I. of his *Novum Organum*. These letters I was unwilling to omit, because the collection, in which they have lately appear-

PREFACE.

appeared, intitled by the very learned and ingenious editor, Sir David Dalrymple, Bart. *Memorials and Letters relating to the History of Britain in the reign of James the First, published from the Originals,* at Glasgow 1762, in 8vo, is likely to be much less known in England, from the smallness of the number of printed copies, than it deserves.

The general rule, which I have prescribed myself, of publishing only what is new, restrained me from adding those letters written in the earlier part of Mr. Francis Bacon's life, which I had before published from the originals, found among the papers of his brother Antony, in the *Memoirs of the Reign of Queen Elizabeth, from the Year* 1581 *to her death.*

The example of the greatest men, in preserving in their editions of the classics the smallest remains of their writings, will be a full justification of my industry in collecting and inserting even the fragments of a writer equal to the most valuable of the ancients. Nor will the candid and intelligent object to the least considerable of the Duke of Buckingham's letters, since they acquire an importance from the rank and character of the writer, as well as from their carrying on the series of his correspondence, acquainting us with new facts, or ascertaining

PREFACE.

taining old ones with additional evidence and circumſtances, and ſhewing the extent of that authority and influence, which his ſituation, as a favourite, gave him in all parts of the government, even as high as the ſeat of juſtice itſelf.

ERRATA.

P. 6. l. 24. *anchor*, as it is in the original, ſhould probably be *anchorite*.

112. paragr. 3. l. 1. for *Provoſt's* r. *Provoſts*.

218. l. 10. for *Vanbore* r. *Vanlore*.

226. l. 5. for *manes* r. *manos*.

291. note *(t)* inſert, at the beginning of that note, *Either* John Murray, *of the King's Bed-Chamber, mentioned* above, p. 45, note *(r)*; or [Thomas, &c.]

336. l. 16. for *eximendi* r. *erigendi*.

L E T-

SUPPLEMENT

TO

LETTERS, SPEECHES, &c.

OF

FRANCIS BACON,

Lord Viscount ST. ALBAN.

A

To Sir THOMAS EGERTON, *Lord Keeper of the Great Seal* (a).

May it please your honourable good Lordship,

OF your Lordship's honourable disposition, both generally and to me, I have that belief, as what I think, I am not afraid to speak; and what I would speak, I am not afraid to write. And therefore I have thought to commit to letter some matter, whereunto [which] I have been [conceived] led [into the same] by two motives; the one, the consideration of my own estate; the other, the appetite, which I have to give your Lordship some evidence of the thoughtful and voluntary desire, which is in me, to merit well of your most honourable Lordship: which desire in me hath been bred chiefly by the consent I have to your great virtue come in good time to do this state pleasure; and next by your loving courses held towards me, especially in your nomination and inablement of me long since to the solicitor's place, as your Lordship best knows. Which your two honourable friendships I esteem so much [in so great sort,] as your countenance and favour in my practise, which are somewhat to my poverty; yet I count them not the best [greatest] part of the obligation, wherein I stand bound to you.

And now, my Lord, I pray you right humbly, that you will vouchsafe your honourable licence and

(a) From the original draught in the library of Queen's College, Oxford, Arch. D. 2. the copy of which was communicated to me by Thomas Tyrwhytt, Esq; clerk of the Honourable House of Commons. Sir William Dugdale in his *Baronage of England*, Vol. II. p. 438, has given two short passages of this letter transcribed by him from the unpublished original.

patience,

patience, that I may exprefs to you, what in a doubtful liberty I have thought fit, partly by way of
praying your help, and partly by way of offering
my good will; partly again by way of pre-occupat-
ing your conceipt, left you may in fome things
miftake.

My eftate, to confefs a truth to your Lordfhip,
is weak and indebted, and needeth comfort; for
both my father, though I think I had greateft
part in his love to all his children, yet in his wifdom ferved me in as a laft comer; and myfelf, in
mine own induftry, have rather referred and af-
pired to virtue than to gain: whereof I am not
yet wife enough to repent me. But the while,
whereas Solomon fpeaketh, that *want cometh* firft
like a way-faring man, and after like *an armed man*,
I muft acknowledge to your Lordfhip myfelf to [be]
in primo gradu; for it ftealeth upon me. But for
the fecond, that it fhould not be able to be refifted,
I hope in God I am not in that cafe; for the preventing whereof, as I do depend upon God's providence all in all, fo in the fame his providence I fee
opened unto me three not unlikely expectations of
help : the one my practife ; the other fome proceeding in the Queen's fervice ; the third [the]
place I have in reverfion; which, as it ftandeth now
unto me, is but like another man's ground reaching
upon my houfe, which may mend my profpect, but
it doth not fill my barn.

For my practife, it prefuppofeth my health, which,
if I fhould judge of, as a man that judgeth of a
fair morrow by a fair evening, I might have reafon
to value well. But myfelf having this error of
mind, that I am apter to conclude in every thing of
change from the prefent tenfe than of a continuance,
do make no fuch appointment. Befides, I am not fo
far deceived in myfelf, but that I know very well,
and I think your Lordfhip is *major corde*, and in
your

your wisdom you note it more deeply than I can in myself, that in practising the law, I play not all my best game, which maketh me accept it with a *nisi quid potius*, as the best of my fortune, and a thing agreeable to better gifts than mine, but not to mine.

For my placing, your Lordship best knows, that when I was much dejected with her Majesty's strange dealing towards me, it pleased you of your singular favour so far to comfort and encourage me, as to hold me worthy to be excited to think of succeeding your Lordship in your second place (*b*); signifying in your plainness, that no man should better content yourself: which your exceeding favour you have not since varied from, both in pleading the like signification into the hands of some of my best friends, and also in an honourable and answerable nomination and commendation of me to her Majesty. Wherein I hope your Lordship, if it please you to call to mind, did find me neither overweening in presuming too much upon it, nor much deceived in my opinion of the event for the continuing it still in yourself, nor sleepy in doing some good offices to the same purpose.

Now upon this matter I am to make your Lordship three humble requests; which had need be very reasonable, coming so many together. First, that your Lordship will hold and make good your wishes towards me in your own time; for no other I mean it; and in thankfulness thereof, I will present your Lordship with the fairest flower of my estate; though it yet bear no fruit; and that is the poor reversion, which of her Majesty's gift I hold;

(*b*) The master-ship of the Rolls; which office the Lord Keeper held till the Lord Bruce was advanced to it, May 18, 1603.

in the which I shall be no less willing Mr. John Egerton (c), if it seem good to you, should succeed me in that, than I would be willing to succeed your Lordship in the other place.

My next humble request is, that your Lordship would believe a protestation, which is, that if there be now against the next term, or hereafter (for a little bought knowledge of the court teacheth me to foresee these things) any heaving or palting at that place, upon mine honesty and troth, my spirit is not in, nor with it; I, for my part, being resolutely resolved not to proceed one pace or degree in this matter but with your Lordship's foreknowledge and approbation. The truth of which protestation will best appear, if by any accident, which I look not for, I shall receive any further strength. For, as I now am, your Lordship may impute it only to policy alone in me, that being without present hope myself, I would be content the matter sleep.

My third humble petition to your Lordship is, that you would believe an intelligence, and not take it for a fiction in court; of which manner I like Cicero's speech well, who writing to Appius Claudius saith; *Sin autem quæ tibi ipsi in mentem veniant, ea aliis tribuere soles, inducis genus sermonis in amicitiam minime liberale.* But I do assure your Lordship, it is both true and fresh, and from a person of that sort, as having some glimpse of it before, I now

(c) second son of the Lord Keeper, whose eldest son Sir Thomas, knighted at Cadiz upon the taking it in 1596 by the Earl of Essex, died in Ireland, whither he attended that Earl in 1599, as Mr. John Egerton likewise did, and was knighted by his Lordship, and at the coronation of King James was made knight of the Bath. He succeeded his father in the titles of Baron of Ellesmere and Viscount Brackley, and on the 17th of May, 1617, was created Earl of Bridgewater.

rest

reſt fully confirmed in it : and it is this, that there ſhould be a plot laid of ſome ſtrength between Mr. Attorney General (*d*), and Mr. Attorney of the Wards (*e*), for the one's remove to the Rolls, and the other to be drawn to his place. Which, to be plain with your Lordſhip, I do apprehend much. For firſt, I know Mr. Attorney General, whatſoever he pretendeth or proteſteth to your Lordſhip, or any other, doth ſeek it ; and I perceive well by his dealing towards his beſt friends, to whom he oweth moſt, how perfectly he hath conned the adage of *proximus egomet mihi :* and then I ſee no man ripened for the place of the Rolls in competition with Mr. Attorney General. And laſtly, Mr. Attorney of the Wards being noted for a pregnant and ſtirring man, the objection of any hurt her Majeſty's buſineſs may receive in her cauſes by the drawing up of Mr. Attorney General, will wax cold. And yet neverthelefs, if it may pleaſe your Lordſhip to pardon me ſo to ſay, of the ſecond of thoſe placings I think with ſome ſcorn ; only I commend the knowledge hereof to your Lordſhip's wiſdom, as a matter not to be neglected.

And now laſtly, my honourable good Lord, for my third poor help, I account [it] will do me ſmall good, except there be a heave ; and that is this place of the Star-Chamber. I do confeſs ingenuouſly to your Lordſhip, out of my love to the publick, beſides my particular, that I am of opinion, that rules without examples will do little good, at leaſt not to continue ; but that there is ſuch a concordance between the time to come, and the time paſſed, as there will be no reforming the one

(*d*) Coke.
(*e*) Probably Sir Thomas Heſkett, who died 15 October 1605, and has a monument erected to his memory in Weſtminſter-Abbey.

with-

without informing of the other. And I will not, as the proverb is, spit against the wind, but yield so far to a general opinion, as there was never a more * * or particular example. But I submit it wholly to your honourable grave consideration; only I humbly pray you to conceive, that it is not any money, that I have borrowed of Mr. Mills, nor any gratification I receive for my aid, that makes me shew myself any ways in it, but simply a desire to preserve the rights of the office, as far as it is meet and incorrupt; and secondly his importunity, who nevertheless, as far as I see, taketh a course to bring this matter in question to his farther disadvantage, and to be principal in his own harm. But if it be true, that I have heard of more than one or two, that besides this fore-running in taking of fees, there are other deep corruptions, which in an ordinary course are intended to be proved against him; surely, for my part, I am not superstitious, as I will not take any shadow of it, nor labor to stop it, since it is a thing medicinable for the office of the realm. And then if the place by such an occasion or otherwise should come in possession, the better to testify my affection to your Lordship, I should be glad, as I offered it to your Lordship by way of [surrender] so in this case to offer it by way of joint-patency, in nature of a reversion, which, as it is now, there wanteth no good will in me to offer, but that both in that condition it is not worth the offering; and besides, I know not whether my necessity may inforce me to sell it away; which, if it were locked in by any reversion or joint-patency, I were disabled to do for my relief.

Thus your Lordship may perceive how assured a persuasion I have of your love towards me, and care of me; which hath made me so freely to communicate of my poor state with your Lordship, as I could have done to my honourable father, if he

had

had lived; which I most humbly pray your Lordship may be private to yourself, to whom I commit it to be used to such purpose, as in your wisdom and honourable love and favour should seem good. And so humbly craving pardon, I commend your Lordship to the divine preservation.

At your Lordship's honourable

commandment humbly and particularly.

In Henricum *Principem Walliæ Elogium* Francisci Baconi (a).

HENRICUS primogenitus Regis Magnæ Britanniæ, Princeps Walliæ, antea spe beatus, nunc memoriâ felix, diem suum obiit 6. Novemb. anno 1612. Is magno totius regni luctu et desiderio extinctus est, utpote adolescens, qui animos hominum nec offendisset nec satiasset. Excitaverat autem propter bonam indolem multiplices apud plurimos omnium ordinum spes, nec ob brevitatem vitæ frustravere. Illud imprimis accessit, quod in causâ religionis firmus vulgo habebatur: prudentioribus quoque hoc animo penitus insiderat, adversus insidias conjurationum (cui malo ætas nostra vix remedium reperit) patri eum instar præsidii et scuti fuisse, adeo ut et religionis et regis apud populum amor in eum redundaret, et in æstimationem jacturæ meritò annumeraretur. Erat corpore validus et erectus, staturâ mediocri,

(a) Harl. MSS. Vol. 1893. fol. 75. It seems to me no improbable supposition, that this character was intended to be sent to Thuanus, in order to be inserted in his excellent history, if he should have continued it to the year 1612, whereas it reached only to 1607.

decorâ

decorâ membrorum compage, inceſſu regio, facie oblongâ et in maciem inclinante, habitu plenior, vultu compoſito, oculorum motu magis ſedato quam forti. Inerant quoque et in fronte ſeveritatis ſigna, et in ore nonnihil faſtûs. Sed tamen ſi quis ultra exteriora illa penetraverat, et eum obſequio debito et ſermone tempeſtivo deliniverat, utebatur eo benigno et facili, ut alius longè videretur colloquio quam aſpectu, talisque prorſus erat, qui famam ſui excitaret moribus diſſimilem. Laudis et gloriæ fuit procul dubio appetens, et ad omnem ſpeciem boni et auram decoris commovebatur; quod adoleſcenti pro virtutibus eſt. Nam et arma ei in honore erant ac viri militares; quin et ipſe quiddam bellicum ſpirabat; et magnificentiæ operum (licet pecuniæ alioquin ſatis parcus) deditus erat : amator inſuper antiquitatis et artium. Literis quoque plus honoris attribuit quam temporis. In moribus ejus nihil laudandum magis fuit, quam quod in omni genere officiorum probè inſtitutus credebatur et congruus : filius Regi patri mirè obſequens, etiam reginam multo cultu demerebat, erga fratrem indulgens; ſororem verò unicè amabat, quam etiam (quantum potuit virilis forma ad eximiam virginalem pulchritudinem collata) referebat. Etiam magiſtri et educatores pueritiæ ejus (quod rarò fieri ſolet) magnâ in gratiâ apud eum manſerant. Sermone verò obſequii idem exactor et memor. Denique in quotidiano vitæ genere, et aſſignatione horarum ad ſingula vitæ munera, magis quam pro ætate conſtans atque ordinatus. Affectus ei inerant non nimium vehementes, et potius æquales quam magni. Etenim de rebus amatoriis mirum in illâ ætate ſilentium, ut prorſus lubricum illud adoleſcentiæ ſuæ tempus in tantâ fortunâ, et valetudine ſatis proſperâ, abſque aliquâ inſigni notâ amorum tranſigeret. Nemo reperiebatur in aulâ ejus apud eum præpotens, aut in animo ejus validus : quin et

studia

ſtudia ipſa, quibus capiebatur maximè, potius tempora patiebantur quàm exceſſus, et magis repetita
erant per vices, quam quod extaret aliquod unum,
quod reliqua ſuperaret et compeſceret, ſive ea mode-
ratio fuit, ſive in naturâ non admodum præcoci, ſed
lentè matureſcente, non cernebantur adhuc quæ
prævalitura erant.   Ingenio certè pollebat, eratque
et curioſus ſatis et capax, ſed ſermone tardior et
tanquam impeditus : tamen ſi quis diligenter ob-
ſervaverat ea, quæ ab eo proferebantur, ſive quæ-
ſtionis vim obtinebant, ſive ſententiæ, ad rem om-
nino erant, et captum non vulgarem arguebant; ut in
illâ loquendi tarditate et raritate judicium ejus magis
ſuſpenſum videretur et anxium, quam infirmum aut
hebes.   Interim audiendi miris modis patiens, etiam
in negotiis, quæ in longitudinem porrigebantur ;
idque cum attentione et ſine tædio, ut rarò animo
peregrinaretur aut feſſâ mente aliquid ageret, ſed
ad ea, quæ dicebantur aut agebantur, animum ad-
verteret atque applicaret; quod magnam ei (ſi vita
ſuppetiiſſet) prudentiam ſpondebat.   Certe in illius
principis naturâ plurima erant obſcura, neque judicio
cujuſpiam patefacienda, ſed tempore, quod ei præ-
reptum eſt.   Attamen quæ apparebant, optima erant,
quod famæ ſatis eſt.   Mortuus eſt ætatis ſuæ anno
decimo nono ex febri contumaci, quæ ubique à
magnis et inſulanis fere inſolitis ſiccitatibus ac fer-
voribus orta per æſtatem populariter graſſabatur,
ſed raro funere ; dein ſub autumnum erat facta
lethalior.   Addidit fama atrocior (ut ille (*b*) ait) erga
dominantium exitus ſuſpicionem veneni.   Sed cum
nulla ejus rei extarent indicia, præſertim in ventri-
culo, quod præcipuè a veneno pati ſolet, is ſermo
citò evanuit.

(*b*) Tacit. Annal. l. iv. 11.

The

The following Tranſlation is an attempt, for the ſake of the Engliſh Reader, to give the ſenſe of the original, without pretending to reach the force and conciſeneſs of expreſſion peculiar to the great Writer as well as to the Roman Language.

HENRY Prince of Wales, eldeſt ſon of the King of Great-Britain, happy in the hopes conceived of him, and now happy in his memory, died on the 6th of Nov. 1612, to the extreme concern and regret of the whole kingdom, being a youth, who had neither offended nor ſatiated the minds of men. He had by the excellence of his diſpoſition excited high expectations among great numbers of all ranks; nor had through the ſhortneſs of his life diſappointed them. One capital circumſtance added to theſe was the eſteem, in which he was commonly held, of being firm to the cauſe of religion : and men of the beſt judgment were fully perſuaded, that his life was a great ſupport and ſecurity to his father from the danger of conſpiracies; an evil, againſt which our age has ſcarce found a remedy; ſo that the people's love of religion and the King overflowed to the prince; and this conſideration deſervedly heightened the ſenſe of the loſs of him. His perſon was ſtrong and erect; his ſtature of a middle ſize; his limbs well made; his gait and deportment majeſtic; his face long and inclining to leanneſs; his habit of body full; his look grave, and the motion of his eyes rather compoſed than ſpirited. In his countenance were ſome marks of ſeverity, and in his air ſome appearance of haughtineſs. But whoever looked beyond theſe outward circumſtances, and addreſſed and ſoftened him with a due reſpect and ſeaſonable diſcourſe, found the prince to be gracious and eaſy; ſo that he ſeemed wholly different in converſation from what he was in appearance,

ance, and in fact raifed in others an opinion of himfelf very unlike what his manner would at firft have
fuggefted. He was unqueftionably ambitious of commendation and glory, and was ftrongly affected by
every appearance of what is good and honourable;
which in a young man is to be confidered as virtue.
Arms and military men were highly valued by him;
and he breathed himfelf fomething warlike. He was
much devoted to the magnificence of buildings and
works of all kinds, though in other refpects rather
frugal; and was a lover both of antiquity and arts.
He fhewed his efteem of learning in general more
by the countenance, which he gave to it, than by the
time, which he fpent in it. His conduct in refpect
of morals did him the utmoft honour; for he was
thought exact in the knowledge and practice of
every duty. His obedience to the King his father
was wonderfully ftrict and exemplary: towards the
Queen he behaved with the higheft reverence: to
his brother he was indulgent; and had an intire affection for his fifter, whom he refembled in perfon
as much as that of a young man could the beauty of
a virgin. The inftructors of his younger years (which
rarely happens) continued high in his favour. In
converfation he both expected a proper decorum,
and practifed it. In the daily bufinefs of life, and
the allotment of hours for the feveral offices of it,
he was more conftant and regular than is ufual at
his age. His affections and paffions were not ftrong,
but rather equal than warm. With regard to that
of love, there was a wonderful filence, confidering
his age, fo that he paffed that dangerous time of
his youth in the higheft fortune, and in a vigorous
ftate of health, without any remarkable imputation
of gallantry. In his court no perfon was obferved
to have any afcendant over him, or ftrong intereft
with him: and even the ftudies, with which he was
moft delighted, had rather proper times affigned
them,

them, than were indulged to excefs, and were rather repeated in their turns, than that any one kind
of them had the preference of, and controlled the
reft ; whether this arofe from the moderation of his
temper, and that in a genius not very forward, but
ripening by flow degrees, it did not yet appear what
would be the prevailing object of his inclination. He
had certainly ftrong parts, and was endued with both
curiofity and capacity ; but in fpeech he was flow,
and in fome meafure hefitating. But whoever dili-
gently obferved what fell from him either by way
of queftion or remark, faw it to be full to the purpofe,
and expreffive of no common genius. So that under
that flownefs and infrequency of difcourfe, his judgment had more the appearance of fufpence and fo-
licitude to determine rightly, than of weaknefs and
want of apprehenfion. In the mean time he was
wonderfully patient in hearing, even in bufinefs of
the greateft length ; and this with unwearied attention, fo that his mind feldom wandered from the
fubject, or feemed fatigued, but he applied himfelf
wholly to what was faid or done : which (if his life
had been lengthened) promifed a very fuperior degree of knowledge. There were indeed in the
prince fome things obfcure, and not to be difcovered by the fagacity of any perfon, but by time only,
which was denied him ; but what appeared were
excellent, which is fufficient for his fame.

He died in the 19th year of his age, of an obfti-
nate fever, which during the fummer, through the
exceffive heat and drynefs of the feafon, unufual
to iflands, had been epidemical, though not fatal,
but in autumn became more mortal. Fame, which,
as Tacitus fays, is more tragical with refpect to
the deaths of princes, added a fufpicion of poifon :
but as no figns of this appeared, efpecially in his
ftomach, which ufes to be chiefly affected by poifon,
this report foon vanifhed.

2.

To the Reverend UNIVERSITY *of* OXFORD (*a*).

AMONGST the gratulations I have received, none are more welcome and agreeable to me than your letters, wherein the lefs I acknowledge of thofe attributes you give me, the more I muft acknowledge of your affection, which bindeth me no lefs to you, that are profeffors of learning, than mine own dedication doth to learning itfelf. And therefore you have no need to doubt, but I will emulate (as much as in me is) towards you the merits of him that is gone, by how much the more I take myfelf to have more propriety in the principal motive thereof. And for the equality you write of, I fhall by the grace of God (far as may concern me) hold the balance as equally between the two Univerfities, as I fhall hold the balance of other juftice between party and party. And yet in both cafes I muft meet with fome inclinations of affection, which neverthelefs fhall not carry me afide. And fo I commend you to God's goodnefs.

Your moft loving

Gorhambury,
April 12, 1617.

And affured friend,

Fr. BACON.

(*a*) This and the following letter are from the collections of the late Robert Stephens, Efq; hiftoriographer royal, and John Locker, Efq; deceafed, now in poffeffion of the editor.

To

To the Lord Keeper BACON.

My Lord,

IF your man had been addressed only to me, I should have been careful to have procured him a more speedy dispatch: but now you have found another way of address, I am excused; and since you are grown weary of employing me, I can be no otherwise in being employed. In this business of my brother's, that you overtrouble yourself with, I understand from London by some of my friends, that you have carried yourself with much scorn and neglect both toward myself and friends; which, if it prove true, I blame not you, but myself, who was ever

Your Lordship's assured friend,

[July 1617.] G. BUCKINGHAM.

LETTERS, &c.

OF

Lord Chancellor BACON.

Mr. FRANCIS BACON *to Sir* JOHN PUCKERING,
Lord Keeper of the Great Seal (a).

My Lord,

IT is a great grief unto me, joined with marvell, that her Majefty fhould retain an hard conceit of my fpeeches in parliament *(b)*. It might pleafe her facred Majefty to think what my end fhould be in thofe fpeeches, if it were not duty, and duty alone. I am not fo fimple, but I know the common beaten way to pleafe. And whereas popularity hath been objected, I mufe what care I fhould take to pleafe many, that take a courfe of life to deal with few. On the other fide, her Majefty's grace and particular favour towards me hath been fuch, as I efteem no worldly thing above the comfort to enjoy it, except it be the confcience to deferve it. But if

(*a*) Harl. MSS. Vol. 286. N° 129. fol. 232.
(*b*) on Wednefday the 7th of March, 159$\frac{2}{3}$, upon the three fubfidies demanded of the houfe of commons; to which he affented, but not to the payment of them under fix years, urging the neceffities of the people, the danger of raifing public difcontentment, and the fetting of an evil precedent againft themfelves and their pofterity. See Sir Simonds D'Ewes's Journals, p. 493. He fat in that parliament, which met November 19, 1592, and was diffolved 10 April, 1593, as one of the knights of the fhire for Middlefex.

the

the not seconding of some particular person's opinion shall be presumption, and to differ upon the manner shall be to impeach the end ; it shall teach my devotion not to exceed wishes, and those in silence. Yet notwithstanding (to speak vainly as in grief) it may be her Majesty hath discouraged as good a heart, as ever looked toward her service, and as void of self-love. And so in more grief than I can well express, and much more than I can well dissemble, I leave your Lordship, being as ever,

Your Lordship's intirely devoted, &c.

The first copy of my discourse touching the safety of the Queen's person.

THESE be the principal remedies, I could think of, for extirping the principal cause of those conspiracies, by the breaking the nest of those fugitive traitors, and the filling them full of terror, despair, jealousy, and revolt. And it is true, I thought of some other remedies, which, because in mine own conceit I did not so well allow, I therefore do forbear to express. And so likewise I have thought, and thought again, of the means to stop and divert as well the attempts of violence, as poison, in the performance and execution. But not knowing how my travell may be accepted, being the unwarranted wishes of a private man, I leave ; humbly praying her Majesty's pardon, if in the zeal of my simplicity I have roved at things above my aim.

The first fragments of a discourse, touching intelligence and the safety of the Queen's person.

THE first remedy, in my poor opinion, is that, against which, as I conceive, least exception can be taken, as a thing, without controversy, honourable and

and politic; and that is reputation of good intelligence. I fay not only *good intelligence*, but the *reputation* and *fame* thereof. For I fee, that where booths are fet for watching thievifh places, there is no more robbing: and though no doubt the watchmen many times are afleep, or away; yet that is more than the thief knoweth; fo as the empty booth is ftrength and fafeguard enough. So likewife, if there be fown an opinion abroad, that her Majefty hath much fecret intelligence, and that all is full of fpies and falfe brethren; the fugitives will grow into fuch a mutual jealoufy and fufpicion one of another, as they will not have the confidence to confpire together, not knowing whom to truft; and thinking all practice bootlefs, as that, which is affured to be difcovered. And to this purpofe, to fpeak reverently, as becometh me, as I do not doubt, but thofe honourable counfellors, to whom it doth appertain, do carefully and fufficiently provide and take order, that her Majefty receive good intelligence; fo yet, under correction, methinks it is not done with that glory and note of the world, which was in Mr. Secretary Walfingham's (c) time: and in this cafe, as was faid, *opinio veritate major.*

The fecond remedy I deliver with lefs affurance, as that, which is more removed from the compafs of mine underftanding: and that is, to treat and negotiate with the King of Spain, or Archduke Erneft (d),
who

(c) Who died April 6, 1590. After his death the bufinefs of fecretary of ftate appears to be chiefly done by Mr. Robert Cecil, who was knighted by Queen Elizabeth at Theobald's, about the beginning of June, 1591, and in Auguft following fworn of the privy-council; but not actually appointed fecretary of ftate till July 5, 1596.

(d) Erneft, Archduke of Auftria, fon of the Emperor Maximilian II, and governor of the Low Countries, upon which government he entered in June, 1594; but held it only a fhort time, dying February $\frac{11}{2}$ following. It was probably in purfuance of the advice of Mr. Francis Bacon in this paper, that

who refides in the place, where thefe confpiracies are moft forged, upon the point of the law of nations, upon which kind of points, princes enemies may with honour negotiate, viz. that, contrary to the fame law of nations, and the facred dignity of kings, and the honour of arms, certain of her Majefty's fubjects (if it be not thought meet to impeach any of his minifters) refuged in his dominions, have confpired and practifed affaffination againft her Majefty's perfon.

(e) *The fpeeches drawn up by Mr.* FRANCIS BACON *for the Earl of Effex in a* device (f) *exhibited by his Lordfhip before Queen* ELIZABETH, *on the anniverfary of her acceffion to the throne, November* 17, 1595.

The SQUIRE's *fpeech.*

MOST excellent and moft glorious Queen, give me leave, I befeech your Majefty, to offer my mafter's complaint and petition ; complaint, that coming

Queen Elizabeth fent to the Archduke, in 1594, to complain of the defigns, which had been formed againft her life by the Count de Fuentes, and Don Diego de Ibarra, and other Spanifh minifters concerned in governing the Low Countries after the death of Alexander Duke of Parma in December 1592, and by the Englifh fugitives there ; and to defire him to fignify thofe facts to the King of Spain, in order that he might vindicate his own character, by punifhing his minifters, and delivering up to her fuch fugitives, as were parties in fuch defigns. *Camdeni Annales Eliz. Reginæ*, p. 625. Edit. Lugduni Bat. 1625.

(e) Bifhop Gibfon's Papers, Vol. V. N° 118.

(f) An account of this *device*, which was much applauded, is given by Mr. Rowland Whyte to Sir Robert Sydney, in a letter dated at London, Saturday the 22d of November, 1595, and printed in the *Letters and Memorials of State* of the Sydney Family, Vol. I. p. 362. According to this letter, the Earl of Effex, fome confiderable time before he came himfelf into the Tilt-yard, fent his page with fome fpeech to the Queen, who returned

coming hither to your Majesty's most happy day, he is tormented with the importunity of a melancholy dreaming hermit, a mutinous brain-sick soldier, and a busy tedious secretary. His petition is, that he may be as free as the rest; and, at least while he is here, troubled with nothing but with care how to please and honour you.

returned with her Majesty's glove; and when his lordship came himself, he was met by an old hermit, a secretary of state, a brave soldier, and an esquire. The first presented him with a book of meditations; the second with political discourses; the third with orations of bravely fought battles; the fourth was his own follower, to whom the other three imparted much of their purpose before the Earl came in. "Another, *adds Mr. Whyte*, "devised with him, persuading him to this and that course of "life, according to their inclinations. Comes into the Tilt-yard, "unthought upon, the ordinary post-boy of London, a ragged "villain, all bemired, upon a poor lean jade, galloping and "blowing for life, and delivered the secretary a packet of let- "ters, which he presently offered my Lord of Essex. And with "this dumb shew our eyes were fed for that time. In the after- "supper, before the Queen, they first delivered a well-penned "speech to move this worthy knight to leave his following of "love, and to betake him to heavenly meditation; the secre- "tary's all tending to have him follow matters of state; the "soldier's persuading him to the war: but the squire answered "them all, and concluded with an excellent, but too plain, "English, that this knight would never forsake his mistress's "love, whose virtue made all his thoughts divine; whose wis- "dom taught him all true policy; whose beauty and worth were "at all times able to make him fit to command armies. He "shewed all the defects and imperfections of all their times; "and therefore thought his course of life to be best in serving "his mistress." Mr. Whyte then mentions, that the part of the old *hermit* was performed by him, who at Cambridge played that of *Giraldi*; that Morley acted the *secretary*; and that the *soldier* was represented by him, who acted the *pedant*, and that Mr. Tobie Matthew was the *squire*. "The world, *says Mr.* "*Whyte*, makes many untrue constructions of these speeches, "comparing the hermit and the secretary to two of the lords; "and the soldier to Sir Roger Williams. But the Queen said, "that if she had thought there had been so much said of her, "she would not have been there that night; and so went to "bed."

The

The HERMIT's *speech in the presence.*

THOUGH our ends be diverse, and therefore may be one more just than another ; yet the complaint of this Squire is general, and therefore alike unjust against us all.   Albeit he is angry, that we offer ourselves to his master uncalled, and forgets we come not of ourselves, but as the messengers of self-love, from whom, all that comes, should be well taken. He saith, when we come, we are importunate.   If he mean, that we err in form, we have that of his master, who being a lover, useth no other form of solliciting.   If he will charge us to err in matter, I for my part will presently prove, that I persuade him to nothing but for his own good.   For I wish him to leave turning over the book of fortune, which is but a play for children ; when there be so many books of truth and knowledge, better worthy the revolving; and not fix his view only upon a picture in a little table, when there be so many tables of histories, yea to life, excellent to behold and admire.   Whether he believe me or no, there is no prison to the prison of the thoughts, which are free under the greatest tyrants.   Shall any man make his conceit, as an anchor, mured up with the compass of one beauty or person, that may have the liberty of all contemplation ? Shall he exchange the sweet travelling through the universal variety, for one wearisome and endless round or labyrinth ? Let thy master, Squire, offer his service to the *muses*.   It is long since they received any into their court.   They give alms continually at their gate, that many come to live upon ; but few they have ever admitted into their palace.   There shall he find secrets not dangerous to know ; sides and parties not factious to hold ; precepts and commandments not penal to disobey. The gardens of love, wherein he now placeth himself,

felf, are frefh to day, and fading to-morrow, as the
fun comforts them, or is turned from them. But
the gardens of the mufes keep the privilege of the
golden age; they ever flourifh, and are in league
with time. The monuments of wit furvive the
monuments of power. The verfes of a poet endure without a fyllable loft, while ftates and empires
pafs many periods. Let him not think he fhall defcend; for he is now upon a hill, as a fhip is
mounted upon the ridge of a wave: but that hill
of the mufes is above tempefts, always clear and
calm; a hill of the goodlieft difcovery, that man
can have, being a profpect upon all the errors and
wanderings of the prefent and former times. Yea,
in fome cliff it leadeth the eye beyond the horizon
of time, and giveth no obfcure divinations of times
to come. So that if he will indeed lead *vitam vitalem,*
a life, that unites fafety and dignity, pleafure and
merit; if he will win admiration without envy; if
he will be in the feaft, and not in the throng; in
the light, and not in the heat; let him embrace the
life of ftudy and contemplation. And if he will accept of no other reafon, yet becaufe the gift of the
mufes will enworthy him in love, and where he now
looks on his miftrefs's outfide with the eyes of fenfe,
which are dazzled and amazed, he fhall then behold
her high perfections and heavenly mind with the eyes
of judgement, which grow ftronger by more nearly
and more directly viewing fuch an object.

The SOLDIER's *fpeech.*

SQUIRE, the good old man hath faid well to you;
but I dare fay, thou wouldft be forry to leave to
carry thy mafter's fhield, and to carry his books:
and I am fure thy mafter had rather be a falcon, a
bird of prey, than a finging bird in a cage. The

mufes

mufes are to ferve martial man, to fing their famous actions ; and not to be ferved by them. Then hearken to me.

It is the war, that giveth all fpirits of valour, not only honour, but contentment. For mark, whether ever you did fee a man grown to any ho-nourable commandment in the wars, but whenfoever he gave it over, he was ready to die with melancho-ly ? Such a fweet felicity is in that noble exercife, that he, that hath tafted it thoroughly, is diftafted for all other. And no marvell ; for if the hunter takes fuch folace in his chace ; if the matches and wagers of fport pafs away with fuch fatisfaction and delight ; if the looker on be affected with pleafure in the reprefentation of a feigned tragedy ; think what contentment a man receiveth, when they, that are equal to him in nature, from the hight of info-lency and fury are brought to the condition of a chaced prey ; when a victory is obtained, whereof the victories of games are but counterfeits and fhadows ; and when, in a lively tragedy, a man's enemies are facrificed before his eyes to his fortune.

Then for the dignity of military profeffion, is it not the trueft and perfecteft practice of all virtues ? of wifdom, in difpofing thofe things, which are moft fubject to confufion and accident : of juftice, in continual diftributing rewards : of temperance, in exercifing of the ftraiteft difcipline : of fortitude, in toleration of all labours and abftinence from effemi-nate delights : of conftancy, in bearing and digefting the greateft variety of fortune. So that when all other places and profeffions require but their feveral virtues, a brave leader in the wars muft be accom-plifhed with all. It is the wars, that are the tribunal feat, where the higheft rights and poffeffions are de-cided ; the occupation of kings, the root of nobi-lity, the protection of all eftates. And laftly, lovers never thought their profeffion fufficiently graced, till
                                          they

they have compared it to a warfare. All, that in any other profeſſion can be wiſhed for, is but to live happily : but to be a brave commander in the field, death itſelf doth crown the head with glory. Therefore, Squire, let thy maſter go with me ; and though he be reſolved in the purſuit of his love, let him aſpire to it by the nobleſt means. For ladies count it no honour to ſubdue them with their faireſt eyes, which will be daunted with the fierce encounter of an enemy. And they will quickly diſcern a champion fit to wear their glove from a page not worthy to carry their pantofle. Therefore I ſay again, let him ſeek his fortune in the field, where he may either loſe his love, or find new argument to advance it.

The STATESMAN's *ſpeech.*

SQUIRE, my advice to thy maſter ſhall be as a token wrapped up in words ; but then will it ſhew itſelf fair, when it is unfolded in his actions. To wiſh him to change from one humour to another, were but as if, for the cure of a man in pain, one ſhould adviſe him to lie upon the other ſide, but not enable him to ſtand on his feet. If from a ſanguine delightful humour of love, he turn to a melancholy retired humour of contemplation, or a turbulent boiling humour of the wars ; what doth he but change tyrants ? Contemplation is a dream ; love a trance ; and the humour of war is raving. Theſe be ſhifts of humour, but no reclaiming to reaſon. I debar him not ſtudies nor books, to give him ſtay and variety of conceit, to refreſh his mind, to cover ſloth and indiſpoſition, and to draw to him from thoſe, that are ſtudious, reſpect and commendation. But let him beware, leſt they poſſeſs not too much of his time ; that they abſtract not his judgement from preſent experience, nor make him preſume upon
knowing

knowing much, to apply the lefs. For the wars, I deny him no enterprife, that fhall be worthy in greatnefs, likely in fuccefs, or neceffary in duty; not mixed with any circumftance of jealoufy, but duly laid upon him. But I would not have him take the alarm from his own humour, but from the occafion; and I would again he fhould know an employment from a difcourting. And for his love, let it not difarm his heart within, as it make him too credulous to favours, nor too tender to unkindneffes, nor too apt to depend upon the heart he knows not. Nay, in his demonftration of love, let him not go too far; for thefe feely lovers, when they profefs fuch infinite affection and obligation, they tax themfelves at fo high a rate, that they are ever under arreft. It makes their fervice feem nothing, and every cavil or imputation very great. But what, Squire, is thy mafter's end? If to make the prince happy he ferves, let the inftructions to employ men, the relations of ambaffadors, the treaties between princes, and actions of the prefent time, be the books he reads: let the orations of wife princes, or experimented counfellors in council or parliament, and the final fentences of grave and learned judges in weighty and doubtful caufes, be the lecturers he frequents. Let the holding of affection with confederates without charge, the fruftrating of the attempts of enemies without battles, the intitling of the crown to new poffeffions without fhew of wrong, the filling of the prince's coffers without violence, the keeping of men in appetite without impatience, be the inventions he feeks out. Let policy and matters of ftate be the chief, and almoft the only thing, he intends. But if he will believe *Philautia*, and feek moft his own happinefs, he muft not of them embrace all kinds, but make choice, and avoid all matter of peril, difpleafure, and charge, and turn them over to fome novices, that know not manacles from brace-

lets,

lets, nor burdens from robes. For himſelf, let him
ſet for matters of commodity and ſtrength, though
they be joined with envy. Let him not trouble
himſelf too laboriouſly to ſound into any matter
deeply, or to execute any thing exactly ; but let
himſelf make himſelf cunning rather in the humours
and drifts of perſons, than in the nature of buſineſs
and affairs. Of that it ſufficeth to know only ſo
much, as may make him able to make uſe of other
men's wits, and to make again a ſmooth and pleaſing
report. Let him entertain the propoſition of others,
and ever rather let him have an eye to the circumſtances, than to the matter itſelf ; for then ſhall he
ever ſeem to add ſomewhat of his own : and beſides,
when a man doth not forget ſo much as a circumſtance, men do think his wit doth ſuperabound for
the ſubſtance. In his counſels let him not be confident ; for that will rather make him obnoxious to
the ſucceſs ; but let him follow the wiſdom of ora-
cles, which uttered that, which might ever be applied to the event. And ever rather let him take
the ſide, which is likelieſt to be followed, than that
which is ſoundeſt and beſt, that every thing may
ſeem to be carried by his direction. To conclude,
let him be true to himſelf, and avoid all tedious
reaches of ſtate, that are not merely pertinent to his
particular. And if he will needs purſue his affection,
and go on his courſe, what can ſo much advance
him in his own way ? The merit of war is too out-
wardly glorious to be inwardly grateful : and it is the
exile of his eyes, which looking with ſuch affection
upon the picture, cannot but with infinite contentment
behold the life. But when his miſtreſs ſhall perceive,
that his endeavours are become a true ſupport of
her, a diſcharge of her care, a watchman of her perſon, a ſcholar of her wiſdom, an inſtrument of her
operation, and a conduit of her virtue ; this, with
his diligences, acceſſes, humility, and patience, may

4

move

move him to give her further degrees and approaches to her favour. So that I conclude, I have traced him the way to that, which hath been granted to some few, *amare et sapere*, to love and be wise.

The reply of the Squire.

Wandering Hermit, storming Soldier, and hollow Statesman, the inchanting orators of *Philautia*, which have attempted by your high charms to turn resolved *Erophilus* into a statue deprived of action, or into a vulture attending about dead bodies, or into a monster with a double heart; with infinite assurance, but with just indignation, and forced patience, I have suffered you to bring in play your whole forces. For I would not vouchsafe to combat you one by one, as if I trusted to the goodness of my breath, and not the goodness of my strength, which little needeth the advantage of your severing, and much less of your disagreeing. Therefore, first, I would know of you all what assurance you have of the fruit, whereto you aspire.

You, Father, that pretend to truth and knowledge, how are you assured, that you adore not vain chimæra's and imaginations? that in your high prospect, when you think men wander up and down; that they stand not indeed still in their place? and it is some smoke or cloud between you and them, which moveth, or else the dazzling of your own eyes? Have not many, which take themselves to be inward counsellors with nature, proved but idle believers, which told us tales, which were no such matter? And, Soldier, what security have you for these victories and garlands, which you promise to yourself? Know you not of many, which have made provision of laurel for the victory, and have been fain to exchange it with cypress for the funeral? of many,

which

which have befpoken fame to found their triumphs, and have been glad to pray her to fay nothing of them, and not to difcover them in their flights?

Corrupt Statefman, you that think by your engines and motions to govern the wheel of fortune; do you not mark, that clocks cannot be long in temper? that jugglers are no longer in requeft, when their tricks and flights are once perceived? Nay, do you not fee, that never any man made his own cunning and practice (without religion and moral honefty) his foundation, but he overbuilt himfelf, and in the end made his houfe a windfall? But give ear now to the comparifon of my mafter's condition, and acknowledge fuch a difference, as is betwixt the melting hail-ftone and the folid pearl. Indeed it feemeth to depend, as the globe of the earth feemeth to hang, in the air; but yet it is firm and ftable in itfelf. It is like a cube, or a die-form, which tofs it or throw it any way, it ever lighteth upon a fquare. Is he denied the hopes of favours to come? He can refort to the remembrance of contentments paft. Deftiny cannot repeal that, which is paft. Doth he find the acknowledgement of his affection fmall? He may find the merit of his affection the greater. Fortune cannot have power over that, which is within. Nay, his falls are like the falls of Antæus; they renew his ftrength. His clouds are like the clouds of harveft, which makes the fun break forth with greater force. His wanes are changes like the moon's, whofe globe is all light towards the fun, when it is all dark towards the world; fuch is the excellency of her nature, and of his eftate. Attend, you beadfman of the mufes, you take your pleafure in a wildernefs of variety; but it is but of fhadows. You are as a man rich in pictures, medals, and cryftals. Your mind is of the water, which taketh all forms and impreffions, but is weak of fubftance. Will you compare fhadows with bodies, picture

with

with life, variety of many beauties with the peerless excellency of one? the element of water with the element of fire? And such is the comparison between knowledge and love.

Come out, Man of war; you must be ever in noise. You will give laws, and advance force, and trouble nations, and remove land-marks of kingdoms, and hunt men, and pen tragedies in blood: and that, which is worst of all, make all the virtues accessary to bloodshed. Hath the practice of force so deprived you of the use of reason, as that you will compare the interruption of society with the perfection of society? the conquest of bodies with the conquest of spirits? the terrestrial fire, which destroyeth and dissolveth, with the celestial fire, which quickeneth and giveth life? And such is the comparison between the soldier and the lover.

And as for you, untrue Politique, but truest bondman to *Philautia*, you, that presume to bind occasion, and to overwork fortune, I would ask you but one question. Did ever any lady, hard to please, or disposed to exercise her lover, injoin him so good tasks and commandments, as *Philautia* exacteth of you? While your life is nothing but a continual acting upon a stage; and that your mind must serve your humour, and yet your outward person must serve your end; so as you carry in one person two several servitudes to contrary masters. But I will leave you to the scorn of that mistress, whom you undertake to govern; that is, to fortune, to whom *Philautia* hath bound you. And yet, you commissioner of *Philautia*, I will proceed one degree farther: if I allowed both of your assurance, and of your values, as you have set them, may not my master enjoy his own felicity; and have all yours for advantage? I do not mean, that he should divide himself in both pursuits, as in your feigning tales towards the conclusion you did yield him; but because

all

all thefe are in the hands of his miftrefs more fully to beftow, than they can be attained by your addreffes, knowledge, fame, fortune. For the *mufes*, they are tributary to her Majefty for the great liberties they have enjoyed in her kingdom, during her moft flourifhing reign ; in thankfulnefs whereof, they have adorned and accomplifhed her Majefty with the gifts of all the fifters. What library can prefent fuch a ftory of great actions, as her Majefty carrieth in her royal breaft by the often return of this happy day ? What worthy author, or favourite of the mufes, is not familiar with her ? Or what language, wherein the mufes have ufed to fpeak, is unknown to her ? Therefore, the hearing of her, the obferving of her, the receiving inftructions from her, may be to *Erophilus* a lecture exceeding all dead monuments of the mufes. For *Fame*, can all the exploits of the war win him fuch a title, as to have the name of favoured and felected fervant of fuch a Queen ? For *Fortune*, can any infolent politique promife to himfelf fuch a fortune, by making his own way, as the excellency of her nature cannot deny to a careful, obfequious, and dutiful fervant ? And if he could, were it equal honour to obtain it by a fhop of cunning, as by the gift of fuch a hand ?

Therefore *Erophilus*'s refolution is fixed : he renounceth *Philautia*, and all her inchantments. For her recreation, he will confer with his mufe : for her defence and honour, he will facrifice his life in the wars, hoping to be embalmed in the fweet odours of her remembrance. To her fervice will he confecrate all his watchful endeavours, and will ever bear in his heart the picture of her beauty ; in his actions, of her will ; and in his fortune, of her grace and favour.

To Sir Thomas Egerton, *Lord Keeper of the Great Seal (g).*

It may pleafe your Lordfhip,

I AM to make humble complaint to your Lord-fhip of fome hard dealing offered me by one Symp-fon, a goldfmith, a man noted much, as I have heard, for extremities and ftoutnefs upon his purfe: but yet I could fcarcely have imagined, he would have dealt either fo difhoneftly towards myfelf, or fo contemptuoufly towards her Majefty's fervice. For this Lombard (pardon me, I moft humbly pray your Lordfhip, if being admonifhed by the ftreet he dwells in, I give him that name) having me in bond for 300 l. principal, and I having the laft term confeffed the action, and by his full and direct confent, refpited the fatisfaction till the beginning of this term to come, without ever giving me warning, either by letter or meffage, ferved an execution upon me, having trained me at fuch time, as I came from the Tower, where, Mr. Waad can witnefs, we attended a fervice of no mean importance (*b*). Neither would he

---

(*g*) From the original in the Hatfield Collection of State Papers, communicated to me by the Rev. William Murdin, B. D. and intended by him for the public in a third volume of the collection of thofe papers, if his death had not prevent-ed him from executing his defign.

(*b*) It is not eafy to determine what this fervice was; but it feems to relate to the examination of fome prifoner; perhaps Edward Squire, executed in November, 1598, for poifoning the Queen's faddle; or Valentine Thomas, who accufed the King of Scots of practices againft Queen Elizabeth [*Hiftorical View*, p. 178.] or one Stanley; concerning whom I fhall infert here paffages from two MS. letters of John Chamberlain, Efq; to his friend, Dudley Carleton, Efq; afterwards ambaffador to Venice, the United Provinces, and France; thefe letters being part of a very large collection, from 1598 to 1625, which I tranfcribed from the originals. " One Stanley, *fays* **Mr. Cham-** " **berlain,**

he fo much as vouchfafe to come and fpeak with me to take any order in it, though I fent for him divers times, and his houfe was juft by; handling it as upon a defpite, being a man I never provoked with a crofs word, no nor with many delays. He would have urged it to have had me in prifon; which he had done, had not Sheriff More, to whom I fent, gently recommended me to an handfome houfe in Coleman-ftreet, where I am. Now becaufe he will not treat with me, I am inforced humbly to defire your Lordfhip to fend for him, according to your place, to bring him to fome reafon; and this forthwith, becaufe I continue here to my farther difcredit and inconvenience, and the trouble of the gentleman, with whom I am. I have an hundred pounds lying by me, which he may have, and the reft upon fome reafonable time and fecurity; or, if need be, the whole; but with my more trouble. As for the contempt he hath offered, in regard her Majefty's

---

" berlain, *in his letter dated at London,* 3 *October,* 1598, *that* " came in fixteen days over land with letters out of Spain, is " lately committed to the Tower. He was very earneft to have " private conference with her Majefty, pretending matter of " great importance, which he would by no means utter to any " body elfe." In another letter, dated 20 November, 1598, Mr. Chamberlain obferves, that on " the day, that they looked " for Stanley's arraignment, he came not himfelf, but fent his " forerunner, one Squire, that had been an under-purveyor of " the ftable, who being in Spain was dealt withall by one Wal- " pole, a Jefuit, to poifon the Queen and the Earl of Effex; and " accordingly came prepared into England, and went with the " Earl in his own fhip the laft journey, and poifoned the arms " or handles of the chair he ufed to fit in, with a confection he " had received of the Jefuit; as likewife he had done the pum- " mel of the Queen's faddle not paft five days before his going " to fea. But becaufe nothing fucceeded of it, the prieft think- " ing he had either changed his purpofe, or betrayed it, " gave Stanley inftructions to accufe him; thereby to get him " more credit, and to be revenged of Squire for breaking pro- " mife. The fellow confeffed the whole practice, and, as it " feemed, died very penitent."

C   fervice;

fervice, to my underftanding, carrieth a privilege *eundo et redeundo* in meaner caufes, much more in matters of this nature, efpecially in perfons known to be qualified with that place and employment, which, though unworthy, I am vouchfafed, I inforce nothing, thinking I have done my part, when I have made it known; and fo leave it to your Lordfhip's honourable confideration. And fo with fignification of my humble duty, &c.

To Sir ROBERT CECIL, *Secretary of State* (*i*).

It may pleafe your Honour,

I Humbly pray you to underftand how badly I have been ufed by the inclofed, being a copy of a letter of complaint thereof, which I have written to the Lord Keeper. How fenfitive you are of wrongs offered to your blood in my particular, I have had not long fince experience. But herein I think your Honour will be doubly fenfitive, in tendernefs alfo of the indignity to her Majefty's fervice. For as for me, Mr. Sympfon might have had me every day in London; and therefore to belay me, while he knew I came from the Tower about her Majefty's fpecial fervice, was to my underftanding very bold. And two days before he brags he forbore me, becaufe I dined with Sheriff More. So as with Mr. Sympfon, examinations at the Tower are not fo great a privilege, *eundo et redeundo,* as Sheriff More's dinner. But this complaint I make in duty; and to that end have alfo informed my Lord of Effex thereof; for otherwife his punifhment will do me no good.

(*i*) From the Hatfield Collection.

So

So with fignification of my humble duty, I commend your Honour to the divine prefervation.

From Coleman-ftreet, this 24th of September [1598.]

At your honourable command particularly,

FR. BACON.

*The Subftance of a Letter I (k) now wifh your Lord-
fhip (l) fhould write to her Majefty.*

THAT you defire her Majefty to believe *id, quod
res ipfa loquitur,* that it is not confcience to
yourfelf of any advantage her Majefty hath towards
you, otherwife than the general and infinite advantage of a queen and a miftrefs; nor any drift or device to win her Majefty to any point or particular;
that moveth you to fend her thefe lines of your own
mind. But firft, and principally, gratitude; next a
natural defire of, you will not fay, the tedious remembrance, for you can hold nothing tedious, that
hath been derived from her Majefty; but the troubled
and penfive remembrance of that, which is paft, of
enjoying better times with her Majefty, fuch as others
have had, and that you have wanted. You cannot
impute the difference to the continuance of time,
which addeth nothing to her Majefty but increafe of
virtue; but rather to your own misfortune or errors.
Wherein neverthelefs, if it were only queftion of your
own indurances, though any ftrength never fo good may
be oppreffed, yet you think you fhould have fuffo-
cated them, as you had often done, to the impairing
of your health, and weighing down of your mind.
But that, which indeed toucheth the quick, is that,
whereas you accounted it the choice fruit of yourfelf

(*k*) Francis Bacon.   (*l*) Robert Earl of Effex.

C 2   to

to be a contentment and entertainment to her Majesty's mind, you found many times to the contrary, that you were rather a disquiet to her, and a distaste.

Again, whereas in the course of her service, though you confess the weakness of your own judgement, yet true zeal, not misled with any mercenary nor glorious respect, made you light sometimes upon the best and soundest counsels ; you had reason to fear, that the distaste particular against yourself made her Majesty farther off from accepting any of them from such a hand. So as you seemed, to your deep discomfort, to trouble her Majesty's mind, and to foil her business ; inconveniencies, which, if you be minded as you ought, thankfulness should teach you to redeem, with stepping down, nay throwing yourself down, from your own fortune. In which intricate case, finding no end of this former course, and therefore desirous to find the beginning of a new, you have not whither to resort, but unto the oracle of her Majesty's direction. For though the true introduction *ad tempora meliora* be by an *amnestia* of that, which is past, except it be in the sense, that the verse speaketh, *Olim hæc meminisse juvabit*, when tempests past are remembered in the calm ; and that you do not doubt of her Majesty's goodness in pardoning and obliterating any of your errors and mistakings heretofore ; refreshing the memory and contemplations of your poor services, or any thing that hath been gratefull to her Majesty from you ; yea, and somewhat of your sufferings ; so though that be, yet you may be to seek for the time to come. For as you have determined your hope in a good hour, not willingly to offend her Majesty, either in matter of court or state, but to depend absolutely upon her will and pleasure ; so you do more doubt and mistrust your wit and insight in finding her Majesty's mind, than your conformities and submission in obeying it ; the rather, because you cannot but nourish a doubt

in

in your breaft, that her Majefty, as princes hearts are infcrutable, hath many times towards you *aliud in ore, et aliud in corde.* So that you, that take her *fecundum literam,* go many times farther out of your way.

Therefore your moft humble fuit to her Majefty is, that fhe will vouchfafe you that approach to her heart, and bofom, *et ad fcrinium pectoris,* plainly, for as much as concerneth yourfelf, to open and expound her mind towards you, fuffering you to fee clear what may have bred any diflike in her Majefty ; and in what points fhe would have you reform yourfelf ; and how fhe would be ferved by you. Which done, you do affure her Majefty, fhe fhall be both at the beginning and the ending of all, that you do, of that regard, as you may prefume to impart to her Majefty.

And fo that hoping, that this may be an occafion of fome farther ferenity from her Majefty towards you, you refer the reft to your actions, which may verify what you have written; as that you have written may interpret your actions, and the courfe you fhall hereafter take.

Indorfed by Mr. Francis Bacon,

A letter framed for my Lord of Effex to the Queen.

To Mr. Secretary C E C I L (*m*).

It may pleafe your Honour,

BECAUSE we live in an age, where every man's imperfections is but another's fable ; and that there fell out an accident in the Exchequer, which I know not how, nor how foon, may be traduced, though I dare truft rumour in it, except it be malicious, or extreme partial; I am bold now to poffefs your

(*m*) From the Hatfield Collection.

Honour,

Honour, as one, that ever I found careful of my advancement, and yet more jealous of my wrongs, with the truth of that, which passed; deferring my farther request, untill I may attend your honour: and so I continue

Your Honour's very humble

and particularly bounden,

F<small>R</small>. B<small>ACON</small>.

Gray's-Inn, this
24th of April,
1601.

A true remembrance of the abuse I received of Mr. Attorney General (n) publicly in the Exchequer the first day of term; for the truth whereof I refer myself to all that were present.

I Moved to have a reseizure of the lands of Geo. Moore, a relapsed recusant, a fugitive, and a practising traytor; and shewed better matter for the Queen against the discharge by plea, which is ever with a *salvo jure*. And this I did in as gentle and reasonable terms as might be.

Mr. Attorney kindled at it, and said, "Mr. Bacon, " if you have any tooth against me, pluck it out; for " it will do you more hurt, than all the teeth in your " head will do you good." I answered coldly in these very words: " Mr. Attorney, I respect you: I fear " you not: and the less you speak of your own great- " ness, the more I will think of it."

He replied, " I think scorn to stand upon terms " of greatness towards you, who are less than little; " less than the least;" and other such strange light terms he gave me, with that insulting, which cannot be expressed.

(n) Edward Coke, knighted by King James at Greenwich in 1603; and made Lord Chief Justice of the Common Pleas, 30 June, 1606.

Here-

Herewith ftirred, yet I faid no more but this : " Mr. Attorney, do not deprefs me fo far ; for I have " been your better, and may be again, when it pleafe " the Queen."

With this he fpake, neither I nor himfelf could tell what, as if he had been born Attorney General; and in the end bade me not meddle with the Queen's bufinefs, but with mine own ; and that I was un- fworn, &c. I told him, fworn or unfworn was all one to an honeft man ; and that I ever fet my fervice firft, and myfelf fecond ; and wifh'd to God, that he would do the like.

Then he faid, it were good to clap a *cap. atlega- tum* upon my back ! To which I only faid he could not ; and that he was at a fault ; for he hunted upon an old fcent.

He gave me a number of difgracefull words be- fides ; which I anfwered with filence, and fhewing, that I was not moved with them.

To ROBERT, *Lord* CECIL (*o*).

It may pleafe your good Lordfhip,

THEY fay late thanks are ever beft. But the reafon was, I thought to have feen your Lord- fhip ere this. Howfoever I fhall never forget this your laft favour amongft others ; and it grieveth me not a little, that I find myfelf of no ufe to fuch an honourable and kind friend.

For that matter, I think, I fhall defire your affift- ance for the punifhment of the contempt ; not that I would ufe the privilege in future time, but becaufe I would not have the dignity of the King's fervice pre- judiced in my inftance. But herein I will be ruled by your Lordfhip.

(*o*) From the Hatfield Collection.

C 4

It

It is fit likewise, though much against my mind, that I let your Lordship know, that I shall not be able to pay the money within the time by your Lordship undertaken, which was a fortnight. Nay money I find so hard to come by at this time, as I thought to have become an humble suitor to your Honour to have sustained me with your credit for the present from urgent debts with taking up 300 l. till I can put away some land. But I am so forward with some sales, as this request, I hope, I may forbear.

For my estate (because your Honour hath care of it) it is thus: I shall be able with selling the skirts of my living in Hertfordshire (*p*) to preserve the body; and to leave myself, being clearly out of debt, and having some money in my pocket, 300 l. land *per ann.* with a fair house, and the ground well timbered. This is now my labour.

For my purpose or course, I desire to meddle, as little as I can, in the King's causes, his Majesty now abounding in council; and to follow my private thrift and practise, and to marry with some convenient advancement. For as for any ambition, I do assure your Honour, mine is quenched. In the Queen's, my excellent mistress's, time, the *quorum* was small: her service was a kind of freehold, and it was a more solemn time. All those points agreed with my nature and judgement. My ambition now I shall only put upon my pen, whereby I shall be able to maintain memory and merit of the times succeeding.

Lastly, for this divulged and almost prostituted title of knighthood, I could without charge, by your Honour's mean, be content to have it, both because of this late disgrace, and because I have three new knights in my mess in Gray's Inn commons; and because I have found out an alderman's daughter (*q*),

an

(*p*) Gorhambury.
(*q*) Probably the lady, whom he afterwards married, Alice,

one

an handſome maiden, to my liking. So as if your Honour will find the time, I will come to the court from Gorhambury upon any warning.

How my ſales go forward, your Lordſhip ſhall in a few days hear. Mean while, if you will not be pleaſed to take farther day with this lewd fellow, I hope your Lordſhip will not ſuffer him to take any part of the penalty, but principal, intereſt, and coſts.

So I remain your Lordſhip's moſt bounden,

3 July, 1603. F ʀ. B ᴀ ᴄ ᴏ ɴ.

To the ſame.

It may pleaſe your good Lordſhip,

IN anſwer of your laſt letter, your money ſhall be ready before your day, principal, intereſt, and coſts of ſuit. So the ſheriff promiſed, when I re-leaſed errors ; and a Jew takes no more. The reſt cannot be forgotten ; for I cannot forget your Lord-ſhip's *dum memor ipſe mei :* and if there have been *aliquid nimis*, it ſhall be amended. And, to be plain with your Lordſhip, that will quicken me now, which ſlackened me before. Then I thought you might have had more uſe of me, than now, I ſuppoſe, you are like to have. Not but I think the impedi-ment will be rather in my mind, than in the matter or times. But to do you ſervice, I will come out of my religion at any time.

For my knighthood *(r)*, I wiſh the manner might be ſuch, as might grace me, ſince the matter will

one of the daughters and coheirs of Benedict Barnham, Eſq; alderman of London. She ſurviv'd her huſband above twenty years. *Life of Lord Bacon, by Dr. William Rawley.*

(*r*) He was knighted at Whitehall, 23 July, 1603.

not :

noc: I mean, that I might not be merely gregarious in a troop. The coronation (s) is at hand. It may please your Lordship to let me hear from you speedily. So I continue

Your Lordship's

From Gorhambury,
this 16th of July,
1603.

ever much bounden,

FR. BACON.

To ISAAC CASAUBON *(t).*

CUM ex literis, quas ad Dominum Carew misisti, cognoscam scripta mea à te probari, et mihi de judicio tuo gratulatus sum, et tibi, quam ea res mihi fuerit voluptati, scribendum existimavi. Atque illud etiam de me recte auguraris, me scientias ex latebris in lucem extrahere vehementer cupere. Neque enim multum interest ea per otium scribi, quæ per otium legantur; sed plane vitam, et res humanas, et medias earum turbas, per contemplationes sanas et veras instructiores esse volo. Quanta autem in hoc genere aggrediar, et quam parvis præsidiis, postmodum fortasse rescisces. Etiam tu pariter gratissimum mihi facies, si quæ in animo habes atque moliris et agitas, mihi nota esse velis. Nam conjunctionem animorum et studiorum plus facere ad amicitias judico, quam civiles necessitates et occasionum officia. Equidem existimo neminem unquam magis verè potuisse dicere de sese, quam me ipsum, illud quod habet psalmus, *multum incola fuit anima*

<hr>

(s) It was solemnised, 24 July, 1603.
(t) This letter appears to have been written after Sir George Carew, mention'd in it, return'd from his embassy in France, in October, 1609; and before the arrival of Casaubon in England, in Octob. 1610.

mea.

mea. Itaque magis videor cum antiquis verfari, quam cum his, quibufcum vivo. Quid ni etiam poffim cum abfentibus potius verfari, quam cum iis, qui præfto funt; et magis electione in amicitiis uti, quam occafionibus de more fubmitti? Verum ad inftitutum revertor ego; fi quâ in re amicitia mea tibi aut tuis ufui aut ornamento efîe poffit, tibi operam meam bonam atque navam polliceor. Itaque falutem tibi dicit

Amieus tuus, &c.

Indors'd, *To Cafaubon.*

The beginning of a letter immediately after my Lord Treafurer's (u) deceafe (w).

May 29, 1612.

It may pleafe your Majefty,

IF I fhall feem in thefe few lines to write *majorâ quam pro fortunâ,* it may pleafe your Majefty to take it to be an effect, not of prefumption, but of affection. For of the one I was never noted; and for the other I could never fhew it hitherto to the full; being as a hawk tied to another's fift, that might fometimes bait and proffer, but could never fly. And therefore if, as it was faid to one, that fpoke great words, *Amice, verba tua defiderant civitatem.* (x), fo your Majefty fay to me, " Bacon, your words re-" quire a place to fpeak them;" I muft anfwer, that place, or not place, is in your Majefty to add or refrain: and though I never grow eager but to ******
yet your Majefty———

(u) Robert Earl of Salifbury, who died 24 May, 1612.
(w) The draught of this imperfect letter is written chiefly in Greek characters.
(x) Thefe words of Themiftocles, are cited likewife by Lord Bacon at the end of his book *De Augmentis Scientiarum.*

To

To the KING, *immediately after the Lord Treafurer's death.*

31 *May*, 1612.

It may pleafe your excellent Majefty,

I Cannot but endeavour to merit, confidering your preventing graces, which is the occafion of thefe few lines.

Your Majefty hath loft a great fubject and a great fervant. But, if I fhould praife him in propriety, I fhould fay, that he was a fit man to keep things from growing worfe; but no very fit man to reduce things to be much better. For he loved to have the eyes of all Ifrael a little too much on himfelf, and to have all bufinefs ftill under the hammer; and, like clay in the hands of the potter, to mould it as he thought good; fo that he was more *in operatione* than *in opere*. And though he had fine paffages of action, yet the real conclufions came flowly on. So that although your Majefty hath grave counfellors and worthy perfons left; yet you do, as it were, turn a leaf, wherein if your Majefty fhall give a frame and conftitution to matters, before you place the perfons, in my fimple opinion it were not amifs. But the great matter, and moft inftant for the prefent, is the confideration of a parliament, for two effects: the one, for the fupply of your eftate; the other, for the better knitting of the hearts of your fubjects unto your Majefty, according to your infinite merit; for both which, parliaments have been, and are, the ancient and honourable remedy.

Now becaufe I take myfelf to have a little fkill in that region, as one, that ever affected, that your Majefty might, in all your caufes, not only prevail, but prevail with fatisfaction of the inner man; and though no man can fay but I was a perfect and peremptory

tory royalift, yet every man makes me believe, that I was never one hour out of credit with the lower houfe : my defire is to know, whether your Majefty will give me leave to meditate and propound unto you fome preparative remembrances, touching the future parliament.

Your Majefty may truly perceive, that, though I cannot challenge to myfelf either invention, or judgement, or elocution, or method, or any of thofe powers ; yet my offering is care and obfervance : and, as my good old miftrefs was wont to call me her watch-candle, becaufe it pleafed her to fay, I did continually burn (and yet fhe fuffered me to waft almoft to nothing ;) fo I muft much more owe the like duty to your Majefty, by whom my fortunes have been fettled and raifed.   And fo craving pardon, I reft,

Your Majefty's moft humble fervant devote,

F. B.

To the K I N G.

It may pleafe your excellent Majefty,

MY principal end being to do your Majefty fervice, I crave leave to make at this time to your Majefty this moft humble oblation of myfelf. I may truly fay with the pfalm, *Multum incola fuit anima mea* ; for my life hath been converfant in things, wherein I take little pleafure.   Your Majefty may have heard fomewhat, that my father was an honeft man ; and fomewhat yet I may have been of myfelf, though not to make any true judgement by, becaufe I have hitherto had only *poteftatem verborum*, nor that neither.   I was three of my young years bred with

. an

an ambaſſadot (y) in France, and ſince I have been an old truant in the ſchool-houſe of your council-chamber, though on the ſecond form; yet longer than any, that now ſitteth, hath been in the head form. If your Majeſty find any aptneſs in me, or if you find any ſcarcity in others, whereby, you may think it fit for your ſervice to remove me to buſineſs of ſtate, although I have a fair way before me for profit, and, by your Majeſty's grace and favour, for honour and advancement, and in a courſe leſs expoſed to the blaſt of fortune; yet now that he (z) is gone, *quo vivente virtutibus certiſſimum exitium*, I will be ready as a cheſſman to be wherever your Majeſty's royal hand ſhall ſet me. Your Majeſty will bear me witneſs, I have not ſuddenly opened myſelf thus far. I have looked on upon others. I ſee the exceptions; I ſee the diſtractions; and I fear Tacitus will be a prophet, *magis alii homines, quam alii mores.* I know mine own heart; and I know not, whether God, that hath touched my heart with the affection, may not touch your royal heart to diſcern it. Howſoever, I ſhall go on honeſtly in mine ordinary courſe, and ſupply the reſt in prayers for you, remaining, &c.

To the KING (a).

*** Laſtly, I will make two prayers unto your Majeſty, as I uſed to do to God Almighty, when I commend to him his own glory and cauſe; ſo I will pray to your Majeſty for yourſelf.

The one is, that theſe cogitations of want do not any ways trouble or vex your mind. I remember,

(y) Sir Amias Poulet, who was ſent ambaſſador to France, in September, 1576. He was ſucceeded by Sir Edward Stafford, in December, 1578.

( ) Lord Treaſurer Saliſbury.

(a) The beginning of this letter is wanting.

Moſes

Moses faith of the land of promise, that it was not like the land of Egypt, that was watered with a river, but was watered with showers from heaven; whereby I gather, God preferreth sometimes uncertainties before certainties, because they teach a more immediate dependance upon his providence. Sure I am, *nil novi accidit vobis.* It is for no new thing for the greatest Kings to be in debt: and, if a man shall *parvis componere magna,* I have seen an Earl of Leicester, a Chancellor Hatton, an Earl of Essex, and an Earl of Salisbury in debt; and yet was it no manner of diminution to their power or greatness.

My second prayer is, that your Majesty, in respect of the hasty freeing of your state, would not descend to any means, or degree of means, which carrieth not a symmetry with your majesty and greatness. He is gone, from whom those courses did wholly flow. So have your wants and necessities in particular, as it were, hanged up in two tablets before the eyes of your Lords and Commons to be talked of for four months together: to have all your courses to help yourself in revenue or profit put into printed books, which were wont to be held *arcana imperii:* to have such worms of aldermen to lend for ten in the hundred upon good assurance, and with such * *, as if it should save the bark of your fortune: to contract still where might be had the readiest payment, and not the best bargain: to stir a number of projects for your profit, and then to blast them, and leave your Majesty nothing but the scandal of them: to pretend an even carriage between your Majesty's rights and the ease of the people, and to satisfy neither. These courses, and others the like, I hope, are gone with the deviser of them; which have turned your Majesty to inestimable prejudice (*b*).

I hope

(*b*) It will be but justice to the memory of the Earl of Salisbury to remark, that this disadvantageous character of him by
Sir

I hope your Majesty will pardon my liberty of writing. I know these things are *majora quam pro fortunâ:* but they are *minora quam pro studio et voluntate.* I assure myself, your Majesty taketh not me for one of a busy nature; for my state being free from all difficulties, and I having such a large field for contemplations, as I have partly, and shall much more make manifest to your Majesty and the world, to occupy my thoughts, nothing could make me active, but love and affection. So praying my God to bless and favour your person and estate, &c.

To the KING.

It may please your excellent Majesty,

I HAVE, with all possible diligence since your Majesty's progress, attended the service committed to the sub-commissioners, touching the repair and improvement of your Majesty's means: and this I have done, not only in meeting, and conference, and debate with the rest; but also by my several and private meditation and inquiry. So that, besides the joint account, which we shall give to the Lords, I hope I shall be able to give your Majesty somewhat *ex proprio.* For as no man loveth better *consulere in commune* than I do; neither am I of those fine ones, that use to keep back any thing, wherein

Sir Francis Bacon seems to have been heightened by the prejudices of the latter against that able Minister, grounded upon some suspicions, that the Earl had not served him with so much zeal, as he might have expected from so near a relation, either in Queen Elizabeth's reign, or that of her successor. Nor is it any just imputation on his Lordship, that he began to decline in King James I's good opinion, when his Majesty's ill œconomy occasioned demands on the Lord Treasurer, which all his skill, in the business of the finances, could not answer, but which drew from him advices and remonstrances still extant, which that King, not being very ready to profit by, conceived some resentment against his old servant, and even retained it against his memory.

they

they think they may win credit apart, and so make the consultation almost *inutile*. So nevertheless, in cases, where matters shall fall in upon the bye, perhaps of no less worth than that, which is the proper subject of the consultation; or where I find things passed over too slightly, or in cases, where that, which I should advise, is of that nature, as I hold it not fit to be communicated to all those, with whom I am joined; these parts of business I put to my private account; not because I would be officious, (though I profess I would do works of supererogation, if I could) but in a true discretion and caution. And your Majesty had some taste in those notes, which I gave you for the wards, (which it pleased you to say were no tricks nor novelties, but true passages of business) that mine own particular remembrances and observations are not like to be unprofitable. Concerning which notes for the wards, though I might say, *sic vos non vobis*; yet let that pass.

I have also considered fully of that great proposition, which your Majesty commended to my care and study, touching the conversion of your revenue of land into a multiplied present revenue of rent: wherein, I say, I have considered of the means and course to be taken, of the assurance, of the rates, of the exceptions, and of the arguments for and against it. For though the project itself be as old as I can remember, and falleth under every man's capacity; yet the dispute and manage of it asketh a great deal of consideration and judgement; projects being like Æsop's tongues, the best meat and the worst, as they are chosen and handled. But surely, *ubi deficiunt remedia ordinaria, recurrendum est ad extraordinaria*. Of this also I am ready to give your Majesty an account.

Generally upon this subject of the repair of your Majesty's means, I beseech your Majesty to give me leave to make this judgement, that your Majesty's recovery muft be by the medicines of the Galenifts and Arabians, and not of the chemifts or Paracelfians. For it will not be wrought by any one fine extract, or ftrong water; but by a fkilful company of a number of ingredients, and thofe by juft weight and proportion, and that of fome fimples, which perhaps of themfelves, or in over-great quantity, were little better than poifons; but mixed, and broken, and in juft quantity, are full of virtue. And fecondly, that as your Majefty's growing behind-hand hath been work of time; fo muft likewife be your Majefty's coming forth and making even. Not but I wifh it were by all good and fit means accelerated; but that I forefee, that if your Majefty fhall propound to yourfelf to do it *per faltum*, it can hardly be without accidents of prejudice to your honour, fafety, or profit.

Indorfed,

My letter to the KING, *touching his eftate in general,*

September 18th, 1612.

To the KING.

May it pleafe your Majefty,

ACCORDING to your Highnefs's pleafure fignified by my Lord Chamberlain (*c*), I have confidered of the petition of certain baronets (*d*) made unto your Majefty for confirmation and extent,

---

(*c*) Thomas Howard, Earl of Suffolk.

(*d*) The order of baronets was created by patent of King James I, dated the 22d of May, 1611. The year following, a decree was made relating to their place and precedence, and four years after, viz. in 1616, another decree to the fame purpofe. See Selden's *Titles of Honour*, Part. II. Ch. V. p. 821. Ch. XI. p. 906, and 910. 2d Edit. fol. 1631.

or

or explanation of certain points mentioned in their charter ; and am of opinion, that firſt, whereas it is deſired, that the baronets be declared a middle degree between baron and knight, I hold this to be reaſonable as to their placing.

Secondly, where it is deſired, that unto the words *degree or dignity of baron*, the word *honour* might be added ; I know very well, that in the preface of the baronets patent it is mentioned, that all honours are derived from the king. I find alſo, that in the patent of the baronets, which are marſhalled under the barons (except it be certain principals) the word *honour* is granted. I find alſo, that the word *dignity* is many times in law a ſuperior word to the word *honour*, as being applied to the King himſelf, all capital indict-ments concluding *contra coronam et dignitatem noſtram*. It is evident alſo, that the word *honour* and *honourable* are uſed in theſe times in common ſpeech very pro-miſcuouſly. Nevertheleſs, becauſe the ſtyle of ho-nour belongs chiefly to peers and counſellors, I am doubtful what opinion to give therein.

Thirdly, whereas it is believed, that if there be any queſtion of precedence touching baronets, it may be ordered, that the ſame be decided by the com-miſſioners marſhal, I do not ſee but it may be granted them for avoiding diſturbances.

Fourthly, for the precedence of baronets, I find no alteration or difficulty, except it be in this, that the daughters of baronets are deſired to be declared to have precedence before the wives of knights eldeſt ſons ; which, becauſe it is a degree hereditary, and that in all examples, the daughters in general have place next the eldeſt brothers wives, I hold conve-nient.

Laſtly, whereas it is deſired, that the apparent heirs males of the bodies of the baronets may be knighted during the life of their fathers ; for that I have received from the Lord Chamberlain a ſignifica-

tion,

tion, that your Majesty did so understand it, I humbly subscribe thereunto, with this, that the baronets eldest sons being knights do not take place of ancient knights, so long as their fathers live.

All which nevertheless I humbly submit to your Majesty's better judgement.

Your Majesty's most humble, and

most bounden servant,

Fr. Bacon.

The Charge against Mr. Whitelocke (e).

My Lords,

THE offence, wherewith Mr. Whitelocke is charged (for as to Sir Robert Mansell, I take it to my part only to be sorry for his error) is a contempt

(e) He had been committed, in May 1613, to the Fleet, for speaking too boldly against the marshal's court, and for giving his opinion to Sir Robert Mansell, Treasurer of the Navy, and Vice-Admiral, that the commission to the Earl of Nottingham, Lord High Admiral, for reviewing and reforming the disorders committed by the officers of the navy, was not according to law; though Mr. Whitelocke had given that opinion only in private to his client, and not under his hand. Sir Robert Mansell was also committed to the Marshalsea, for animating the Lord Admiral against the commission. [Sir Ralph Windwood's *Memorials of State*, Vol. III. p. 460.] This Mr. Whitelocke was probably the same with James Whitelocke, who was born in London, 28 November 1572, educated at Merchant Taylor's school there, and St. John's college in Oxford, and studied law in the Middle Temple, of which he was summer reader in 1619. In the preceding year, 1618, he stood for the place of recorder of the city of London, but was not elected to it, Robert Heath, Esq; being chosen on the 10th of November, chiefly by the recommendation of the King, the city having been told, that they must choose none, whom his Majesty should refuse, as he did in particular

ticular

tempt of an high nature, and resting upon two parts : on the one, a presumptuous and licentious censure and defying of his Majesty's prerogative in general ; the other, a slander and traducement of one act or emanation hereof, containing a commission of survey and reformation of abuses in the office of the navy.

This offence is fit to be opened and set before your Lordships (as it hath been well begun,) both in the true state, and in the true weight of it. ' For as I desire, that the nature of the offence may appear in its true colours ; so, on the other side, I desire, that the shadow of it may not darken or involve any thing, that is lawful, or agreeable with the just and reasonable liberty of the subject.

First, we must and do agree, that the asking, and taking, and giving of counsel in law is an essential part of justice ; and to deny that, is to shut the gate of justice, which in the Hebrews commonwealth was therefore held in the gate, to shew all passage to justice must be open : and certainly counsell in law is one of the passages. But yet, for all that, this liberty is not infinite and without limits.

If a jesuited papist should come, and ask counsel (I put a case not altogether feigned) whether all the acts of parliament made in the time of Queen Elizabeth and King James are void or no ; because there are no lawful bishops sitting in the upper house, and a parliament must consist of lords spiritual and temporal and commons ; and a lawyer will set it under his hand, that they be all void, I will touch him for high treason upon this his counsel.

ticular except to Mr. Whitelocke by name [MS. letter of Mr. Chamberlain to Sir Dudley Carleton, November 14, 1618.] Mr. Whitelocke, however, was call'd to the degree of serjeant in Trinity Term 1620, knighted, made Chief Justice of Chester ; and at last, on the 18th of October, 1624, one of the Justices of the King's Bench ; in which post he died June 1632. He was father of Bulstrode Whitelocke, Esq; Commissioner of the Great Seal.

So,

So, if a puritan preacher will afk counfel, whether he may ftyle the King Defender of the Faith, becaufe he receives not the difcipline and prefbytery ; and the lawyer will tell him, it is no part of the King's ftyle, it will go hard with fuch a lawyer.

Or if a tribunitious popular fpirit will go and afk a lawyer, whether the oath and band of allegiance be to the kingdom and crown only, and not to the King (as was Hugh Spenfer's cafe,) and he deliver his opinion as Hugh Spenfer did ; he will be in Hugh Spenfer's danger.

So as the privilege of giving counfel proveth not all opinions : and as fome opinions given are traitorous ; fo are there others of a much inferior nature, which are contemptuous. And among thefe I reckon Mr. Whitelocke's ; for as for his loyalty and true heart to the King, God forbid I fhould doubt it.

Therefore let no man miftake fo far, as to conceive, that any lawful and due liberty of the fubject for afking counfel in law is called in queftion, when points of difloyalty or of contempt are reftrained. Nay, we fee it is the grace and favour of the King and his courts, that if the cafe be tender, and a wife lawyer in modefty and difcretion refufeth to be of council (for you have lawyers fometimes too nice as well as too bold) they are then ruled and affigned to be of council. For certainly counfell is the blind man's guide ; and forry I am with all my heart, that in this cafe the blind did lead the blind.

For the offence, for which Mr. Whitelocke is charged, I hold it great, and to have, as I faid at firft, two parts ; the one a cenfure, and (in as much as in him is) a circling, nay a clipping, of the King's prerogative in general : the other, a flander and depravation of the King's power and honour in this commiffion.

And for the firft of thefe, I confider it again in three degrees : firft, that he prefumed to cenfure
the

the King's prerogative at all. Secondly, that he runneth into the generality of it more than was pertinent to the present question. And laftly, that he hath erroneoufly, and falfely, and dangeroufly given opinion in derogation of it.

Firft, I make a great difference between the King's grants and ordinary commmiffions of juftice, and the King's high commiffions of regiment, or mixed with caufes of ftate.

For the former, there is no doubt but they may be freely queftioned and difputed (and any defect in matter or form ftood upon,) though the King be many times the adverfe party :

But for the latter fort, they are rather to be dealt with (if at all) by a modeft, and humble intimation or remonftrance to his Majefty and his council, than by bravery of difpute or peremptory oppofition.

Of this kind is that properly to be underftood, which is faid in Bracton, *De chartis et factis regiis non debent aut poffunt juftitiarii aut privatæ perfonæ difputare, fed tutius eft, ut expectetur fententia regis.*

And the King's courts themfelves have been exceeding tender and fparing in it ; fo that there is in all our law, not three cafes of it. And in that very cafe of 24 Ed. 3. afs. pl. s. which Mr. Whitelocke vouched, where, as it was a commiffion to arreft a man, and to carry him to prifon, and to feize his goods without any form of juftice or examination preceding ; and that the Judges faw it was obtained by furreption : yet the Judges faid they would keep it by them, and fhew it to the King's council.

But Mr. Whitelocke did not advife his client to acquaint the King's council with it, but prefumptuoufly giveth opinion, that it is void. Nay, not fo much as a claufe or paffage of modefty, as that he fubmits his opinion to cenfure : that it is too great a matter for him to deal in ; or this is my opinion, which is nothing, &c. But *illotis manibus,*

he

he takes it into his hands, and pronounceth of it, as a man would scarcely do of a warrant of a justice of peace, and speaks like a dictator, that *this is law*, and *this is against law*, &c. (*f*).

ROBERT *Earl of* SOMERSET *to Sir* THOMAS OVERBURY (*g*). *From a Copy among Lord* BACON's *papers in the Lambeth library.*

SIR,

I HAVE considered, that my answer to you, and what I have otherwise to say, will exceed the bounds of a letter; and now having not much

(*f*) Sir H. Wotton in a letter of his to Sir Edmund Bacon [*Reliq. Wotton.* p. 421. Edit. 3d] written about the beginning of June, 1613, mentions, that Sir Robert Mansell and Mr. Whitelocke were, on the Saturday before, called to a very honourable hearing in the Queen's presence-chamber at Whitehall, before the Lords of the Council, with intervention of the Lord Chief Justice Coke, the Lord Chief Baron Tanfield, and the Master of the Rolls; the Lord Chief Justice of the King's Bench, Fleming, being kept at home by some infirmity. There the Attorney and Sollicitor first undertook Mr. Whitelocke, and the Recorder [Henry Montagu], as the King's Serjeant, Sir Robert Mansell, charging the one as a counsellor, the other as a questioner, in matters of the King's prerogative and sovereignty upon occasion of a commission intended for a research into the administration of the admiralty. "Whitelocke in his answer, *adds Sir Henry* "*Wotton,* spake more confusedly than was expected from a lawyer; "and the knight more temperately than was expected from a "soldier. . . . Whitelocke ended his speech with an absolute "confession of his own offence, and with a promise of employing "himself hereafter in defence of the King's prerogative. . . . "In this they generally agreed, both counsellors and judges, "to represent the humiliation of both the prisoners to the King "in lieu of innocency, and to intercede for his gracious par- "don: which was done, and accordingly the next day they "were inlarged upon a submission under writing."

(*g*) He was committed to the Tower on the 21st of April, 1613, and died there of poison on the 15th of September following.

time

time to ufe betwixt my waiting on the King, and the removes we do make in this our little progrefs, I thought fit to ufe the fame man to you, whom I have heretofore many times employed in the fame bufinefs. He has, befides an account and a better defcription of me to give you, to make a repetition of the former carriages of all this bufinefs, that you may diftinguifh that, which he did by knowledge of mine and direction, and betwixt that he did out of his own difcretion without my warrant. With all this he has to renew to you a former defire of mine, which was the ground-work of this, and the chief errand of his coming to you, wherein I defire your anfwer by him. I would not employ this gentleman to you, if he were, as you conceit of him, your unfriend, or an ill inftrument betwixt us. So owe him the teftimony of one, that has fpoken as honeftly, and given more praifes of you, than any man, that has fpoken to me.

My hafte at this time makes me to end fooner than I expected : but the fubject of my next fending fhall be to anfwer that part you give me in your love, with a return of the fame from

Your affured loving friend,

R. SOMERSET.

Indorfed, *Lord Somerfet's firft letter.*

To the KING.

It may pleafe your moft excellent Majefty,

HAVING underftood of the death of the Lord Chief Juftice *(b)*, I do ground in all humble-

(b) Sir Thomas Fleming, who died about Auguft 1613.

nefs

nefs an affured hope, that your Majefty will not
think of any other but your poor fervants, your Attorney (*i*), and your Sollicitor (*k*), one of them,
for that place. Elfe we fhall be like Noah's dove,
not knowing where to reft our feet. For the places
of reft, after the extreme painful places, wherein
we ferve, have ufed to be either the Lord Chancellor's place, or the Mafterfhip of the Rolls, or the
places of the Chief Juftices: whereof, for the firft,
I could be almoft loth to live to fee this worthy
counfellor fail. The Mafterfhip of the Rolls is
blocked with a reverfion (*l*). My Lord Coke is
like to outlive us both. So as, if this turn fail, I
for my part know not whither to look. I have
ferved your Majefty above a prenticehood, full feven
years and more, as your Sollicitor, which is, I
think, one of the painfulleft places in your kingdom,
fpecially as my employments have been; and God
hath brought mine own years to fifty two, which
I think is older than ever any Sollicitor continued unpreferred. My fuit is principally, that you
would remove Mr. Attorney to the place. If he
refufe, then I hope your Majefty will feek no farther than myfelf, that I may at laft, out of your
Majefty's grace and favour, ftep forwards to a place
either of more comfort or more eafe. Befides, how neceffary it is for your Majefty to ftrengthen your fervice amongft the Judges by a Chief Juftice, which
is fure to your prerogative, your Majefty knoweth.
Therefore I ceafe farther to trouble your Majefty,
humbly craving pardon, and relying wholly upon

(*i*) Sir Henry Hobart, who was made Lord Chief Juftice of
the Common Pleas, November 26, 1613, in the room of Sir
Edward Coke, removed to the poft of Lord Chief Juftice of the
King's Bench, October 25.

(*k*) Sir Francis Bacon himfelf, who was appointed Attorney
General, October 27, 1613.

(*l*) to Sir Julius Cæfar.

your

your goodneſs and remembrance, and reſting in all
true humbleneſs,

Your Majeſty's moſt devoted,

and faithful ſubject and ſervant,

Fr. Bacon.

*Reaſons why it ſhould be exceeding much for his Majeſty's
ſervice to remove the Lord* Coke *from the place he
now holdeth* (m) *to be Chief Juſtice of England* (n),
and the Attorney (o) *to ſucceed him, and the Sollicitor* (p) *the Attorney.*

First, it will ſtrengthen the King's cauſes greatly
amongſt the Judges: for both my Lord Coke will
think himſelf near a Privy Counſellor's place, and
thereupon turn obſequious; and the Attorney General, a new man, and a grave perſon, in a Judge's
place, will come in well to the other, and hold him
hard to it, not without emulation between them,
who ſhall pleaſe the King beſt.

Secondly, the Attorney General ſorteth not ſo
well with his preſent place, being a man timid and
ſcrupulous both in parliament and other buſineſs,
and one, that in a word was made fit for the late
Lord Treaſurer's bent, which was to do little with
much formality and proteſtation: whereas the now
Sollicitor going more roundly to work, and being
of a quicker and more earneſt temper, and more effectual in that he dealeth in, is like to recover that

(m) of Chief Juſtice of the Common Pleas, having been appointed to that office June 30, 1606.

(n). He was advanced to that office October 25, 1613.

(o) Sir Henry Hobart, who had been appointed Attorney
General July 4, 1606.

(p) Sir Francis Bacon, who had been ſworn Sollicitor General June 25, 1607.

ſtrength

ftrength to the King's prerogative, which it hath had in times paft, and which is due unto it. And for that purpofe there muft be brought in to be Sollicitor fome man of courage and fpeech, and a grounded lawyer ; which done, his Majefty will fpeedily find a marvellous change in his bufinefs. For it is not to purpofe for the Judges to ftand well-difpofed, except the King's council, which is the active and moving part, put the Judges well to it ; for in a weapon, what is a back without an edge ?

Thirdly, the King fhall continue and add reputation to the Attorney's and Sollicitor's place, by this orderly advancement of them ; which two places are the champions places for his rights and prerogative ; and being ftripped of their expectations and fucceffions to great place, will wax vile ; and then his Majefty's prerogative goeth down the wind. Befides, the remove of my Lord Coke to a place of lefs profit (though it be with his will) yet will be thought abroad a kind of difcipline to him for oppofing himfelf in the King's caufes ; the example whereof will contain others in more awe.

Laftly, whereas now it is voiced abroad touching the fupply of places, as if it were a matter of labour and canvafs, and money ; and other perfons are chiefly fpoken of to be the men and the great fuitors ; this will appear to be the King's own act, and is a courfe fo natural and regular, as it is without all fufpicion of thefe by-courfes, to the King's infinite honour. For men fay now, the King can make good fecond Judges (as he hath done lately (*q*) ;) but that is no maftery, becaufe men fue to be kept from thefe places. But now is the trial in thofe great places, how his Majefty can hold good, where there is great fuit and means.

(*q*) Sir John Dodderidge was made a Judge of the King's Bench, November 25, 1612, and Sir Auguftin Nichols of the Common Pleas the day following.

4

To Mr. JOHN MURRAY (r) *of the Bed-chamber to the King* (*).

Mr. Murray,

I KEEP the same measure in a proportion with my master and with my friend; which is, that I will never deceive them in any thing, which is in my power; and when my power faileth my will, I am sorry.

Monday is the day appointed for performing his Majesty's commandment. Till then I cannot tell what to advise you farther, except it should be this, that in case the Judges should refuse to take order in it themselves, then you must think of some warrant to Mr. Secretary, who is your friend, and constant in the businesses, that he see forth-with his Majesty's commandment executed, touching the double lock; and, if need be, repair to the place, and see by view the manner of keeping the seal; and take order, that there be no stay of working of the seal for justice, nor no prejudice to Killegrew's farm, nor to the duty of money paid to the Chief Justice. Whether this may require your presence, as you write, that yourself can best judge. But of this more, when we have received the Judges answer. It is my duty, as much as in me is, to procure my master to be obeyed. I ever rest,

Your friend and assured,

January 21,
1614.
FR. BACON.

I pray deliver the inclosed letter to his Majesty.

To his very good friend, Mr. John Murray, *of his Majesty's Bed-chamber.*

(r) He was created Viscount of Annan in Scotland, in August, 1622. *Negotiations of Sir Thomas Roe, in his embassy to the Ottoman Porte, p.* 93. In April, 1624, the Lord Annan was created Earl of Annandale in Scotland. Ibid. p. 250.

(*) This, and the three following letters, are printed from Harl. MSS. Vol. 6986. *To*

To Mr. MURRAY.

Mr. Murray,

MY Lord Chancellor, yesterday in my presence, had before him the Judges of the Common Pleas, and hath performed his Majesty's royal command in a very worthy fashion, such as was fit for our master's greatness; and because the King may know it, I send you the inclosed. This seemeth to have wrought the effect desired; for presently I sent for Sir Richard Cox (s), and willed him to present himself to my Lord Hobart, and signify his readiness to attend. He came back to me, and told me, all things went on. I know not what afterwards may be; but I think this long chace is at an end.

I ever rest,

                                Your's assured,

January 25,
    1614.   FR. BACON.

To Mr. MURRAY.

Mr. Murray,

I PRAY deliver the inclosed to his Majesty, and have care of the letter afterwards. I have written also to his Majesty about your reference to this purpose, that if you can get power over the whole title, it may be safe for his Majesty to assent, that you may try the right upon the deed. This is the farthest I can go.

I ever rest,

                                Your's assured,

February 28,
    1614,   FR. BACON.

(s) He was one of the Masters of the Green Cloth, and had had a quarrel at court during the Christmas holy-days of the year 1614, with Sir Thomas Erskine; which quarrel was made up by the Lords of the Marshal's Court, Sir Richard being obliged to put up with very foul words. MS. letter of Mr. Chamberlain to Sir Dudley Carleton, January 12, 1614.

                                                To

To the K I N G.

May it pleafe your moft excellent Majefty,

I SEND your Majefty inclofed a copy of our laft examination of Peacham (*t*), taken the 10th of this prefent; whereby your Majefty may perceive, that

(*t*) Edmund Peacham, a minifter in Somerfetfhire [MS. letter of Mr. Chamberlain, dated January 5, 1614]. I find one of both his names, who was inftituted into the vicarage of Ridge in Hertfordfhire July 22, 1581, and refigned it in 1587 [New-court, *Reporter.* Vol. I. p. 864.] Mr. Peacham was committed to the Tower for inferting feveral treafonable paffages in a fer-mon *never preached, nor,* as Mr. Juftice Croke remarks in his *Reports* during the reign of King Charles I, p. 125, *ever intended to be preached.* Mr. Chamberlain, in a letter of the 9th of Fe-bruary, 1614, to Sir Dudley Carleton, mentions Mr. Peacham's having been " ftretched already, though he be an old man, " and, they fay, much above threefcore : but they could " wring nothing out of him more than they had at firft in his " papers. Yet the King is extremely incenfed againft him, " and will have him profecuted to the uttermoft." In another letter, dated February 23, we are informed, that the King, fince his coming to London on the 15th, had had " the opinion " of the Judges feverally in Peacham's cafe ; and it is faid, that " moft of them concur to find it treafon : yet my Lord Chief " Juftice [Coke] is for the contrary ; and if the Lord Hobart, " that rides the weftern circuit, can be drawn to jump with his " collegue, the Chief Baron [Tanfield,] it is thought he fhall " be fent down to be tried, and truffed up in Somerfetfhire." In a letter of the 2d of March, 1614, Mr. Chamberlain writes, " Peacham's trial at the weftern affizes is put off, and his journey " ftayed, though Sir Randall Crew, the King's Serjeant, and " Sir Henry Yelverton, the Sollicitor, were ready to go to horfe " to have waited on him there." " Peacham, the minifter, *adds he in a letter of the* 13th *of July,* 1615, that hath been " this twelve month in the Tower, is fent down to be tried for " treafon in Somerfetfhire before the Lord Chief Baron and Sir " Henry Montagu, the Recorder. The Lord Hobart gave " over that circuit the laft affizes. Sir Randall Crew and Sir " Henry Yelverton, the King's Serjeant and Sollicitor, are fent " down that this miscreant wretch goeth back from all, and denieth his hand and all. No doubt, being fully of belief, that he should go presently down to his trial, he meant now to repeat his part, which he purposed to play in the country, which was to deny all. — But your Majesty in your wisdom perceiveth, that this denial of his hand, being not possible to be counterfeited, and to be sworn by Adams, and so oft by himself formerly confessed and admitted, could not mend his case before any jury in the world, but rather aggravateth it by his notorious impudency and falshood, and will make him more odious. He never deceived me ; for when others had hopes of discovery, and thought time well spent that way, I told your Majesty, *pereuntibus mille figuræ* ; and that he now did but turn himself into divers shapes, to save or delay his punishment. And therefore submitting myself to your Majesty's high wisdom, I think myself bound in conscience to put your Majesty in remembrance, whether Sir John Sydenham (*u*) shall be detained upon this man's impeaching, in whom there is no truth. Notwithstanding, that farther inquiry be made of this other Peacham, and that information

---

" down to prosecute the trial." The event of this trial, which was on the 7th of August, appears from Mr. Chamberlain's letter of the 14th of that month, wherein, it is said, that " seven knights were taken from the bench, and appointed to be " of the jury, He defended himself very simply, but obsti- " nately and doggedly enough. But his offence was so foul " and scandalous, that he was condemned of high treason ; " yet not hitherto executed, nor perhaps shall be, if he have " the grace to submit himself, and shew some remorse." He died, as appears from another letter of the 27th of March, 1616, in the jail at Taunton, where he was said to have " left behind " a most wicked and desperate writing, worse than that he was " convicted for."

(*u*) He had been confronted about the end of February, or beginning of March, 161$\frac{4}{5}$, with Mr. Peacham, about certain speeches, which had formerly passed between them. MS. letter of Mr. Chamberlain to Sir Dudley Carleton, from London, March 2, 161$\frac{4}{5}$.

and

and light be taken from Mr. Poulet (*w*) and his fervants, I hold it, as things are, neceffary.

God preferve your Majefty.

Your Majefty's moft humble and

devoted fubject and fervant,

March 12,
1614.   Fr. Bacon.

Supplement of two paffages omitted in the edition of Sir
  Francis Bacon's *fpeech in the King's Bench againft*
  Owen (*x*), *as printed in his works. After the words*
  [it is bottomlefs] *in the paragraph beginning* [For
  the treafon itfelf, which is the fecond point, &c.]
  add

[I said in the beginning, that this treafon in the nature of it was old. It is not of the treafons, whereof it may be faid, *from the beginning it was not fo.* You are indicted, Owen, not upon any ftatute made againft the Pope's fupremacy, or other matters, that have reference to religion; but merely upon that

(*w*) John Poulet, Efq; Knight of the Shire for the county of Somerfet in the parliament, which met April 5, 1614. He was created Lord Poulet of Henton St. George, June 23, 1627.

(*x*) He was of the family of that name at Godftow in Oxford-fhire [*Camdeni Annales Regis Jacobi I, p. 12.*] He was a young man, who had been in Spain; and was condemned at the King's Bench, on Wednefday May 17, 1615, " for divers moft vile
" and traiterous fpeeches confeffed and fubfcribed with his
" own hand; as, among others, that it was as lawful for any
" man to kill a King excommunicated, as for the hangman to
" execute a condemned perfon. He could fay little for himfelf,
" or in maintenance of his defperate pofitions, but only that he
" meant it not by the King, and he holds him not excommuni-
" cate." MS. letter of Mr. Chamberlain to Sir Dudley Carle-ton from London, May 20, 1615.

E   law,

law, which was born with the kingdom, and was law even in superstitious times, when the Pope was received. The compassing and imagining of the King's death was treason. The statute of the 25th of Edward III, which was but declaratory, begins with this article, as the capital of capitals in treason, and of all others the most odious and the most perilous.] And so the civil law, &c.

At the conclusion of this speech, after the words [*the Duke of Anjou and the Papists*] add

[As for subjects, I see not, or ever could discern, but that by infallible consequence, it is the case of all subjects and people, as well as of Kings ; for it is all one reason, that a Bishop, upon an excommunication of a private man, may give his lands and goods in spoil, or cause him to be slaughtered, as for the Pope to do it towards a King ; and for a Bishop to absolve the son from duty to the father, as for the Pope to absolve the subject from his allegiance to his King. And this is not my inference, but the very affirmative of Pope Urban the Second, who in a brief to Godfrey, Bishop of Luca, hath these very words, which Cardinal Baronius reciteth in his Annals, Tom. XI. p. 802. *Non illos homicidas arbitramur, qui adversus excommunicatos zelo catholicæ matris ardentes eorum quoslibet trucidare contigerit*, speaking generally of all excommunications.]

To Mr. MURRAY (*).

Good Mr. Murray,

ACCORDING to his Majesty's pleasure by you signified unto me, we have attended my Lord Chancellor (*y*), my Lord Treasurer (*z*), and Mr.

(*) Harl. MSS. Vol. 6986.   (*y*) Ellesmere.
(*z*) Thomas Howard, Earl of Suffolk.

Chancellor

Chancellor of the Exchequer (*a*), concerning Sir
Gilbert Houghton's patent stayed at the seal; and
we have acquainted them with the grounds and state
of the suit, to justify them, that it was just and be-
neficial to his Majesty. And for any thing we could
perceive by any objection or reply they made, we
left them in good opinion of the same, with this,
that because my Lord Chancellor (by the advice, as
it seemeth, of the other two) had acquainted the
council-table (for so many as were then present) with
that suit amongst others, they thought fit to stay till
his Majesty's coming to town, being at hand, to
understand his farther pleasure. We purpose, upon
his Majesty's coming, to attend his Majesty, to give
him a more particular account of this business, and
some other. Mean while, finding his Majesty to
have care of the matter, we thought it our duty
to return this answer to you in discharge of his Majesty's direction. We remain,

Your assured friends,

July 6, 1615.

FRANCIS BACON,
HENRY YELVERTON.

To the KING (*).

It may please your excellent Majesty,

I RECEIVED this very day, in the forenoon,
your Majesty's several directions touching your
cause prosecuted by my Lord Hunsdon (*b*), as your
farmer. Your first direction was by Sir Christopher
Parkins, that the day appointed for the judicial sen-

(*a*) Sir Fulk Grevile, advanced to that post October 1, 1614,
in the room of Sir Julius Cæsar, made Master of the Rolls.
(*) Harl. MSS. Vol. 6986.
(*b*) John Carey, Baron of Hunsdon. He died in April, 1617.

E 2

tence

tence fhould hold : and if my Lord Chief Juftice, upon my repair to him, fhould let me know, that he could not be prefent, then my Lord Chancellor fhould proceed, calling to him my Lord Hobart, except he fhould be excepted to ; and then fome other Judge by confent. For the latter part of this your direction, I fuppofe, there would have been no difficulty in admitting my Lord Hobart ; for after he had affifted at fo many hearings, it would have been too late to except to him. But then your Majefty's fecond and later direction (which was delivered unto me from the Earl of Arundel, as by word of mouth, but fo as he had fet down a remembrance thereof in writing frefhly after the fignification of his pleafure) was to this effect, that before any proceeding in the Chancery, there fhould be a conference had between my Lord Chancellor, my Lord Chief Juftice, and myfelf, how your Majefty's intereft might be fecured. This later direction I acquainted my Lord Chancellor with ; and finding an impoffibility, that this conference fhould be had before to-morrow, my Lord thought good, that the day be put over, taking no occafion thereof other than this, that in a caufe of fo great weight it was fit for him to confer with his affiftants, before he gave any decree, or final order. After fuch time as I have conferred with my Lords, according to your commandment, I will give your Majefty account with fpeed of the conclufion of that conference.

Farther, I think fit to let your Majefty know, that in my opinion I hold it a fit time to proceed in the bufinefs of the *Rege inconfulto*, which is appointed for Monday. I did think thefe greater caufes would Have come to period or paufe fooner : but now they are in the hight, and to have fo great a matter as this of the *Rege inconfulto* handled, when men do *aliud agere*, I think it no proper time. Befides, your Majefty in your great wifdom knoweth, that this
bufinefs

bufinefs of Mr. Murray's is fomewhat againft the ftream of the Judges inclination : and it is no part of a fkilful mariner to fail on againft a tide, when the tide is at ftrongeft. If your Majefty be pleafed to write to my Lord Coke, that you would have the bufinefs of the *Rege inconfulto* receive a hearing, when he fhould be *animo fedato et libero*, and not in the midft of his affiduous and inceffant cares and induftries in other practices, I think your Majefty fhall do your fervice right.   Howfoever, I will be provided againft the day.

Thus praying God for your happy prefervation, whereof God giveth you fo many great pledges;

I reft your Majefty's moft humble and

devoted fubject and fervant,

November 17,   Fr. Bacon.
   1615.

Innovations introduced into the laws and government (c).

1. The ecclefiaftical commiffion.

In this he prevailed, and the commiffion was pared, and namely the point of alimony left out, whereby wives are left wholly to the tyranny of their hufbands. This point, and fome others, may require a review, and is fit to be reftored to the commiffion.

(c) This paper was evidently defigned againft the Lord Chief Juftice Coke.

E 3   2. Againft

2. Againſt the provincial councils.

In this he prevailed in ſuch ſort, as the preſidents are continually ſuitors for the enlargement of the inſtructions, ſometimes in one point, ſometimes in another; and the juriſdictions grow into contempt, and more would, if the Lord Chancellor did not ſtrengthen them by injunctions, where they exceed not their inſtructions.

3. Againſt the Star-chamber for levying damages.

In this he was over-ruled by the ſentence of the court; but he bent all his ſtrength and wits to have prevailed; and ſo did the other Judges by long and laborious arguments: and if they had prevailed, the authority of the court had been overthrown. But the plurality of the court took more regard to their own precedents, than to the Judges opinion.

4. Againſt the Admiralty.

In this he prevaileth, for prohibitions fly continually; and many times are cauſe of long ſuits, to the diſcontent of foreign ambaſſadors, and the King's diſhonour and trouble by their remonſtrances.

5. Againſt the court of the duchy of Lancaſter prohibitions go; and the like may do to the Court of Wards and Exchequer.

This is new, and would be forthwith reſtrained, and the others ſettled.

6. Againſt

6. Againſt the Court of Requeſts.

In this he prevaileth ; and this but lately brought in queſtion.

7. Againſt the Chancery for decrees after judgment.

In this his Majeſty hath made an eſtabliſhment : and he hath not prevailed, but made a great noiſe and trouble.

8. Præmunire for ſuits in the Chancery.

This his Majeſty hath alſo eſtabliſhed, being a ſtrange attempt to make the Chancellor ſit under a hatchet, inſtead of the King's arms.

9. Diſputed in the Common Pleas, whether that court may grant a prohibition to ſtay ſuits in the Chancery, and time given to ſearch for precedents.

This was but a bravery, and dieth of itſelf, eſpecially the authority of the Chancery by his Majeſty's late proceedings being ſo well eſtabliſhed.

10. Againſt the new boroughs in Ireland.

This in good time was overruled by the voice of eight Judges of ten, after they had heard your Attorney. And had it prevailed, it had overthrown the parliament of Ireland, which would have been imputed to a fear in this ſtate to have proceeded ; and ſo his Majeſty's authority and reputation loſt in that kingdom.

11. Againſt the writs *Dom. Rege inconſulto.*

This is yet *ſub judice :* but if it ſhould prevail, it maketh the Judges abſolute over the patents of the King, be they of power and profit, contrary

to

to the antient, and ever continued law of the crown; which doth call those causes before the King himself, as he is represented in Chancery.

12. Against contribution, that it was not lawful neither to levy it, nor to move for it.

In this he prevailed, and gave opinion, that the King by his great seal could not so much as move any his subjects for benevolence. But this he retracted after in the Star-chamber; but it marred the benevolence in the mean time.

13. Peacham's case.

In this, for as much as in him was, and in the court of King's Bench, he prevailed, though it was holpen by the good service of others. But the opinion, which he held, amounted in effect to this, that no word of scandal or defamation, importing, that the King was utterly unable or unworthy to govern, were treason, except they disabled his title, &c.

14. Owen's case.

In this we prevailed with him to give opinion, it was treason: but then it was upon a conceit of his own, that was no less dangerous, than if he had given his opinion against the King: for he proclaimed the King excommunicate in respect of the anniversary bulls of *Cæna Domini*, which was to expose

15. The value of benefices not to be according to the tax in the King's book of taxes.

16. Suits for legacies ought to be in their proper dioceses, and not in the prerogative court; although the will be proved in the prerogative court upon *bona notabilia* in several dioceses, commendams,&c.

expose his person to the fury of any jesuited conspirator.

By this the intent of the statute of 21 Henry VIII. is frustrated; for there is no benefice of so small an improved value as 8l. by that kind of rating. For this the Judges may be assembled in the Exchequer for a conference.

The practice hath gone against this; and it is fit, the suit be where the probate is. And this served but to put a pique between the archbishops courts and the bishops courts. This may be again propounded upon a conference of the Judges.

To Sir GEORGE VILLIERS.

SIR,

THE message, which I received from you by Mr. Shute, hath bred in me such belief and confidence, as I will now wholly rely upon your excellent and happy self. When persons of greatness and quality begin speech with me of the matter, and offer me their good offices, I can but answer them civilly. But those things are but toys: I am your's surer to you than to mine own life; for, as they speak of the Turquois stone in a ring, I will break

into

into twenty pieces, before you have the leaft fall. God keep you ever.

Your trueft fervant,

February 15, 1615,

Fr. Bacon.

My Lord Chancellor is prettily amended. I was with him yefterday almoft half an hour. He ufed me with wonderful tokens of kindnefs. We both wept, which I do not often.

Indorfed,

A letter to Sir G. Villiers touching a meffage brought to him by Mr. Shute of a promife of the Chancellor's place.

Mr. Tobie Matthew (d) *to Sir* Francis Bacon, *Attorney General.*

May it pleafe you, Sir,

THE notice I have from my Lord Roos, Sir Henry Goodere, and other friends, of the extreme obligation, wherein I continue towards you, together with the confcience I have of the knowledge, how dearly and truly I honour and love you, and daily pray, that you may rife to that hight, which

---

(d) Son of Dr. Tobie Matthew, Archbifhop of York. He was born at Oxford in 1578, while his father was Dean of Chrift-church, and educated there. During his travels abroad, he was feduced to the Romifh religion by Father Parfons. This occafioned his living out of his own country from the year 1607 to 1617, when he had leave to return to England. He was again ordered to leave it in October 1618; but in 1622 was recalled to affift in the match with Spain; and on account of his endeavours to promote it, was knighted by King James I. at Royfton, on the 10th of October, 1623. He tranflated into Italian Sir Francis Bacon's *Effays*, and died at Ghent in Flanders, October 13, 1655, N. S.

the

the ftate, wherein you live, can give you, hath taken away the wings of fear, whereby I was almoft carried away from daring to importune you in this kind. But I know how good you have always been, and are ftill, towards me; or rather becaufe I am not able to comprehend how much it is, I will prefume there is enough for any ufe, whereupon an honeft humble fervant may employ it.

It imports the bufinefs of my poor eftate, that I be reftored to my country for fome time; and I have divers friends in that court, who will further my defire thereof, and particularly Mr. Secretary Lake and my Lord Roos, whom I have defired to confer with you about it. But nothing can be done therein, unlefs my Lord of Canterbury (*e*) may be made propitious, or at leaft not averfe; nor do I know in the world how to charm him but by the mufic of your tongue. I befeech you, Sir, lofe fome minutes upon me, which I fhall be glad to pay by whole years of fervice; and call to mind, if it pleafe you, the laft fpeech you made me, that if I fhould continue as I then was, and neither prove ill-affected to the ftate, nor become otherwife than a meer fecular man in my religion, you would be pleafed to negotiate for my return. On my part the conditions are performed; and it remains, that you do the like: nor can I doubt but that the noblenefs of your nature, which loves nothing in the world fo well as to be doing of good, can defcend from being the Attorney General to a great King, to be follicitor for one of the meaneft fubjects that he hath.

I fend my letter to my Lord's Grace open, that before you feal it (if you fhall think fit to feal it, and rather not to deliver it open) you may fee the reafons that I have; which, if I be not partial, are very pregnant. Although I confefs, that till it was now very lately

(*e*) Dr. George Abbot.

2   motioned

motioned to me by some honourable friends, who have already procured to disimpression his Majesty of some hard conceit he had me in, I did not greatly think thereof; and now I am full of hope, that I shall prevail. For supposing, that my Lord of Canterbury's mind is but made of iron, the adamant of your persuasion will have power to draw it. It may please you either to send a present answer hereunto; or, since I am not worthy of so much favour, to tell either of those honourable persons aforenamed what the answer is, that accordingly they may co-operate.

This letter goes by Sir Edward Parham, a gentleman, whom I have been much beholding to. I know him to be a perfect honest man; and since, I protest, I had rather die than deceive you, I will humbly pray, that he may rather receive favor from you, than otherwise, when he shall come in your way, which at one time or other all the world there must do. And I shall acknowledge myself much bound to you, as being enabled by this means to pay many of my debts to him.

I presume to send you the copy of a piece of a letter, which Galileo, of whom, I am sure, you have heard, wrote to a monk of my acquaintance in Italy, about the answering of that place in Joshua, which concerns the sun's standing still, and approving thereby the pretended falshood of Copernicus's opinion. The letter was written by occasion of the opposition, which some few in Italy did make against Galileo, as if he went about to establish that by experiments, which appears to be contrary to Holy Scripture. But he makes it appear the while by this piece of a letter, which I send you, that if that passage of Scripture doth expresly favour either side, it is for the affirmative of Copernicus's opinion, and for the negative of Aristotle's. To an Attorney General in the midst of a town, and such a one, as is employed in the weightiest affairs of the kingdom, it might

seem

feem unfeafonable for me to interrupt you with matter of this nature. But I know well enough in how high account you have the truth of things; and that no day can pafs, wherein you give not liberty to your wife thoughts of looking upon the works of nature. It may pleafe you to pardon the fo much trouble, which I give you in this kind; though yet, I confefs, I do not deferve a pardon, becaufe I find not in myfelf a purpofe of forbearing to do the like hereafter. I moft humbly kifs your hand.

Your moft faithful and affectionate fervant,

Bruffels, this 21ft
of April, 1616.
TOBIE MATTHEW.

Queftions legal for the Judges [in the Cafe of the Earl and Countefs of Somerfet.]

WHETHER the ax is to be carried before the prifoner, being in the cafe of felony?

Whether, if the Lady make any digreffion to clear his Lordfhip, fhe is not by the Lord Steward to be interrupted and filenced?

Whether, if my Lord of Somerfet fhould break forth into any fpeech of taxing the King, he be not prefently by the Lord Steward to be interrupted and filenced; and, if he perfift, he be not to be told, that if he take that courfe, he is to be withdrawn, and evidence to be given in his abfence? And whether that may be; and what elfe to be done?

Whether if there fhould be twelve votes to condemn, and twelve or thirteen to acquit, it be not a verdict for the King?

Queftions of Convenience, whereupon his Majefty may confer with fome of his Council.

WHETHER, if Somerfet confefs at any time before his trial, his Majefty fhall ftay trial in refpect of farther examination concerning practice of treafon, as

the

the death of the late Prince, the conveying into Spain of the now Prince, or the like ; for till he confess the less crime, there is [no] likelihood of confessing the greater ?

Whether, if the trial upon that reason shall be put off, it shall be discharged privately by dissolving the commission, or discharging the summons ? Or whether it shall not be done in open court, the peers being met, and the solemnity and celebrity preserved ; and that with some declaration of the cause of putting off the farther proceeding ?

Whether the days of her trial and his shall be immediate, as it is now appointed ; or a day between, to see, if, after condemnation, the Lady will confess of this Lord ; which done, there is no doubt but he will confess of himself ?

Whether his trial shall not be set first, and hers after, because then any conceit, which may be wrought by her clearing of him, may be prevented ; and it may be he will be in the better temper, hoping of his own clearing, and of her respiting?

What shall be the days ; for Thursday and Friday can hardly hold in respect of the summons ; and it may be as well Friday and Saturday, or Monday and Tuesday, as London makes it already?

A particular remembrance for his Majesty.

IT were good, that after he is come into the Hall, so that he may perceive he must go to trial, and shall be retired into the place appointed, till the court call for him, then the Lieutenant should tell him roundly, that if in his speeches he shall tax the King (f), that the justice of England is, that he shall be

---

(f) The King's apprehension of being *taxed* by the Earl of Somerset on his trial, though for what is not known, accounts
in

be taken away, and the evidence shall go on without him; and then all the people will cry *away with him*; and then it shall not be in the King's will to save his life, the people will be so set on fire.

Indorfed,

Memorial touching the courfe to be had in my Lord of Somerfet's arraignment.

The heads of the charge againft ROBERT *Earl of* SOMERSET.

Apoftyle of the King.

YE will doe well to remember lykewayes in your præamble, that infigne, that the only zeal to juftice maketh me take this courfe. I

FIRST it is meant, that Somerfet fhall not be charged with any thing by way of aggravation, otherwife than as conduceth to the proof of the impoifonment.

in fome meafure for his Majefty's extreme uneafinefs of mind till that trial was over, and for the management ufed by Sir Francis Bacon in particular, as appears from his letters, to prevail upon the Earl to fubmit to be tried, and to keep him in temper during his trial, *left he*, as the King expreffed it in an apoftille on Sir Francis's letter of the 28th of April, 1616, *upon the one part commit unpardonable errors, and I on the other feem to punifh him in the fpirit of revenge.* See more on this fubject in Mr. Mallet's *Life of the Lord Chancellor Bacon*, who clofes his remarks with a reference to a letter of Somerfet to the King, printed in the *Cabala*, and written in an high ftyle of expoftulation, and fhewing, through the affected obfcurity of fome expreffions, that there was an important fecret in his keeping, of which his Majefty dreaded a difcovery. The Earl and his Lady were releafed from their confinement in the Tower in January 162½, the latter dying Auguft 23, 1632, leaving one daughter Anne, then fixteen years of age, afterwards married to William Lord Ruffel, afterwards Earl, and at laft Duke of Bedford. The Earl of Somerfet furviv'd his Lady feveral years, and died in July 1645, being interr'd on the 17th of that month in the church of St. Paul's, Covent-Garden.

have

have commandit you not to expatiate, nor digresse upon any other points, that maye not serve clearlie for probation or inducement of that point, quhairof he is accused.

For the proofs themselves, they are distributed into four :

The first to prove the malice, which Somerset bore to Overbury, which was the motive and ground of the impoisonment.

The second is to prove the preparations unto the impoisonment, by plotting his imprisonment, placing his keepers, stopping access of friends, &c.

The third is the acts of the impoisonments themselves.

And the fourth is acts subsequent, which do vehemently argue him to be guilty of the impoisonment.

For the first two heads, upon conference, whereunto I called Serjeant Montagu and Serjeant Crew, I have taken them two heads to myself ; the third I have allotted to Serjeant Montagu ; and the fourth to Serjeant Crew.

In the first of these, to my understanding, is the only tenderness : for, on the one side, it is most necessary to lay a foundation, that the malice was a deep malice, mixed with fear, and not only matter of revenge upon his Lordship's quarrel : for *periculum periculo vincitur* ; and the malice must have a proportion to the effect of it, which was the impoisonment : so that if this foundation be not laid, all the evidence is weakened.

On the other side, if I charge him, or could charge him, by way of aggravation, with matters tending to disloyalty or treason, then he is like to grow desperate.

Therefore

Therefore I shall now set down perspicuously what course I mean to hold, that your Majesty may be pleased to direct and correct it, preserving the strength of the evidence : and this I shall now do, but shortly, and without ornament.

First, I shall read some passages of Overbury's letters, namely these : " Is this the fruit of nine " years love, common secrets, and common dan- " gers ?" In another letter ; " Do not drive me to " extremity to do that, which you and I shall be " forry for ?" In another letter ; " Can you forget " him, between whom such secrets of all kinds have " passed ? &c."

Then will I produce Simcock, who deposeth from Weston's speech, that Somerset told Weston, that, *if ever Overbury came out of prison, one of them must die for it.*

Then will I say what these secrets were. I mean not to enter into particulars, nor to charge him with disloyalty, because he stands to be tried for his life upon another crime. But yet by some taste, that I shall give to the peers in general, they may conceive of what nature those secrets may be. Wherein I will take it for a thing notorious, that Overbury was a man, that always carried himself insolently, both towards the Queen, and towards the late Prince : that he was a man, that carried Somerset on in courses separate and opposite to the privy-council : that he was a man of nature fit to be an incendiary of a state, full of bitterness and wildness of speech and project : that he was thought also lately to govern Somerset, insomuch that in his own letters he vaunted, *that from him proceeded Somerset's fortune, credit, and understanding.*

This course I mean to run in a kind of generality, putting the imputations rather upon Overbury than Somerset ; and applying it, that such a nature was like to hatch dangerous secrets and practices. I mean to shew likewise what jargons there were and

F   cyphers

cyphers between them, which are great badges of secrets of eftate, and ufed either by princes and their minifters of ftate, or by fuch, as practife againft Princes. That your Majefty was called *Julius*, in refpect of your empire; the Queen *Agrippina* (though Somerfet now faith it was *Livia,* and that my Lady of Suffolk was *Agrippina*;) the Bifhop of Canterbury *Unctius*; Northampton, *Dominic*; Suffolk, firft *Lerma,* after *Wolfey*; and many others: fo as it appears they made a play both of your court and kingdom; and that their imaginations wrought upon the greateft men and matters.

Neither will I omit Somerfet's breach of truft to your Majefty, in trufting Overbury with all the difpatches, things, wherewith your council of eftate itfelf was not many times privy or acquainted: and yet this man muft be admitted to them, not curforily, or by glimpfes, but to have them by him, to copy them, to regifter them, to table them, &c.

Apoftyle of the King.

This evidence cannot be given in without making me his accufer, and that upon a very flight ground. As for all the fubfequent evidences, they are all fo little evident, as una litura *may ferve thaime all.*

I fhall alfo give in evidence, in this place, the flight account of that letter, which was brought to Somerfet by Afhton, being found in the fields foon after the late Prince's death, and was directed to Antwerp, containing thefe words, that "the firft branch was cut "from the tree; and that he "fhould, ere long, fend hap-"pier and joyfuller news." Which is a matter I would not ufe, but that my Lord Coke, who hath filled this part with many frivolous things, would think all loft, except he hear

fomewhat

somewhat of this kind. But this it is to come to the leavings of a bufinefs.

And for the reft of that kind, as to fpeak of that particular, that Mrs. Turner did at Whitehall fhew to Franklin the man, who, as fhe faid, poifoned the Prince, which, he fays, was a phyfician with a red beard.

Nothing to Somerfet, and declared by Franklin after condemnation.

That there was a little picture of a young man in white wax, left by Mrs. Turner with Forman the conjurer, which my Lord Coke doubted was the Prince.

Nothing to Somerfet, and a loofe conjecture.

That the Vice-Roy of the Indies at Goa reported to an Englifh factor, that Prince Henry came to an untimely death by a miftrefs of his.

No better than a gazette, or paffage of Gallo Belgicus.

That Somerfet, with others, would have preferred Lowbell, the apothecary, to Prince Charles.

Nothing yet proved againft Lowbell.

That the Countefs laboured Forman and Grefham, the conjurers, to inforce the Queen by witchcraft to favour the Countefs.

Nothing to Somerfet.

That the Countefs told Franklin, that when the Queen died, Somerfet fhould have Somerfet-houfe.

Declared by Franklin after condemnation.

That Northampton faid, the Prince, if ever he came to reign, would prove a tyrant.

Nothing to Somerfet.

F 2 *Nothing*

Nothing to Somer-
fet.

That Franklin was moved by the Countefs to go to the Palfgrave, and fhould be furnifhed with money.

The particular reafons, why I omit them, I have fet in the margin; but the general is partly to do a kind of right to juftice, and fuch a folemn trial, in not giving that In evidence, which touches not the delinquent, or is not of weight; and partly to obferve your Majefty's direction, to give Somerfet no juft occafion of defpair, or flufhes.

But I pray your Majefty to pardon me, that I have troubled your Majefty with repeating them, left you fhould hear hereafter, that Mr. Attorney hath omitted divers material parts of the evidence.

Indorfed,

Somerfet's bufinefs and charge, with his Majefty's poftiles.

To Sir GEORGE VILLIERS.

SIR,

YOUR man made good hafte; for he was with me yefterday about ten of the clock the forenoon. Since I held him.

The reafon, why I fet fo fmall a diftance of time between the ufe of the little charm, or, as his Majefty better terms it, *the evangile (g)*, and the day of his trial (*h*), notwithftanding his Majefty's being fo far off, as advertifement of fuccefs and order thereupon could not go and come between, was chiefly, for that his Majefty, from whom the overture of that

(*g*) Cicero, Epift. ad Atticum, Lib. XIII. Ep. 40. ufes this word, εὐαγγέλια; which fignifies both good news, and the reward given to him, who brings good news. See Lib. II. Epift. 3.
(*h*) The Earl of Somerfet's.

firft

firſt moved, did write but of a few hours, that this ſhould be done, which I turned into days. Secondly, becauſe the hope I had of effect by that mean, was rather of attempting him at his arraignment, than of confeſſion before his arraignmet. But I ſubmit it to his Majeſty's better judgement.

The perſon, by your firſt deſcription, which was without name, I thought had been meant of Packer (*i*) : but now I perceive it is another, to me unknown, but, as it ſeemeth, very fit. I doubt not but he came with ſufficient warrant to Mr. Lieutenant to have acceſs. In this I have no more to do, but to expect to hear from his Majeſty how this worketh.

The letter from his Majeſty to myſelf and the Serjeants I have received, ſuch as I wiſhed; and I will ſpeak with the commiſſioners, that he may, by the Lieutenant, underſtand his Majeſty's care of him, and the tokens herein of his Majeſty's compaſſion towards him.

I ever had a purpoſe to make uſe of that circumſtance, that Overbury, the perſon murdered, was his Majeſty's priſoner in the Tower; which indeed is a ſtrong preſſure of his Majeſty's juſtice. For Overbury is the firſt priſoner murdered in the Tower, ſince the murder of the young Princes by Richard the Third, the tyrant.

I would not trouble his Majeſty with any points of preamble, nor of the evidence itſelf, more than that part nakedly, wherein was the tenderneſs, in which I am glad his Majeſty, by his poſtils, which he returned to me, approveth my judgement.

Now I am warranted, I will not ſtick to ſay openly, I am commanded, not to exaſperate, nor to aggravate the matter in queſtion of the impoiſonment with any other collateral charge of diſloyalty, or

(*i*) John, of whom there are ſeveral letters in Winwood's *Memorials*, Vol. II.

others

otherwife; wherein, befides his Majefty's principal intention, there will be fome ufe to fave the former bruits of Spanifh matters (*k*).

There is a direction given to Mr. Lieutenant by my Lord Chancellor and myfelf, that as yefterday Mr. Whiting (*l*), the preacher, a difcreet man, and one that was ufed to Helwiffe, fhould preach before the Lady (*m*), and teach her, and move her generally to a clear confeffion. That after the fame preacher fhould fpeak as much to him at his going away in private; and fo proof to be made, whether this good mean, and the laft night's thoughts, will produce any thing. And that this day the Lieutenant fhould declare to her the time of her trial, and likewife of his trial, and perfuade her, not only upon Chriftian duty, but as good for them both, that fhe deal clearly touching him, whereof no ufe can be made, nor need to be made, for evidence, but much ufe may be made for their comfort.

It is thought, at the day of her trial the Lady will confefs the indictment; which if fhe do, no evidence ought to be given. But becaufe it fhall not be a dumb fhew, and for his Majefty's honour in fo folemn an affembly, I purpofe to make a declaration of the proceedings of this great work of juftice, from the beginning to the end, wherein, neverthelefs, I

(*k*) Secretary Winwood, in a private letter to Sir Thomas Edmondes, dated March 26, 1616, mentions, that there was great expectation, that Sir John Digby, juft then returned from Spain, where he had been Ambaffador, could charge the Earl of Somerfet with *fome treafons and plots with Spain. Hiftorical View of the Negotiations between the Courts of England, France, and Bruffels,* p. 392.

(*l*) John Whiting, D. D. Rector of St. Martin Vintry, in London, and Vicar of Eaft-Ham in Effex, Prebendary of Ealdftreet in the church of St. Paul's, and Chaplain to King James I. He attended Sir Gervafe Helwiffe, who had been Lieutenant of the Tower, at his execution upon Tower-Hill, on Monday the 20th of November, 1615, for the murder of Sir Thomas Overbury. (*m*) Frances, Countefs of Somerfet,

will

will be careful no ways to prevent or difcover the evidence of the next day.

In this my Lord Chancellor and I have likewife ufed a point of providence : for I did forecaft, that if in that narrative, by the connection of things, any thing fhould be fpoken, that fhould fhew him guilty, fhe might break forth into paffionate pro-teftations for his clearing ; which, though it mȳ be juftly made light of, yet it is better avoided. Therefore my Lord Chancellor and I have devifed, that upon the entrance into that declaration fhe fhall, in refpect of her weaknefs, and not to add farther affliction, be withdrawn. ·

It is impoffible, neither is it needful, for me, to exprefs all the particulars of my care in this bufinefs. But I divide myfelf into all cogitations as far as I can forefee ; being very glad to find, that his Majefty doth not only accept well of my care and advices, but that he applieth his directions fo fitly, as guideth me from time to time.

I have received the commiffions figned.

I am not forgetful of the goods and eftate of So-merfet, as far as is feafonable to inquire at this time. My Lord Coke taketh upon him to anfwer for the jewels, being the chief part of his moveable value : and this, I think, is done with his Majefty's privity. But my Lord Coke is a good man to anfwer for it.

God ever preferve and profper you.   I reft,

Your true and devoted fervant,

May 10, Friday at 7
  of the clock in the
  morning [1616.]

                Fr. Bacon.

The charge of the Attorney General, Sir FRANCIS
BACON, *against* FRANCES, *Countess of* SOMER-
SET, *intended to have been spoken by him at her arraignment, on Friday, May 24, 1616, in case she
had pleaded not guilty (n).*

IT may please your Grace, my Lord High Steward of England (o), and you my Lords the Peers.

You have heard the indictment against this Lady
well opened; and likewise the point in law, that
might make some doubt, declared and solved;
wherein certainly the policy of the law of England
is much to be esteemed, which requireth and re-
specteth form in the indictment, and substance in the
proof.

This scruple it may be hath moved this Lady to
plead not guilty, though for the proof I shall not
need much more than her own confession, which she
hath formerly made, free and voluntary, and therein
given glory to God and Justice. And certainly confession, as it is the strongest foundation of Justice, so
it is a kind of corner-stone, whereupon Justice and
Mercy may meet.

The proofs, which I shall read in the end for the
ground of your verdict and sentence, will be very
short; and, as much as may, serve to satisfy your
honours and consciences for the conviction of this
Lady, without wasting of time in a case clear and confessed; or ripping up guiltiness against one, that hath
prostrated herself by confession; or preventing or de-
flowering too much of the evidence. And therefore
the occasion itself doth admonish me to spend this
day rather in declaration, than in evidence, giving
God and the King the honour, and your Lordships
and the hearers the contentment, to set before you

(n) She pleaded guilty, on which occasion the Attorney General
spoke a charge somewhat different from this, printed in his works.
(o) Thomas Egerton, Viscount Ellesmere, Lord High Chancellor.

the

the proceeding of this excellent work of the King's juſtice, from the beginning to the end ; and ſo to conclude with the reading the confeſſions and proofs.

My Lords, this is now the ſecond time *(p)* within the ſpace of thirteen years reign of our happy Sovereign, that this high tribunal-ſeat of Juſtice, ordained for the trial by peers, hath been opened and erected ; and that, with a rare event, ſupplied and exerciſed by one and the ſame perſon ; which is a great honour to you, my Lord Steward.

In all this mean time, the King hath reigned in his white robe, not ſprinkled with any drop of blood of any of his nobles of this kingdom. Nay, ſuch hath been the depths of his mercy, as even thoſe noblemen's bloods, (againſt whom the proceeding was at Wincheſter,) Cobham and Grey, were attainted and corrupted, but not ſpilt or taken away ; but that they remained rather ſpectacles of juſtice in their continual impriſonment, than monuments of juſtice in the memory of their ſuffering.

It is true, that the objects of his juſtice then and now were very differing. For then, it was the revenge of an offence againſt his own perſon and crown, and upon perſons, that were malcontents, and contraries to the ſtate and government. But now, it is the revenge of the blood and death of a particular ſubject, and the cry of a priſoner. It is upon perſons, that were highly in his favour ; whereby his Majeſty, to his great honour, hath ſhewed to the world (as if it were written in a ſun-beam) that he is truly the Lieutenant of him, with whom there is no reſpect of perſons ; that his affections royal are above his affections private : that his favours and nearneſs about him are not like popiſh ſanctuaries to privilege malefactors : and that his being the beſt maſter of the world doth not let him from being the beſt King of

(p) The firſt time was on the trials of the Lords Cobham and Grey, in November 1603.

the

the world. His people, on the other side, may fay to themfelves, *I will lie down in peace ; for God and the King and the law protect me againft great and fmall.* It may be a difcipline alfo to great men, efpecially fuch, as are fwoln in fortunes from fmall beginnings, that the King is as well able to level mountains, as to fill vallies, if fuch be their defert.

But to come to the prefent cafe ; the great frame of juftice, my Lords, in this prefent action, hath a vault, and it hath a ftage : a vault, wherein thefe works of darknefs were contrived ; and a ftage with fteps, by which they were brought to light. And therefore I will bring this work of juftice to the period of this day ; and then go on with this day's work.

Sir Thomas Overbury was murthered by poifon in the 15th of September, 1613, 11 *Reg.* This foul and cruel murther did, for a time, cry fecretly in the ears of God ; but God gave no anfwer to it, otherwife than by that voice, which fometimes he ufeth, which is *vox populi*, the fpeech of the people. For there went then a murmur, that Overbury was poifoned : and yet this fame fubmifs and foft voice of God, the fpeech of the vulgar people, was not without a counter-tenor, or counter-blaft of the devil (who is the common author both of murder and flander :) for it was given out, that Overbury was dead of a foul difeafe, and his body, which they had made a *corpus Judaicum* with their poifons, fo as it had no whole part, muft be faid to be leprofed with vice, and fo his name poifoned as well as his body. For as to diffolutenefs, I never heard the gentleman noted with it : his faults were infolency, and turbulency, and the like of that kind : the other part of the foul not the voluptuous.

Mean time, there was fome induftry ufed (of which I will not now fpeak) to lull afleep thofe, that were the revengers of blood ; the father and the bro-

ther

ther of the murthered. And in these terms things stood by the space almost of two years ; during which time, God so blinded the two great procurers, and dazzled them with their own greatness, and bind and nail fast the actors and instruments, with security upon their protection, as neither the one looked about them, nor the other stirred or fled, nor were conveyed away ; but remained here still, as under a privy arrest of God's judgments ; insomuch as Franklin, that should have been sent over to the Palsgrave with good store of money, was, by God's providence, and the accident of a marriage of his, diverted and stayed.

But about the beginning of the progress last summer, God's judgments began to come out of their depths : and as the revealing of murthers is commonly such, as a man may say, *a Domino hoc factum est* ; it is God's work, and it is marvellous in our eyes : so in this particular it was most admirable ; for it came forth by a compliment and matter of courtesy.

My Lord of Shrewsbury (*q*), that is now with God, recommended to a counsellor, of state of especial trust by his place, the late Lieutenant Helwisse (*r*);

(*q*) Gilbert, Earl of Shrewsbury, Knight of the Garter, who died May 8, 1616.

(*r*) Sir Gervase Helwisse, appointed Lieutenant of the Tower, upon the removal of Sir William Waad on the 6th of May, 1613. [*Reliquiæ Wottonianæ*, p. 412, 3d Edit. 1672.] Mr. Chamberlain, in a MS. letter to Sir Dudley Carleton, dated at London, May 13, 1613, speaks of Sir Gervase's promotion in these terms. " One " Sir Gervase Helwisse of Lincolnshire, somewhat an unknown " man, is put into the place [of Sir W. Waad's] by the favour " of the Lord Chamberlain [Earl of Somerset] and his Lady. " The gentleman is of too mild and gentle a disposition for such " an office. He is my old friend and acquaintance in France, " and lately renewed in town, where he hath lived past a year, " nor followed the court many a day." Sir Henry Wotton, in a letter of the fourteenth of May, 1613, [*ubi supra*, p. 13.] says, that Sir Gervase had been before *one of the Pensioners*.

only

only for acquaintance as an honeft worthy gentleman; and defired him to know him, and to be acquainted with him. That counfellor anfwered him civilly, that my Lord did him a favour; and that he fhould embrace it willingly: but he muft let his Lordfhip know, that there did lie a heavy imputation upon that gentleman, Helwiffe; for that Sir Thomas Overbury, his prifoner, was thought to have come to a violent and untimely death. When this fpeech was reported back by my Lord of Shrewfbury to Helwiffe, *perculit illico animum*, he was ftricken with it; and being a politic man, and of likelihood doubting, that the matter would break forth at one time or other, and that others might have the ftart of him, and thinking to make his own cafe by his own tale, refolved with himfelf, upon this occafion, to difcover to my Lord of Shrewfbury and that counfellor, that there was an attempt, whereto he was privy, to have poifoned Overbury by the hands of his under-keeper, Wefton; but that he checked it, and put it by, and diffuaded it, and related fo much to him indeed: but then he left it thus, that was but an attempt, or untimely birth, never executed; and, as if his own fault had been no more, but that he was honeft in forbidding, but fearful of revealing and impeaching or accufing great perfons; and fo with this fine point thought to fave himfelf.

But that great counfellor of ftate wifely confidering, that by the Lieutenant's own tale it could not be fimply a permiffion or weaknefs; for that Wefton was never difplaced by the Lieutenant, notwithftanding that attempt: and coupling the fequel by the beginning, thought it matter fit to be brought before his Majefty, by whofe appointment Helwiffe fet down the like declaration in writing.

Upon this ground, the King playeth Solomon's part, *Gloria Dei celare rem; et Gloria Regis inveftigare rem*; and fets down certain papers of his own hand, which

which I might term to be *claves juſtitiæ*, keys of juſtice ; and may ſerve for a precedent both for Princes
to imitate, and for a direction for Judges to follow :
and his Majeſty carried the balance with a conſtant
and ſteady hand, evenly and without prejudice,
whether it were a true accuſation of the one part,
or a practice and factious device of the other : which
writing, becauſe I am not able to expreſs according
to the worth thereof, I will deſire your Lordſhip
anon to hear read.

This excellent foundation of juſtice being laid by
his Majeſty's own hand, it was referred unto ſome
counſellors to examine farther, who gained ſome degrees of light from Weſton, but yet left it imperfect.

After it was referred to Sir Edward Coke, Chief
Juſtice of the King's Bench, as a perſon beſt practiſed
in legal examinations, who took a great deal of indefa-
tigable pains in it, without intermiſſion, having, as
I have heard him ſay, taken at leaſt three hundred
examinations in this buſineſs.

But theſe things were not done in a corner. I
need not ſpeak of them. It is true, that my Lord
Chief Juſtice, in the dawning and opening of the
light, finding that the matter touched upon theſe
great perſons, very diſcreetly became ſuitor to the
King to have greater perſons than his own rank joined with him. Whereupon, your Lordſhip, my Lord
High Steward of England, to whom the King commonly reſorteth *in arduis*, and my Lord Steward of
the King's houſe, and my Lord Zouch, were joined
with him.

Neither wanted there this while practice to ſup-
preſs teſtimony, to deface writings, to weaken the
King's reſolution, to ſlander the juſtice, and the like.
Nay when it came to the firſt ſolemn act of juſtice,
which was the arraignment of Weſton, he had his
leſſon to ſtand mute ; which had arreſted the wheel
of juſtice. But this dumb devil, by the means of
ſome

some discreet divines, and the potent charm of justice, together, was cast out. Neither did this poisonous adder stop his ear to those charms, but relented, and yielded to his trial.

Then follow the proceedings of justice against the other offenders, Turner, Helvisse, Franklin.

But all these being but the organs and instruments of this fact, the actors and not the authors, justice could not have been crowned without this last act against these great persons. Else Weston's censure or prediction might have been verified, when he said, he hoped the small flies should not be caught, and the great escape. Wherein the King being in great straits, between the defacing of his honour and of his creature, hath, acording as he useth to do, chosen the better part, reserving always mercy to himself.

The time also of this justice hath had its true motions. The time until this Lady's deliverance was due unto honour, Christianity, and humanity, in respect of her great belly. The time since was due to another kind of deliverance too; which was, that some causes of estate, that were in the womb, might likewise be brought forth, not for matter of justice, but for reason of state. Likewise this last procrastination of days had the like weighty grounds and causes. And this is the true and brief representation of this extreme work of the King's justice.

Now for the evidence against this Lady, I am sorry I must rip it up. I shall first shew you the purveyance or provisions of the poisons; that they were seven in number brought to this Lady, and by her billetted and laid up till they might be used: and this done with an oath or vow of secrecy, which is like the Egyptian darkness, a gross and palpable darkness, that may be felt.

Secondly, I shall shew you the exhibiting and sorting of this same number or volley of poisons: white
arsenic

arfenic was fit for falt, becaufe it is of like body and colour. The poifon of great fpiders, and of the venomous fly cantharides, was fit for pig's fauce, or partridge fauce, becaufe it refembled pepper. As for mercury-water, and other poifons, they might be fit for tarts, which is a kind of hotch-pot, wherein no one colour is fo proper : and fome of thefe were delivered by the hands of this Lady, and fome by her direction.

Thirdly, I fhall prove and obferve unto you, the cautions of thefe poifons ; that they might not be too fwift, left the world fhould ftartle at it by the fuddennefs of the difpatch : but they muft abide long in the body, and work by degrees : and for this purpofe there muft be effays of them upon poor beafts, &c.

And laftly, I fhall fhew you the rewards of this impoifonment, firft demanded by Wefton, and denied, becaufe the deed was not done ; but after the deed done and perpetrated, that Overbury was dead, then performed and paid to the value of 180 l.

And fo without farther aggravation of that, which in itfelf bears its own tragedy, I will conclude with the confeffions of this Lady herfelf, which is the ftrongeft fupport of juftice ; and yet is the foot-ftool of mercy. For, as the Scripture fays, *Mercy and Truth have kiffed each other* ; there is no meeting or greeting of mercy, till there be a confeffion, or trial of truth. For thefe read,

Franklin, November 16,	Helwiffe, October 2,
Franklin, November 17,	The Countefs's letter
Rich. Wefton, October 1,	without date,
Rich. Wefton, October 2,	The Countefs's confeffion,
Will. Wefton, October 2,	January 8.
Rich. Wefton, October 3,	

Mr.

Mr. Tobie Matthew *to Sir* Francis Bacon, *Attorney General.*

May it pleafe your Honour,

SUCH, as know your Honour, may congratulate with you the favour, which you have lately received from his Majefty, of being made a Counfellor of State (*s*): but as for me, I muft have leave to congratulate with the council-table, in being fo happy as to have you for an affeffor. I hope thefe are but beginnings, and that the marriage, which now I perceive that Fortune is about to make with Virtue, will be confummate in your perfon. I cannot diffemble, though I am afhamed to mention, the exceffive honour, which you have vouchfafed to do unto my picture. But fhame ought not to be fo hateful as fin; and without fin I know not how to conceal the extreme obligation, into which I am entered thereby, which is incomparably more than I can exprefs, and no lefs than as much as I am able to conceive. And as the copy is more fortunate than the original, becaufe it hath the honour to be under your eye; fo the original being much more truly your's than the copy can be, afpires by having the happinefs to fee you, to put the picture out of countenance.

I underftand by Sir George Petre (*t*), who is arrived here at the Spa, and is fo wife as to honour you extremely, though he have not the fortune to be known to your Honour, that he had heard how my Lord of Canterbury had been moved in my behalf; and that he gave way unto my return. This,

(*s*) Sir Francis Bacon was fworn at Greenwich of the privy-council, June 9, 1616.
(*t*) Grandfon of John, the firft Lord Petre, and fon of William, fecond Baron of that name.

if

if it be true, cannot have happened without some endeavour of your Honour; and therefore, howsoever I have not been particularly advertised, that your Honour had delivered my letter to his Grace; yet now methinks I do as good as know it, and dare adventure to present you with my humblest thanks for the favour. But the main point is, how his Majesty should be moved; wherein my friends are straining courtesy; and unless I have your Honour for a master of the ceremonies, to take order, who shall begin, all the benefit, that I can reap by this negotiation, will be to have the reputation of little judgment in attempting that, which I was not able to obtain; and that howsoever I have shot fair, I know not how to hit the mark. I have been directed by my Lord Roos, who was the first mover of this stone, to write a letter, which himself would deliver to the Master of the Horse (*u*), who doth me the honour to wish me very well: and I have obeyed his Lordship, and beseech your Honour, that you will be pleased to prevent, or to accompany, or second it with your commendation, lest otherwise the many words, that I have used, have but the virtue of a single *o*, or cypher. But indeed, if I had not been over-weighed by the authority of my Lord Roos's commandment, I should rather have reserved the Master of the Horse's favour to some other use afterward. In conformity whereof, I have also written to his Lordship; and perhaps he will thereupon forbear to deliver my letter to the Master of the Horse: whereas, I should be the less sorry, if your Honour's self would not think it inconvenient to make the suit of my return to his Majesty; in which case I should, to my extreme contentment, have all my obligations to your Honour only.

(*u*) Sir George Villiers, who was appointed to that office, January 4, 161⅝.

G

His

His Majesty's being now in progress will give some impediment to my suit, unless either it be my good fortune, that your Honour do attend his person; or else that you will be pleased to command some one of the many servants your Honour hath in court, to procure the expedition of my cause; wherein I can foresee no difficulty, when I consider the interest, which your Honour alloweth me in your favour, and my innocent carriage abroad for so many years; whereunto all his Majesty's ministers, who have known me, I am sure, will give an attestation, according to the contents of my letter to his Grace of Canterbury.

If I durst, I would most humbly intreat your Honour to be pleased, that some servant of your's may speedily advertise me, whether or no his Grace of Canterbury hath received my letter; what his answer was; and what I may hope in this my suit. I remember, that the last words, which I had the honour to hear from your mouth, were, that if I continued any time, free both from disloyalty and priesthood, your Honour would be pleased to make yourself the intercessor for my return. Any letter sent to Mr. Trumball for me will come safely and speedily to my hands.

The term doth now last with your Honour all the year long; and therefore the sooner I make an end, the better service I shall do you. I presume to kiss your hands, and continue

Your Honour's most intirely, and

Spa, this 16th of .July, *stylo novo*, 1616.   humbly ever at commandment,

TOBIE MATTHEW.

POSTSC.

POSTSC. It is no small penance, that I am forced to apparel my mind in my man's hand, when it speaks to your Honour.   But God Almighty will have it so, through the shaking I have in my right hand ; and I do little less than want the use of my fore finger.

To Sir FRANCIS BACON, *Attorney General.*

It may please your Honour,

I PRESUMED to importune your Honour with a letter of the 16th of this month, whereby I signified, how I had written to the Master of the Horse, that he would be pleased to move his Majesty for my return into England ; and how that I had done it upon the direction of my Lord Roos, who offered to be the deliverer thereof.   Withal I told your Honour, that I expressed thereby an act rather of obedience, than prudence, as not holding his Lordship a fit man, whom, by presenting that letter, the King might peradventure discover to be my favourer in this business.   In regard whereof I besought him, that, howsoever I had complied with his command in writing, yet he would forbear the delivery : and I gave him divers reasons for it.   And both in contemplation of those reasons, as also of the hazard of miscarriage, that letters do run into between these parts and those, I have now thought fit to send your Honour this inclosed, accompanied with a most humble intreaty, that you will be pleased to put it into the Master of the Horse's hands, with such a recommendation as you can give.   Having read it, your Honour may be pleased to seal it ; and if his Honour have received the former by other hands, this may serve in the nature of a duplicate or copy : if not, it may be the original.   And indeed, though it should be but the

copy,

copy, if it may be touched by your Honour, it would have both greater grace and greater life, than the principal itfelf; and therefore, howfoever, I humbly pray, that this may be delivered.

If my bufinefs fhould be remitted to the counciltable (which yet, I hope, will not be) I am moft a ftranger to my Lord Chancellor and my Lord Chamberlain (*w*), of whom yet I truft, by means of your Honour's good word in my behalf, that I fhall receive no impediment.

The bearer, Mr. Becher (*x*), can fay what my carriage hath been in France, under the eye of feveral Ambaffadors; which makes me the more glad to ufe him in the delivery of this letter to your Honour: and if your Honour may be pleafed to command me any thing, he will convey it to my knowledge.

I hear, to my unfpeakable joy of heart, how much power you have with the Mafter of the Horfe; and how much immediate favour you have alfo with his moft excellent Majefty: fo that I cannot but hope for all good fuccefs, when I confider withal the protection, whereinto you have been pleafed to take me, the

Moft humble and moft obliged of

Spa, this laft of
July, *ftyle novo*,
1616.

your Honour's many fervants,

TOBIE MATTHEW.

(*w*) William, Earl of Pembroke.
(*x*) William, afterwards knighted. He had been fecrerary to Sir George Calvert, Ambaffador to the court of France, and was afterwards agent at that court; and at laft made Clerk of the Council.

To

To Sir FRANCIS BACON, *Attorney General.*

May it pleafe your Honour,

I HAVE been made happy by your Honour's noble and dear lines of the two and twentieth of July: and the joy, that I took therein, was only kept from excefs by the notice they gave me of fome intentions and advices of your Honour, which you have been pleafed to impart to others of my friends, with a meaning, that they fhould acquaint me with them; whereof they have intirely failed. And therefore, if ftill it fhould import me to underftand what they were, I muft be inforced to beg the know-ledge of them from yourfelf. Your Honour hath, by this fhort letter, delivered me otherwife from a great deal of laborious fufpénce. For, befides the great hope you give me of being fo fhortly able to do you reverence, I am come to know, that by the dili-gence of your favour towards me, my Lord of Can-terbury hath been drawn to give way, and the Ma-fter of the Horfe hath been induced to move. That motion, I truft, will be granted howfoever; but I fhould be out of fear thereof, if, when he moves the King, your Honour would caft to be prefent; that if his Majefty fhould make any difficulty, fome fuch reply, as is wont to come from you in fuch cafes, may have power to difcharge it.

I have been told rather confidently, than credibly (for in truth I am hardly drawn to believe it) that Sir Henry Goodere fhould under hand (upon the reafon of certain accounts, that run between him and me, wherein I might juftly lofe my right, if I had fo little wit, as to trouble your Honour's infinite bufinefs, by a particular relation thereof,) oppofe himfelf to my return; and perform ill offices in conformity of

that

that unkind affection, which he is said to bear me. But, as I said, I cannot absolutely believe it, though yet I could not so far despise the information, as not to acquaint your Honour with what I heard. I offer it not as a ruled case, but only as a query, as I have also done to Mr. Secretary Lake, in this letter, which I humbly pray your Honour may be given him, together with your best advice, how my business is to be carried in this conjuncture of his Majesty's drawing near to London, at which time I shall receive my sentence. I have learned from your Honour to be confident, that it will be pronounced in my favour: but, if the will of God should be otherwise, I shall yet frame for myself a good proportion of contentment; since, howsoever I was so unfortunate, as that I might not enjoy my country, yet withal, I was so happy, as that my return thither was desired and negotiated by the affection, which such a person as yourself vouchsafed to bear me. When his Majesty shall be moved, if he chance to make difficulty about my return, and offer to impose any condition, which, it is known, I cannot draw myself to digest; I desire it may be remembered, that my case is common with many of his subjects, who breath in the air of their country, and that my case is not common with many, since I have lived so long abroad with disgrace at home; and yet have ever been free, not only from suspicion of practice, but from the least dependence upon foreign Princes. My King is wise; and I hope, that he hath this just mercy in store for me. God Almighty make and keep your Honour ever happy, and keep me so in his favour, as I will be sure to continue

Your Honour's ever most obliged,

and devoted servant,

Antwerp, this first
of Sept. *stylo novo,*
1616.

TOBIE MATTHEW.

POST-

P O S T S C R I P T.

May it pleafe your Honour,

I have written to Sir John Digby; and I think he would do me all favour, if he were handfomely put upon it. My Lady of Pembroke *(y)* hath written, and that very earneftly, to my Lord Chamberlain in my behalf.

This letter goes by Mr. Robert Garret, to whom I am many ways beholden, for making me the beft prefent, that ever I received, by delivering me your honour's laft letter.

Sir FRANCIS BACON *to the* KING.

May it pleafe your excellent Majefty,

BECAUSE I have ever found, that in bufinefs the confideration of perfons, who are *inftrumenta animata*, is no lefs weighty than of matters, I humbly pray your Majefty to perufe this inclofed paper, containing a diligence, which I have ufed *in omnem eventum*. If Towerfon *(z)*, as a paffionate man, have overcome himfelf in his opinion, fo it is. But if his company make this good, then I am very glad to fee in the cafe, wherein we now ftand, there is this hope left, and your Majefty's honour preferved in the *extier*. God have your Majefty in his divine protection.

Your Majefty's moft devoted, and

moft bounden fervant, &c.

(y) Mary, widow of Henry, Earl of Pembroke, who died January 19, 160½, daughter of Sir Henry Sidney, and fifter of Sir Philip. She died September 25, 1621.

(z) Whofe brother, Captain Gabriel Towerfon, was one of the Englifh merchants executed by the Dutch at Amboyna, in 1623,

This

This is a secret to all men but my Lord Chancellor; and we go on this day with the new company, without discouraging them at all.

September 18, 1616.

Indorsed,

To the King, upon Towerson's propositions about the cloth business.

RICHARD MARTIN, *Esq; (a) to Sir* FRANCIS BACON.

Right Honourable,

MY attendance at court two days (in vain, considering the end of my journey) was no loss unto me, seeing thereby I made the gain of the overture and assurance of your Honour's affection. These comforts have given new life and strength to my hopes, which before began to faint. I know, what your Honour promiseth, you will undertake; and what you undertake, you seldom fail to compass; for such proof of your prudence and industry your Honour hath of late times given to the swaying world. There is, to my understanding, no great intricacy in my affair, in which I plainly descry the course to the shore I would land at; to which neither I, nor any other, can attain, without the direction of our great master-pilot, who will not stir much without the beloved mate found the way. Both these none

(a) Born about 1570, entered a commoner of Broad-gate's Hall, now Pembroke-College, Oxford, in 1585, whence he removed to the Middle-Temple. In the Parliament of 1601, he served for the borough of Barnstable in Devon; and in the first parliament of King James I, he served for Cirencester in Gloucestershire. He was chosen Recorder of London in September 1618; but died in the last day of the following month. He was much esteemed by the men of learning and genius of that age.

4   can

can fo well fet awork as yourfelf, who have not only their ear, but their affection, and that with good right, as I hope, in time, to good and public pur-pofe. It is· fit likewife,. that your Honour know all my advantages. The prefent incumbent is tied to me by firm promife, which gives an impediment to the competitors, whereof one already, according to the heavinefs of his name and nature, *petit deorfum.* And though I be a bad courtier, yet I know the ftyle of gratitude, and fhall learn as I am inftructed. Whatfoever your Honour fhall undertake for me, I will make good. Therefore I humbly and earneftly intreat your beft endeavour, to affure to yourfelf and your mafter a fervant, who both can and will, though as yet miftaken, advance his honour and fervice with advantage. Your love and wifdom is my laft ad-drefs ; and on the real noblenefs of your nature (whereof there is fo good proof) ftands my laft hope. If I now find a ftop, I will refolve it is *fatum Cartha-ginis,* and fit down in perpetual peace. In this bu-finefs I defire all convenient filence ; for though I can endure to be refufed, yet it would trouble me to have my name blafted. If your Honour return not, and you think it requifite, I will attend at court. Mean time, with all humble and hearty wifhes for increafe of all happinefs, I kifs your Honour's hands.

Your Honour's humbly at command,

September 27,
1616.

R. MARTIN.

To the Right Honourable Sir Francis Bacon, Knight,
his Majefty's Attorney General, and one of his Ma-
jefty's moft honourable privy council, my fingular pa-
tron, at court.

To

To the KING.

It may pleafe your Majefty,

THIS morning, according to your Majefty's command, we have had my Lord Chief Juftice of the King's Bench (b) before us, we being affifted by all your learned council, except Serjeant Crew, who was then gone to attend your Majefty. It was delivered unto him, that your Majefty's pleafure was, that we fhould receive an account from him of the performance of a commandment of your Majefty laid upon him, which was, that he fhould enter into a view and retractation of fuch novelties, and errors, and offenfive conceits, as were difperfed in his *Reports*; that he had had good time to do it; and we doubted not but he had ufed good endeavour in it, which we defired now in particular to receive from him.

His fpeech was, that there were of his *Reports* eleven books, that contained about five hundred cafes: that heretofore, in other *Reports*, as namely, thofe of Mr. Plowden (c), which he reverenced much, there hath been found neverthelefs errors, which the wifdom of time had difcovered, and later judgments controlled; and enumerated to us four cafes in Plow-

---

(b) Sir Edward Coke.
(c) Edmund Plowden, born of an ancient family of that name at Plowden in Shropfhire, about the year 1518. He was educated at Cambridge and Oxford, in both which univerfities he ftudied phyfic for fome time, being admitted, in November 1552, by the latter to practife chirurgery and phyfic. After this, he applied himfelf to the ftudy of the common law, in which he foon became eminent, and in 1557 was autumn reader to the Middle-Temple, and three years after lent reader, having been made Serjeant, October 27, 1558. He died February 6, 158⅓, at the age of fixty feven, in the profeffion of the Roman catholic faith.

den,

den, which were erroneous : and thereupon delivered in to us the inclofed paper, wherein your Majefty
may perceive, that my Lord is an happy man, that
there fhould be no more errors in his five hundred
cafes, than in a few cafes of Plowden. Your Majefty may alfo perceive, that your Majefty's direction
to my Lord Chancellor and myfelf, and the travail
taken by us and Mr. Sollicitor *(d)*, in following and
performing your direction, was not altogether loft ;
for that of thofe three heads, which we principally
refpected, which were the rights and liberties of the
church, your prerogative, and the jurifdiction of
other your courts, my Lord hath fcarcely fallen upon
any, except it be the Prince's cafe, which alfo yet
feemeth to ftand but upon the grammatical, of French
and Latin.

My Lord did alfo give his promife, which your
Majefty fhall find in the end of his writing, thus far
in a kind of common place or thefis, that it was fit
for a man to go againft his own confcience, though
erroneous, except his confcience be firft informed and
fatisfied.

The Lord Chancellor in the conclufion fignified to
my Lord Coke your Majefty's commandment, that
until report made, and your pleafure thereupon
known, he fhall forbear his fitting at Weftminfter,
&c. not reftraining neverthelefs any other exercife
of his place of Chief Juftice in private.

Thus having performed, to the beft of our underftanding, your royal commandment, we reft ever

Your Majefty's moft faithful, and

moft bounden fervants, &c.

(d) Sir Henry Yelverton.

The

The Lord Viscount VILLIERS *to Sir* FRANCIS BACON, *Attorney General.*

SIR,

I HAVE acquainted his Majesty with my Lord Chancellor's and your report, touching my Lord Coke ; as also with your opinion therein ; which his Majesty doth dislike for these three reasons : first, because, that by this course you propound, the process cannot have a beginning, till after his Majesty's return ; which, how long it may last after, no man knoweth. He therefore thinketh it too long and uncertain a delay, to keep the bench so long void from a Chief Justice. Secondly, although his Majesty did use the council's advice in dealing with the Chief Justice upon his other misdemeanors ; yet he would be loth to lessen his prerogative, in making the council judges, whether he should be turned out of his place or no, if the case should so require. Thirdly, for that my Lord Coke hath sought means to kiss his Majesty's hands, and withal, to acquaint him with some things of great importance to his service ; he holdeth it not fit to admit him to his presence, before these points be determined, because that would be a grant of his pardon before he had his trial. And if those things, wherewith he is to acquaint his Majesty, be of such consequence, it would be dangerous and prejudicial to his Majesty, to delay him too long. Notwithstanding, if you shall advise of any other reasons to the contrary, his Majesty would have you, with all the speed you can, to send them unto him ; and in the mean time to keep back his Majesty's letter, which is herein sent unto you, from my Lord Coke's knowledge,

ledge, until you receive his Majesty's further direction for your proceeding in his business.

And so I rest,

Your ever assured friend at command,

Theobalds, the
3d of October, 1616.

GEORGE VILLIERS.

*To the Right Honourable Sir Francis Bacon, Knight,
his Majesty's Attorney General, and of his most honourable privy council.*

To the KING.

It may please your most excellent Majesty,

WE have considered of the letters, which we received from your Majesty, as well that written to us both, as that other written by my Lord Villiers to me, the Attorney, which I thought good to acquaint my Lord Chancellor withal, the better to give your Majesty satisfaction. And we most humbly desire your Majesty to think, that we are, and ever shall be, ready to perform and obey your Majesty's directions; towards which, the first degree is to understand them well.

In answer therefore to both the said letters, as well concerning matter as concerning time, we shall in all humbleness offer to your Majesty's high wisdom the considerations following:

First, we did conceive, that after my Lord Coke was sequestered from the table and his circuits (e), when your Majesty laid upon him your command-

(e) On the 30th of June, 1616. *Camdeni Annales Regis Jacobi I.* p. 19; and Peck, *Desiderata Curiosa,* Vol. I. Lib. VI. p. 18.

ment

ment for the expurging of his *Reports*, and commanded also our service to look into them, and into other novelties introduced into the government, your Majesty had in this your doing two principal ends :

The one, to see, if upon so fair an occasion, he would make any expiation of his former faults ; and also shew himself sensible of those things in his *Reports*, which he could not but know were the likest to be offensive to your Majesty.

The other, to perform *de vero* this right to your crown and succession, and your people also ; that those errors and novelties might not run on, and authorize by time, but might be taken away, whether he consented to it or no.

But we did not conceive your Majesty would have had him charged with those faults of his book, or those other novelties ; but only would have had them represented to you for your better information.

Now your Majesty seeth what he hath done; you can better judge of it than we can. If, upon this probation added to former matters, your Majesty think him not fit for your service, we must in all humbleness subscribe to your Majesty, and acknowledge, that neither his displacing (considering he holdeth his place but during your will and pleasure) nor the choice of a fit man to be put in his room, are council-table matters, but are to proceed wholly from your Majesty's great wisdom, and gracious pleasure. So that in this course, it is but the signification of your pleasure, and the business is at an end as to him. Only there remaineth the actual expurgation or animadversions of the books.

But if your Majesty understand it, that he shall be charged, then, as your Majesty best knoweth, justice requireth, that he be heard and called to his answer, and then your Majesty will be pleased to consider, before whom he shall be charged ; whether before the body of your council (as formerly he was,) or
                                                        some

some selected commissioners ; for we conceive your Majesty will not think it convenient it should be before us two only. Also the manner of his charge is considerable, whether it shall be verbal by your learned council, as it was last ; or whether, in respect of the multiplicity of matters, he shall not have the collections, we have made in writing, delivered to him. Also the matter of his charge is likewise considerable, whether any of those points of novelty, which by your Majesty's commandment we collected, shall be made part of his charge ; or only the faults of his books, and the prohibitions and *habeas corpus*, collected by my Lord of Canterbury. In all which course we foresee length of time, not so much for your learned council to be prepared (for that is almost done already,) but because himself, no doubt, will crave time of advice to peruse his own books, and to see, whether the collections be true, and that he be justly charged ; and then to produce his proofs, that those things, which he shall be charged with, were not conceits or singularities of his own, but the acts of court, and other like things, tending to excusation or extenuation ; wherein we do not see, how the time of divers days, if not of weeks, can be denied him.

Now for time, (if this last course of charging him be taken) we may only inform your Majesty thus much, that the absence of a Chief Justice, though it should be for a whole term, as it hath been often upon sickness, can be no hindrance to common justice. For the business of the King's Bench may be dispatched by the rest of the Judges : his voice in the Star-Chamber may be supplied by any other Judge, that my Lord Chancellor shall call ; and the trials by *nisi prius* may be supplied by commission.

But as for those great matters of discovery, we can say nothing more than this, that either they are old or new. If old, he is to blame for having kept

2 them

them fo long : if new, or whatfoever, he may advertife your Majefty of them by letter, or deliver them by word to fuch counfellor, as your Majefty will affign.

Thus we hope your Majefty will accept of our fincerity, having dealt freely and openly with your Majefty, as becometh us : and when we fhall receive your pleafure and direction, we fhall execute and obey the fame in all things; ending with our prayers for your Majefty, and refting

Your Majefty's moft faithful, and

moft bounden fervants,

October 6, 1616.

T. ELLESMERE CANE.
FRANCIS BACON.

Remembrances of his Majefty's declaration, touching the Lord COKE.

THAT although the difcharging and removing of his Majefty's officers and fervants, as well as the choice and advancement of men to place, be no council-table matters, but belong to his Majefty's princely will, and fecret judgement; yet his Majefty will do his council this honour, that in his refolutions of that kind, his council fhall know them firft before others, and fhall know them, accompanied by their caufes, making as it were a private manifefto, or revealing of himfelf to them without parables.

Then to have the report of the Lords touching the bufinefs of the Lord Coke, and the laft order of the council read.

That done, his Majefty farther to declare, that he might, upon the fame three grounds in the order mentioned,

mentioned, of deceit, contempt, and flander of his government, very juftly have proceeded then, not only to have put him from his place of Chief Juftice, but to have brought him in queftion in the Star-Chamber, which would have been his utter over-throw; but then his Majefty was pleafed for that time only to put him off from the council-table, and from the public exercife of his place of Chief Juftice, and to take farther time to deliberate.

That in this his Majefty's deliberation (befides the prefent occafion) he had in fome things looked back to the Lord Coke's former carriage, and in fome things looked forward, to make fome farther trial of him.

That for things paffed, his Majefty had noted in him a perpetual turbulent carriage, firft towards the liberties of his church and eftate ecclefiaftical; to-wards his prerogative royal, and the branches there-of; and likewife towards all the fettled jurifdictions of all his other courts, the High Commiffion, the Star-Chamber, the Chancery, the Provincial Coun-cils, the Admiralty, the Duchy, the Court of Re-quefts, the Commiffion of Inquiries, the new Bo-roughs of Ireland; in all which he had raifed trou-bles and new queftions; and laftly, in that, which might concern the fafety of his royal perfon, by his expofition of the laws in cafes of high treafon.

That, befides the actions themfelves, his Majefty, in his princely wifdom, hath made two fpecial obfer-vations of him; the one, that he having in his na-ture not one part of thofe things, which are popular in men, being neither civil, nor affable, nor mag-nificent, he hath made himfelf popular by defign only, in pulling down government. The other, that whereas his Majefty might have expected a change in him, when he made him his own, by taking him to be of his council, it made no change at all, but to the worfe, he holding on all his former channel, and running feparate courfes from the reft of his council; and rather bufying himfelf in cafting fears before his council, concerning what they could not do, than joining his advice what they fhould do.

- That his Majefty, defirous yet to make a farther trial of him, had given him the fummer's vacation to reform his *Reports*, wherein there be many dangerous conceits of his own uttered for law, to the prejudice of his crown, parliament, and fubjects; and to fee, whether by this he would in any part redeem his fault. But that his Majefty hath failed of the redemption he defired, but hath met with another kind of redemption from him, which he little expected. For as to the *Reports*, after three months time and confideration, he had offered his Majefty only five animadverfions, being rather a fcorn, than a fatisfaction to his Majefty; whereof one was, that in the Prince's cafe he had found out the French ftatute, which was *filz aifné*, whereas the Latin was *primogenitus*; and fo the Prince is Duke of Cornwall in French, and not Duke of Cornwall in Latin. And another was, that he had fet Montagu to be Chief Juftice in Henry VIII's time, when it fhould have been in Edward VI's, and fuch other ftuff; not falling upon any of thofe things, which he could not but know were offenfive.

That hereupon his Majefty thought good to refrefh his memory, and out of many cafes, which his Majefty caufed to be collated, to require his anfwer to five, being all fuch, as were but expatiations of his own, and no judgments; whereunto he returned fuch an anfwer, as did either juftify himfelf, or elude the matter, fo as his Majefty feeth plainly *antiquum obtinet*.

To Sir FRANCIS BACON, *Attorney General* (*).

SIR,

I HAVE kept your man here thus long, becaufe I thought there would have been fome occafion for me to write after Mr. Sollicitor General's being with the King. But he hath received fo full inftruction from his Majefty, that there is nothing left for me to add in the bufinefs. And fo I reft,

Your faithful fervant,

Royfton, the 13th of Octob. 1616. GEORGE VILLIERS.

To the Right Honourable Sir Francis Bacon, Knight, one of his Majefty's Privy Council, and his Attorney General.

Sir EDMUND BACON (f) *to Sir* FRANCIS BACON, *Attorney General.*

My Lord,

I AM bold to prefent unto your hands by this bearer, whom the law calls up, fome falt of wormwood, being uncertain, whether the regard of your health makes you ftill continue the ufe of that medicine. I could wifh it otherwife; for I am perfuaded, that all diuretics, which carry with them that punctuous nature and cauftic quality by calci-

(*) Harl. MSS. Vol. 7006.
(f) Nephew of Sir Francis Bacon, being eldeft fon of Sir Nicolas Bacon, eldeft fon of Sir Nicolas Bacon, Lord Keeper of the Great Seal. Sir Edmund died without iffue, April 10, 1649. There are feveral letters to him from Sir Henry Wotton, printed among the works of the latter.

nation, are hurtful to the kidneys, if not enemies to the other principal parts of the body. Wherein, if it shall please you, for your better satisfaction, to call the advice of your learned physicians, and that they shall resolve of any medicine for your health, wherein my poor labour may avail you, you know where your faithful apothecary dwells, who will be ready at your commandment; as I am bound both by your favours to myself, as also by those to my nephew, whom you have brought out of darkness into light, and, by what I hear, have already made him, by your bounty, a subject of emulation to his elder brother. We are all partakers of this your kindness towards him; and, for myself, I shall be ever ready to deserve it by any service, that shall lie in the power of

Your Lordship's poor nephew,

Redgrave, this
19th of Octo-
ber, 1616.

EDM. BACON.

For the Right Honourable Sir Francis Bacon, Knight, his Majesty's Attorney General, and one of his most Honourable Privy Counsellors, be these delivered at London.

To the KING.

May it please your excellent Majesty,

I SEND your Majesty a form of discharge for my Lord Coke from his place of Chief Justice of your Bench (g).

(g) Sir Edward Coke was removed from that post on the 15th of November, 1616.

I send

I fend alfo a warrant to the Lord Chancellor, for making forth a writ for a new Chief Juftice, leaving a blank for the name to be fupplied by your Majefty's prefence ; for I never received your Majefty's exprefs pleafure in it.

If your Majefty refolve of Montagu (*b*) (as I conceive and wifh) it is very material, as thefe times are, that your Majefty have fome care, that the Recorder fucceeding be a temperate and difcreet man, and affured to your Majefty's fervice. If your Majefty, without too much harfhnefs, can continue the place within your own fervants, it is beft : if not, the man, upon whom the choice is like to fall, which is Coventry (*i*), I hold doubtful for your fervice ; not but that he is a well learned, and an honeft man ; but he hath been, as it were, bred by Lord Coke, and feafoned in his ways.

God preferve your Majefty.

Your Majefty's moft humble, and

moft bounden fervant,

Fr. Bacon.

I fend not thefe things, which concern my Lord Coke, by my Lord Villiers, for fuch reafons as your Majefty may conceive.

November 13, at noon [1616].

(*b*) Sir Henry Montagu, Recorder of London, who was made Lord Chief Juftice of the King's Bench, November 16, 1616. He was afterwards made Lord Treafurer, and created Earl of Manchefter.

(*i*) Thomas Coventry, Efq; afterwards Lord Keeper of the Great Seal.

To the KING.

It may please your most excellent Majesty,

I SEND your Majesty, according to your commandment, the warrant for the review of Sir Edward Coke's *Reports*.   I had prepared it before I received your Majesty's pleasure: but I was glad to see
it was in your mind, as well as in my hands.   In the
nomination, which your Majesty made of the Judges,
to whom it should be directed, your Majesty could
not name the Lord Chief Justice, that now is (*k*),
because he was not then declared: but you could
not leave him out now, without discountenance.

I send your Majesty the state of Lord Darcy's
cause (*l*) in the Star-Chamber, set down by Mr.
Sollicitor,

(*k*) Sir Henry Montagu.
(*l*) This is just mentioned in a letter of Sir Francis Bacon to
the Lord Viscount Villiers, printed in his works; but is more
particularly stated in the *Reports* of Sir Henry Hobart, Lord
Chief Justice of the Common Pleas, p. 120, 121. Edit. London,
1658, fol. as follows.   The Lord Darcy of the North sued
Gervase Markham, Esq; in the Star-Chamber, in 1616, on
this occasion.   They had hunted together, and the defendant
and a servant of the plaintiff, one Beckwith, fell together by
the ears in the field; and Beckwith threw him down, and was
upon him cuffing him, when the Lord Darcy took his servant off, and reproved him.   However, Mr. Markham expressing
some anger against his Lordship, and charging him with maintaining his man, Lord Darcy answered, that he had used Mr.
Markham kindly; for if he had not rescued him from his man,
the latter would have beaten him to rags.   Mr. Markham, upon
this, wrote five or six letters to Lord Darcy, subscribing them
with his name; but did not send them, and only dispersed them
unsealed in the fields; the purport of them being this: that
whereas the Lord Darcy had said, that, but for him, his servant
Beckwith had beaten him to rags, he lied; and, as often as he
should speak it, he lied; and that he would maintain this with
his life: adding, that he had dispersed those letters, that his
Lordship might find them, or somebody else bring them to him;
and

Sollicitor (*m*), and mentioned in the letters, which your Majefty received from the Lords. I leave all in humblenefs to your Majefty's royal judgement : but this is true, that it was the clear opinion of my Lord Chancellor, and myfelf, and the two Chief Juftices, and others, that it is a caufe moft fit for the cenfure of the court, both for the repreffing of duels, and the encouragement of complaints in courts of juftice. If your Majefty be pleafed it fhall go on, there refteth but Wednefday next for the hearing ; for the laft day of term is commonly left for orders, though fometimes, upon extraordinary occafion, it hath been fet down for the hearing of fome great caufe.

I fend your Majefty alfo Baron Bromley's (*n*) report, which your Majefty required ; whereby your Majefty may perceive things go not fo well in Cumberland (which is the feat of the party your Majefty named to me) as was conceived. And yet if there were land-winds, as there be fea-winds, to bind men in, I could wifh he were a little wind-bound, to keep him in the fouth.

But while your Majefty paffeth the accounts of Judges in circuits, your Majefty will give me leave to think of the Judges here in their upper region. And becaufe Tacitus faith well, *opportuni magnis conatibus tranfitus rerum ;* now upon this change, when he, that letteth, is gone, I fhall endeavour, to the beft of my power and fkill, that there may be a confent and united mind in your Judges to ferve you, and ftrengthen your bufinefs. For I am perfuaded there cannot be a facrifice, from which there may come up to you

and that if his Lordfhip were defirous to fpeak with him, he might fend his boy, who fhould be well ufed. For this offence, Mr. Markham was cenfured, and fined 500 l. by the Star-Chamber.

(*m*) Sir Henry Yelverton.

(*n*) Edward Bromley, made one of the Barons of the Exchequer, February 6, 16⅝.

a fweeter

a fweeter odour of reft, than this effect, whereof I fpeak.

For this wretched murderer, Bertram (*o*), now gone to his place, I have, perceiving your Majefty's good liking of what I propounded, taken order, that there fhall be a declaration concerning the caufe in the King's Bench, by occafion of punifhment of the offence of his keeper ; and another in Chancery, upon the occafion of moving for an order, according to his juft and righteous report. And yet withal, I have fet on work a good pen (*p*) (and myfelf will overlook it) for making fome little pamphlet fit to fly abroad in the country.

For your Majefty's proclamation touching the wearing of cloth, after I had drawn a form as near as I could to your Majefty's direction, I propounded it to the Lords, my Lord Chancellor being then abfent ; and after their Lordfhips good approbation, and fome points by them altered, I obtained leave of them to confer thereupon with my Lord Chancellor and fome principal Judges, which I did this afternoon ; fo as, it being now perfected, I fhall offer it to the board to-morrow, and fo fend it to your Majefty.

So humbly craving your Majefty's pardon for troubling you with fo long a letter, fpecially being accompanied with other papers, I ever reft,

Your Majefty's moft humble, and

bounden fervant,

This 21ft of November, at ten at night [1616].

FR. BACON.

(*o*) John Bertram, a grave man, above feventy years of age, and of a clear reputation, according to Camden, *Annales Regis Jacobi I, p.* 21. He killed with a piftol, in Lincoln's Inn, on the 12th of November 1616, Sir John Tyndal, a Mafter in Chancery, for having made a report againft him in a caufe, wherein the fum contended for did not exceed 200l. He hanged himfelf in prifon on the 17th of that month. (*p*) Mr. Trott.

Remembrances

Remembrances for the King before his going into Scotland.

May it pleafe your Majefty,

ALTHOUGH your journey be but as a long progrefs, and that your Majefty fhall be ftill within your own land ; and therefore any extraordinary courfe neither needful, nor in my opinion fit ; yet neverthelefs, I thought it agreeable to my duty and care of your fervice, to put you in mind of thofe points of form, which have relation, not fo much to a journey into Scotland, as to an abfence from your city of London for fix months, or to a diftance from your faid city near three hundred miles ; and that in an ordinary courfe, wherein I lead myfelf, by calling to confideration what things there are, that require your fignature, and may feem not fo fit to expect fending to and fro ; and therefore to be fupplied by fome precedent warrants.

Firft, your ordinary commiffions of juftice, of affize, and the peace, need not your fignature, but pafs of courfe by your Chancellor. And your commiffions of lieutenancy, though they need your fignature, yet if any of the Lieutenants fhould die, your Majefty's choice and pleafure may be very well attended. Only I fhould think fit, under your Majeft's correction, that fuch of your Lord Lieutenants, as do not attend your perfon, were commanded to abide within their countries refpectively.

For grants, if there were a longer ceffation, I think your Majefty will eafily believe it will do no hurt. And yet if any be neceffary, the continual difpatches will fupply that turn.

That, which is chiefly confiderable, is proclamations, which all do require your Majefty's fignature, except you leave fome warrant under your great feal to your ftanding council here in London.

It'

It is true, I cannot foresee any case of such sudden necessity, except it should be the apprehension of some great offenders, or the adjournment of the term upon sickness, or some riot in the city, such as hath been about the liberties of the Tower, or against strangers, &c. But your Majesty, in your great wisdom, may perhaps think of many things, that I cannot remember, or foresee: and therefore it was fit to refer those things to your better judgement.

Also my Lord Chancellor's age and health is such, as it doth not only admit, but require the accident of his death (q) to be thought of; which may fall in such a time, as the very commissions of ordinary justice before mentioned, and writs, which require present dispatch, cannot well be put off. Therefore your Majesty may be pleased to take into consideration, whether you will not have such a commission, as was prepared about this time twelvemonth in my Lord's extreme sickness, for the taking of the seal into custody, and for the seal of writs and commissions for ordinary justice, till you may advise of a Chancellor or Keeper of the Great Seal.

Your Majesty will graciously pardon my care, which is assiduous; and it is good to err in caring even rather too much than too little. These things, for so much as concerneth forms, ought to proceed from my place, as Attorney, unto which you have added some interest in matter, by making me of your privy council. But for the main they rest wholly in your princely judgement, being well informed; because miracles are ceased, though admiration will not cease, while you live.

Indorsed, *February* 21, 1616.

(q) He died at the age of seventy, on the 15th of March, 161⅚, having resigned the great seal on the 3d of that month; which was given on the 7th to Sir Francis Bacon.

2

Sir

Sir EDWARD COKE *to the* KING.

Moft gracious Sovereign,

I THINK it now my duty to inform your Majefty of the motives, that induced the Lord Chancellor and Judges to refolve, that a murder of felony, committed by one Englifhman upon another in a foreign kingdom, fhall be punifhed before the Conftable and Marfhal here in England.

Firft, in the book-cafe, in the 13th year of King Henry the Fourth, in whofe reign the ftatute was made, it is exprefsly faid, one liege-man was killed in Scotland by another liege-man ; and the wife of him, that was killed, did fue an appeal of murder in the Conftable's Court of England. *Vide Statutum*, faith the book, *de primo Henrici IV*. Cap. 14. *Et contemporanea expofitio eft fortiffima in Lege*. Stanford (r), an author without exception, faith thus, *fol.* 65. *a*. : " By the " ftatute of Henry IV. Cap. 14. if any fubject kill " another fubject in a foreign kingdom, the wife of " him, that is flain, may have an appeal in Eng- " land before the Conftable and Marfhal : which is " a cafe *in terminis terminantibus*. And when the " wife, if the party flain have any, fhall have an ap- " peal, there, if he hath no wife, his next heir fhall " have it."

If any fact be committed out of the kingdom, upon the high fea, the Lord Admiral fhall determine it. If in a foreign kingdom, the cognizance belongeth to the Conftable, where the jurifdiction pertains to him.

(r) Sir William, the moft ancient writer on the Pleas of the Crown. He was born in Middlefex, Auguft 22, 1509, educated in the univerfity of Oxford, ftudied the law at Gray's Inn, in which he was elected autumn reader in 1545, made Serjeant in 1552, the year following Queen's Serjeant, and, in 1554, one of the Juftices of the Common Pleas. He died Auguft 28, 1558.

And

And these authorities being seen by Bromley, Chancellor, and the two Chief Justices, they clearly resolved the case, as before I have certified your Majesty.

I humbly desire I may be so happy, as to kiss your Majesty's hands, and to my exceeding comfort to see your sacred person ; and I shall ever rest

Your Majesty's faithful and loyal subject,

February 25 [161⅚].

EDW. COKE.

To the King's most Excellent Majesty.

To the KING (s).

May it please your most excellent Majesty,

MY continual meditations upon your Majesty's service and greatness have, amongst other things, produced this paper inclosed, which I most humbly pray your Majesty to excuse, being that, which, in my judgement, I think to be good both *de vero*, and *ad populum*. Of other things I have written to my Lord of Buckingham. God for ever preserve and prosper your Majesty.

Your Majesty's humble servant, most devoted and most bounden,

March 23, 1616.

FR. BACON.

Indorsed,

My Lord Keeper to his Majesty, with some additional instructions for Sir John Digby.

(s) His Majesty had begun his journey towards Scotland, on the 14th of March, 161⅚.

Additional

Additional Instructions to Sir JOHN DIGBY (*t*).

BESIDES your instructions directory to the substance of the main errand, we would have you in the whole carriage and passages of the negotiation, as well with the King himself, as the Duke of Lerma, and council there, intermix discourse upon fit occasions, that may express ourselves to the effect following:

That you doubt not, but that both Kings, for that which concerns religion, will proceed sincerely, both being intire and perfect in their own belief and way. But that there are so many noble and excellent effects, which are equally acceptable to both religions, and for the good and happiness of the Christian world, which may arise of this conjunction, as the union of both Kings in actions of state, as may make the difference in religion as laid aside, and almost forgotten.

As first, that it will be a means utterly to extinguish and extirpate pirates, which are the common enemies of mankind, and do so much infest Europe at this time.

Also, that it may be a beginning and seed (for the like actions heretofore have had less beginnings) of a holy war against the Turk ; whereunto it seems the events of time do invite Christian Kings, in respect of the great corruption and relaxation of discipline of war in that empire ; and much more in respect of the utter ruin and enervation of the Grand Signor's navy and forces by sea ; which openeth a way (with congregating vast armies by land) to suffocate and starve Constantinople, and thereby to put those provinces into mutiny and insurrection.

(*t*) Ambassador to the court of Spain.

Also,

Also, that by the same conjunction there will be erected a tribunal, or prætorian power, to decide the controversies, which may arise amongst the princes and estates of Christendom, without effusion of Christian blood ; for so much as any estate of Christendom will hardly recede from that, which the two Kings shall mediate and determine.

Also, that whereas there doth, as it were, creep upon the ground a disposition in some places to make popular estates and leagues to the disadvantage of monarchies, the conjunction of the two Kings will be able to stop and impedite the growth of any such evil.

These discourses you shall do well frequently to treat upon, and therewithal to fill up the spaces of the active part of your negotiation ; representing, that it stands well with the greatness and majesty of the two Kings to extend their cogitations and the influence of their government, not only to their own subjects, but to the state of the whole world besides, specially the Christian portion thereof.

Account of Council Business.

FOR remedy against the infestation of pirates, than which there is not a better work under heaven, and therefore worthy of the great care his Majesty hath expressed concerning the same, this is done :

First, Sir Thomas Smith (*u*) hath certified in writing, on the behalf of the merchants of London,
that

(*u*) of Biborough in Kent, second son of Thomas Smith, of Ostenhanger, of that county, Esq. He had farmed the customs in the reign of Queen Elizabeth, and was sent, by King James I, Ambassador to the court of Russia, in March 1604; from whence returning, he was made governor of the Society of Merchants trading to the East Indies, Muscovy,
the

that there will be a contribution of 20,000 l. a year, during two years space, towards the charge of repressing the pirates; wherein we do both conceive, that this, being as the first offer, will be increased. And we consider also, that the merchants of the West, who have sustained in proportion far greater damage than those of London, will come into the circle, and follow the example: and for that purpose letters are directed unto them.

Secondly, for the consultation *de modo* of the arming and proceeding against them, in respect that my Lord Admiral (*w*) cometh not yet abroad, the table hath referred it to my Lord Treasurer (*x*), the Lord Carew (*y*), and Mr. Chancellor of the Exchequer (*z*), who heretofore hath served as Treasurer of the Navy, to confer with the Lord Admiral, calling to that conference Sir Robert Mansell, and others expert in sea-service; and so to make report unto the board. At which time some principal merchants shall likewise attend for the Lords better information.

So that, when this is done, his Majesty shall be advertised from the table: whereupon his Majesty may be pleased to take into his royal consideration, both the business in itself, and as it may have relation to Sir John Digby's embassage.

For safety and caution against tumults and disorders in and near the city, in respect of some idle fly-

---

the French and Summer Islands; and Treasurer for the colony and company of Virginia. He built a magnificent house at Deptford, which was burnt on the 30th of January, 1618; and in April, 1619, he was removed from his employments of Governor and Treasurer, upon several complaints of frauds committed by him.

(*w*) Charles Howard, Earl of Nottingham.

(*x*) Thomas Howard, Earl of Suffolk.

(*y*) George, Lord Carew, who had been president of Munster in Ireland, and was now Master of the Ordnance. He was created Earl of Totness by King Charles I, in 1626.

(*z*) Sir Fulk Grevile.

ing

ing papers, that were caft abroad of a May-day, &c. the Lords have wifely taken a courfe neither to nurfe it, or nourifh it, by too much apprehenfion, nor much lefs to neglect due provifion to make all fure. And therefore order is given, that as well the trained bands, as the military bands, newly erected, fhall be in mufter as well weekly, in the mean time, on every Thurfday (which is the day upon which May-day falleth) as in the May-week itfelf, the Monday, Tuefday, Wednefday, and Thurfday. Befides, that the ftrength of the watch fhall that day be increafed.

For the buildings in and about London, order is given for four felected Aldermen, and four felected Juftices, to have the care and charge thereof laid upon them; and they anfwerable for the obferving of his Majefty's proclamation, and for ftop of all farther building; for which purpofes the faid *Eflus* are warned to be before the board, where they fhall receive a ftrait charge, and be tied to a continual account.

For the Provoft's Marfhalls, there is already direction given for the city and the counties adjacent; and it fhall be ftrengthened with farther commiffion, if there be caufe.

For the proclamation, that Lieutenants (not being counfellors) Deputy-Lieutenants, Juftices of the Peace, and gentlemen of quality, fhould depart the city, and refide in their countries; we find the city fo dead of company of that kind for the prefent, as we account it out of feafon to command that, which is already done. But after men have attended their bufinefs the two next terms, in the end of Trinity term, according to the cuftom, when the Juftices fhall attend at the Star-Chamber, I fhall give a charge concerning the fame: and that fhall be corroborated by a proclamation, if caufe be.

For

For the information given againſt the Withering-tons, that they ſhould countenance and abet the ſpoils and diſorders in the middle ſhires ; we find the informers to faulter and fail in their accuſation. Ne-vertherleſs, upon my motion, the table hath or-dered, that the informer ſhall attend one of the clerks of the council, and ſet down articulately what he can ſpeak, and how he can prove it, and againſt whom, either the Witheringtons or others.

For the cauſes of Ireland, and the late letters from the Deputy (*a*), we have but entered into them, and have appointed Tueſday for a farther conſulta-tion of the ſame ; and therefore of that ſubject I for-bear to write more for this preſent.

Indorſed,

March 30, 1617. *An account of council buſineſs.*

To the L O R D K E E P E R (*).

My honourable Lord,

WHEREAS the late Lord Chancellor thought it fit to diſmiſs out of the Chancery a cauſe touching Henry Skipwith to the common law, where he deſireth it ſhould be decided ; theſe are to intreat your Lordſhip (*b*) in the gentleman's favour, that if

(*a*) Sir Oliver St. John, afterwards Viſcount Grandiſon.
(*) Harl. MSS. Vol. 7006.
(*b*) This is the firſt of many letters, which the Marquis of Buckingham wrote to Lord Bacon in favour of perſons, who had cauſes depending in, or likely to come into, the court of Chan-cery. And it is not improbable, that ſuch recommendations were conſidered in that age as leſs extraordinary and irregular, than they would appear now. The Marquis made the ſame kind of applications to Lord Bacon's ſucceſſor, the Lord Keeper Williams, in whoſe *Life*, by Biſhop Hacket, Part I, p. 107, we are informed, that " there was not a cauſe of moment, but, as " ſoon as it came to publication, one of the parties brought letters " from this mighty Peer, and the Lord Keeper's patron."

I

the

the adverse party ſhall attempt to bring it now back again into your Lordſhip's court, you would not retain it there, but let it reſt in the place, where now it is, that without more vexation unto him in poſting him from one to another, he may have a final hearing and determination thereof. And ſo I reſt

Your Lordſhip's ever at command,

G. Buckingham.

My Lord,

This is a buſineſs, wherein I ſpake to my Lord Chancellor (c); whereupon he diſmiſſed the ſuit.

Lincoln, the 4th of
 April, 1617.

The Lord Keeper *to his* Niece, *touching her Marriage.*

Good Niece,

AMONGST your other virtues, I know there wanteth not in you a mind to hearken to the advice of your friends. And therefore you will give me leave to move you again more ſeriouſly than before in the match with Mr. Comptroller (d). The ſtate, wherein you now are, is to be preferred before

---

(c) Elleſmere.

(d) Sir Thomas Edmondes, who had been appointed to that office, December 21, 1616; and, January 19, 161⁷⁄₈, was made Treaſurer of the Houſhold. He had been married to Magdalen, one of the daughters and coheirs of Sir John Wood, Knight, Clerk of the Signet; which Lady died at Paris, December 31, 1614.

The propoſal for a ſecond marriage between him and the Lord Keeper's niece does not appear to have had ſucceſs.

marriage,

marriage, or changed for marriage, not simply the one or the other, but according as, by God's providence, the offers of marriage are more or lefs fit to be embraced. This gentleman is religious, a perfon of honour, being Counfellor of State, a great officer, and in very good favour with his Majefty. He is of years and health fit to be comfortable to you, and to free you of burdenfome cares. He is of good means, and a wife and provident man, and of a loving and excellent good nature; and, I find, hath fet his affections upon you; fo as I forefee you may fooner change your mind, which, as you told me, is not yet towards marriage, than find fo happy a choice. I hear he is willing to vifit you, before his going into France, which, by the King's commandment, is to be within fome ten days: and I could wifh you ufed him kindly, and with refpect. His return out of France is intended before Michaelmafs. God direct you, and be with you. I reft

Your very loving uncle, and affured friend,

Dorfet-houfe, this
28th of Apr. 1617.   FR. BACON.

To the LORD KEEPER (*).

My honourable Lord,

I HAVE acquainted his Majefty with your letters, who liked all your proceedings well, faving only the point, for which you have fince made amends, in obeying his pleafure touching the proclamation. His Majefty would have your Lordfhip go thoroughly about the bufinefs of Ireland, whereinto you are fo well entered, efpecially at this time, that the Chief

(*) Harl. MSS. Vol. 7006.
I 2   Juftice

Juſtice (e) is come over, who hath delivered his opinion thereof to his Majeſty, and hath underſtood
what his Majeſty conceived of the ſame; wherewith
he will acquaint your Lordſhip, and with his own ob-
ſervation and judgement of the buſineſſes of that
country.

I give your Lordſhip hearty thanks for your care
to ſatisfy my Lady of Rutland's (f) deſire; and will
be as careful, when I come to York, of recommend-
your ſuit to the Biſhop (g). So I reſt

Your Lordſhip's ever at command,

Newark, the 5th
of April, 1617. G. BUCKINGHAM.

*To my very honourable Lord, Sir Francis Bacon, Knight,
Lord Keeper of the Great Seal of England.*

(e) Sir John Denham, one of the Lords Juſtices of Ireland
in 1616. He was made one of the Barons of the Exchequer
in England, May 2, 1617. He died January 6, 1638, in the
eightieth year of his age. He was the firſt, who ſet up cuſtoms
in Ireland (not but there were laws for the ſame before;) of
which the firſt year's revenue amounted but to 500 l; but before
his death, which was about twenty-two years after, they were
let for 54,000 l. *per annum. Borlaſe's Reduction of Ireland to the
Crown of England,* p. 200. Edit. London, 1675.

(f) Frances, Counteſs of Rutland, firſt wife of Francis, Earl
of Rutland, and daughter and coheir of Sir Henry Knevet, of
Charleton in Wiltſhire, Knight. She had by the Earl an only
daughter and heir, Catharine, firſt married to George, Marquis,
and afterwards Duke, of Buckingham; and ſecondly to Randolph Mac-Donald, Earl, and afterwards Marquis, of Antrim
in Ireland.

(g) relating to York-houſe.

To

To the LORD KEEPER (*).

My honourable Lord,

I SPAKE at York with the Archbishop (*b*), touching the house, which he hath wholly put into your hands, to do with it what your Lordship shall be pleased.

I have heretofore, since we were in this journey, moved his Majesty for dispatch of my Lord Brackley's (*i*) business : but because his Majesty never having heard of any precedent in the like case, was of opinion, that this would be of ill consequence in making that dignity as easy, as the pulling out of a sword to make a man a knight, and so make it of little esteem, he was desirous to be assured, first, that it was no new course, before he would do it in that fashion. But since he can receive no assurance from your Lordship of any precedent in that kind, his Majesty intendeth not so to precipitate the business, as to expose that dignity to censure and contempt, in omitting the solemnities required, and usually belonging unto it.

His Majesty, though he were a while troubled with a little pain in his back, which hindered his hunting, is now, God be thanked, very well, and as merry as ever he was ; and we have all held out well.

(*) Harl. MSS. Vol. 7006.   (*b*) Dr. Tobie Matthew.
(*i*) who desired to be created Earl in an usual manner, by letters patents, without the delivering of the patent by the King's own hand, or without the ordinary solemnities of creation. He was accordingly created Earl of Bridgewater, May 27, 1617.

I shewed

I shewed his Majesty your letter, who taketh very well your care and desire to hear of his health.

So I commit you to God, and rest

Your Lordship's most assured friend

to do you service,

Aukland, the 18th
of Apr. 1617.   G. Buckingham.

Since the writing of this letter, I have had some farther speech with his Majesty, touching my Lord Brackley; and find, that if, in your Lordship's information in the course, you write any thing, that may tend to the furthering of the dispatch of it in that kind, he desireth it may be done.

To the Lord Keeper (*).

My honourable Lord,

I SEND your Lordship the warrant for the Queen (*k*) signed by his Majesty, to whom I have likewise delivered your Lordship's letter. And touching the matter of the pirates, his Majesty cannot yet resolve; but within a day or two your Lordship shall see a dispatch, which he purposeth to send to the Lords of his Council in general, what his opinion and pleasure is in that point.

I would not omit this opportunity to let your Lordship know, that his Majesty, God be thanked, is in very good health, and so well pleased with his journey, that I never saw him better, nor merrier.

So I rest

Your Lordship's ever at command,

From Newcastle, the
23d of Apr. 1617.   G. Buckingham.

(*) Harl. MSS. Vol. 7006.
(*k*) relating to her house. See the Lord Keeper's letter of April 7, 1617, printed in his works.

To

To the LORD KEEPER (*).

My honourable Lord,

I UNDERSTAND, that Sir Lewis Trefham hath a fuit depending in the Chancery before your Lordſhip ; and therefore, out of my love and refpect toward him, I have thought fit to recommend him unto your favour fo far only, as may ftand with juftice and equity, which is all he defireth, having to encounter a ſtrong party. And becauſe he is ſhortly to go into Spain about fome other bufinefs of his own, I farther defire your Lordſhip to give him what expedition you can, that he may receive no prejudice by his journey.

Your Lordſhip's ever at command,

G. BUCKINGHAM.

Indorfed, *May* 6, 1616,

To the LORD KEEPER (*).

My honourable Lord,

I HAVE, by reports, heard that, which doth much grieve and trouble me, that your Lordſhip hath, through a pain in one of your legs, been forced to keep your chamber. And being defirous to underftand the true eftate of your health, which reports do not always bring, I intreat your Lordſhip to favour me with a word or two from yourfelf, which, I hope, will bring me the comfort I defire, who

(*) Harl. MSS. Vol. 7006.
I 4   cannot

cannot but be very senfible of whatfoever happeneth to your Lordfhip, as being

Your Lordfhip's moft affectionate

to do you fervice,

G. BUCKINGHAM.

His Majefty, God be thanked, is very well, and fafely returned from his hunting journey.

From Edinburgh, the
3d of June, 1617.

To the Earl of BUCKINGHAM.

My very good Lord,

THIS day I have made even with the bufinefs of the kingdom for common juftice; not one caufe unheard; the lawyers drawn dry of all the motions they were to make; not one petition unanfwered. And this, I think, could not be faid in our age before. This I fpeak not out of oftentation, but out of gladnefs, when I have done my duty. I know men think I cannot continue, if I fhould thus opprefs my felf with bufinefs: but that account is made. The duties of life are more than life; and, if I die now, I fhall die before the world be weary of me, which in our times is fomewhat rare. And all this while I have been a little unperfect in my foot. But I have taken pains more like the beaft with four legs, than like a man with fcarce two legs. But if it be a gout, which I do neither acknowledge, nor much difclaim, it is a good-natured gout; for I have no rage of it, and it goeth away quickly. I have hope it is but an accident of changing from a field-

air

air (*l*) to a Thames-air (*m*) ; or rather, I think, it is the diſtance of the King and your Lordſhip from me, that doth congeal my humours and ſpirits.

When I had written this letter, I received your Lordſhip's letter of the third of this preſent, wherein your Lordſhip ſheweth your ſollicitous care of my health, which did wonderfully comfort me. And it is true, that at this preſent I am very well, and my ſuppoſed gout quite vaniſhed.

I humbly pray you to commend my ſervice, infinite in deſire, howſoever limited in ability, to his Majeſty, to hear of whoſe health and good diſpoſition is to me the greateſt beatitude, which I can receive in this world. And I humbly beſeech his Majeſty to pardon me, that I do not now ſend him my account of council buſineſs, and other his royal commands, till within theſe four days ; becauſe the flood of buſineſs of juſtice did hitherto wholly poſſeſs me ; which, I know, worketh this effect, as it contenteth his ſubjects, and knitteth their hearts more and more to his Majeſty, though, I muſt confeſs, my mind is upon other matters, as his Majeſty ſhall know, by the grace of God, at his return. God ever bleſs and proſper you.

> Your Lordſhip's true, and moſt
> 　　　　devoted friend and ſervant,

Whitehall, this 8th
　of June, 1617.　　　　　　　　Fr. Bacon.

To the Lord Keeper (*).

My honourable Lord,

YOUR Lordſhip will underſtand, by Sir Thomas Lake's letter, his Majeſty's directions touching

(*l*) Gray's Inn,
(*m*) Dorſet-houſe, originally belonging to the Biſhops of Saliſbury, afterwards the houſe of Sir Richard Sackville, and then of his ſon, Sir Thomas, Earl of Dorſet, and Lord Treaſurer.
(*) Harl. MSS. Vol. 7006.

the

the Surveyor's Deputy of the Court of Wards. And though I affure myfelf of your Lordfhip's care of the bufinefs, which his Majefty maketh his own; yet my refpect to Sir Robert Naunton (*n*) maketh me add my recommendation thereof to your Lordfhip, whom I defire to give all the furtherance and affiftance you can to the bufinefs, that no prejudice or imputation may light upon Sir Robert Naunton, through his zealous affection to attend his Majefty in this journey.

I will not omit to let you know, that his Majefty is very well, and receiveth much contentment in his journey. And with this conclufion, I reft

　　　　　Your Lordfhip's moft affectionate

　　　　　　　　　　　　to do you fervice,

Edinburgh, the 11th
　of June, 1617.　　　　　　G. BUCKINGHAM.

　　　　To the Lord Vifcount FENTON (*o*).

My very good Lord,

I THANK your Lordfhip for your courteous letter; and, if I were afked the queftion, I would always choofe rather to have a letter of no news, than a letter of news; for news imports alteration: but letters of kindnefs and refpect bring that, which, though it be no news amongft friends, is more welcome.

I am exceedingly glad to hear, that this journey of his Majefty, which I never efteemed more than a

(*n*) Surveyor of the Court of Wards.
(*o*) Sir Thomas Erfkine, who for his fervice to the King, in the attempt of the Earl of Gowry, was, upon his Majefty's acceffion to the throne of England, made Captain of his guard in the room of Sir Walter Ralegh. He was afterwards created Earl of Kelly.

　　　　　　　　　　　　　　　　　long

long progress, save that it had reason of state joined with pleasure, doth sort to be so joyful and so comfortable.

For your parliament, God speed it well : and for ours, you know the sea would be calm, if it were not for the winds : and I hope the King, whensoever that shall be, will find those winds reasonably well laid. Now that the sun is got up a little higher, God ordains all things to the happiness of his Majesty, and his monarchy.

My health, I thank God, is good ; and I hope this supposed gout was but an incomer. I ever rest

Your Lordship's affectionate

and assured friend,

Whitehall, June 18
  [1617].

Fr. Bacon.

To the Lord Keeper, *written from Scotland* *June* 28, 1618 (*p*).

I WILL begin to speak of the business of this day ; *opus hujus diei in die suo*, which is of the parliament. It began on the 7th of this month, and ended this day, being the 28th of June. His Majesty, as I perceived by relation, rode thither in great state the first day. These eyes are witnesses, that he rode in an honourable fashion, as I have seen him in England, this day. All the Lords rode in English robes ; not an English Lord on horseback, though all the parliament-house at his Majesty's elbow, but my Lord of Buckingham, who waited upon the King's stirrup in his collar, but not in his robes. His Majesty the first day, by way prepara-

(*p*) From a copy in the Paper-office.

tion

tion to the subject of the parliament, made a declaratory speech, wherein he expressed himself what he
would not do, but what he would do.   The relation
is too prolix for a sheet of paper; and I am promised
a copy of it, which I will bring myself unto your
Lordship with all the speed I may.   But I may not
be so reserved, as not to tell your Lordship, that in
that speech his Majesty was pleased to do England
and Englishmen much honour and grace; and that
he studied nothing so much, sleeping and waking,
as to reduce the barbarity (I have warrant to use the
King's own word) of this country unto the sweet ci-
vility of ours; adding farther, that if the Scottish
nation would be as docible to learn the goodness of
England, as they are teachable to limp after their ill,
he might with facility prevail in his desire: for they
had learned of the English to drink healths, to wear
coaches and gay cloaths, to take tobacco, and to
speak neither Scottish nor English.   Many such dis-
eases of the times his Majesty was pleased to enume-
rate, not fit for my pen to remember, and graciously
to recognize, how much he was beholden to the English nation for their love and conformity to his desires.
The King did personally and infallibly sit amongst
them of the parliament every day; so that there fell
not a word amongst them, but his Majesty was of
council with it.

The whole assembly, after the wonted manner,
was abstracted into eight Bishops, eight Lords, eight
Gentlemen, Knights of the Shires, and eight Lay
Burgesses for towns.   And this epitome of the whole
parliament did meet every day in one room to treat and
debate of the great affairs of the kingdom.   There
was exception taken against some of the lower-house,
which were returned by the country, being pointed
at as men averse in their appetites and humours to
the business of the parliament, who were deposed
of their attendance by the King's power; and others,

2   better

better affected, by the King's election, placed in their room.

The greateſt and weightieſt articles, agitated in this parliament, were ſpecially touching the government of the kirk and kirkmen, and for the aboliſhing of hereditary Sheriffs to an annual charge ; and to enable Juſtices of the Peace to have as well the real execution, as the title of their places. ' For now the Sheriff doth hold *jura regalia* in his circuit without check or controlment ; and the Juſtices of the Peace do want the ſtaff of their authority. For the church and commonwealth, his Majeſty doth ſtrive to ſhape the frame of this kingdom to the method and degrees of the government of England, as by reading of the ſeveral acts it may appear. The King's deſire and travail herein, though he did ſuffer a momentary oppoſition, (for his countrymen will ſpeak boldly to him,) hath in part been profitable. For though he hath not fully and complementally prevailed in all things, yet he hath won ground in moſt things, and hath gained acts of parliament to authorize particular commiſſioners, to ſet down orders for the church and churchmen, and to treat with Sheriffs for their offices by way of pecuniary compoſition. But all theſe proceedings are to have an inſeparable reference to his Majeſty. If any prove unreaſonably and undutifully refractory, his Majeſty hath declared himſelf, that he will proceed againſt him by the warrant of the law, and by the ſtrength of his royal power.

His Majeſty's ſpeech this day had a neceſſary connexion with his former diſcourſe. He was pleaſed to declare what was done and determined in the progreſs of this parliament ; his reaſons for it ; and that nothing was gotten by ſhouldering or wreſtling, but by debate, judgement, and reaſon, without any interpoſition of his royal power in any thing. He commanded the Lords in ſtate of judicature, to give life, by a careful execution, unto the law, which
otherwiſe

otherwife was but *mortuum cadaver et bona peri-tura.*

Thus much touching the legal part of my adver-tifement unto you. I will give your Lordfhip an account in two lines of the complement of the coun-try, time, and place.

The country affords more profit, and better con-tentment, than I could ever promife myfelf, by my reading of it.

The King was never more chearful in body and mind, never fo well pleafed : and fo are the Englifh of all conditions.

The entertainment very honourable, very general, and very full : every day feafts and invitations. I know not who paid for it. They ftrive, by direction, to give us all fair contentment, that we may know, that the country is not fo contemptible, but that it is worth the cherifhing.

The Lord Provoft of this town, who in Englifh is the Mayor, did feaft the King and all the Lords this week ; and another day all the gentlemen. And, I confefs, it was performed with ftate, with abun-dance, and with a general content.

There is a general, and a bold expectation, that Mr. John Murray fhall be created a Baron of this country ; and fome do chat, that my Lord of Buck-ingham's Mr. Wray fhall be a Groom of the Bed-chamber in his place.

There hath been yet no creation of Lords, fince his Majefty did touch Scotland : but of Knights many, yet not fo many as we heard in England ; but it is thought all the Penfioners will be Knights to-morrow. Neither are there any more Englifh Lords fworn of the privy-council here, fave my Lord of Buckingham.

The Earl of Southamton, Montgomery, and Hay, are already gone for England.

I have made good profit of my journey hither ; for I have gotten a tranfcript of the fpeech, which

4   your

your Lordſhip did deliver at your firſt and happy ſitting in Chancery; which I could not gain in England. It hath been ſhewed to the King, and received due approbation. The God of heaven, all-wiſe and all-ſufficient, guard and aſſiſt your Lordſhip in all your actions: for I can read here whatſoever your Lordſhip doth act there; and your courſes be ſuch, as you need not to fear to give copies of them. But the King's ears be wide and long, and he ſeeth with many eyes. All this works for your honour and comfort. I pray God nothing be ſoiled, heated, or cooled in the carriage. Envy ſometimes attends virtues, and not for good; and theſe bore certain proprieties and circumſtances inherent to your Lordſhip's mind; which men may admire, I cannot expreſs. But I will wade no farther herein, leſt I ſhould ſeem eloquent. I have been too ſaucy with your Lordſhip, and held you too long with my idleneſs. He, that takes time from your Lordſhip, robs the public. God give your body health, and your ſoul heaven.

My Lord of Pembroke, my Lord of Arundel, my Lord Zouch, and Mr. Secretary Lake, were new ſworn of the council here.

To the Earl of B U C K I N G H A M.

My very good Lord,

I HAVE ſent incloſed a letter to his Majeſty concerning the ſtrangers; in which buſineſs I had formerly written to your Lordſhip a joint letter with my Lord of Canterbury, and my Lord Privy-Seal (*q*), and Mr. Secretary Winwood.

I am, I thank God, much relieved with my being in the country-air, and the order I keep; ſo that of late years I have not found my health better.

(*q*) Edward, Earl of Worceſter.

Your

Your Lordſhip writeth ſeldomer than you were wont; but when you are once gotten into England, you will be more at leiſure. God bleſs and proſper you.

Your Lordſhip's true and devoted

friend and ſervant,

Gorhambury, July 29, 1617.

FR. BACON.

To the LORD KEEPER (*).

My honourable Lord,

I HAVE acquainted his Majeſty with your letter, who, in this buſineſs of Sir John Bennet's (r), hath altogether followed your Lordſhip's direction.

His Majeſty hath at length been pleaſed to diſpatch Mr. Lowder (s), according to your Lordſhip's deſire, for the place in Ireland. What the cauſe of the ſtay was, I ſhall impart to your Lordſhip, when I ſee you, being now too long to relate.

His Majeſty hath not yet had leiſure to read the little book you ſend me to preſent unto him; but, as ſoon as I ſee the fitteſt opportunity, I will offer it to him again.

His Majeſty, God be thanked, is very well; and I am exceeding glad to hear of your health, that you

(*) Harl. MSS. Vol. 7006.
(r) of Godſtow in Oxfordſhire, who was ſent to Bruſſels to the Archduke, to expoſtulate with him concerning a Libel on the King, imputed to Erycius Puteanus, and intitled, *Iſaaci Caſauboni Corona Regia.*
(s) He had been Sollicitor to the Queen; but finding her diſlike of him, he was willing to part with his place for that of one of the Barons of the Exchequer in Ireland; for which he was recommended by the Lord Keeper to the Earl of Buckingham, in a letter dated at Whitehall, May 25, 1617.

are

are of so good term-proof, which is the best of it, being you are in those businesses put most to the trial, which I wish may long continue in that strength, that you may still do his Majesty and your country that good service, whereof we hear so general approbation, that it much rejoiceth me, who rest

Your Lordship's ever at command,

Falkland, the 5th
of July, 1617.   G. Buckingham.

To the King (*t*).

May it please your most excellent Majesty,

I DO very much thank your Majesty for your letter, and think myself much honoured by it. For though it contain some matter of dislike, in which respect it hath grieved me more than any event, which hath fallen out in my life : yet because I know reprehensions from the best masters to the best servants are necessary ; and that no chastisement is pleasant for the time, but yet worketh good effects ; and for that I find intermixed some passages of trust and grace ; and find also in myself inwardly sincerity of intention, and conformity of will, howsoever I may have erred ; I do not a little comfort myself, resting upon your Majesty's accustomed favour ; and most humbly desiring, that any one of my particular notions may be expounded by the constant and direct course, which, your Majesty knoweth, I have ever held in your service.

And because it hath pleased your Majesty, of your singular grace and favour, to write fully and freely

(*t*) This letter appears, from the indorsement of the King's answer to it, to have been written at Gorhambury, July 25, 1617. That printed with this date in his *Works*, should be August 2, 1617, as I find by the original draught of it.

K   unto

unto me ; it is duty and decorum in me not to write shortly to your Majesty again, but with some length ; not so much by way of defence or answer, which yet, I know, your Majesty would always graciously admit ; as to shew, that I have, as I ought, weighed every word of your Majesty's letter.

First, I do acknowledge, that this match of Sir John Villiers is *magnum in parvo* in both senses, that your Majesty speaketh. But your Majesty perceiveth well, that I took it to be in a farther degree, *majus in parvo*, in respect of your service. But since your Majesty biddeth me to confide upon your act of empire, I have done. For, as the Scripture saith, *to God all things are possible* ; so certainly, to wise Kings much is possible. But for that second sense, that your Majesty speaketh of, *magnum in parvo*, in respect of the stir ; albeit it being but a most lawful and ordinary thing, I most humbly pray your Majesty to pardon me, if I signify to you, that we here take the loud, and vocal, and, as I may call it, streperous carriage to have been far more on the other side, which indeed is inconvenient, rather than the thing itself.

Now for the manner of my affection to my Lord of Buckingham, for whom I would spend my life, and that, which is to me more, the cares of my life ; I must humbly confess, that it was in this a little parent-like (this being no other term, than his Lordship hath heretofore vouchsafed to my counsels ;) but in truth (and it please your Majesty) without any grain of disesteem of his Lordship's discretion. For I know him to be naturally a wise man, of a sound and staid wit, as I ever said unto your Majesty. And again, I know he hath the best tutor in Europe. But yet I was afraid, that the hight of his fortune might make him too secure ; and, as the proverb is, a looker-on sometimes seeth more than a gamester.

For

For the particular part of a true friend, which your Majesty witnesseth, that the Earl hath lately performed towards me, in palliating some errors of mine; it is no new thing with me to be more and more bound to his Lordship; and I am most humbly to thank (whatsoever it was) both your Majesty and him; knowing well, that I may, and do commit many errors, and must depend upon your Majesty's gracious countenance and favour for them, and shall have need of such a friend near your Majesty. For I am not so ignorant of mine own case, but that I know I am come in with as strong an envy of some particulars, as with the love of the general.

For my opposition to this business, which, it seemeth, hath been informed your Majesty, I think it was meant (if it be not a thing merely feigned, and without truth or ground) of one of these two things; for I will dissemble nothing with your Majesty. It is true, that in those matters, which, by your Majesty's commandment and reference, came before the table concerning Sir Edward Coke, I was sometimes sharp (it may be too much;) but it was with end to have your Majesty's will performed; or else, when me thought he was more peremptory than became him, in respect of the honour of the table. It is true also, that I disliked the riot or violence, whereof we of your council gave your Majesty advertisement by our joint letter: and I disliked it the more, because he justified it to be law; which was his old song. But in that act of council, which was made thereupon, I did not see but all my Lords were as forward as myself, as a thing most necessary for preservation of your peace, which had been so carefully and firmly kept in your absence. And all this had a fair end, in a reconcilement made by Mr. Attorney (*y*), whereby both husband and wife and child

(*y*) Sir Henry Yelverton.

K 2

should

should have kept together.　Which, if it had continued, I am perfuaded the match had been in better and fairer forwardnefs, than now it is.

Now for the times of things, I befeech your Majefty to underftand that, which my Lord of Buckingham will witnefs with me, that I never had any word of letter from his Lordfhip of the bufinefs, till I wrote my letter of advice; nor again, after my letter of advice, till five weeks after, which was now within this fennight.　So that although I did in truth prefume, that the Earl would do nothing without your Majefty's privity; yet I was in fome doubt, by this his filence of his own mind, that he was not earneft in it, but only was content to embrace the officious offers and endeavours of others.

But, to conclude this point, after I had received, by a former letter of his Lordfhip, knowledge of his mind, I think Sir Edward Coke himfelf, the laft time he was before the Lords, might particularly perceive an alteration in my carriage.　And now that your Majefty hath been pleafed to open yourfelf to me, I fhall be willing to further the match by any thing, that fhall be defired of me, or that is in my power.

And whereas your Majefty conceiveth fome dregs of fpleen in me by the word *Mr. Bacon*; truly it was but to exprefs in thankfulnefs the comparative of my fortune unto your Majefty, the author of the latter, to fhew how little I needed to fear, while I had your favour.　For, I thank God, I was never vindicative nor implacable.

As for my opinion of prejudice to your Majefty's fervice, as I touched it before, I have done; I do humbly acquiefce in your Majefty's fatisfaction, and rely upon your Majefty's judgement, who unto judgement have alfo power, fo to mingle the elements, as may conferve the fabric.

For

For the intereſt, which I have in the mother, I do not doubt but it was increaſed by this, that I in judgement, as I then ſtood, affected that, which ſhe did in paſſion. But I think the chief obligation was, that I ſtood ſo firmly to her in the matter of her aſſurance, wherein I ſuppoſed I did your Majeſty ſervice, and mentioned it in a memorial of council-buſineſs, as half craving thanks for it. And ſure I am now, that, and the like, hath made Sir Edward Coke a convert, as I did write to your Majeſty in my laſt.

For the collation of the two ſpirits, I ſhall eaſily ſubſcribe to your Majeſty's anſwer ; for Solomon were no true man, if in matter of malice the woman ſhould not be the ſuperior.

To conclude, I have gone through, with the plainneſs of truth, the parts of your Majeſty's letter ; very humbly craving pardon for troubling your Majeſty ſo long ; and moſt humbly praying your Majeſty to maintain me in your grace and favour, which is the fruit of my life upon the root of a good conſcience. And although time in this buſineſs have caſt me upon a particular, which, I confeſs, may have probable ſhew of paſſion or intereſt ; yet God is my witneſs, that the thing, that moſt moved me, was an anxious and ſollicitous care of your Majeſty's ſtate and ſervice, out of conſideration of the time paſt and preſent.

God ever preſerve and bleſs your Majeſty, and ſend you a joyful return after your proſperous journey.

The K I N G *to the* L O R D K E E P E R, *in anſwer to his Lordſhip's Letter from Gorhambury of* July 25, 1617.

J A M E S R.

RIGHT truſty and well-beloved Counſellor, we greet you well.

Al-

Although our approach doth now begin to be near London, and that there doth not appear any great neceffity of anfwering your laft letter, fince we are fo fhortly to be at home ; yet we have thought good to make fome obfervations to you upon the fame, that you may not err, by miftaking our meaning.

The firft obfervation we are to make is, that, whereas you would invert the fecond fenfe, wherein we took your *magnum in parvo*, in accounting it to be made *magnum* by their ftreperous carriage, that were for the match, we cannot but fhew you your miftaking therein. For every wrong muft be judged by the firft violent and wrongous ground, whereupon it proceeds. And was not the thefteous ftealing away of the daughter from her own father (*u*) the firft ground, whereupon all this great noife hath fince proceeded ? For the ground of her getting again came upon a lawful and ordinary warrant, fubfcribed by one of our council (*w*), for redrefs of the former violence : and except

(*u*) Lady Hatton had firft removed her daughter to Sir Edmund Withipole's houfe, near Oatlands, without the knowledge of Sir Edward Coke ; and from thence, according to a letter of Mr. Chamberlain, dated July 19, 1617, the young lady was privately conveyed to a houfe of the Lord of Argyle's by Hampton-Court. " Whence, *adds Mr. Chamberlain*, her father, with a warrant " from Mr. Secretary [Winwood] fetched her ; but indeed went " farther than his warrant, and brake open divers doors before " he got her."

(*w*) Secretary Winwood, who, as Mr. Chamberlain obferves in the letter cited in the note above, was treated with ill language at the council-board by the Lord Keeper, and threatened with a *præmunire*, on account of his warrant granted to Sir Edward Coke. His Lordfhip, at the fame time, told the Lady Compton, mother of the Earl of Buckingham, that they wifhed well to her and her fons, and would be ready to ferve the Earl with all true affection ; whereas others did it out of *faction* and *ambition*. Which words glancing directly at Secretary Winwood, he alledged, that what he had done was by the direction of the Queen and the other parties, and fhewed a letter of approbation of all his courfes from the King, making the whole table judge
what

except the father of a child might be proved to be either lunatic, or idiot, we never read in any law, that either it could be lawful for any creature to steal his child from him ; or that it was a matter of noise and streperous carriage for him to hunt for the recovery of his child again.

Our next observation is, that whereas you protest your affection to Buckingham, and thereafter confess, that it is in some sort *parent-like* ; yet, after that you have praised his natural parts, we will not say, that you throw all down by a direct imputation upon him ; but we are sure you do not deny to have had a greater jealousy of his discretion, than, so far as we conceive, he ever deserved at your or any man's hands. For you say, that you were afraid, that the hight of his fortune might make him too secure ; and so, as a looker-on, you might sometime see more than a gamester. Now we know not how to interpret this in plain English otherwise, than that you were afraid, that the hight of his fortune might make him misknow himself. And surely, if that be your *parent-like affection* toward him, he hath no obligation to you for it. And, for our part, besides our own proof, that we find him farthest from that vice of any courtier, that ever we had so near about us ; so do we fear, that you shall prove the only phenix in that jealousy of all the kingdom. For we would be very sorry, that the world should apprehend that conceit of him. But we cannot conceal, that we think it was least your part of any to enter into that

---

what *faction* or *ambition* appeared in his carriage : to which no answer was returned. The Queen, some time after, taking notice of the disgust, which the Lord Keeper had conceived against Secretary Winwood, and asking his Lordship, what occasion the Secretary had given him to oppose himself so violently against him, his Lordship answered, " Madam, I can say no more but he is " proud, and I am proud." MS. letter of Mr. Chamberlain, October 11, 1717.

jealousy

jealoufy of him, whom of we have heard you oft
fpeak in a contrary ftyle. And as for that error of
yours, which he lately palliated, whereof you feem
to pretend ignorance ; the time is fo fhort fince you
commended to him one (*x*) to be of the Barons of
our Exchequer in Ireland, as we cannot think you
to be fo fhort of memory, as to have forgotten how
far you undertook in that bufinefs, before acquainting
us with it ; what a long journey you made the poor
man undertake, together with the flight recommendation you fent of him ; which drave us to thofe ftraits,
that both the poor man had been undone, and your
credit a littled blafted, if Buckingham had not, by his
importunity, made us both grant you more than fuit
(for you had already acted a part of it,) and likewife
run a hazard of the hindrance of our own fervice, by
preferring a perfon to fo important a place, whom
you fo flightly recommended.

Our third obfervation is upon the point of your
oppofition to this bufinefs, wherein you either do,
or at leaft would feem to, miftake us a little. For
firft, whereas you excufe yourfelf of the oppofitions
you made againft Sir Edward Coke at the council-
table, both for that, and other caufes ; we never took
upon us fuch a patrociny of Sir Edward Coke, as if
he were a man not to be meddled withall in any cafe.
For whatfoever you did againft him, by our employment and commendation, we ever allowed it, and
ftill do, for good fervice on your part. *De bonis
operibus non lapidamus vos.* But whereas you talk of
the riot and violence committed by him, we wonder
you make no mention of the riot and violence of
them, that ftole away his daughter, which was the
firft ground of all that noife, as we faid before. For
a man may be compelled by manifeft wrong beyond

(*x*) Mr Lowder.   See the letter of the Earl of Buckingham of
the 5th of July.

his

his patience ; and the firſt breach of that quietneſs, which hath ever been kept ſince the beginning of our journey, was made by them, that committed the theft.   And for your laying the burden of your oppoſition upon the council, we meddle not with that queſtion ; but the oppoſition, which we juſtly find fault with you, was the refuſal to ſign a warrant for the father to the recovery of his child, clad with thoſe circumſtances (as is reported) of your ſlight carriage to Buckingham's mother, when ſhe repaired to you upon ſo reaſonable an errand.   What farther oppoſition you made in that buſineſs, we leave it to the due trial in the own time.   But whereas you would diſtinguiſh of times, pretending ignorance either of our meaning or his, when you made your oppoſition ; that would have ſerved for a reaſonable excuſe not to have furthered ſuch a buſineſs, till you had been firſt employed in it : but that can ſerve for no excuſe of croſſing any thing, that ſo nearly concerned one, whom you profeſs ſuch friendſhip unto. We will not ſpeak of obligation ; for ſurely we think, even in good manners, you had reaſon not to have croſſed any thing, wherein you had heard his name uſed, till you had heard from him.   For if you had willingly given your conſent and hand to the recovery of the young gentlewoman ; and then written both to us and to him what inconvenience appeared to you to be in ſuch a match ; that had been the part indeed of a true ſervant to us, and a true friend to him.   But firſt to make an oppoſition ; and then to give advice by way of friendſhip, is to make the plow go before the horſe.

Thus leaving all the particulars of your carriage, in this buſineſs, to the own proper time, which is ever the diſcoverer of truth, we commend you to God.   Given under our ſignet at Nantwich, in the fifteenth year of our reign of Great Britain, &c.

To

To the LORD KEEPER.

My Lord,

I HAVE received your Lordfhip's letter by your man; but having fo lately imparted my mind to you in my former letters, I refer your Lordfhip to thofe letters, without making a needlefs repetition, and reft

Your Lordfhip's at command,

Afhton, the 25th
of Aug. 1617.

G. BUCKINGHAM.

*To my honourable Lord, Sir Francis Bacon, Knight,
Lord Keeper of the Great Seal of England.*

Sir HENRY YELVERTON, *Attorney General, to the* LORD KEEPER BACON.

My moft worthy and honourable Lord,

I DARE not think my journey loft, becaufe I have with joy feen the face of my mafter, the King, though more clouded towards me than I looked for.

Sir Edward Coke hath not forborne, by any engine, to heave at your Honour, and at myfelf; and he works by the weightieft inftrument, the Earl of Buckingham, who, as I fee, fets him as clofe to him as his fhirt, the Earl fpeaking in Sir Edward's praife, and, as it were, menacing in his fpirit.

My Lord, I emboldened myfelf to affay the temper of my Lord of Buckingham to myfelf, and found it very fervent, mifled by information, which yet I find he embraced as truth, and did nobly and plainly tell me, he would not fecretly bite; but whofoever had had any intereft, or tafted of the oppofition to his

brother's

brother's marriage, he would as openly oppofe them to their faces, and they fhould difcern what favour he had, by the power he would ufe.

In the paffage between him and me, I ftood with much confidence upon thefe grounds :

Firft, that neither your Lordfhip, nor myfelf, had any way oppofed, but many ways had furthered, the fair paffage to the marriage.

Secondly, that we only wifhed the manner of Sir Edward's proceedings to have been more temperate, and more nearly refembling the Earl's fweet difpofition.

Thirdly, that the chiefeft check in this bufinefs was Sir Edward himfelf, who liftened to no advice, who was fo tranfported with paffion, as he purpofely declined the even way, which your Lordfhip and the reft of the Lords left both him, his Lady, and his daughter, in.

Fourthly, I was bold to ftand upon my ground ; and fo I faid I knew your Lordfhip would, that thefe were flanders, which were brought him of us both ; and that it ftood not with his honour to give credit to them.

After I had paffed thefe ftraits with the Earl, leaving him leaning ftill to the firft relation of envious and odious adverfaries, I adventured to approach his Majefty, who gracioufly gave me his hand to kifs, but intermixed withall, that I deferved not that favour, if three or four things were true, which he had to object againft me. I was bold to crave his princely juftice ; firft, to hear, then to judge ; which he gracioufly granted, and faid, he wifhed I could clear myfelf. I anfwered, I would not appeal to his mercy in any of the points, but would endure the fevereft cenfure, if any of them were true. Whereupon he faid, he would referve his judgement till he heard me ; which could not be then, his other occafions preffed him fo much. All this was in the hear-

ing

ing of the Earl ; and I proteft, I think the confidence in my innocency made me depart half juftified ; for I likewife kiffed his Majefty's hand at his departure ; and though out of his grace he commanded my attendance to Warwick, yet upon my fuit he eafily inclined to give me the choice, to wait on him at Windfor, or at London.

Now, my Lord, give me leave, out of all my affections, that fhall ever ferve you, to intimate touching yourfelf :

1. That every courtier is acquainted, that the Earl profeffeth openly againft you, as forgetful of his kindnefs, and unfaithful to him in your love, and in your actions.

2. That he returneth the fhame upon himfelf, in not liftening to counfel, that diffuaded his affection from you, and not to mount you fo high, not forbearing in open fpeech (as divers have told me, and this bearer, your gentleman, hath heard alfo) to tax you, as if it were an inveterate cuftom with you, to be unfaithful to him, as you were to the Earls of Effex and Somerfet.

3. That it is too common in every man's mouth in court, that your greatnefs fhall be abated ; and as your tongue hath been as a razor to fome, fo fhall theirs be to you.

4. That there is laid up for you, to make your burden the more grievous, many petitions to his Majefty againft you.

My Lord, Sir Edward Coke, as if he were already upon his wings, triumphs exceedingly ; hath much private conference with his Majefty ; and in public doth offer himfelf, and thruft upon the King, with as great boldnefs of fpeech, as heretofore.

It is thought, and much feared, that at Woodftock he will again be recalled to the council-table ; for neither are the Earl's ears, nor his thoughts, ever off him.

Sir

Sir Edward Coke, with much audacity, affirmeth his daughter to be moſt deeply in love with Sir John Villiers ; that the contract pretended with the Earl of Oxford is counterfeit ; and the letter alſo, that is pretended to come from the Earl.

My noble Lord, if I were worthy, being the meaneſt of all to interpoſe my weakneſs, I would humbly deſire,

1. That your Lordſhip fail not to be with his Majeſty at Woodſtock. The ſight of you will fright ſome.

2. That you ſingle not yourſelf from the other Lords ; but juſtify the proceedings as all your joint acts ; and I little fear but you paſs conqueror.

3. That you retort the clamour and noiſe in this buſineſs upon Sir Edward Coke, by the violence of his carriage.

4. That you ſeem not diſmayed, but open your-ſelf bravely and confidently, wherein you can excell all ſubjects ; by which means I know you ſhall amaze ſome, and daunt others.

I have abuſed your Lordſhip's patience long ; but my duty and affection towards your Lordſhip ſhall have no end : but I will ſtill wiſh your Honour greater, and reſt myſelf

Your Honour's ſervant,

Daventry, Sept. 3,
  1617.
H E N R Y   Y E L V E R T O N.

I beſeech your Lordſhip burn this letter.

To the Right Honourable his ſingular good Lordſhip, the Lord Keeper of the Great Seal.

To the L O R D   K E E P E R.

My Lord,

I HAVE received ſo many letters lately from your Lordſhip, that I cannot anſwer them ſeverally : but the ground of them all being only this, that your
Lordſhip

Lordſhip feareth I am ſo incenſed againſt you, that I will hearken to every information, that is made unto me; this one letter may well make anſwer unto them all. As his Majeſty is not apt to give ear to any idle report againſt men of your place; ſo, for myſelf, I will anſwer, that it is far from my diſpoſition to take any advantage in that kind. And for your Lordſhip's unkind dealing with me in this matter of my brother's, time will try all. His Majeſty hath given me commandment to make this anſwer in his name to your letter to him, that he needeth not to make any other anſwer to you, than that, which in that letter you make to yourſelf, that you know his Majeſty to be ſo judicious, that whatſoever he heareth, he will keep one ear open to you. Which being indeed his own princely diſpoſition, you may be aſſured of his gracious favour in that kind.

I will not trouble your Lordſhip with any longer diſcourſe at this time, being to meet you ſo ſhortly, where will be better trial of all, that hath paſſed, than can be made by letters. So I reſt

Your Lordſhip's at command,

Warwick, Sept. 5
[1617].

G. BUCKINGHAM.

To the Right Honourable Sir Francis Bacon, Knight, Lord Keeper of the Great Seal of England.

Advice to the KING, *for reviving the commiſſion of ſuits.*

THAT, which for the preſent I would have ſpoken with his Majeſty about, was a matter, wherein time may be precious, being upon the tendereſt point of all others. For though the particular occaſion occafion may be defpifed (and yet nothing ought to be defpifed in this kind,) yet the counfel thereupon I conceive to be moft found and neceffary, to avoid future perils.

There is an examination taken within thefe few days by Mr. Attorney, concerning one Baynton, or Baynham (for his name is not yet certain,) atteſted by two witneffes, that the faid Baynton, without any apparent fhew of being overcome with drink, otherwife than fo as might make him lefs wary to keep fecrets, faid, that he had been lately with the King, to petition him for reward of fervice ; which was denied him. Whereupon it was twice in his mind to have killed his Majefty. The man is not yet apprehended, and faid by fome to be mad, or halfmad ; which, in my opinion, is not the lefs dangerous ; for fuch men commonly do moft mifchief ; and the manner of his fpeaking imported no diftraction. But the counfel I would out of my care ground hereupon, is, that his Majefty would revive the commiffion for fuits, which hath been now for thefe three years, or more, laid down. For it may prevent any the like wicked cogitations, which the devil may put into the mind of a roarer or fwaggerer upon a denial : and befides, it will free his Majefty from much importunity, and fave his coffers alfo. For I am fure, when I was a commiffioner, in three whole years fpace there paffed fcarce ten fuits, that were allowed. And I doubt now, upon his Majefty's coming home from this journey, he will be much troubled with petitions and fuits ; which maketh me think this remedy more feafonable. It is not meant, that fuits generally fhould pafs that way, but only fuch fuits, as his Majefty would be rid on.

Indorfed,

September 21, 1617.
To revive the commiffion of fuits. For the King.

The

The Earl of BUCKINGHAM *to the* LORD KEEPER, *Sir* FRANCIS BACON (z).

My Lord,

I HAVE made his Majesty acquainted with your note concerning that wicked fellow's speeches, which his Majesty contemneth, as is usual to his great spirit in these cases. But, notwithstanding, his Majesty is pleased, that it shall be exactly tried, whether this foul-mouthed fellow was taken either with drunkenness or madness, when he spake it. And as for your Lordship's advice for setting up again the commissioners for suits, his Majesty saith, there will be time enough for thinking upon that, at his coming to Hampton-Court.

But his Majesty's direction, in answer of your letter, hath given me occasion to join hereunto a discovery upon the discourse you had with me this day (a). For I do freely confess, that your offer of submission unto me, and in writing, if so I would have it, battered so the unkindness, that I had conceived in my heart for your behaviour towards me in my absence, as out of the sparks of my old affection towards you, I went to found his Majesty's intention towards you, specially in any public meeting; where I found, on the one part, his Majesty so little satisfied with your late answer unto him, which he counted (for I protest I use his own terms) *confused* and *childish*, and his rigorous resolution, on the other part, so fixed, that he would put some public exemplary mark upon you; as I protest the sight of his deep-conceived in-

(z) This seems to be the letter, to which the Lord Keeper returned an answer, September 22, 1617, printed in his works.
(a) at Windsor, according to Sir Antony Weldon, who may perhaps be believed in such a circumstance as this. See *Court and Coar. &er of King James I,* p. 122.

dignation

dignation quenched my paſſion, making me upon the inſtant change from the perſon of a party into a peace-maker; ſo as I was forced upon my knees to beg of his Majeſty, that he would put no public act of diſgrace upon you. And as, I dare ſay, no other perſon would have been patiently heard in this ſuit by his Majeſty but myſelf; ſo did I (though not without difficulty) obtain thus much, that he would not ſo far diſable you from the merit of your future ſervice, as to put any particular mark of diſgrace upon your perſon. Only thus far his Majeſty pro-teſteth, that upon the conſcience of his office he cannot omit (though laying aſide all paſſion) to give a kindly reprimand, at his firſt ſitting in council, to ſo many of his counſellors, as were then here behind, and were actors in this buſineſs, for their ill behaviour in it. Some of the particular errors committed in this buſineſs he will name, but without accuſing any particular perſons by name.

Thus your Lordſhip ſeeth the fruits of my natural inclination. I proteſt, all this time paſt it was no ſmall grief unto me to hear the mouth of ſo many, upon this occaſion, open to load you with innumera-ble malicious and detracting ſpeeches, as if no muſic were more pleaſing to my ear, than to rail of you: which made me rather regret the ill nature of man-kind, that, like dogs, love to ſet upon them, that they ſee ſnatched at.

And, to conclude, my Lord, you have hereby a fair occaſion, ſo to make good hereafter your repu-tation, by your ſincere ſervice to his Majeſty, as alſo by your firm and conſtant kindneſs to your friends, as I may (your Lordſhip's old friend) participate of the comfort and honour, that will thereby come to you. Thus I reſt at laſt

Your Lordſhip's faithful friend and ſervant,

G. B.

L   The

The force of your old kindnefs hath made me fet down this in writing unto you, which fome, that have deferved ill of me in this action, would be glad to obtain by word of mouth, though they be far enough from it, for ought I yet fee. But I befeech your Lordfhip to referve this fecretly to yourfelf only, till our meeting at Hampton-Court, left his Majefty fhould be highly offended, for a caufe that I know.

Indorfed,

A letter of reconciliation from Lord Buckingham, after his Majefty's return from Scotland.

To the Earl of BUCKINGHAM.

My very good Lord,

IT may pleafe your Lordfhip to let his Majefty underftand, that I have fpoken with all the Judges, fignifying to them his Majefty's pleafure touching the commendams. They all *una voce* did re-affirm, that his Majefty's powers, neither the power of the Crown, nor the practifed power by the Archbifhop, as well in the commendam *ad recipiendum*, as the commendam *ad retinendum*, are intended to be touched ; but that the judgement is built upon the particular defects and informalities of this commendam now before them. They received with much comfort, that his Majefty took fo well at their hands the former ftay, and were very well content and defirous, that when judgement is given, there be a faithful report made of the reafon thereof.

The accounts of the fummer-circuits, as well as that of the lent-circuit, fhall be ready againft his Majefty's coming. They will alfo be ready with fome account of their labours concerning Sir Edward Coke's *Reports*: wherein I told them his Majefty's
meaning

meaning was, not to disgrace the person, but to rectify the work, having in his royal contemplation rather posterity than the present.

The two points touching the peace of the middle shires, I have put to a consult with some selected Judges.

The cause of the Egertons I have put off, and shall presently enter into the treaty of accord, according to his Majesty's commandment, which is well tasted abroad in respect of his compassion towards those ancient families.

God ever preserve and prosper your Lordship, according to the faithful and fervent wishes of

Your Lordship's true friend,

and devoted servant,

York-house, Octo-
ber 11, 1617.   Fr. Bacon.

To the Earl of Buckingham.

My very good Lord,

I HAVE reformed the ordinance according to his Majesty's corrections, which were very material. And for the first of *phrasis non placet*, I understand his Majesty, nay farther, I understand myself, the better for it.   I send your Lordship therefore six privy seals; for every court will look to have their several warrant. I send also two bills for letters patents to the two reporters : and for the persons, I send also four names, with my commendations of those two, for which I will answer upon my knowledge.   The names must be filled in the blanks; and so they are to be returned.

L 2

For

For the bufinefs of the Court of Wards, your Lordfhip's letter found me in the care of it. Therefore, according to his Majefty's commandment, by you fignified, I have fent a letter for his Majefty's fignature. And the directions themfelves are alfo to be figned. Thefe are not to be returned to me, left the fecret come out; but to be fent to my Lord of Wallingford, as the packets ufe to be fent.

I do much rejoice to hear of his Majefty's health and good difpofition. For me, though I am inceffantly in bufinefs, yet the re-integration of your love maketh me find all things eafy.

God preferve and profper you.

Your Lordfhip's true friend,

and devoted fervant,

York-houfe, October 18, 1617.

Fr. Bacon.

To the Lord Keeper (*).

My honourable Lord,

I HAVE delivered the Judges advice, touching the middle fhires, unto his Majefty, who liketh it very well. As for the point of law, his Majefty will confider of it at more leifure, and then fend you his opinion thereof. And fo I reft

Your Lordfhip's faithful friend and fervant,

Hinchingbroke, the 22d of October, 1617.

G. Buckingham.

(*) Harl. MSS. Vol. 7006.

Te

To the LORD KEEPER (*).

My honourable Lord,

HIS Majesty hath spent some time with Sir Lionel Cranfield about his own business, wherewith he acquainted his Majesty. He hath had some conference with your Lordship, upon whose report to his Majesty of your zeal and care of his service, which his Majesty accepteth very well at your hands, he hath commanded Sir L. Cranfield to attend your Lordship, to signify his farther pleasure for the furtherance of his service; unto whose relation I refer you. His Majesty's farther pleasure is, you acquaint no creature living with it, he having resolved to rely upon your care and trust only.

Thus, wishing you all happiness, I rest

Your Lordship's faithful friend and servant,

October 26, 1617.

G. BUCKINGHAM.

Sir FRANCIS ENGLEFYLD (b) to the LORD KEEPER.

Right Honourable,

GIVE me leave, I beseech your Lordship, for want of other means, by this paper to let your Lordship understand, that notwithstanding I rest in

no

(*) Harl. MSS. Vol. 7006.
(b) This gentleman was very unfortunate in his behaviour, with regard to those, who had the great seal; for in Hilary Term of the year 162¼, he was fined 3000l. by the Star-Chamber, for casting an imputation of bribery on the Lord Keeper Williams, Bishop of Lincoln. MS. Letter of Mr. Chamberlain to Sir Dudley Carleton, dated at London, 162¼. Sir

Francis

no contempt, nor have to my knowledge broken any order made by your Lordſhip concerning the truſt, either for the payment of money, or aſſignment of land; yet, by reaſon of my cloſe impriſonment, and the unuſual carriage of this cauſe againſt me, I can get no council, who will in open court deliver my caſe unto your Lordſhip. I muſt therefore humbly leave unto your Lordſhip's wiſdom, how far your Lordſhip will, upon my adverſary's fraudulent bill, exhibited by the wife without her huſband's privity, extend the moſt powerful arm of your authority againſt me, who deſire nothing but the honeſt performance of a truſt, which I know not how to leave, if I would. So, nothing doubting but your Lordſhip will do what appertaineth to juſtice, and the eminent place of equity your Lordſhip holdeth, I muſt, ſince I cannot underſtand from your Lordſhip the cauſe of my late cloſe reſtraint, reſt, during your Lordſhip's pleaſure,

Your Lordſhip's cloſe priſoner in the Fleet,

October 28, 1617.

FR. ENGLEFYLD.

Francis had been committed to the Fleet for a contempt of a decree in Chancery; upon which he was charged, by Sir John Bennet, with having ſaid before ſufficient witneſs, " that he " could prove this holy Biſhop Judge had been bribed by ſome, " that fared well in their cauſes." A few days after the ſentence in the Star-Chamber, the Lord Keeper ſent for Sir Francis, and told him, he would refute his foul aſperſions, and prove upon him, that he ſcorned the pelf of the world, or to exact, or make lucre of any man: and that for his own part, he forgave him every penny of his fine, and would crave the ſame mercy towards him from the King. Biſhop Hacket's *Life of Archbiſhop Williams*, Part I. p. 83, 84.

To

To the LORD KEEPER (*).

My honourable Lord,

I HAVE thought good to renew my motion to your Lordship, in the behalf of my Lord of Huntingdon, my Lord Stanhope, and Sir Thomas Gerard ; for that I am more particularly acquainted with their defires ; they only feeking the true advancement of the charitable ufes, unto which the land, given by their grandfather, was intended : which, as I am informed, was meant by way of a corporation, and by this means, that it might be fettled upon the fchool-mafter, ufher, and poor, and the coheirs to be vifitors. The tenants might be confcionably dealt withall ; and fo it will be out of the power of any feoffees to abufe the truft ; which, it hath been lately proved, have been hitherto the hindrance of this good work. Thefe coheirs defire only the honour of their anceftor's gift, and wifh the money, mifemployed and ordered to be paid into court by Sir John Harper, may rather be beftowed by your Lordfhip's difcretion for the augmentation of the foundation of their anceftors, than by the cenfure of any other. And fo I reft

Your Lordfhip's fervant,

Theobalds, November 12.

G. BUCKINGHAM.

Indorfed, 1617.

To the LORD KEEPER (*).

My honourable Lord,

THOUGH I had refolved to give your Lordfhip no more trouble in matters of controverfy depending before you, with what importance foever

(*) Harl. MSS. Vol. 7006.

my

my letters had been; yet the refpect I bear unto this gentleman hath fo far forced my refolution, as to recommend unto your Lordfhip the fuit, which, I am informed by him, is to receive a hearing before you on Monday next, between Barneby Leigh and Sir Edward Dyer, plaintiffs, and Sir Thomas Thynne (*c*), defendant; wherein I defire your Lordfhip's favour on the plaintiffs fo far only, as the juftice of their caufe fhall require. And fo I reft

Your Lordfhip's faithful fervant,

Newmarket, the
15th of Nov.

G. B U C K I N G H A M.

Indorfed, 1617.

To the L O R D K E E P E R (*).

My honourable Lord,

THE certificate being returned upon the commiffion touching Sir Richard Haughton's alummines, I have thought fit to defire your Lordfhip's furtherance in the bufinefs, which his Majefty (as your Lordfhip will fee by his letter) much affecteth as a bargain for his advantage, and for the prefent relief of Sir Richard Haughton. What favour your Lordfhip fhall do him therein, I will not fail to acknowledge, and will ever reft

Your Lordfhip's faithful fervant,

G. B U C K I N G H A M.

Indorfed, *Received November* 16, 1617.

(*c*) eldeft fon of Sir John Thynne, Knight, who died November 21, 1604. This Sir Thomas's younger fon by his firft wife, Mary, daughter of George, Lord Audley, was father of Thomas Thynne, Efq; affaffinated by the followers of Count Coningfmark, February 12, 168$\frac{2}{3}$.

(*) Harl. MSS. Vol. 7906,

To

To the LORD KEEPER (*).

My honourable Lord,

I HAVE acquainted his Majesty with your Lord-ship's letter, who liketh well of the Judges opinion you sent unto him, and hath pricked the Sheriff of Buckinghamshire in the roll you sent, which I return signed unto your Lordship.

His Majesty takes very well the pains you have taken in sending to Sir Lionel Cranfield; and desireth you to send to him again, and to quicken him in the business.

Your Lordship's faithful friend and servant,

G. BUCKINGHAM.

His Majesty liketh well the course taken about his houshold, wherewith he would have your Lordship, and the rest of his council, to go forward.

Newmarket, the 17th
of November, 1617.

Indorsed,

My Lord of Buckingham shewing his Majesty's approbation of the courses held touching the houshold.

To the LORD KEEPER (*).

My honourable Lord,

UNDERSTANDING, that Thomas Huke-ley, a merchant of London, of whom I have heard a good report, intendeth to bring before your Lordship in Chancery a cause depending between him, in the right of his wife, daughter of William

(*) Harl. MSS. Vol. 7006.

Austen,

Auften, and one John Horfemendon, who married another daughter of the faid Auften; I have thought fit to defire your Lordſhip to give the faid Thomas Hukeley a favourable hearing, when his caufe ſhall come before you; and fo far to refpect him for my fake, as your Lordſhip ſhall fee him grounded upon equity and reafon; which is no more than, I aſſure myſelf, your Lordſhip will grant readily, as it is defired by

Your Lordſhip's faithful friend and ſervant,

G. BUCKINGHAM,

Indorfed, *November* 17, 1617.

To the Earl of BUCKINGHAM *(d).*

My very good Lord,

THE laſt letter of my Lords, whereof the con-cluſion indeed is a little *blunt*, as the King calleth it, was concluded in my abſence, which hath been but once fince I came to this town; and brought me by the Clerk of the Council, as I fat in Chancery. Whereupon I retired to a little cloſet I have there, and ſigned it, not thinking fit to fever.

For my opinion, I difpatched it the morrow following. And till Sir Lionel Cranfield (e) be able to

(d) In anſwer to his Lordſhip's letter from Newmarket, November 19, 1617, printed in Lord Bacon's works.

(e) He was originally a merchant in the city of London, introduced to the King's knowledge by the Earl of Northampton, and into his ſervice by the Earl of Buckingham, being the great projector for reforming the King's houſhold, advancing the cuſtoms, and other ſervices; for which he was made Lord Treaſurer, Baron Cranfield, and Earl of Middleſex; but being accuſed by the houfe of commons for mifdemeanors in his office, he had a fevere fentence paſſed upon him by the Lords in 1624.

execute

execute his part in the fub-commiffion, it will, in my opinion, not be fo fit to direct it. He crept to me yeftetnight, but he is not well. I did his Majefty's meffage to him touching the tobacco ; and he faid he would give his Majefty very real and folid fatisfaction touching the fame.

This is all for the prefent I fhall trouble your Lordfhip withall, refting ever

Your Lordfhip's true friend,

and devoted fervant,

November 20, 1617.

Fr. Bacon.

To the Lord Keeper (*).

My honourable Lord,

HIS Majefty liketh very well of the draught your Lordfhip fent of the letter for the fub-commiffion, and hath figned it, as it was, without any alteration, and fent it to the Lords. Which is all I have to write at this time, but that I ever reft

Your Lordfhip's faithful friend and fervant,

Newmarket, the 2d
of Decemb. 1617.

G. Buckingham.

To the Lord Keeper (*).

My honourable Lord,

HIS Majefty hath been pleafed to refer a petition of one Sir Thomas Blackftones to your Lordfhip, who being brother-in-law to a gentleman, whom I much refpect, Sir Henry Conftable, I have,

(*) Harl. MSS. Vol. 7006.

at

at his requeſt, yielded to recommend his buſineſs ſo far to your Lordſhip's favour, as you ſhall find his caſe to deſerve compaſſion, and may ſtand with the rules of equity. And ſo I reſt

Your Lordſhip's faithful friend and ſervant,

Newmarket, the 4th of December.
G. BUCKINGHAM.

Indorſed, 1617.

To the Earl *of* BUCKINGHAM.

My very good Lord,

YOUR Lordſhip may marvel, that together with the letter from the board, which, you ſee, paſſed ſo well, there came no particular letter from myſelf; wherein, though it be true, that now this very evening I have made even with the cauſes of Chancery, and comparing with the cauſes heard by my Lord *(f)*, that dead is, of Michaelmaſs-term was twelvemonth, I find them to be double ſo many and one more; beſides that the cauſes, that I diſpatch, do ſeldom turn upon me again, as his many times did; yet nevertheleſs, I do aſſure your Lordſhip, that ſhould have been no excuſe to me, who ſhall ever aſſign both to the cauſes of the ſubject, yea, and to my health, but the leavings of times after his Majeſty's buſineſs done. But the truth is, I could not ſpeak with Sir Lionel Cranfield, with whom of neceſſity I was to confer about the names, till this afternoon. Firſt, therefore, I ſend the names, by his advice, and with mine own good allowance of thoſe, which we wiſh his Majeſty ſhould ſelect; wherein I have had

(f) Chancellor Elleſmere.

respect

respect somewhat to form, more to the avoiding of opposition, but most to the service.

Two most important effects his Majesty's letter hath wrought already : the one, that we perceive his Majesty will go through stitch ; which goeth to the root of our disease. The other, that it awaketh the particular officers, and will make their own endeavours and propositions less perfunctory, and more solid and true for the future. Somewhat is to be done presently, and somewhat by seasonable degrees. For the present, my advice is, his Majesty would be pleased to write back to the table, that he doth well approve, that we did not put back or retard the good ways we were in of ourselves ; and that we understood his Majesty's right : that his late direction was to give help, and not hindrance, to the former courses ; and that he doth expect the propositions we have in hand, when they are finished : and that for the sub-commissions, he hath sent us the names he hath chosen out of those by us sent and propounded ; and that he leaveth the particular directions from time to time, in the use of the sub-commissioners, wholly to the table.

This I conceive to be the fairest way ; first to seal the sub-commission without opening the nature of their employments, and without seeming, that they should have any immediate dependance upon his Majesty, but merely upon the table.

As for that, which is to be kept in breast, and to come forth by parts, the degrees are these :

First, to employ the sub-commissioners in the re-considering of those branches, which the several officers shall propound.

Next, in taking consideration of other branches of retrenchment, besides those, which shall be propounded.

The third, to take into consideration the great and huge arrears and debts in every office ; whether there

there be caufe to abate them upon deceit or abufe; and at leaft how to fettle them beft, both for the King's honour, and avoiding of clamour, and for the taking away, as much as may be, that fame ill influence and effect, whereby the arrear paft deftroys the good hufbandry and reformation to come.

The fourth is to proceed from the confideration of the retrenchments and arrears to the improvements.

All thefe four, at leaft the laft three, I wifh not to be ftirred in till his Majefty's coming.

God ever preferve and profper you.

Your Lordfhip's true friend,

and devoted fervant,

FR. BACON:

Your Lordfhip will be pleafed to have a little care of the beftowing of this letter.

York-houfe, this 6th
of December, 1617.

To the LORD KEEPER (*).

My honourable Lord,

LEST Mr. Secretary (g) fhould be come away before the delivery of this packet, I have thought fit to direct it to your Lordfhip, with this letter to your Lordfhip about the Court of Wards, and another to the Lords from his Majefty. Which is all I have now to write, but that I ever reft

Your Lordfhip's faithful friend and fervant,

Newmarket, the
7th of Decem-
ber, 1617.   G. BUCKINGHAM.

(*) Harl. MSS. Vol. 7006.

(g) Sir Thomas Lake. His collegue, Secretary Winwood, died October 27, 1617; and Sir Robert Naunton fucceeded to the poft of Secretary, January 8, 1617, from that of Surveyor of the Court of Wards.

4

To

To the LORD KEEPER (*).

My honourable Lord,

I HAVE acquainted his Majesty with your Lordship's letter, who hath followed your directions
therein, and written to the Lords accordingly. Which
is all I have now to write to your Lordship, but that
I shall ever rest

Your Lordship's faithful friend and servant,

Newmarket, the
  9th day of De-   G. BUCKINGHAM.
  cember, 1617.

Indorsed,

*My Lord of Buckingham to your Lordship, shewing the
King's liking of your opinion and choice of names for
sub-commission.*

To the Earl of BUCKINGHAM.

My very good Lord,

YOUR Lordship's letters patents (*b*) are ready.
I would be glad to be one of the witnesses at
the delivery ; and therefore, if the King and your
Lordship will give me leave, I will bring it to-morrow
at any hour shall be appointed.

Your Lordship's ever,

New-Year's eve, 1617.

FR. BACON.

(*) Harl. MSS. Vol. 7006.
(*b*) for the title of Marquis of Buckingham to himself and the
male-heirs of his body.

I was

I was bold to send your Lordship, for your New-Year's gift, a plain cap of essay, in token, that if your Lordship in any thing shall make me your sayman, I will be hurt before your Lordship shall be hurt. I present therefore to you my best service, which shall be my All-Years gift.

To the Earl of BUCKINGHAM.

My very good Lord,

SIR George Chaworth and I am agreed, so that now I shall retain the grace of my place, and yet he rewarded. The King hath no ill bargain; for he hath four times as much as he was offered by Sir George of increase; and yet I take upon me to content my servants, and to content him. Nevertheless, I shall think myself pleasured by his Majesty, and do acknowledge, that your Lordship hath dealt very honourably and nobly with me.

I send inclosed a letter, whereby your Lordship signifieth his Majesty's pleasure to me; and I shall make the warrant to Mr. Attorney. I desire it may be carried in privateness. I ever rest

Your Lordship's true friend,

and devoted servant,

This New-Year's
eve, 1617.

FR. BACON.

To Sir JAMES FULLERTON (i).

I PRESUME to send his Highness this pair of small candlesticks, that his light, and the light of his posterity, upon the church and commonwealth,

(i) He had been Surveyor of the Lands to Prince Charles, when Duke of York; and was Groom of the Stole to him, when King. He died in January, 163¾.

may

may never fail. I pray you do me the favour to prefent it to his Highneſs, with my beſt and humbleſt ſervice.

Your moſt affectionate and aſſured friend,

Fr. Bacon, C. S.

To the Lord Chancellor (*k*).

My honourable Lord,

I HAVE heretofore recommended unto your Lordſhip the determination of the cauſe between Sir Rowland Egerton and Edward Egerton (*l*), who, I underſtand, did both agree, being before your Lordſhip, upon the values of the whole lands. And as your Lordſhip hath already made ſo good an entrance into the buſineſs, I doubt not but you will be as noble in furthering the full agreement between the parties: whereunto, I am informed, Sir Rowland Egerton is very forward, offering on his part that, which to me ſeemeth very reaſonable, either to divide the lands, and his adverſe party to chooſe; or the other to divide, and he to chooſe. Whereupon my deſire to your Lordſhip is, that you would accordingly make a final end between them, in making a diviſion, and ſetting forth the lands, according to the values agreed upon by the parties themſelves. Wherein, beſides the charitable work your Lordſhip ſhall do in making an end of a controverſy between thoſe, whom

(*k*) Sir Francis Bacon had that title given him January 4.
(*l*) This was one of the cauſes mentioned in the charge of the Houſe of Commons againſt the Lord Bacon; in his anſwer to which, he acknowledged, that ſome days after perfecting his award, which was done with the advice and conſent of the Lord Chief Juſtice Hobart, and publiſhing it to the parties, he received 300*l*. of Mr. Edward Egerton, by whom, ſoon after his coming to the ſeal, he had likewiſe been preſented with 400*l*. in a purſe.

M name

name and blood fhould tie together, and keep in unity, I will acknowledge your favour as unto my-felf, and will ever reft

Your Lordfhip's faithful fervant,

Theobalds, the 9th of
January, 1617.   G. BUCKINGHAM.

To the LORD CHANCELLOR (*).

My honourable Lord,

HIS Majefty having given order to Mr. Sollicitor (*m*) to acquaint your Lordfhip with a bufinefs touching ale-houfes (*n*), that upon confideration thereof you might certify your opinion unto his Majefty, whether it be fit to be granted or not; I have thought fit to defire your Lordfhip to give it what favour and furtherance you may, if you find it reafonable, and not prejudicial to his Majefty's fervice, becaufe it concerneth Mr. Patrick Maule, and my brother, Chriftopher Villiers, whofe benefit I have reafon to wifh and advance by any juft courfes. And fo I reft

Your Lordfhip's faithful fervant,

Royfton, the 11th
of Jan. 1617.   G. BUCKINGHAM.

(*) Harl. MSS. Vol. 7006.   (*m*) Sir Thomas Coventry.
(*n*) The Lord Chancellor, in his letter to the Marquis of Buckingham, dated January 25, 1617, printed in his works, has the following paffage : " For the fuit of the *ale-houfes,* which " concerneth your brother, Mr. Chriftopher Villiers, and Mr. " Patrick Maule, I have conferred with my Lord Chief Juftice " and Mr. Sollicitor thereupon, and there is a fcruple in it, that " it fhould be one of the grievances put down in parliament : " which if it be, I may not, in my duty and love to you, advife " you to deal in it ; if it be not, I will meuld in the beft man- " ner, and help it forward." A patent for licenfing ale-houfes being afterwards granted to Sir Giles Mompeffon and Sir Francis Mitchel, and greatly abufed by them, they were punifhed for thofe abufes by the parliament, which met January 30, 162$\frac{9}{7}$.

To

To the LORD CHANCELLOR (*).

My honourable Lord,

SIR John Cotton (*o*) having acquainted me with a petition he intended to exhibit to his Majesty, that, without any apparent fault committed by him, he was put from his office of *Custos Rotulorum*; I have persuaded him to forbear the presenting of his petition until I had written to your Lordship, and received your answer. I have therefore thought fit to signify unto your Lordship, that he is a gentleman, of whom his Majesty maketh good esteem, and hath often occasion to use his service : and therefore, besides that he is a man of good years, and hath served long in the place, I know his Majesty, out of these respects, will be loth he should receive any disgrace. I desire therefore to understand from your Lordship the reasons of his remove, that, if I cannot give satisfaction to the gentleman himself, I may at least make answer to his Majesty for that act of your Lordship's, which is alledged to be very unusual, unless upon some precedent misdemeanor of the party. Thus, having in this point discharged my part in taking the best course I could, that no complaint should come against you to the King, I rest

Your Lordship's faithful friend,

Newmarket, the 16th
of January, 1617.

G. BUCKINGHAM.

(*) Harl. MSS. Vol. 7006.
(*o*) of Landwade, in Cambridgeshire, Knight. He served many years as knight of the shire for that county, and died in 1620, at the age of seventy-seven. His eldest son, Sir John Cotton, was created a Baronet, July 14, 1641.

M 2

To

To Sir HENRY YELVERTON, *Attorney General.*

Mr. Attorney,

WHEREAS there dependeth before me in Chancery a great cause of tythes concerning the benefices of London, though in a particular, yet, by confequence, leading to a general; his Majefty, out of a great and religious care of the ftate, both of church and city, is gracioufly pleafed, that before any judicial fentence be pronounced in Chancery, there be a commiffion directed unto me, the Lord Chancellor, Lord Treafurer, the Lord Privy-Seal, and the Lord Chamberlain; and likewife to the Lord Archbifhop, the Lord Bifhop of Winchefter *(p)*, and the Bifhop of Ely *(q)*, and alfo to the Mafter of the Rolls *(r)*, the two Lord Chief Juftices *(s)*, Juftice Dodderidge, and Juftice Hutton, who formerly affifted me in the caufe, to treat of fome concord in a reafonable moderation between the minifters and the Mayor and the commonalty of London in the behalf of the citizens; and to make fome pact and tranfaction between them by confent, if it may be; or otherwife to hear and certify their opinions touching the caufe, that thereupon his Majefty may take fuch farther order, by directing of a proceeding in Chancery, or by fome other courfe, as to his wifdom fhall feem fit.

You will have care to draw the commiffion with fome preface of honour to his Majefty, and likewife to infert in the beginning of the commiffion, that it

---

(p) Dr. James Montagu.   *(q)* Dr. Lancelot Andrews.
(r) Sir Julius Cæfar.
(s) Sir Henry Montagu of the King's Bench, and Sir Henry Hobart of the Common Pleas.

was

was *de advifamento cancellarii* (as it was indeed) left it fhould feem to be taken from the court. So I commit you to God's &c.

January 19, 1617.

FR. BACON, *Canc.*

To the Marquis of BUCKINGHAM.

My very good Lord,

I DO not eafily fail towards gentlemen of quality to difgrace them. For I take myfelf to have fome intereft in the good wills of the gentlemen of England, which I keep and cherifh for his Majefty's fpecial fervice. And for this gentleman, of whom you write, Sir John Cotton, I know no caufe in the world, why I fhould have difplaced him, but that it was certified unto me, that it was his own defire to refign : wherein if I was abufed, I will reftore him. But if he did confent, and, now it is done, changeth his mind, then I would be loth to difgrace the other, that is come in. Therefore I pray your Lordfhip, that I may know and be informed from himfelf what paffed touching his confent ; and I will do him reafon.

Thus, with my thanks to your Lordfhip, I will ever reft

Your Lordfhip's true friend,

and moft devoted fervant,

January 20, 1617.

FR. BACON, *Canc.*

Indorfed,

To the Marquis of Buckingham, concerning Sir John Cotton's refigning the place of Cuftos Rotulorum of Cambridgefhire.

M 3

To the Lord Chancellor (*).

My honourable Lord,

I THANK your Lordship for your favour to Sir George Tipping, in giving liberty unto him to make his appearance before you after the holy-days, at my request ; who, as I understand by some friends of mine, who moved me to recommend him to your Lordship's favour, is willing to conform himself in performance of the decree made in the Chancery by your Lordship's predecessor, but that he is persuaded, that presently, upon the performance thereof, his son will make away the land, that shall be conveyed unto him : which being come to Sir George from his ancestors, he desireth to preserve to his posterity. I desire your Lordship's farther favour therefore unto him, that you will find out some course, how he may be exempted from that fear of the sale of his lands, whereof he is ready to acknowledge a fine to his son, and to his heirs by Anne Pigot ; and, they failing, to his son's heirs males, and, for want thereof, to any of his son's or brethren's heirs males, and so to the heirs general of his father and himself by lineal descent, and the remainder to the crown. This offer, which seemeth very reasonable, and for his Majesty's advantage, I desire your Lordship to take into your consideration, and to shew him what favour you may for my sake ; which I will readily acknowledge, and ever rest

Your Lordship's faithful servant,

Newmarket, the 23d
of January, 1617.

G. Buckingham.

(*) Harl. MSS. Vol. 7006.

To

To *the* LORD CHANCELLOR (*).

My honourable Lord,

SINCE I received your Lordship's letter, Sir Lionel Cranfield being here, hath informed his Majesty of the whole proceeding in his business of the houshold ; which his Majesty liketh very well, and is glad it is approved by your Lordship, of whose care and pains therein he receiveth very good satisfaction.

In the business touching Sir John Cotton, your Lordship dealeth as nobly as can be desired ; and so, if it should come in question before his Majesty, I would answer in your behalf. I leave Sir John Cotton to inform your Lordship by his letter of the business, and ever rest

Your Lordship's fathful servant,

Newmarket, the 24th
of January, 1617.   G. BUCKINGHAM.

To *the* LORD CHANCELLOR (*).

My honourable Lord,

I HAVE been intreated by a gentleman, whom I much respect, to recommend to your Lordship's favour Mr. John Huddy, between whom and Mr. Richard Huddy there is, as I am informed, a cause to be heard before your Lordship in the Chancery on Saturday next. My desire unto your Lordship is, that you would shew the said John Huddy what favour you lawfully may, and as his cause will bear, when it cometh before you, for my fake. Which I will not fail to acknowledge, ever resting

Your Lordship's faithful servant,

Newmarket, the 28th
of January, 1617.   G. BUCKINGHAM,

To the LORD CHANCELLOR (*).

My honourable Lord,

I UNDERSTAND, that his Majesty hath been pleased to refer a suit unto him by two of his servants, Robert Maxwell and John Hunt, for the making of Sheriffs and Escheators patents, to your Lordship's consideration. My desire unto your Lordship on their behalf is, that you would shew them thus much favour for my fake, as with as much expedition, as may be, and your Lordship's other occasions may permit, to certify your opinion thereof unto his Majesty; which I will be ready to acknowledge, and ever rest

Your Lordship's faithful servant,

Newmarket, the 4th day
of February, 1617.   G. BUCKINGHAM,

To the LORD CHANCELLOR (*).

My honourable Lord,

THOUGH I had resolved not to write to your Lordship in any matter between party and party; yet at the earnest request of my noble friend, the Lord Norris, to whom I account myself much be-

(*) Harl. MSS. Vol. 7006.

holden,

holden, I could not but recommend unto your Lord-ship's favour a special friend of his, Sir Thomas Monk, who hath a suit before your Lordship in the Chancery (*t*) with Sir Robert Baffet; which, upon the report made unto me thereof, seemeth so reason-able, that I doubt not but the cause itself will move your Lordship to favour him, if, upon the hearing thereof, it shall appear the same unto your Lordship, as at the first sight it doth unto me. I therefore desire your Lordship to shew in this particular what favour you lawfully may, for my sake, who will ac-count it as done unto myself; and will ever rest

Your Lordship's faithful servant,

Newmarket, the 4th
  day of Feb. 1617.   G. BUCKINGHAM,

To the Marquis of BUCKINGHAM,

My very good Lord,

I HAVE sent inclosed a letter to his Majesty about the public charge I am to give the last Star-Chamber day, which is this day sevennight, to the Judges and Justices before the circuits. I pray de-liver it to his Majesty with speed. I send also some papers appertaining to that business, which I pray your Lordship to have in readiness, if his Majesty call for them. I ever rest

Your Lordship's true friend,

and devoted servant,

February 6, 1617.

FR. BACON, *Canc.*

(*t*) Lord Bacon was afterwards accused by the House of Com-mons of having received of Sir Thomas Monk 100 pieces; which he did not deny, but alledged, that it was after the suit was ended.

2   *To*

To the LORD CHANCELLOR (*).

My honourable Lord,

HIS Majesty marvelleth, that he heareth nothing of the business touching the gold and silver thread (*u*) ; and therefore hath commanded me to write unto your Lordship to hasten the dispatch of it ; and to give him as speedy an account thereof, as you can. And so I rest

Your Lordship's faithful servant,

Newmarket, 7th
of February.

G. BUCKINGHAM.

Indorsed, 1617.

To the LORD CHANCELLOR (*).

My honourable Lord,

I UNDERSTAND by this bearer, Edward Hawkins, how great pains your Lordship hath taken, in the business, which I recommended to you concerning him, and how favourably your Lordship hath used him for my sake. For which I give your Lordship many thanks, and will be ever ready to acknowledge your favour toward him by all the testimonies of

Your Lordship's faithful friend,

Theobalds, the 12th
of February, 1617.

G. BUCKINGHAM.

(*) Harl. MSS. Vol. 7006.
(*u*) A patent for the monopoly of which was granted to Sir Giles Mompesson and Sir Francis Mitchel, who were punished, for the abuse of that patent by the parliament, which met January 30, 162⁰/₁.

To

To the LORD CHANCELLOR (*).

My honourable Lord,

I HAVE acquainted his Majesty with your letter, who liketh well of the courfe you mention in the end of your letter, and will fpeak with you farther of it at his return to London. In the mean time, he would have your Lordfhip give direction to the Mafter of the Rolls (*x*) and Mr. Attorney (*y*) to ftay the examination. And fo I reft

Your Lordfhip's moft affured

to do you fervice,

Hampton-Court, the
18th of March,
1617.

G. BUCKINGHAM.

To the LORD CHANCELLOR *of Ireland* (*z*).

My Lord Chancellor,

I WILL not have you account the days of my not anfwering your letter. It is a thing impofed up-on the multitude of my bufinefs to lodge many things faithfully, though I make no prefent return.

Your conjunction and good underftanding with the Deputy (*a*) I approve and commend ; for I ever loved intire and good compofitions, which was the old phyfic, better than fine feparations.

Your friendly attributes I take as effects of affec-tion ; which muft be caufes of any good offices, wherewith I can requite you.

(*) Harl. MSS. Vol. 7006.
(*x*) Sir Julius Cæfar. (*y*) Sir Henry Yelverton.
(*z*) Dr. Thomas Jones, Archbifhop of Dublin, who died April 10, 1619.
(*a*) Sir Oliver St. John, afterwards Vifcount Grandifon. He died at Batterfea in Surrey, December 29, 1630, aged feventy.

We

We conceive that kingdom is in growth. God send foundnefs to the increafe; wherein I doubt not but your Lordfhip will do your part. God keep you.

Your Lordfhip's very loving friend,

York-houfe, April 15,
1618.
    F R. B A C O N, *Canc.*

To the LORD CHIEF JUSTICE *of Ireland* (*b*).

My Lord Chief Juftice,

I THANK you for your letter, and affure you, that you are not deceived, neither in the care I have of the public in that ftate, nor in my good wifhes, and the effects thereof, when it fhall lie in my power towards yourfelf.

I am glad to receive your teftimony of my Lord Deputy, both becaufe I efteem your judgement, and becaufe it concurreth with my own.

The materials of that kingdom, which is trade and wealth, grow on apace. I hope the form, which giveth the beft living of religion and juftice, will not be behind, the rather by you, as a good inftrument. I reft

Your Lordfhip's affured friend,

York-houfe * * of
April, 1618.
    F R. B A C O N, *Canc.*

To the LORD CHANCELLOR (*).

My honourable Lord,

UNDERSTANDING, that there is a fuit depending before your Lordfhip between Sir

(*b*) Sir William Jones, to whom, upon his being called to that poft, the Lord Keeper made a fpeech, printed in his works.
(*) Harl. MSS. Vol. 7006.

Rowland

Rowland Cotton (*c*), plaintiff, and Sir John Gawen, defendant, which is shortly to come to a hearing; and having been likewise informed, that Sir Rowland Cotton hath undertaken it in the behalf of certain poor people; which charitable endeavour of his, I assure myself, will find so good acceptation with your Lordship, that there shall be no other use of recommendation: yet, at the earnest request of some friends of mine, I have thought fit to write to your Lordship in his behalf, desiring you to shew him what favour you lawfully may, and the cause may bear, in the speedy dispatch of his business; which I shall be ever ready to acknowledge, and rest

Your Lordship's most devoted to serve you,

Whitehall, the 20th
day of Apr. 1618.   G. BUCKINGHAM.

To the LORD CHANCELLOR (*).

My honourable Lord,

I WILL not go about to excuse mine own fault, by making you believe his Majesty was backward in your business; but upon the first motion, he gave me directions for it; which it was my negligence, as I freely confess, that I have no sooner performed,

(*c*) a gentleman eminent for his learning, especially in the Hebrew language, in which he had been instructed by the famous Hugh Broughton, who died in 1612. He was son of Mr. William Cotton, citizen and draper of London, and had an estate at Bellaport in Shropshire, where he resided, till he came to live at London at the request of Sir Allen Cotton, his father's younger brother, who was Lord Mayor of that city in 1625. Sir Rowland was the first patron of the learned Dr. Lightfoot, and encouraged him in the prosecution of his studies of the Hebrew language and antiquities.

(*) Harl. MSS. Vol. 7006.

having

having not been flack in moving his Majefty, but in difpatching your man. All is done, which your Lordfhip defired, and I will give order, according to his Majefty's directions, fo that your Lordfhip fhall not need to trouble yourfelf any farther, but only to expect the fpeedy performance of his Majefty's gracious pleafure.

I will take the firft opportunity to acquaint his Majefty with the other bufinefs, and will ever reft

Your Lordfhip's faithful friend and fervant,

Theobalds, the 8th
of May [1618].

G. B U C K I N G H A M.

To the L O R D C H A N C E L L O R (*).

My honourable good Lord,

WHEREAS in Mr. Hanfbye's caufe *(d)*, which formerly, by my means, both his Majefty and myfelf recommended to your Lordfhip's favour, your Lordfhip thought good, upon a hearing thereof, to decree fome part for the young gentleman, and to refer to fome Mafters of the Chancery, for your farther fatisfaction, the examination of witneffes to this point ; which feemed to your Lordfhip to be the main thing your Lordfhip doubted of, whether or no the leafes, conveyed by old Hanfbye to young Hanfbye by deed, were to be liable to the legacies, which he

(*) Harl. MSS. Vol. 7006.
(d) This feems to be one of the caufes, on account of which Lord Bacon was afterwards accufed by the Houfe of Commons ; in anfwer to whofe charge he admits, that in the caufe of Sir Ralph Hanfbye there being two decrees, one for the inheritance, and the other for goods and chattels ; fome time after the firft decree, and before the fecond, there was 500 l. delivered to him by Mr. Tobie Matthew ; nor could his Lordfhip deny, that this was upon the matter *pendente lite.*

gave

gave by will ; and that now I am credibly informed, that it will appear upon their report, and by the depositions of witnesses, without all exception, that the said leases are no way liable to those legacies : these shall be earnestly to intreat your Lordship, that upon consideration of the report of the masters, and depositions of the witnesses, you will, for my sake, shew as much favour and expedition to young Mr. Hansbye in this cause, as the justness thereof will permit. And I shall receive it at your Lordship's hands as a particular favour.

So I take my leave of your Lordship, and rest

Your Lordship's faithful friend and servant,

Greenwich, the
12th of June,
1618.

G. BUCKINGHAM.

To the LORD CHANCELLOR (*).

My honourable Lord,

UNDERSTANDING, that the cause depending in the Chancery between the Lady Vernon and the officers of his Majesty's houshold is now ready for a decree ; though I doubt not, but, as his Majesty hath been satisfied of the equity of the cause on his officers behalf, who have undergone the business, by his Majesty's command, your Lordship will also find their cause worthy of your favour : yet I have thought fit once again to recommend it to your Lordship, desiring you to give them a speedy end of it, that both his Majesty may be freed from farther importunity, and they from the charge and trouble of following

(*) Harl. MSS. Vol. 7006.

it :

it : which I will be ever ready to acknowledge as a favour done unto myfelf, and always reft

　　　Your Lordfhip's faithful friend and fervant,

Greenwich, the
　15th day of　　　　　　　　G. BUCKINGHAM,
June, 1618.

　　　To the LORD CHANCELLOR (*).

My honourable Lord,

I WROTE unto your Lordfhip lately in the be-half of Sir Rowland Cotton, that then had a fuit in dependance before your Lordfhip and the reft of my Lords in the Star-Chamber. The caufe, I un-derftand, hath gone contrary to his expectation ; yet he acknowledges himfelf much bound to your Lord-fhip for the noble and patient hearing he did then re-ceive ; and he refts fatisfied, and I much beholden to your Lordfhip, for any favour it pleafed your Lord-fhip to afford him for my caufe. It now refts only in your Lordfhip's power for the affeffing of cofts ; which, becaufe, I am certainly informed, Sir Rowland Cotton had juft caufe of complaint, I hope your Lordfhip will not give any againft him. And I do the rather move your Lordfhip to refpect him in it, becaufe it concerns him in his reputation, which I know he tenders, and not the money, which might be impofed upon him ; which can be but a trifle. Thus prefuming of your Lordfhip's favour herein, which I fhall be ready ever to account to your Lord-fhip for, I reft

　　　Your Lordfhip's moft devoted to ferve you,
June 19, 1618.

　　　　　　　G. BUCKINGHAM.

　　　(*) Harl. MSS. Vol. 7006.

　　　　　　　　　　　　　　　　　To

To the LORD CHANCELLOR (*).

My honourable Lord,

WHEREAS it hath pleafed his Majefty to recommend unto your confideration a petition exhibited by Mr Fowle, together with the grievances and requeft for the rectifying of the work of gold and filver thread; and now underftandeth, that your Lordfhip hath called unto you the other commiffioners in that cafe, and fpent fome time to hear what the oppofers could object, and perceiveth by a relation of a good entrance you have made into the bufinefs; and is now informed, that there remaineth great ftore of gold and filver thread in the merchants hands, brought from foreign parts, befides that, which is brought in daily by ftealth, and wrought here by underhand workers; fo that the agents want vent, with which inconveniencies, it feemeth the ordinary courfe of law cannot fo well meet: and yet they are inforced, for freeing of clamour, to fet great numbers of people on work; fo that the commodity lying dead in their hands, will in a very fhort time grow to a very great fum of money: To the end therefore, that the undertakers may not be difheartened by thefe wrongs and loffes, his Majefty hath commanded me to write unto your Lordfhip, to the end you might beftow more time this vacation in profecuting the courfe you have fo worthily begun, that all differences being reconciled, the defects of the commiffion may be alfo amended, for prevention of farther abufes therein; fo as the agents may receive encouragement to

(*) Harl. MSS. Vol. 7006.

N

go

go on quietly in the work without disturbance. And
I rest

Your Lordship's faithful friend and servant,

From Bewly, the 20th
day of Aug. 1618.
G. BUCKINGHAM.

To the LORD CHANCELLOR.

Most honourable Lord,

HEREWITHALL I presumed to send a note
inclosed, both of my business in Chancery,
and with my Lord Roos, which it pleased your Lordship to demand of me, that so you might better do
me good *in utroque genere.* It may please your Lordship, after having perused it, to commend it over to
the care of Mr. Meautys for better custody.

At my parting last from your Lordship, the grief
I had to leave your Lordship's presence, though but
for a little time, was such, as that being accompanied
with some small corporal indisposition, that I was in,
made me forgetful to say that, which now for his
Majesty's service I thought myself bound not to silence. I was credibly informed and assured, when
the Spanish Ambassador went away, that howsoever
Ralegh and the prentices (*e*) should fall out to be
proceeded withall, no more instances would be made
hereafter on the part of Spain for justice to be done
ever in these particulars: but that if slackness were

(*e*) who on the 12th of July, 1618, had insulted Gondomar,
the Spanish Ambassador, on account of a boy's being hurt by him
as he was riding. [*Camdeni Annales Regis Jacobi I.* p. 33.]
They were proceeded against by commissioners at Guildhall
on Wednesday the 12th of August following; seven being found
guilty, and adjudged to six months imprisonment, and to pay
500 l. a piece. Two others were acquitted. MS. letter of
Mr. Chamberlain to Sir Dudley Carleton, London, August 15,
1618.

used

tifed here, they would be laid up in the deck, and would ferve for materials (this was the very word) of future and final difcontentments. Now as the humour and defign of fome may carry them towards troubling of the waters; fo I know your Lordfhip's both nature and great place require an appeafing them at your hands. And I have not prefumed to fay this little out of any mind at all, that I may have, to meddle with matters fo far above me, but out of a thought I had, that I was tied in duty to lay thus much under your Lordfhip's eye; becaufe I know and confider of whom I heard that fpeech, and with how grave circumftances it was delivered.

I befeech Jefus to give continuance and increafe to your Lordfhip's happinefs; and that, if it may ftand with his will, myfelf may one day have the honour of cafting fome fmall mite into that rich treafury. So I humbly do your Lordfhip reverence, and continue

The moft obliged of your Lordfhip's

many faithful fervants,

Nottingham, this 21ft
of Auguft, 1618.   T O B I E   M A T T H E W.

To Mr. (afterwards Sir) I s a a c   W a k e, *his Ma-jefty's Agent at the court of Savoy.*

Mr. Wake,

I HAVE received fome letters from you; and hearing from my Lord Cavendifh (f) how well he affects you, and taking notice alfo of your good abilities and fervices in his Majefty's affairs, and not forgetting the knowledge I had, when young, of your

(f) William Cavendifh, fon and heir of William, created Baron Cavendifh Hardwicke in Derbyfhire, in May 1605, and Earl of Devonfhire, July 12, 1618.

N 2   good

good father (g), I thought myself in some measure tied not to keep from you my good opinion of you, and my desire to give you any furtherance in your fortunes and occasions, whereof you may take knowledge and liberty to use me for your good. Fare you well.

Your very loving friend,

York-house, this 1st
of Sept. 1618.

Fr. Verulam (b), Canc.

To the Lord Chancellor (*).

My honourable Lord,

HIS Majesty is desirous to be satisfied of the fitness and conveniency of the gold and silver thread-business; as also of the profit, that shall any way accrue unto him thereby. Wherefore his pleasure is, that you shall, with all convenient speed, call unto you the Lord Chief Justice of the King's Bench (i), the Attorney General (k), and the Sollicitor (l); and consider with them of every of the said particulars, and return them to his Majesty, that thereupon he may resolve what present course to take for the advancement of the execution thereof. And so I rest

Your Lordship's faithful servant,

Theobalds, the 4th
of Octob. 1618.

G. Buckingham.

(g) Arthur Wake, Rector of Billing in Northamptonshire, Master of the Hospital of St. John in Northampton, and Canon of Christ-Church, Oxford.

(b) He had been created Lord Verulam on the 12th of July, 1618.

(*) Harl. MSS. Vol. 7006.

(i) Sir Henry Montagu.   (k) Sir Henry Yelverton.

(l) Sir Thomas Coventry.

To

To the LORD CHANCELLOR (*).

My honourable Lord,

I HAVE been defired by fome friends of mine, in the behalf of Sir Francis Englefyld, to recommend his caufe fo far unto your Lordfhip, that a peremptory day being given by your Lordfhip's order for the perfecting of his account, and for the affignment of the truft, your Lordfhip would take fuch courfe therein, that the gentleman's eftate may be redeemed from farther trouble, and fecured from all danger, by engaging thofe, to whom the truft is now transferred by your Lordfhip's order, to the performance of that, whereunto he was tied. And fo not doubting but your Lordfhip will do him what lawful favour you may herein, I reft

Your Lordfhip's faithful friend and fervant,

G. BUCKINGHAM.

Indorfed, *Received October* 14, 1618.

To the KING, *concerning the form and manner of proceeding againft Sir* WALTER RALEGH (*m*).

May it pleafe your moft excellent Majefty,

A CCORDING to your commandment given unto us, we have, upon divers meetings and conferences, confidered what form and manner of proceeding againft Sir Walter Ralegh might beft ftand with your Majefty's juftice and honour, if you fhall be pleafed, that the law fhall pafs upon him.

(*) Harl. MSS. Vol. 7006.
(*m*) He was beheaded October 29, 1618, the day of the inauguration of the Lord Mayor of London.

And,

And, firſt, we are of opinion, that Sir Walter Ra-legh being attainted of high-treaſon (which is the higheſt and laſt work of law,) he cannot be drawn in queſtion judicially for any crime or offence ſince committed. And therefore we humbly preſent two forms of proceeding to your Majeſty: the one, that together with the warrant to the Lieutenant of the Tower (if your Majeſty ſhall ſo pleaſe) for his execution, to publiſh a narrative in print of his late crimes and offences; which, albeit your Majeſty is not bound to give an account of your actions in theſe caſes to any but only to God alone, we humbly offer to your Majeſty's conſideration, as well in reſpect of the great effluxion of time ſince his attainder, and of his employment by your Majeſty's commiſſion, as for that his late crimes and offences are not yet publicly known. The other form (whereunto, if your Majeſty ſo pleaſe, we rather incline) is, that where your Majeſty is ſo renowned for your juſtice, it may have ſuch a proceeding, as is neareſt to legal proceeding; which is, that he be called before the whole body of your Council of State, and your principal Judges, in your Council-Chamber; and that ſome of the nobility and gentlemen of quality be admitted to be preſent to hear the whole proceeding, as in like caſes hath been uſed. And after the aſſembly of all theſe, that ſome of your Majeſty's Counſellors of State, that are beſt acquainted with the caſe, ſhould openly declare, that this form of proceeding againſt Sir Walter is holden, for that he is civilly dead. After this your Majeſty's council learned to charge his acts of hoſtility, depredation, abuſe as well of your Majeſty's commiſſion, as of your ſubjects under his charge, impoſtures, attempt of eſcape, and other his miſdemeanors. But for that, which concerns the French, wherein he was rather paſſive than active, and without which the charge is compleat, we humbly refer to your Majeſty's conſideration.

tion, how far that shall be touched. After which charge so given, the examinations read, and Sir Walter heard, and some to be confronted against him, if need be, then he is to be withdrawn and sent back; for that no sentence is, or can be, given against him. And after he is gone, then the Lords of the Council and Judges to give their advice to your Majesty, whether in respect of these subsequent offences, upon the whole matter, your Majesty, if you so please, may not with justice and honour give warrant for his execution upon his attainder. And of this whole proceeding we are of opinion, that a solemn act of council should be made, with a memorial of the whole presence. But before this be done, that your Majesty may be pleased to signify your gracious direction herein to your Council of State; and that your Council learned, before the calling of Sir Walter, should deliver the heads of the matter, together with the principal examinations touching the same, wherewith Sir Walter is to be charged, unto them, that they may be perfectly informed of the true state of the case, and give their advice accordingly. All which nevertheless we, in all humbleness, present and submit to your princely wisdom and judgement, and shall follow whatsoever it shall please your Majesty to direct us herein, with all dutiful readiness.

Your Majesty's most humble,

York-house, this 18th of October, 1618.   and faithful servants, &c.

To the LORD CHANCELLOR (*).

My honourable Lord,

WHEREAS there is a cause depending in the court of Chancery between one Mr. Francis Follambe and Francis Hornsby, the which

(*) Harl. MSS. Vol. 7006.

N 4

already

already hath received a decree, and is now to have another hearing before yourself; I have thought fit to defire you to fhew fo much favour therein, feeing it concerns the gentleman's whole eftate, as to make a full arbitration and final end, either by taking the pains in ending it yourfelf, or preferring it to fome other, whom your Lordfhip fhall think fit: which I fhall acknowledge as a courtefy from your Lordfhip; and ever reft

Your Lordfhip's faithful friend and fervant,

Hinchingbroke,
  the 22d of Octo-
ber, 1618.

G. BUCKINGHAM.

To the Marquis of BUCKINGHAM.

My very good Lord,

I SEND the commiffion for making Lincoln's Inn-Fields into walks for his Majefty's fignature. It is without charge to his Majefty.

We have had my Lord of Ormonde (*n*) before us. We could not yet get him to anfwer directly, whether he would obey the King's award or no. After we had endured his importunity and impertinences, and yet let him down to this, that his Majefty's award was not only juft and within his fubmiffion, but in his favour; we concluded in few words,

(*n*) Walter, Earl of Ormonde, grandfather of James the firft Duke of Ormonde. This Earl, upon the death of Thomas, Earl of Ormonde and Offory, fucceeding to thofe honours, fhould have inherited likewife the greateft part of the eftate: but his right was contefted by Sir Richard Prefton Lord Dingwell, fupported by the favour of King James I, who made an award, which Walter, Earl of Ormonde, conceiving to be unjuft, refufed to fubmit to, and was, by the King's order, committed to the Fleet, where he remained eight years before the death of that King; but in 1625 recovered his liberty.

that

that the award muſt be obeyed, and if he did refuſe or impugn the execution of it in Ireland, he was to be puniſhed by the juſtice of Ireland: if he did murmur or ſcandalize it here, or trouble his Majeſty any more, he was to be puniſhed in England. Then he aſked, whether he might be gone. For that, we told him, his Majeſty's pleaſure was to be known.

Sir Robert Manſell hath promiſed to bring his ſummer account this day ſevennight. God preſerve and proſper you.

Your Lordſhip's moſt obliged friend,

and-faithful ſervant,

November 12, 1618.

Fr. Verulam, *Canc.*

To the Lord Chancellor (*).

My honourable Lord,

I SEND your Lordſhip the commiſſion ſigned by his Majeſty, which he was very willing to diſpatch as a buſineſs very commendable and worthy to be taken in hand.

For the Earl of Ormonde, his Majeſty made no other anſwer, but that he hopeth he is not ſo unmannerly, as to go away without taking leave of his Majeſty.

For Sir Robert Manſell's account, his Majeſty ſaith he is very ſlow, eſpecially being but a ſummary account, and that he promiſed to bring it in before: and therefore would have him tied to the day he hath now ſet, without any farther delay.

(*) Harl. MSS. Vol. 7006.

This

This laft his Majefty commanded me to put in after I had written and figned my letter.

Your Lordfhip's faithful friend and fervant,

Royfton, the 13th of
November, 1618.   G. BUCKINGHAM.

To the LORD CHANCELLOR (*).

My honourable Lord,

HAVING formerly moved your Lordfhip in the bufinefs of this bearer, Mr. Wyche, of whom, as I underftand, your Lordfhip hath had a fpecial care to do him favour, according to the equity of his caufe ; now feeing, that the caufe is fhortly to be heard, I have thought fit to continue my recommendation of the bufinefs unto you, defiring your Lordfhip to fhew what favour you lawfully may unto Mr. Wyche, according as the juftnefs of the caufe fhall require : which I will acknowledge as a courtefy from your Lordfhip, and ever reft

Your Lordfhip's faithful friend and fervant,

Newmarket, the 18th
of November, 1618.   G. BUCKINGHAM.

To the LORD CHANCELLOR (*).

My honourable Lord,

I SEND your Lordfhip the bill of the Sheriff of Hereford and Leicefter, pricked and figned by his Majefty, who hath likewife commanded me to fend unto your Lordfhip thefe additions of inftructions, fent unto him by the Surveyor and Receiver of the Court of Wards ; wherein, becaufe he knoweth not

(*) Harl. MSS. Vol. 7006.

2   what

what to prescribe without understanding what objections can be made, his pleasure is, that your Lordship advise and consider of them, and send him your opinion of them, that he may then take such course therein, as shall be fit.

His Majesty commanded me to give you thanks for your care of his service; and so I rest

Your Lordship's faithful servant,

Newmarket, 22d
of November.   G. B U C K I N G H A M.

Indorsed, 1618.

To the Marquis of B U C K I N G H A M.

My very good Lord,

WE have put the *Declaration* (*o*) touching Ralegh to the press with his Majesty's additions, which were very material, and fit to proceed from his Majesty.

For the prisoners, we have taken an account, given a charge, and put some particulars in examination for punishment and example.

For the pursuivants, we staid a good while for Sir Edward Coke's health; but he being not yet come abroad, we have entered into it; and we find faults, and mean to select cases for example: but in this swarm of priests and recusants we are careful not to discourage in general. But the punishment of some, that are notoriously corrupt, concerned not the good, and will keep in awe those, that are but indifferent.

(*o*) *Declaration of the Demeanor and Carriage of Sir* Walter Ralegh, *Knight, as well in his Voyage, as in and since his return,* &c. printed at London, 1618, in 4to.

The

The balance of the King's eftate is in hand, whereof I have great care, but no great help.

The fub-committees for the feveral branches of treafure are well chofen and charged.

This matter of the King's eftate for means is like a quarry, which digs and works hard; but then, when I confider it buildeth, I think no pains too much; and after term it fhall be my chief care.

For the Mint, by my next I will give account; for our day is Wednefday.

God ever preferve and profper you.

Your Lordfhip's

November 22, 1618.

Fr. VERULAM, *Canc.*

Indorfed, *Of council-bufinefs.*

To the LORD CHANCELLOR (*).

My honourable Lord,

I HAVING underftood by Dr. Steward, that your Lordfhip hath made a decree againft him in the Chancery, which he thinks very hard for him to perform; although I know it is unufual to your Lordfhip to make any alterations, when things are fo far paft: yet in regard I owe him a good turn, which I know not now how to perform but this way, I defire your Lordfhip, if there be any place left for mitigation, your Lordfhip would fhew him what favour you may, for my fake, in his defires, which I fhall be ready to acknowledge as a great courtefy done unto myfelf; and will ever reft

Your Lordfhip's faithful friend and fervant,

Newmarket, the 2d
of Decemb. 1618.

G. BUCKINGHAM.

(*) Harl. MSS. Vol. 7006.

To

To the L O R D C H A N C E L L O R (*).

My honourable Lord,

I HAVE written a letter unto your Lordfhip, which will be delivered unto you in behalf of Dr. Steward ; and befides, have thought fit to ufe all freedom with you in that, as in other things ; and therefore have thought fit to tell you, that he being a man of very good reputation, and a ftout man, that will not yield to any thing, wherein he conceiveth any hard courfe againft him, I fhould be forry he fhould make any complaint againft you. And therefore, if you can advife of any courfe, how you may be eafed of that burden, and freed from his complaint, without fhew of any fear of him, or any thing he can fay, I will be ready to join with you for the accomplifhment thereof : And fo defiring you to excufe the long ftay of your man, I reft

Your Lordfhip's faithful friend and fervant,

From Newmarket, 3d of
   December, 1618.   G. B U C K I N G H A M.

To the Marquis of B U C K I N G H A M.

My very good Lord,

Y ESTERNIGHT we difpatched the Lord Ridgeway's account. Good fervice is done. Seven or eight thoufand pounds are coming to the King, and a good precedent fet for accounts.

There came to the feal about a fortnight fince a ftrange book paffed by Mr. Attorney to one Mr. Hall ; and it is to make fubjects (for fo is deniza-

(*) Harl. MSS. Vol. 7006.

                                                                tion,)

tion,) and this to go to a private use, till some thousand pounds be made of it. The number one hundred denizens. And whereas all books of that nature had an exception of merchants (which importeth the King not much in his customs only, for that is provided for in the book, but many other ways) this takes in merchants and all. I acquainted the commissioners with it, and by one consent it is stayed. But let me counsel his Majesty to grant forth a commission of this nature, so to raise money for himself, being a flower of the crown: and Hall may be rewarded out of it; and it would be to principal persons, that it may be carried with election and discretion, whom to admit to denization, and whom not.

God ever bless and prosper you.

Your Lordship's most faithful,

and obliged friend and servant,

December 8, 1618.

Fr. Verulam, *Canc.*

To the Lord Chancellor (*).

My honourable Lord,

I THANK your Lordship for the favour, which, I understand, Sir Francis Englefyld hath received from your Lordship upon my last letter, whereunto I desire your Lordship to add this one favour more (which is the same, that I understand your Lordship granted him at Christmass last) to give him liberty, for the space of a fortnight, to follow his business in his own person; whereby he may bring it to the more speedy end, putting in security, according to the ordinary course, to render himself prisoner again,

(*) Harl. MSS. Vol. 7006.

as

as foon as that time is expired : which is all that I defire for him, and in which I will acknowledge your Lordfhip's favour towards him ; and ever reft

Your Lordfhip's faithful friend and fervant,

Newmarket, the 10th
of Decemb. 1618.   G. B u c k i n g h a m.

To the Marquis of B u c k i n g h a m.

My very good Lord,

I SEND you herewith the copy of a letter, which we, the commiffioners for Ormonde's caufe, have written to the Deputy of Ireland, according to his Majefty's pleafure fignified by Sir Francis Blundell ; which I humbly defire his Majefty would perufe, that, if it do not attain his meaning, as we conveyed it, we may fecond it with a new letter.

We have appointed Monday morning for thefe Mint bufineffes, referred by his Majefty to certain commiffioners, and we will carry it *fine ftrepitu*.

The patent touching Guinea and Bynny for the trade of gold, ftaid firft by myfelf, and after by his Majefty's commandment, we have now fettled by confent of all parties.

Mr. Attorney, by my direction, hath made, upon his information exhibited into the Star-Chamber, a thundering motion againft the tranfportation of gold by the Dutch ; which all the town is glad of ; and I have granted divers writs of *ne exeat regnum*, according to his Majefty's warrant.

Sir Edward Coke keeps in ftill, and we have mifs of him ; but I fupply it as I may by my farther diligence. God ever blefs you and keep you.

Your Lordfhip's moft faithful and
bounden friend and fervant,

December 11, 1618.

F r. V e r u l a m, *Canc.*
I forget

I forget not your Doctor's *(p)* matter. I shall speak with him to-day, having received your Lordship's letter ; and what is possible, shall be done. I pray pardon my scribbling in haste.

To the LORD CHANCELLOR (*).

My honourable Lord,

I HAVE acquainted his Majesty with your letters, who is very well pleased with your care of his service, in making stay of the grant of denizens upon the reason you alledge, whereof his Majesty will speak farther with you at his return.

The letter, which you sent me about my Lord of Ormonde's son, is not according to his Majesty's meaning ; but I would have you frame another to my Lord Deputy to this purpose : " That his Majesty
" having seen a letter of his to Sir Francis Blundell,
" advertising, that the Earl of Ormonde's son, and
" some other of his kindred, did victual and fortify
" their houses ; his Majesty hath thereupon com-
" manded you to write unto him, that if the ground
" of his information be true (which he may best
" know,) that then he send for the said Earl's
" son, and the principal of his kindred, to appear
" before him : and if they appear, and give him
" satisfaction, it is well ; but if they refuse to ap-
" pear, or give him not satisfaction, though they
" appear ; that then he assemble what forces he can,
" be they never so few, and go against them, that
" he may crush the rebellion in the egg."

I have remembered his Majesty, as I promised your Lordship, about the naming you for a commissioner to treat with the Hollanders : But besides that you have so many businesses, both of the Star-

(p) Steward's. See above, p. 183.
(*) Harl. MSS. Vol. 7006.

Chamber,

Chamber, and others in the term-time, when this muſt be attended as well as in the vacation, whereby this would be either too great a toil to you, or a hindrance to his Majeſty's ſervice ; he thinketh it could not ſtand with the honour of your place to be balanced with thoſe, that are ſent from the ſtate, ſo far unequal to his Majeſty, and being themſelves none of the greateſt of the ſtate. Therefore his Majeſty holdeth it not fit or worthy of you to put you into ſuch an employment, in which none of your predeceſſors, or any of the chief Counſellors, have been ever uſed in this kind, but only in a treaty of marriage or concluſion of a peace ; as when the Conſtable of Caſtile was here, when the commiſſioners on both ſides had their authority under the great ſeal of either kingdom, with direct relation to their Sovereigns, far differing from this commiſſion, which is now given to theſe men, and whereunto his Majeſty is to frame the courſe of his. As for the part, which concerneth Scotland, the choice hath not been made of the Chancellor or Archbiſhop of St. Andrew's, but of men nearer the rank of thoſe, that come hither to treat. As yet his Majeſty delayeth to give any commiſſion at all, becauſe he would firſt be informed from the Lords, both of the points and form of their commiſſion, which his Majeſty hitherto underſtandeth to be, with authority to over-rule and direct their merchants in what they ſhall think fit ; which if it be ſo, then his Majeſty holdeth it fit, for his part, to appoint the whole body of the council with like power over his merchants. As for me, I ſhall be ever ready upon any occaſion to ſhew myſelf

Your Lordſhip's faithful friend and ſervant,

Newmarket, the 14th of
 December, 1618.

G. BUCKINGHAM.

O

To

To the Lady CLIFFORD.

My good Lady and cousin,

I SHALL not be wanting in any thing, that may express my good affection and wishes towards your Ladyship, being so near unto me, and the daughter of a father, to whom I was in the passages of my fortune much obliged. So with my loving commendations, in the midst of business, I rest

Your affectionate kinsman and assured friend,

York-house, this 25th
of January, 1618.   FR. VERULAM, *Canc.*

To the LORD CHANCELLOR (*).

My honourable Lord,

L EST my often writing may make your Lordship conceive, that this letter hath been drawn from you by importunity, I have thought fit, for preventing of any such conceit, to let your Lordship know, that Sir John Wentworth, whose business I now recommend, is a gentleman, whom I esteem in more than an ordinary degree. And therefore I desire your Lordship to shew him what favour you can for my sake in his suit, which his Majesty hath referred to your Lordship : which I will acknowledge as a courtesy unto me, and rest

Your Lordship's faithful friend and servant,

Newmarket, January 26, 1618.   G. BUCKINGHAM.

(*) Harl. MSS. Vol. 7006.

To

To the LORD CHANCELLOR (*).

My honourable Lord,

I BEING defired by a fpecial friend of mine to recommend unto your Lordfhip's favour the cafe of this petitioner, have thought fit to defire you, for my fake, to fhew him all the favour you may in this his defire, as you fhall find it in reafon to deferve; which I fhall take as a courtefy from your Lordfhip, and ever reft

Your Lordfhip's faithful friend and fervant,

G. BUCKINGHAM.

I thank your Lordfhip for your favour to Sir John Wentworth, in the difpatch of his bufinefs.

Newmarket, March 15, 1618.

To the LORD CHANCELLOR.

Moft honourable Lord,

IT may pleafe your Lordfhip, there was with me this day one Mr. Richard White, who hath fpent fome little time at Florence, and is now gone into England. He tells me, that Galileo had anfwered your difcourfe concerning the flux and reflux of the fea, and was fending it unto me; but that Mr. White hindered him, becaufe his anfwer was grounded upon a falfe fuppofition, namely, that there was in the ocean a full fea but once in twenty-four hours. But now I will call upon Galileo again. This Mr. White is a

(*) Harl. MSS. Vol. 7006.

difcreet

difcreet and underftanding gentleman, though he feem a little foft, if not flow ; and he hath in his hands all the works, as I take it, of Galileo, fome printed, and fome unprinted. He hath his difcourfe of the flux and reflux of the fea, which was never printed ; as alfo a difcourfe of the mixture of metals. Thofe, which are printed, in his hand are thefe : the *Nuncius fidereus* ; the *Macchie folari*, and a third *Delle Cofe, che ftanno fu l'acqua*, by occafion of a difputation, that was amongft learned men in Florence about that, which Archimedes wrote, *de infidentibus humido*.

I have conceived, that your Lordfhip would not be forry to fee thefe difcourfes of that man ; and therefore I have thought it belonging to my fervice to your Lordfhip to give him a letter of this date, though it will not be there fo foon as this. The gentleman hath no pretence or bufinefs before your Lordfhip, but is willing to do your Lordfhip all humble fervice ; and therefore, both for this reafon, as alfo upon my humble requeft, I befeech your Lordfhip to beftow a countenance of grace upon him. I am beholden to this gentleman ; and, if your Lordfhip fhall vouchfafe to afk him of me, I fhall receive honour by it. And I moft humbly do your Lordfhip reverence.

Your Lordfhip's moft obliged fervant,

Bruffels, from my
   bed, the 14th of   TOBIE MATTHEW.
   April, 1619.

To the LORD CHANCELLOR (*).

My honourable Lord,

HIS Majefty hath commanded me to fignify unto your Lordfhip, that it is his pleafure you put off the hearing of the caufe between Sir Arthur

(*) Harl. MSS. Vol. 7006.

Manwaring

Manwaring and Gabriel Dennis till toward the end of the term.; becaufe his Majefty is gracioufly pleafed to be at the hearing thereof himfelf. And fo I reft

Your Lordfhip's faithful friend and fervant,

Royfton, April 13, 1619.   G. B U C K I N G H A M.

To the L O R D C H A N C E L L O R, *and Sir* L I O N E L T A N F I E L D, *Lord Chief Baron of the Exchequer* (*).

My Lords,

H I S Majefty having been moved by the Duke of Savoy's Ambaffador in the behalf of Philip Bernardi, whom he is to fend about fome fpecial employment over the feas to the Duke of Savoy, that, before his going, the bufinefs mentioned in this petition may be ended, hath commanded me to recommend the fame unto your Lordfhips care, that with all expedition the caufe may be heard and ended by your Lordfhips, according to his Majefty's reference; or left to the determination of the Court of Chancery, where it is depending, and where the party affureth himfelf of a fpeedy end. And fo I reft

Your Lordfhips very affured friend

at command,

Royfton, the 19th of April, 1619.   G. B U C K I N G H A M.

(*) Harl. MSS. Vol. 7006.

To the Marquis of BUCKINGHAM.

My very good Lord,

I THINK fit to let your Lordſhip underſtand what paſſed yeſterday in the Star-Chamber touching Suffolk's *(p)* buſineſs.

There came to me the Clerk of the Court in the inner chamber, and told me, that my Lord of Suffolk deſired to be heard by his council at the * ſitting of the court, becauſe it was pen * * * him.

I marvelled I heard not of it by Mr. Attorney, who ſhould have let me know as much, that I might not be taken on the ſudden in a cauſe of that weight.

I called preſently Mr. Attorney to me, and aſked him, whether he knew of the motion, and what it was, and how he was provided to anſwer it. He ſignified to me, that my Lord would deſire to have the commiſſion for examinations in Ireland to be returnable in Michaelmaſs term. I ſaid, it might not be, and preſently drew the council, then preſent, to me, and made Mr. Attorney repeat to them the paſſages paſt, and ſettled it, that the commiſſion ſhould be returnable the firſt day of the next term, and then republication granted, that it might, if accidents of wind and weather permit, come to hearing in the term. And upon motion in open court it was ordered accordingly.

(p) Thomas Howard, Earl of Suffolk, who had been made Lord Treaſurer in 1614. He was accuſed of ſeveral miſdemeanors in that office, together with his Lady, and Sir John Bingley, his Ladyſhip's agent; and an information preferred againſt them all in the Star-Chamber.

God

God ever preserve and prosper you.   I pray God this great easterly wind agree well with his Majesty.

Your Lordship's most obliged friend,

and faithful servant,

May 6, 1619.

Fr. Verulam, *Cana.*

Indorsed, *Sent by Sir Gilbert Houghton.*

To the Marquis of Buckingham.

My very good Lord,

I AM much bounden to his Majesty, and likewise to your Lordship.   I see, by the late accesses I have had with his Majesty, and now by his royal and real favour (*q*), that he loveth me, and acknowledgeth me for the servant, that I am, or desire to be.   This in me must turn to a great alacrity to honour and serve him with a mind less troubled and divided. And for your Lordship, my affection may and doth daily receive addition, but cannot, nor never could, receive alteration.   I pray present my humble thanks to his Majesty ; and I am very glad his health confirmeth ; and I hope to see him this summer at Gorhambury : There is sweet air as any is.   God preserve and prosper you both.   I ever rest

Your Lordship's most obliged friend,

and faithful servant,

May 9, 1619.

Fr. Verulam, *Canc.*

(*q*) probably the grant made to him about this time of 1200 l. a year.

O 4   *Minuet*

Minute of a Letter to the Count PALATINE of the Rhine.

Monseigneur,

JE me tiens a grand honneur, qu'il plaise à vostre Alteffe de me cognoistre pour tel, que je suis, ou pour le moins voudrois éstre, envers vous et vostre service : et m'estimeray heureux, si par mes Conseils auprès du Roy, ou autre devoir, je pourroy contribuer à vostre grandeur, dont il semble que Dieu vous a basti de belles occasions, ayant en contemplation vostre tres-illustre personne, non seulement comme tres-cher allié de mon maistre, mais aussi, comme le meilleur appui, apres les Roys de Grande Bretagne, de la plus saine partie de la Chrestieneté.

Je ne puis aussi passer sous silence la grande raison, que vostre Altesse fait a vostre propre honneur en choississtant tels Conseilleurs et Ministres d'Estat, comme se monstre tres-bien estre Monsieur le Baron de Dhona et Monsieur de Plessen, estants personages si graves, discretes et habiles ; en quoy vostre jugement reluict assez.

Vostre Altesse de vostre grace excusera la faulte de mon language François, ayant esté tant versé es vielles Loix de Normandie : mais le coeur supplera la plume, en priant Dieu de vous tenir en sa digne et saincte garde,

Monseigneur,

De vostre Altesse le plus humble,

et plus affectionné serviteur.

Indorsed, *May* 13, 1619.

Te

To the Lord Chancellor (*).

My honourable Lord,

HIS Majesty was pleased, at the suit of some, who have near relation to me, to grant a license for transportation of butter out of Wales unto one Lewis and Williams, who in consideration, that the patent should be passed in their names, entered into articles for the performance of certain conditions agreed upon between them, which, now that the patent is under the great seal, they utterly refuse to perform. My desire therefore to your Lordship is, that you would call the said Lewis and Williams before you, with the other parties, or some of them, who shall be ready at all times to attend your Lordship; and out of your consideration of the matter, according to equity, to take such course therein, that either the said agreement may be performed; or that they, which refuse it, may receive no benefit of the patent; which upon reason thereof was passed in their names. And herein I desire your Lordship to make what expedition you can; because now is the season to make provision of the butter, that for this year is to be transported, whereof they take advantage to stand out. And so I rest

Your Lordship's faithful friend and servant,

Greenwich, May
  14, 1619.   G. Buckingham.

(*). Harl. MSS. Vol. 7006.

To the Marquis of BUCKINGHAM.

My very good Lord,

THOUGH it be nothing, and all is but duty; yet I pray shew his Majesty the paper inclosed, that his Majesty may see, how careful his poor servant is upon every emergent occasion to do him what honour he can. The motion made in court by the King's serjeant, Crew (*q*), that the declaration might be made parcell of the record, and that I hear otherwise of the great satisfaction abroad, encourageth me to let his Majesty know what passed.

God ever preserve and prosper you both.

Your Lordship's obliged friend,

and faithful servant,

FR. VERULAM, *Canc.*

Indorsed, *June* 29, 1619,
My Lord to my Lord Marquis, inclosing the form of a declaration used in point of acknowledgment in the Lady Exeter's (r) cause.

To the Marquis of BUCKINGHAM.

My very good Lord,

I PURPOSED to have seen you to day, and receive your commandments before the progress. But I came not to London till it was late, and found

(*q*) Sir Randolph Crew, made Chief Justice of the King's Bench, January 26, 1624.

(*r*) Countess of Exeter, accused of incest and other crimes by the Lady Lake, wife of Secretary Lake, and their daughter the Lady Roos.

2

you

you were gone before I came. Neverthelefs, I would not fail to let your Lordfhip underftand, that as I find every day more and more occafions, whereby you bind me to you ; fo this morning the King of himfelf did tell me fome teftimony, that your Lordfhip gave of me to his Majefty even now, when you went from him, of fo great affection and commendation (for I muft afcribe your commendation to affection, being above my merit) as I muft do contrary to that, that painters do ; for they defire to make the picture to the life, and I muft endeavour to make the life to the picture, it hath pleafed you to make fo honourable a defcription of me. I can be but your's, and defire to better myfelf, that I may be of more worth to fuch an owner.

I hope to give the King a good account of my time this vacation.

If your Lordfhip pafs back by London, I defire to wait on you, and difcourfe a little with you : if not, my prayers fhall go progrefs with you, and my letters attend you, as occafion ferveth.

God ever preferve and profper you.

Your Lordfhip's moft obliged friend,

and faithful fervant,

July 19, 1619.

FR. VERULAM, *Canc.*

To the Marquis of BUCKINGHAM.

My very good Lord,

THIS day, according to the firft appointment, I thought to have waited upon his Majefty, and to have given him an account of my cares and preparations for his fervice, which is my progrefs. And therefore, fince his coming to Windfor is prolonged,

longed, I thought to keep day by letter, praying your Lordſhip to commend my moſt humble ſervice to his Majeſty, and to let him know, that ſince I ſee his Majeſty doth me the honour, as to rely upon my care and ſervice, I loſe no time in that, which may pertain thereunto. I ſee the ſtraits, and I ſee the way out; and what lieth in one man, whom he hath made great, and trained, ſhall not be wanting. And I hope, if God give me life for a year or two, to give his Majeſty cauſe to think of me ſeven years after I am dead.

I am glad the time approacheth, when I ſhall have the happineſs to kiſs his Majeſty's hands, and to embrace your Lordſhip, ever reſting

Your Lordſhip's moſt obliged friend,

and faithful ſervant,

York-houſe, Aug. 28, 1619.

Fr. Verulam, *Canc.*

To the Lord Chancellor (*).

My honourable Lord,

HIS Majeſty, upon a petition delivered by Mr. Thomas Digby, wherein he complaineth of great wrongs done unto him, hath been pleaſed, for his more ſpeedy relief and redreſs, if it prove as he alledgeth, to refer the conſideration thereof unto your Lordſhip. And becauſe he is a gentleman, whom I have long known and loved, I could not but add my deſire to your Lordſhip, that, if you find he hath been wronged, you would do him ſo much.

(*) Harl. MSS. Vol. 7006.

favour,

favour, as to give him such remedy, as the equity of his case may require. For which I will ever rest

Your Lordship's faithful friend and servant,

Royston, Octob. 8,
1619.

G. Buckingham.

To the Lord Chancellor (*).

My honourable Lord,

I HAVE acquainted his Majesty with your letter, who hath given order to Mr. Secretary Calvert to signify his pleasure for the proceeding in that business, whereof you write, without any farther delay, as your Lordship will more fully understand by Mr. Secretary, who for that purpose is to return to London against the day of hearing.

I have no answer to make to your former letter, and will add no more to this, but that his Majesty hath a great confidence in your care of his service. And so I rest

Your Lordship's faithful friend and servant,

Royston, Octob. 10,
1619.

G. Buckingham.

Indorsed,

Shewing his Majesty's acceptation of your Lordship's care, in particular in the business against the Earl of Suffolk.

(*) Harl. MSS. Vol. 7006.

To

To the Marquis of BUCKINGHAM.

My very good Lord,

AFTER my last letter yesterday, we entered into conference, touching the Suffolk cause, myself, and the commissioners, and the two Chief Justices (s). The fruit of this conference is, that we all conceive the proceedings against my Lord himself to be, not only just and honourable, but in some principal parts plausible in regard of the public ; as namely, those three points, which touch upon the ordnance, the army of Ireland, and the money of the cautionary towns ; and the two Chief Justices are firm in it.

I did also in this cause, by the assent of my Lords, remove a part ; for Mr. Attorney had laid it upon Serjeant Davies (t) to open the information, which is that, which gives much life or coldness to the cause. But I will have none but trained men in this cause ; and I cannot forget, that the allotting of the opening of the information in this cause of the Dutch (I mean the main cause) to a mean fellow, one Hughes, did hurt, and was never well recovered.

By my next I will write of the King's estate : and I ever rest

Your Lordship's most obliged friend,

and faithful servant,

October 14, 1619.

FR. VERULAM, *Canc.*

(s) Sir Henry Montagu of the King's Bench, and Sir Henry Hobart of the Common Pleas.
(t) Sir John Davies, author of *Nosce teipsum*, knighted in February, 1607, and made Serjeant at Law in 1612. He had been Attorney General of Ireland.

To

To the Marquis of B U C K I N G H A M.

My very good Lord,

THIS morning the Duke (*u*) came to me, and told me the King's cause was yesterday left fair; and if ever there were a time for my Lord of Suffolk's submission, it was now; and that, if my Lord of Suffolk should come into the court, and openly acknowledge his delinquency, he thought it was a thing considerable. My answer was, I would not meddle in it; and, if I did, it must be to dissuade any such course; for that all would be but a play upon the stage, if justice went not on in the right course. This I thought it my duty to let the King know by your Lordship.

I cannot express the care I have had of this cause in a number of circumstances and discretions, which, though they may seem but small matters, yet they do the business, and guide it right.

God ever keep your Lordship.

Your Lordship's most obliged friend,

and faithful servant,

October 21, 1619.

Fr. Verulam, *Canc.*

To the Marquis of B U C K I N G H A M.

My very good Lord,

I AM doubly bounden to the King for his Majesty's trust and acceptation; whereof the one I will never deceive; the other, though I cannot deserve, yet

(*u*) Lodowick, Duke of Lennox. He was created Duke of Richmond, May 17, 1623; and died February 11, 162⅔.

I will

I will do my beſt, and perhaps as much as another man.

This day the evidence went well; for the Sollici-tor (*w*) did his part ſubſtantially: and, a little to warm the buſineſs, when the miſemployment of treaſure, which had relation to the army of Ireland, was handled, I ſpake a word, that he, that did draw or milk treaſure from Ireland, did not *emulgere*, milk money, but blood. But this is but one of the little things, that I wrote of before.

The King, under pardon, muſt come hither with two reſolutions; the one, to remit all importunity, touching this cauſe, to the Lords in Court of Juſtice; the other, to purſue the deſigns firſt taken at Wind-ſor, and then at Hampton-Court, for his commiſſion of treaſury: wherein I do my part, and it is reaſona-bly well; but better would it be, if inſtruments were not impediments. I ever reſt

Your Lordſhip's moſt obliged friend,

and faithful ſervant,

Oĉtober 27, Wedneſday.

Fr. Verulam, *Canc.*

Friday will not end the buſineſs; for to-morrow will but go through with the King's evidence.

To the Lord Chancellor (*).

My honourable Lord,

THIS bearer, a Frenchman belonging to the Ambaſſador, having put an Engliſhman in ſuit for ſome matters between them, is much hindered

(*w*) Sir Thomas Coventry, afterwards Lord Keeper of the Great Seal.
(*) Harl. MSS. Vol. 7006.

and

and molefted by often removing of the caufe from one court to another. Your Lordfhip knows, that the French are not acquainted with our manner of proceedings in the law, and muft therefore be ignorant of the remedy in fuch a cafe. His courfe was to his Majefty ; but I thought it more proper, that your Lordfhip would be pleafed to hear and underftand this cafe from himfelf, and then to advife and take order for his relief, as your Lordfhip in your wifdom fhall think fit. So commending him to your honourable favour, I reft

Your Lordfhip's faithful friend and fervant,

Royfton, 27th of
October, 1619.   G. B U C K I N G H A M.

Your Lordfhip fhall do well to be informed of every particular, becaufe his Majefty will have account of it at his coming.

To the L O R D C H A N C E L L O R (*).

My honourable Lord,

I HAVE acquainted his Majefty with your letter, who commanded me to give your Lordfhip thanks for your fpeed in advertifing thofe things, that pafs, and for the great care he feeth you ever have of his fervice.

I fend your Lordfhip back the bill of Sheriffs for Suffex, wherein his Majefty hath pricked the firft, as your Lordfhip wifhed.

His Majefty would not have you omit this opportunity of fo grofs an over-fight in the Judges, to admonifh them of their negligence in fuffering fuch a thing to come to his Majefty, which needed his

(*) Harl. MSS. Vol. 7006.

P   amending

amending afterward : and withall, to let them know, that his Majesty observeth, that every year they grow more and more careless of presenting fit men unto him for that place ; and that you advise them to be more wary hereafter, that they may give his Majesty better satisfaction. And so I rest

Your Lordship's faithful friend and servant,

Royston, November
14, 1619.   G. BUCKINGHAM.

To the Marquis of BUCKINGHAM.

My very good Lord,

THIS day afternoon, upon our meeting in council, we have planed those rubs and knots, which were mentioned in my last, whereof I thought good presently to advertise his Majesty. The days hold without all question, and all delays diverted and quieted.

Sir Edward Coke was at Friday's hearing, but in his night-cap ; and complained to me, he was ambulant, and not current. I would be sorry he should fail us in this cause. Therefore I desire his Majesty to signify to him by your Lordship (taking knowledge of some light indisposition of his) how much he should think his service disadvantaged in this cause, if he should be at any day away ; for then he cannot sentence.

By my next I will give his Majesty some account of the tobacco and the currants. I ever rest

Your Lordship's most obliged friend,

and faithful servant,

November 20, at evening, 1619.   FR. VERULAM, *Canc.*

To

To the Marquis of BUCKINGHAM.

My very good Lord,

I KNOW well his Majesty taketh to heart this bu-
finess of the Dutch (x), as he hath great reason,
in respect both of honour and profit. And because
my first letter was written in the epitasis, or trouble
of the business; and my second in the beginning of
the catastrophe, or calming thereof, (wherein nevertheless I was fain to bear up strongly into the weather,
before the calm followed) and since every day hath
been better and better, I thought good to signify so
much, that his Majesty may be less in suspence.

The great labour was to get entrance into the business; but now the portcullis is drawn up. And
though, I must say, there were some blots in the
tables, yet, by well playing, the game is good.

Rowland is passing well justified; for both his
credit is by very constant and weighty testimony
proved, and those vast quantities, which were
thought incredible, or at least improbable, are now
made manifest truth.

Yet I find a little of the old leven towards the first
defendants, carried in this style and character: " I
" would this, that appears now, had appeared at
" first. But this cometh of haste and precipitation;"
and the like. But yet, I hope, the corruption and
practice upon the *ore tenus,* and the rectifying of
Rowland's credit, will satisfy my Lords upon the
former proofs. For I would be very sorry, that
these new defendants (which, except one or two,
are the smaller flies) should be in the net, and the old

(x) Merchants, accused in the Star-Chamber for exporting the
gold and silver coin.

defendants,

defendants, which are the greater flies, fhould get through. God preferve you.

Your Lordfhip's moft obliged friend,

and faithful fervant,

This November
26, 1619.   FR. VERULAM, *Canc.*

Indorfed, *Touching the Dutch bufinefs.*

To the LORD CHANCELLOR (*).

My honourable Lord,

I DO, from time to time, acquaint his Majefty with your letters, wherein he ever perceiveth your vigilant care in any thing, that concerneth his fervice; and hath commanded me to give you thanks in his name, who is fure your endeavours will never be wanting, when any thing is to be done for the advancement of his affairs.

According to your Lordfhip's advice, his Majefty hath written to the Commiffioners of the Treafury, both touching the currants and the tobacco (y), the plantation whereof his Majefty is fully refolved to reftrain; and hath given them order forthwith to fet out a proclamation to that effect; not intending in that point to ftand upon any doubt of law, nor to expect the Judges interpretation; nor to allow any

_____

(*) Harl. MSS. Vol. 7006.
(y) Lord Bacon, in his letter of November 22, 1619, mentions, that there was offered 2000 l. increafe yearly for the tobacco, to begin at Michaelmafs, as it now is, and 3000 l. increafe, if the plantations here within land be reftrained.

freehold

freehold in that cafe ; but holding this the fafeft
rule, *Salus reipublicæ fuprema lex efto.*   And fo I reft

Your Lordſhip's faithful friend and fervant,

Newmarket, Nov.
    27, 1619.   G. B U C K I N G H A M.

To the L O R D C H A N C E L L O R (*).

My honourable Lord,

I HAVE prefented both the fubmiffions to his
Majefty.   His anfwer is, he cannot alter that,
which was allowed of by the Lords of the laft Star-
Chamber-day, except firft they be acquainted with it,
and the confent of the Lady Exeter be likewife had,
becaufe the decree dqth neceffarily require it.   So I
reft

Your Lordſhip's humble fervant,

G. B U C K I N G H A M.

Indorfed,

Touching the fubmiffions of Sir Thomas Lake and his Lady.

To the Marquis of B U C K I N G H A M.

My very good Lord,

I ACQUAINTED this day the bearer with his
Majefty's pleafure touching Lake's (z) fubmiffion ;
which, whether it fhould be done in perfon, or in
writing, his Majefty fignified his will thus ; that it
fhould be fpared in open court, if my Lady of Exeter fhould confent, and the board think fit.   The

---

(*) Harl. MSS. Vol. 7006.   (z) Sir Thomas Lake's.
P 3   board

board liked it well,.and appointed my Lord Digby and Secretary Calvert to speak with my Lady, who returned her answer in substance, that she would, in this and all things, be commanded by his Majesty: but if his Majesty left it to her liberty and election, she humbly prayed to be excused. And though it was told her, that this answer would be cause, that it could not be performed this term; yet she seemed willing rather it should be delayed, than dispensed with.

This day also Traske *(a)*, in open court, made a retractation of his wicked opinions in writing. The form was as good as may be. I declared to him, that this court was the judgement-seat; the mercy-seat was his Majesty: but the court would commend him to his Majesty: and I humbly pray his Majesty to signify his pleasure speedily, because of the misery of the man; and it is a rare thing for a sectary, that

(a) John Traske, a Minister, who was prosecuted in the Star-Chamber for maintaining, as we find mentioned in the *Reports* of the Lord Chief Justice Hobart, p. 236, that the Jewish Sabbath ought to be observed, and not ours; and that we ought to abstain from all manner of swine's flesh, and those meats, which the Jews were forbidden in Leviticus, according to Bishop Andrews, in his speech in the Star-Chamber on that occasion, printed among his Lordship's works. Mr. Traske being examined in that court, confessed, that he had divulged those opinions, and had laboured to bring as many to them as he could; and had also written a letter to the King, wherein he seemed to tax his Majesty with hypocrisy, and expresly inveighed against the Bishops High Commissioners, as bloody and cruel in their proceedings against him, and a papal clergy. He was sentenced to fine and imprisonment, not for holding those opinions (for those were examinable in the Ecclesiastical Court, and not there,) but for making of conventicles and commotions, and for scandalizing the King, the bishops, and clergy. Dr. Fuller, in his *Church History of Britain*, Book X. p. 77. § 64. mentions his having heard Mr. Traske preach, and remarks, that his *voice had more strength than any thing else he delivered*; and that after his recantation he relapsed, not into the same, but other opinions, *rather humorous than hurtful*, and died obscurely at Lambeth in the reign of King Charles I.

hath

hath once fuffered fmart and fhame, to turn fo un-
feignedly, as he feemed to do.

God ever blefs and keep you.

Your moft obliged friend, and faithful fervant,

December 1, 1619. FR. VERULAM, *Canc.*

To the Marquis of BUCKINGHAM.

My very good Lord,

ON Friday I left London, to hide myfelf at Kew;
for two months and a half together to be ftrong-
bent is too much for my bow. And yet, that the
King may perceive, that in my times of leifure I am
not idle, I took down with me Sir Giles Mompeffon (*b*), and with him I have quietly conferred of
that propofition, which was given me in charge by
his Majefty, and after feconded by your Lordfhip.
Wherein I find fome things I like very well, and fome
other, that I would fet by. And one thing is much
to my liking, that the propofition for bringing in his
Majefty's revenue with fmall charge is no invention,
but was on foot heretofore in King Philip's and Queen
Mary's time, and had a grave and mighty opinion for
it. The reft I leave to his relation, and mine own
attendance.

I hope his Majefty will look to it, that the fines
now to come in may do him moft good. Both
caufes produce fines of one hundred and fourfcore
thoufand pounds, whereof one hundred thoufand

(*b*) who in the parliament, which began January 30, 162⁹⁄₀,
was fentenced to be degraded, and rendered incapable of bearing
any office, for practifing feveral abufes, in fetting up new inns
and ale-houfes, and exacting great fums of money of the people,
by pretence of letters patents granted him for that purpofe. But
he fled into foreign parts, finding himfelf abandoned by the
Marquis of Buckingham, on whom he had depended for protection.

P 4 may

may clear the anticipations; and then the affignations may pafs under the great feal, to be inrollable; fo as we fhall need to think of nothing but the arrears in a manner, of which I wifh the 20,000 l. to the ftrangers (with the intereft) be prefently fatisfied. The remain may ferve for the King's prefent and urgent occafions. And if the King intend any gifts, let them ftay for the fecond courfe (for all is not yet done,) but nothing out of thefe, except the King fhould give me the 20,000 l. I owe Peter Vanbore out of his fine, which is the chief debt I owe. But this I fpeak merrily. I ever reft

Your Lordfhip's moft obliged friend,

and faithful fervant,

Kew, Decemb. 12, 1619.

Fr. Verulam, *Canc.*

After I had written this letter, I received from your Lordfhip, by my fervant, his Majefty's acceptation of my poor fervices; for which I pray your Lordfhip to prefent to his Majefty my moft humble thanks. I have now other things in my mind for his Majefty's fervice, that no time be loft.

To the LORD CHANCELLOR (*).

My honourable Lord,

HIS Majefty hath been pleafed, out of his gracious care of Sir Robert Killigrew, to refer a fuit of his, for certain concealed lands, to your Lordfhip and the reft of the Commiffioners for the Treafury; the like whereof hath been heretofore granted to many others. My defire to your Lordfhip is, that he be-

(*) Harl. MSS. Vol 7006.

2

ing

ing a gentleman, whom I love and wish very well unto, your Lordship would shew him, for my sake, all the favour you can, in furthering his suit. Wherein your Lordship shall do me a courtesy, for which I will ever rest

Your Lordship's faithful friend and servant,

Royston, December
15, 1619.

G. BUCKINGHAM.

To the LORD CHANCELLOR (*).

My honourable Lord,

I HAVE acquainted his Majesty with your letter, who for that business, whereof Mr. Chancellor of the Exchequer brought the message to his Majesty to Theobalds, returned the answer by him.

As for that, whereof Sir Giles Mompesson spake to your Lordship, his Majesty liketh very well, and so do all others, with whom his Majesty hath spoken of it; and therefore he recommendeth it to your care, not doubting but your Lordship will give all your furtherance to it, being your own work, and so much concerning his Majesty's honour and profit; and will speak farther with your Lordship of it at his return to London.

For those other businesses of the Star-Chamber, which his Majesty hath recommended to your Lordship, he hopeth you will keep the clock still going, his profit being so much interested therein, especially seeing Mr. Chancellor of the Exchequer (c) hath promised his Majesty, that he will be no more sick, whereby you shall have this comfort, that the burden will not lie upon your Lordship alone.

(*) Harl. MSS. Vol. 7006.
(c) Sir Fulke Greville, who surrendered that office in September, 1621, being succeeded in it by Sir Richard Weston. He had been created Lord Brooke of Beauchamp's Court, Jan. 9, 1620.
The

The little leisure I had at Theobalds made me bring your man down hither for this answer, which I hope your Lordship will excuse; and ever hold me for

Your Lordship's faithful friend and servant,

Royston, 19th of Jan.   G. BUCKINGHAM.

Indorsed, 1619.

To the Marquis of BUCKINGHAM.

My very good Lord,

IN the midst of business, as in the midst of a way, one should not stay long, especially when I crave no direction, but only advertise.

This day we met about the commission, the commonwealth's commission, for the poor and vagabonds, &c. We have put it into an exceeding good way, and have appointed meetings once in fourteen days, because it shall not be a-slack. I was glad to hear from the two Chief Justices, that whatsoever appears in the country to come from *primum mobile* (that is, the King's care) works better, than if it came from the law. Therefore we have ordered, that this commission shall be published in the several circuits in the charges of the Judges. For the rest hereafter.

For the proposition of Sir Giles Mompesson, we have met once. Exchequer-men will be Exchequer-men still; but we shall do good.

For the account, or rather imparting, of the Commissioners of Treasury to the council, I think it will but end in a compliment. But the real care (and I hope good purpose) I will not give over, the better, because I am not alone.

For

-For the Star-Chamber bufinefs, I fhall, as you write, keep the clock on going, which is hard to do, when fometimes the wheels are too many, and fometimes too few. But we fhall do well, efpecially if thofe, whom the King hath hitherto made bond-men (I mean, which have given bonds for their fines) he do not hereafter make free-men.

For Suffolk's bufinefs, it is a little ftrange, that the Attorney made it a queftion to the Commiffioners of Treafury, whether Suffolk fhould not be admitted to the leafe of the extent of his own land, which is the way to encourage him not to pay his fine. But when it was told him, that the contrary courfe was held with the Earl of Northumberland, and that thereby he was brought to agree for his fine; then he turned, as his manner is.

For the errors, we have yet fo much ufe of the fervice of Sir Henry Britten in bringing in the fines (indeed more than of the Attorney) as we cannot, without prejudice to his Majefty's fervice, enter yet into them; and befides, Sir Edward Coke comes not abroad.

Mr. Kirkham hath communicated with me, as matter of profit to his Majefty, upon the coals referred by his Majefty to us of the Treafury; wherein I hope we fhall do good, the rather, becaufe I am not alone.

The proclamation for light gold Mr. Secretary Calvert, I know, hath fent to his Majefty; and therefore of that I fay no more.

For the raifing of filver by ordinance, and not by proclamation, and that for the time to come, we have given order to finifh it. I hear a whifpering, that thereupon the Commiffioners of the Navy, the Officers of the Houfhold, the Wardrobe, may take occafion to break the book and the undertakings, becaufe the prices may rife, which I thought good to fignify to his Majefty. And, to fpeak plainly, I

fear

fear more the pretence, than the natural effect. God ever more preferve your Lordfhip. I reft

Your Lordfhip's moft obliged friend,

and faithful fervant,

January 20, 1619.

FR. VERULAM, *Canc.*

To the LORD CHANCELLOR (*).

My honourable Lord,

I HAVE acquainted his Majefty with your letter, who is very well pleafed therewith, finding in you a continual care of his fervice. In that point of the Star-Chamber bufinefs, his Majefty faith, there is a miftaking; for he meant not the Dutchmen's bufinefs, but that motion, which your Lordfhip made unto him, of fitting in the Star-Chamber about the commiffions, which you had not leifure to read till he came down to Royfton, and hath reafon to give you thanks for it, defiring you to prepare it, and ftudy the point (of which he will fpeak more with you at his return to London,) being a matter worthy your thinking on, and his Majefty's practice.

For the laft point of your letter, his Majefty faith, it cannot but proceed of malice, that there fhould be any fuch plot, which he will not endure, but he will account thofe, that whifper of it in that fort, enemies of his fervice; and will put them out of their places, that practife it. And fo I reft

Your Lordfhip's faithful friend and fervant,

Newmarket, January
22, 1619.

G. BUCKINGHAM.

(*) Harl. MSS. Vol. 7006.

To

To Mr. Secretary C A L V E R T.

Mr. Secretary,

I HAVE received your letter of the 3d of this
present, signifying his Majesty's pleasure touching Peacock's *(d)* examinations, of which I will
have special care.

My Lord Coke is come to town, and hath sent
me word, he will be with me on Monday, though he
be somewhat lame. Howsoever, the service shall
be done.

I was made acquainted, by your letter to Secretary
Naunton, with his Majesty's dislike of the sending to
him of the jolly letter from Zealand. I will now speak
for myself, that, when it was received, I turned to the
Master of the Wards *(e)*, and said, " Well, I think
" you and I shall ever advise the King to do more
" for a Burlamachi, when he seeketh to his Majesty
" by supplication and supplying the King at the first
" word, than for all the rest upon any bravados from
" the Burgomasters of Holland and Zealand :" Who
answered very honestly, that it was in the King's
power to make them alter their style when he would.
But when another of us said, we could not but in our
own discharge send the King the letter, *scilicet negan-
dum non fuit* ; though indeed my way is otherwise.

I have at last recovered from these companions,
Harrison and Dale, a copy of my Lord of Ban-

(d) He was a Minister of the university of Cambridge. He
was committed to the Tower, for pretending, that he had, by sor-
cery, infatuated the King's judgement in the cause of Sir Thomas Lake. *Camd. Annal. Regis Jacobi I.* p. 54.
(e) Sir Lionel Cranfield.

gor's

gor's (f) book, the great one, and will prefently fet in hand the examinations. God keep you.

Your affured friend,

February 5, 1619.

FR. VERULAM, *Canc.*

To the KING.

May it pleafe your Majefty,

SIR Edward Coke is now a-foot, and, according to your command, fignified by Mr. Secretary Calvert, we proceed in Peacock's examinations. For although there have been very good diligence ufed, yet certainly we are not at the bottom; and he, that would not ufe the utmoft of his line to found fuch a bufinefs as this, fhould not have due regard, neither to your Majefty's honour, nor fafety.

A man would think he were in Luke Hutton's cafe again; for as my Lady Roos perfonated Luke Hutton, fo, it feemeth, Peacock perfonateth Atkins. But I make no judgement yet, but will go on with all diligence; and, if it may not be done otherwife, it is fit Peacock be put to torture. He deferveth it as well as Peacham did.

I befeech your Majefty not to think I am more bitter, becaufe my name is in it; for, befides that I always make my particular a cypher, when there

(f) Dr. Lewis Bayly, born at Caermarthen in Wales, and educated in Exeter-College, Oxford. He had been Minifter of Evefham in Worcefterfhire, and Chaplain to Prince Henry, and Rector of St. Matthew's, Friday-Street, in London. He was promoted to the Bifhopric of Bangor in 1616. On the 15th of July, 1621, he was committed to the Fleet, but on what account is not related by Camden, *Annales Regis Jacobi I.* p. 72. who mentions the Circumftance of the Bifhop's imprifonment; but that he was foon after fet at liberty. He was the author of the well-known book, *the Practice of Piety.*

is

is queftion of your Majefty's honour and fervice, I think myfelf honoured, for being brought into fo good company. And as, without flattery, I think your Majefty the beft of Kings, and my noble Lord of Buckingham the beft of perfons favoured; fo I hope, without prefumption, for my honeft and true intentions to ftate and juftice, and my love to my mafter, I am not the worft of Chancellors.

God ever preferve your Majefty.

Your Majefty's moft obliged,

and moft obedient fervant,

10th of February, 1619.

Fr. Verulam, *Canc.*

To the Lord Chancellor.

Moft honoured Lord,

I PRESUME, now after term (if there be any fuch thing as an after-term with your Lordfhip,) to offer this inclofed paper (g) to your fight, concerning the Duke of Lerma; which, if your Lordfhip have not already read, will not, I think, be altogether unpleafing, becaufe it is full of particular circumftances. I know not how commonly it paffeth up and down more or lefs. My friend, Mr. Gage, fent it me lately out of Spain. But howfoever, I build upon a fure ground; for though it fhould be vulgar, yet for my defire to ferve your Lordfhip, I cannot demerit fo much, as not to deferve a pardon at your Lordfhip's moft noble hand.

(g) I have, out of a ragged hand in Spanifh tranflated it, and accompanied it with fome marginal notes for your Lordfhip's greater eafe. Note of Mr. Matthew.

Before

Before the departure of the Duke of Lermà from that court, there was written upon the gate for a pafquinade, that the houfe was governed *por el Padre, y el Hijo, y un Santo*; as in Paris about the fame time was written upon the Louvre-Gate, *C'eft icy l'hoftel des troys Roys*; for Luynes's brother is almoft as great as himfelf. But the while there is good ftore of Kings now in Chriftendom, though there be one fewer than there was.

In Spain, there are very extraordinary preparations for a great armada. Here is lately in this court a current fpeech, as that the enterprize (whatfoever it fhould have been) is laid wholly afide: but that were ftrange. Yet this is certain, that the forces of men, to the number of almoft two thoufand, which were to have gone into Spain from hence, are difcharged, together with fome munition, which was alfo upon the point of being fent. Another thing is alfo certain, that both in the court of Spain and this, there is at this time a ftrange ftraitnefs of money; which I do not conceive, for my part, to proceed fo much from want, as defign to employ it. The rendezvous, where the forces were to meet, was at Malaga, within the Straits; which makes the enterprife upon Algiers moft likely to be intended. For I take that to be a wild conceit, which thinks of going by the Adriatic *per far in un Viaggio duoi fervitii*; as the giving a blow to Venice, and the landing of forces in aid of the King of Bohemia about Triefte.

Perhaps the King of Spain would be glad to let the world fee, that now he is *hors de payé*; and by fhewing himfelf in fome action, to intitle the Duke of Lerma to all his former floth; or perhaps he now makes a great preparation, upon the pretence of fome enterprize, that he will let fall, that fo he may with the lefs noife affemble great forces fome other year, for fome other attempt not fpoken of now.

My

My Lord Compton (*b*) is in this court, and goes shortly towards Italy. His fashion is sweet, and his disposition noble, and his conversation fair and honest.

Diego, my Lord Roos's man, is come hither. I pray God it be to do me any good towards the recovery of the debt his Lord owes me.

Most honoured Lord, I am here at good leisure to look back upon your Lordship's great and noble goodness towards me, which may go for a great example in this age; and so it doth. That, which I am sure of, is, that my poor heart, such as it is, doth not only beat, but even boil in the desires it hath to do your Lordship all humble service.

I crave leave, though it be against good manners, that I may ever present my humblest service to my most honoured Lady, my Lady Verulam, and Lady Constable, with my best respects to my dear friend, Sir John Constable; who, if your Lordship want the leisure, would perhaps cast an eye upon the inclosed paper.

I do, with more confidence, presume to address this other letter to Mr. Meautys, because the contents thereof concern your Lordship's service.

I beseech sweet Jesus to make and keep your Lordship intirely happy. So I humbly do you reverence, remaining ever

Your Lordship's most obliged servant,

TOBIE MATTHEW.

(*b*) Spencer, Lord Compton, only son of William, Earl of Northampton. This nobleman, who succeeded his father in his title and estate, in June, 1630, was killed at Hopton-Heath, near Stafford, on Sunday, March 19, 164¾, fighting for King Charles I.

Q   POST.

Po st. I ſhould be glad to receive ſome of your Lordſhip's philoſophical labours, if your Lordſhip could ſo think fit. I do now receive a letter from the Conde de Gondomar, who, thinking that it ſhould find me in England, ſaith thus : *Beſo las manes mil vezes a mi ſennor, el ſennor Gran Chancilor, con my coracon; como eſtoy en ſu buena gracia.* The Empreſs is dead long ſince, and the Emperor is ſo ſickly, or rather ſo ſick, that they forbear to bury her with ſolemnity, as conceiving, that he will ſave charge by dying ſhortly. They ſay here, that the buſineſs of Bohemia is growing towards an end by compoſition.

Bruſſels, this 14th of
February, 1619.

To the Marquis of BUCKINGHAM.

My very good Lord,

FOR the ſervices committed to Sir Lionel Cranfield, after his Majeſty hath ſpoken with him, I ſhall attend and follow his Majeſty's pleaſure and directions, and yield my beſt care, advice, and endeavour for performance.

In the pretermitted duty I have ſome profit, and more was to have had, if Queen Anne had lived. Wherefore I ſhall become an humble ſuitor to his Majeſty, that I may become no loſer, ſpecially ſeeing the buſineſs had been many a time and oft quite overthrown, if it had not been upheld only, or chiefly, by myſelf; ſo that whatſoever ſervice hath been ſince done, is upon my foundation.

Mr. Attorney (*i*) groweth pretty pert with me of late ; and I ſee well who they are, that maintain him. But be they flies, or be they waſps, I neither care for buzzies nor ſtings, moſt eſpecially in any thing, that

(*i*) Sir Henry Yelverton.

concerneth

concerneth my duty to his Majesty, or my love to your Lordship.

I forgot not, in my public charge, the last Star-Chamber-day, to publish his Majesty's honour for his late commission for the relief of the poor, and suppressing vagabonds; as also his gracious intention touching informers, which, I perceive, was received with much applause. That of projectors I spake not of, because it is not yet ripe, neither doth it concern the execution of any law, for which my speech was proper.

God ever preserve and prosper you.

Your Lordship's most obliged friend,

and faithful servant,

February 17, 1619.

FR. VERULAM, *Canc.*

To the Marquis of B U C K I N G H A M.

My very good Lord,

I SEND, by post, this sealed packet, containing my Lord of Suffolk's answer in the Star-Chamber. I received it this evening at six of the clock, by the hands of the Master of the Rolls (*k*), sealed as it is with my Lord of Suffolk's seal, and the Master's of the Rolls. But neither I, nor the Master of the Rolls, know what is in it; but it cometh first to his Majesty's sight. Only I did direct, that because the authentic copy (unto which my Lord is sworn, according to the course of the court) is not so fit for his Majesty's reading, my Lord of Suffolk should send withall a paper copy, which his Majesty might read with less trouble.

(*k*) Sir Julius Cæsar.

Q 2

My

My Lady Suffolk is so ill of the small-pox, as she is not yet fit to make any answer.

Bingley's *(l)* answer is come in, a long one; and, as I perceive, with some things impertinent, yea, and unfit. Of that I confer with Mr. Sollicitor *(m)* to-morrow; and then, I will farther advertise your Lordship

God ever preserve and prosper you.

Your Lordship's most obliged friend,

and faithful servant,

York-house, this 23d
of Febr. 1619, at 9
of the clock [16$\frac{1}{8}$].

Fr. Verulam, *Canc.*

To the Lord Chancellor.

Most honoured Lord,

I DO even now receive this letter from the Conde de Gondomar, with direction I should send it (since I am not there to deliver it) to Mr. Wyche, that so he may present it to your Lordship's hand at such time, as it may be of most use to him. He commands me besides, that for his sake I should become a humble sollicitor to your Lordship for this friend of his; which I presume to do the more willingly, because this party is a great friend of mine, and so are also many of his friends my friends. Besides, he wills me to represent his great thanks to your Lordship, for the just favours you have been pleased to vouchsafe to Mr. Wyche already, the rather, in contemplation of the Conde, as he hath been informed. And if in the company, or rather in the attendance, of so great an intercessor, it be not an un-

(l) Sir John Bingley's.   *(m)* Sir Thomas Coventry.

pardonable

pardonable kind of ill manners to intrude myself, I presume to caft myself at your Lordfhip's feet, with proteftation, that I fhall be very particularly bound to your Lordfhip's goodnefs for any favour, with juftice, that he fhall obtain.

I befeech Jefus keep your Lordfhip ever intirely happy ; and fo doing all humble reverence, I take leave.

Your Lordfhip's moft humble,

and moft obliged fervant,

Bruffels, this 26th of
February, 1619.   T O B I E M A T T H E W.

To the L O R D C H A N C E L L O R (*).

My honourable Lord,

UNDERSTANDING, that there hath been a long and tedious fuit depending in the Chancery between Robert D'Oyley and his wife, plaintiffs, and Leonard Lovace, defendant ; which caufe hath been heretofore ended by award, but is now revived again, and was, in Michaelmafs term laft, fully heard before your Lordfhip ; at which hearing your Lordfhip did not give your opinion thereof, but were pleafed to defer it, untill breviats were delivered on both fides ; which, as I am informed, hath been done accordingly : now my defire unto your Lordfhip is, that you will be pleafed to take fome time, as fpeedily as your Lordfhip may, to give your opinion thereof, and fo make a final end, as your Lordfhip fhall find the fame in equity to deferve. For which I will ever reft

Your Lordfhip's faithful friend and fervant,

Windfor, 18th of
May, 1620.   G. B U C K I N G H A M.

(*) Harl. MSS. Vol. 7006.

To the Marquis of BUCKINGHAM.

My very good Lord,

I WENT to Kew for pleasure, but I met with pain. But neither pleasure, nor pain, can withdraw my mind, from thinking of his Majesty's service. And because his Majesty shall see how I was occupied at Kew, I send him these papers of rules for the Star-Chamber, wherein his Majesty shall erect one of the noblest and durablest pillars for the justice of this kingdom in perpetuity, that can be, after, by his own wisdom, and the advice of his Lords, he shall have revised them, and established them. The manner and circumstances I refer to my attending his Majesty. The rules are not all set down; but I will do the rest within two or three days. I ever remain

Your Lordship's most obliged friend,
and faithful servant,

June 9, 1620.

FR. VERULAM, *Canc.*

To the LORD CHANCELLOR (*).

My very good Lord,

SUCH is my haste at this time, that I cannot write so largely to yourself, as I would, in the business of the steel, in which once already I sent to your Lordship, and in which I only desire the good of the commonwealth, and the service of my master. I therefore have sent this bearer, my servant, unto you, and committed the relation of the business to

(*) Harl. MSS. Vol. 7000.

him,

him.   And I do intreat your Lordſhip to give credit
to what he ſhall deliver your Lordſhip therein, with
your lawful aſſiſtance of my deſires ; wherein I doubt
not but you ſhall do a very good office.   And I ſhall
reſt ready to requite your courteſy ; and, with my
beſt wiſhes, continue

Your very loving friend,

Egham, July 6,
    162c.
G. B U C K I N G H A M.

Indorſed,

*My Lord Marquis in the behalf of his ſervant, Mr.
Porter, and Mr. Dallington.*

To the L O R D C H A N C E L L O R (*).

My honourable Lord,

HIS Majeſty having made a reference of buſineſs
to your Lordſhip, concerning Sir Robert Doug-
las and Mr. David Ramſey, two of his Highneſs's
ſervants, whom he loveth, and whom I wiſh very
well unto ; I have thought fit to deſire you to ſhew
them all the favour your Lordſhip may therein :
which I will acknowledge, and ever reſt

Your Lordſhip's faithful friend and ſervant,

G. B U C K I N G H A M.

The reference comes in the name of my brother
Chriſtopher, becauſe they thought it would ſucceed
the better : but the Prince wiſheth well to it.

Farnham, the laſt of
    Auguſt, 1620.

Indorſed, *Touching the buſineſs of wills.*

(*) Harl. MSS. Vol. 7000.

Q 4

To

To the KING (*n*).

AMONGST the counfels, which, fince the time I had the honour to be firft of your learned, and after of your privy council, I have given your Majefty faithfully, according to my fmall ability; I do take comfort in none more, than that I was the firft, that advifed you to come in perfon into the Star-Chamber; knowing very well, that thofe virtues of your Majefty, which I faw near hand, would out of that throne, both as out of a fphere, illuftrate your own honour, and, as out of a fountain, water and refrefh your whole land. And becaufe your Majefty, in that you have already done, hath fo well effected that, which I forefaw and defired, even beyond my expectation; it is no marvel, if I refort ftill to the branches of that counfel, that hath borne fo good fruit.

The Star-Chamber, in the inftitution thereof, hath two ufes; the one as a fupreme court of judicature; the other as an open council. In the firft kind, your Majefty hath fat there now twice: the firft time, in a caufe of force, concerning the duels; the fecond time, in a caufe of fraud, concerning the forgeries and confpiracies againft the Lady of Exeter; which two natures of crimes, force and fraud, are the proper objects of that court.

In the fecond kind, your Majefty came the firft time of all, when you did fet in frame and fabric the feveral jurifdictions of your courts. There wants a fourth part of the fquare to make all complete, which is, if your Majefty will be pleafed to publifh

(*n*) This letter appears to have been written after the proceedings againft Sir Thomas Lake, and his Lady and daughter, in the Star-Chamber, in January 16$\frac{1}{2}$?, and before the refolution of calling the parliament, which met January 30, 162$\frac{9}{7}$.

certain

certain commonwealth commiſſions ; which, as your Majeſty hath well begun to do in ſome things, and to ſpeak of in ſome others ; ſo, if your Majeſty will be pleaſed to make a ſolemn declaration of them in that place, this will follow :

Firſt, that your Majeſty ſhall do yourſelf an infinite honour, and win the hearts of your people to acknowledge you, as well the moſt politic King, as the moſt juſt.

Secondly, it will oblige your Commiſſioners to a more ſtrict account, when they ſhall be engaged by ſuch a public charge and commandment. And, thirdly, it will invite and direct any man, that finds himſelf to know any thing concerning thoſe commiſſions, to bring in their informations. So as I am perſuaded it will eterniſe your name and merit, and that King James's commiſſions will be ſpoken of, and put in ure, as long as Britain laſts ; at the leaſt, in the reign of all good Kings.

For the particulars, beſides the two commiſſions of the navy, and the buildings about London (wherein your Majeſty may conſider, whether you will have any thing altered or ſupplied,) I wiſh theſe following to be added.

Commiſſion for advancing the clothing of England, as well the old drapery as the new, and all the incidents thereunto.

Commiſſion for ſtaying treaſure within the realm, and the reiglement of monies.

Commiſſion for the proviſion of the realm with corn and grain, and the government of the exportation and importation thereof ; and directing of public granaries, if cauſe be.

Commiſſion for introducing and nouriſhing manufactures within the realm, for the ſetting people a-work, and the conſidering of all grants and privileges of that nature.

Commiſſion

Commiffion to prevent the depopulation of towns and houfes of hufbandry, and for nuifances and high-ways.

Commiffion for the recovery of drowned lands.

Commiffion for the fuppreffion of the grievances of informers.

Commiffion for the better proceedings in the plantations of Ireland.

Commiffion for the provifion of the realm with all kind of warlike defence, ordnance, powder, munition, and armour.

Of thefe you may take and leave, as it fhall pleafe you: and I wifh the articles concerning every one of them (firft allowed by your council) to be read openly, and the Commiffioners names.

For the good, that comes of particular and felect committees and commiffions, I need not commonplace, for your Majefty hath found the good of them; but nothing to that, that will be, when fuch things are publifhed; becaufe it will vindicate them from neglect, and make many good fpirits, that we little think of, co-operate in them.

I know very well, that the world, that commonly is apt to think, that the care of the commonwealth is but a pretext in matters of ftate, will perhaps conceive, that this is but a preparative to a parliament. But let not that hinder your Majefty's magnanimity, *in opere operato*, that is fo good; and befides, that opinion, for many refpects, will do no hurt to your affairs.

To the LORD CHANCELLOR (*).

My very good Lord,

BY his Majefty's directions, Sir Francis Blundell will deliver you a petition of Sir Francis Annefly, his Majefty's Secretary of Ireland, with his

(*) Harl. MSS. Vol. 7000.

Majefty's

Majefty's pleafure thereupon. To the gentleman I wifh very well, and do therefore recommend him and his caufe to your Lordfhip's good favour; and your refpect of him, in his abfence, I will thankfully acknowledge. So I take my leave.

Your Lordfhip's very loving friend,

Theobalds, the 2d
of Octob. 1620.　　　　　G. B U C K I N G H A M.

To the K I N G.

It may pleafe your moft excellent Majefty,

IT being a thing to fpeak or write, fpecially to a King, in public, another in private, although I have dedicated a work (*o*), or rather a portion of a work, which, at laft, I have overcome, to your Majefty by a public epiftle, where I fpeak to you in the hearing of others; yet I thought fit alfo humbly to feek accefs for the fame, not fo much to your perfon, as to your judgement, by thefe private lines.

The work, in what colours foever it may be fet forth, is no more but a new logic, teaching to invent and judge by induction, as finding fyllogifm incompetent for fciences of nature; and thereby to make philofophy and fciences both more true and more active.

This tending to inlarge the bounds of reafon, and to endow man's eftate with new value, was no improper oblation to your Majefty, who, of men, is the greateft mafter of reafon, and author of beneficence.

There be two of your council, and one other bifhop (*p*) of this land, that know I have been about

(*o*) *Novum Organum.*
(*p*) Dr. Lancelot Andrews, Bifhop of Winchefter.

fome

some such work near thirty years (q); so as I made no haste. And the reason, why I have published it now, specially being unperfect, is, to speak plainly, because I number my days, and would have it saved. There is another reason of my so doing, which is to try, whether I can get help in one intended part of this work, namely, the compiling of a natural and experimental history, which must be the main foundation of a true and active philosophy.

This work is but a new body of clay, whereinto your Majesty, by your countenance and protection, may breathe life. And, to tell your Majesty truly what I think, I account your favour may be to this work as much as an hundred years time: for I am persuaded, the work will gain upon men's minds in ages, but your gracing it may make it take hold more swiftly; which I would be very glad of, it being a work meant, not for praise or glory, but for practice, and the good of men. One thing, I confess, I am ambitious of, with hope, which is, that after these beginnings, and the wheel once set on going, men shall seek more truth out of Christian pens, than hitherto they have done out of heathen. I say with hope; because I hear my former book of the *Advancement of Learning*, is well tasted in the universities here, and the English colleges abroad: and this is the same argument sunk deeper.

(q) Mr. Chamberlain, in a letter to Sir Dudley Carleton, Ambassador at Holland, dated at London, October 28, 1620, mentions, that Mr. Henry Cuffe, who had been Secretary to Robert, Earl of Essex, and executed for being concerned in his treasons, *having long since perused* this work, *gave this censure, that a fool could not have written such a work, and a wise man would not.* And, in another letter, dated February 3, 162⁰⁄₁, Mr. Chamberlain takes notice, that the King could not forbear sometimes, in reading that book, to say, that it *was like the peace of God, that passeth all understanding.*

And

And so I ever humbly rest in prayers, and all other duties,

Your Majesty's most bounden

and devoted servant,

York-house, this 12th
of October, 1620.

FR. VERULAM, *Canc.*

To the LORD CHANCELLOR (*).

My honourable Lord,

THERE is a business in your Lordship's hands, with which Sir Robert Lloyd did acquaint your Lordship ; whereof the Prince hath demanded of me what account is given. And because I cannot inform his Highness of any proceeding therein, I desire your Lordship to use all expedition, that may be, in making your answer to me, that I may give his Highness some satisfaction, who is very desirous thereof. And so I rest

Your Lordship's faithful friend and servant,

Royston, 14th of
October, 1620.

G. BUCKINGHAM.

Indorsed, *Touching the register of wills.*

To the LORD CHANCELLOR (*).

My honourable Lord,

I DESIRE your Lordship to continue your favour to Sir Thomas Gerrard, in the business concerning him, wherein I signified his Majesty's pleasure to your Lordship. And one favour more I am to intreat of your Lordship in his behalf, that you will be pleased to speak to one of the assistants of the

(*) Harl. MSS. Vol. 7000.

Chancellor

Chancellor of the Duchy, in whofe court he hath a caufe depending, as he will more fully inform your Lordfhip himfelf, to fee, that he may have a fair proceeding, according to juftice: for which I will ever reft

Your Lordfhip's faithful friend and fervant,

Royfton, 15th of
October, 1620.   G. BUCKINGHAM.

To the Marquis of BUCKINGHAM.

My very good Lord,

YOUR Lordfhip defiring to underftand what cometh of the bufinefs, after which the Prince hearkeneth, I was in doubt which of the two bufineffes you meant; that of the Duchy, or that of the Prerogative-Court for wills; for both are recommended from the Prince. But be it one, or be it the other, no time hath been loft in either; for Mr. Secretary Naunton and I have entered into both. For the Duchy, we have already ftayed all proceeding to the King's differvice for thofe manors, which are not already paffed under feal. For that, which is paffed, we have heard the Attorney (r) with none, or little, fatisfaction hitherto. The Chancellor (s) is not yet come, though fent for. For the other, we have heard Sir John Bennet (t), and given him leave to acquaint my Lord of Canterbury; and have required the Sollicitor (u) to come well prepared for the King. So that in neither we can certify yet; and to trouble

(r) Sir Henry Yelverton.
(s) Sir Humphrey May, made Chancellor of the Duchy, March 9, 1617.
(t) Judge of the Prerogative-Court of Canterbury. In 1621 he was fined 20000 l. for bribery, corruption, and exaction in that office. He died in 1627.   (u) Sir Thomas Coventry.

your

your Lordſhip, while buſineſs is but in paſſage, were time loſt. I ever reſt

Your Lordſhip's moſt obliged friend,

and faithful ſervant,

October 16, 1620.

FR. VERULAM, *Canc.*

To the K I N G, *thanking his Majeſty for his gracious acceptance of his book.*

May it pleaſe your Majeſty,

I CANNOT expreſs, how much comfort I received by your laſt letter of your own royal hand (*w*). I ſee your Majeſty is a ſtar, that hath benevolent aſpect and gracious influence upon all things, that tend to a general good.

> *Daphni, quid antiquos ſignorum ſuſpicis artus?*
> *Ecce Dionæi proceſſit Cæſaris aſtrum ;*
> *Aſtrum, quo ſegetes gauderent frugibus, et quo*
> *Duceret apricis in collibus uva colorem* (*x*).

This work, which is for the bettering of men's bread and wine, which are the characters of temporal bleſſings and ſacraments of eternal, I hope, by God's holy providence, will be ripened by Cæſar's ſtar.

Your Majeſty ſhall not only do to myſelf a ſingular favour, but to your buſineſs a material help, if you will be graciouſly pleaſed to open yourſelf to me in thoſe things, wherein you may be unſatisfied. For though this work, as by poſition and principle, doth diſclaim to be tried by any thing but by experience,

(*w*) of the 16th of October, 1620, printed in Lord Bacon's works.

(*x*) Virgil, *Eclog. IX. verſ.* 46—50.

and

and the refults of experience in a true way ; yet the fharpnefs and profoundnefs of your Majefty's judgement ought to be an exception to this general rule ; and your queftions, obfervations, and admonifhments, may do infinite good.

This comfortable beginning makes me hope farther, that your Majefty will be aiding to me, in fetting men on work for the collecting of a natural and experimental hiftory ; which is *bafis totius negotii*, a thing, which I affure myfelf, will be from time to time an excellent recreation unto you ; I fay, to that admirable fpirit of yours, that delighteth in light : and I hope well, that even in your times many noble inventions may be difcovered for man's ufe. For who can tell, now this mine of truth is opened, how the veins go ; and what lieth higher, and what lieth lower ? But let me trouble your Majefty no farther at this time. God ever preferve and profper your Majefty.

[October 19, 1620.]

To the Marquis of BUCKINGHAM.

My very good Lord,

I SEND now only to give his Majefty thanks for the fingular comfort, which I received by his Majefty's letter of his own hand, touching my book. And I muft alfo give your Lordfhip of my beft thanks, for your letter fo kindly and affectionately written.

I did even now receive your Lordfhip's letter touching the proclamation, and do approve his Majefty's judgement and forefight about mine own. Neither would I have thought of inferting matter of ftate for the vulgar, but that now-a-days there is no vulgar, but all ftatefmen. But, as his Majefty doth excellently

cellently confider, the time of it is not yet proper.
I ever reft

　　Your Lordfhip's moft obliged friend,

　　　　　　and faithful fervant,

October 19, 1620.

　　　　　　　　Fr. Verulam, *Canc.*

　　　　　Indorfed,
*In anfwer to his Majefty's directions touching the pro-
clamation for a parliament.*

Notes of a Speech of the Lord Chancellor
in the Star-Chamber, in the caufe of Sir Henry
Yelverton, *Attorney General (y).*

SORRY for the perfon, being a gentleman, that
I lived with in Grey's-Inn; ferved with him
when I was Attorney; joined with him in many fervices, and one, that ever gave me more attributes
in public, than I deferved; and, befides, a man of
very good parts, which with me is friendfhip at firft
fight; much more, joined with fo ancient an acquaintance.

But, as a Judge, I hold the offence very great,
and that without preffing meafure; upon which I
will only make a few obfervations, and fo leave it.

(*y*) He was profecuted in the Star-Chamber, for having paffed
certain claufes in a charter, lately granted to the city of London,
not agreeable to his Majefty's warrant, and derogatory to his
honour. But the chief reafon of the feverity againft him was
thought to be the Marquis of Buckingham's refentment againft
him, for having oppofed, according to the duty of his office,
fome oppreffive, if not illegal, patents, which the projectors of
thofe times were bufy in preparing.

　　　　　　R　　　　　　　1. Firft

1. First I observe the danger and consequence of the offence: for if it be suffered, that the learned council shall practise the art of multiplication upon their warrants, the crown will be destroyed in small time. The great seal, the privy seal, signet, are solemn things; but they follow the King's hand. It is the bill drawn by the learned council and the docquet, that leads the King's hand.

2. Next I note the nature of the defence. As first, that it was error in judgement: for this surely, if the offence were small, though clear, or great, but doubtful, I should hardly sentence it. For it is hard to draw a strait line by steadiness of hand; but it could not be the swerving of the hand. And herein I note the wisdom of the law of England, which termeth the highest contempts and excesses of authority, *misprisions*; which, if you take the sound and derivation of the words, is but *mistaken*: but if you take the use and acceptation of the word, it is high and heinous contempts and usurpations of authority; whereof the reason I take to be, and the name excellently imposed; for that main mistaking, it is ever joined with contempt; for he, that reveres, will not easily mistake; but he, that slights, and thinks more of the greatness of his place than of the duty of his place, will soon commit misprisions.

Indorsed, *Star-Chamber, October* 24, 1620.
Notes upon Mr. Attorney's cause.

To the Marquis of Buckingham.

My very good Lord,

IT may be, your Lordship will expect to hear from me what passed yesterday in the Star-Chamber, touching Yelverton's cause, though we desired Secretary Calvert to acquaint his Majesty therewith.

2

To

To make short, at the motion of the Attorney, in person at the bar, and at the motion of my Lord Steward (z) in court, the day of proceeding is deferred till the King's pleasure is known. This was against my opinion, then declared plain enough; but put to votes, and ruled by the major part, though some concurred with me.

I do not like of this course, in respect that it puts the King in a strait; for either the note of severity must rest upon his Majesty, if he go on; or the thanks of clemency is in some part taken away, if his Majesty go not on.

I have *cor unum et via una*; and therefore did my part as a Judge and the King's Chancellor. What is farther to be done, I will advise the King faithfully, when I see his Majesty and your Lordship. But before I give advice, I must ask a question first.

God ever preserve and prosper you.

Your Lordship's most obliged friend,

and faithful servant,

October 28, 1620.

Fr. Verulam, *Canc.*

To the KING.

It may please your most excellent Majesty,

IN performance of your royal pleasure, signified by Sir John Suckling (a), we have at several times considered of the petition of Mr. Christopher Villiers (b), and have heard, as well the registers and ministers of the Prerogative-Court of Canterbury, and their

(z) The Duke of Lenox.
(a) He was afterwards Comptroller of the Houshold to King Charles I, and father of the poet of the same name.
(b) Youngest brother to the Marquis of Buckingham. He was created, April 23, 1623, Baron of Daventry and Earl of Anglesey. He died September 24, 1624.

R 2   council,

council, as also the council of the Lord Archbishop of Canterbury. And setting aside such other points, as are desired by the petition, we do think, that your Majesty may by law, and without inconvenience, appoint an officer, that shall have the ingrossing of the transcripts of all wills to be sealed with the seal of either of the Prerogative-Courts, which shall be proved *in communi formâ*; and likewise of all inventories, to be exhibited in the same courts.

We see it necessary, that all wills, which are not judicially controverted, be ingrossed before the probate. Yet, as the law now stands, no officer of those courts can lawfully take any fee or reward for ingrossing the said wills and inventories, the statute of the 21st of King Henry the VIIIth restraining them. Wherefore we hold it much more convenient, that it should be done by a lawful officer, to be appointed by your Majesty, than in a cause not warrantable by law. Yet our humble opinion and advice is, that good consideration be had in passing this book, as well touching a moderate proportion of fees to be allowed for the pains and travel of the officer, as for the expedition of the suitor, in such sort, that the subject may find himself in better case than he is now, and not in worse.

But however we conceive this may be convenient in the two courts of prerogative, where there is much business; yet in the ordinary course of the Bishop's diocesans, we hold the same will be inconvenient, in regard of the small employment.

Your Majesty's most faithful,

and obedient servant,

November 15, 1620.

Fr. Verulam, *Canc.*
Robert Naunton,
Henry Montagu (*c*).

(*c*) Lord Chief Justice of the King's Bench, who, on the 3d of December following, was advanced to the post of Lord High Treasurer.

To

To the LORD CHANCELLOR (*).

AFTER my very hearty commendations, I have acquainted his Majefty with your letter, who commanded me to tell you, that he had been thinking upon the fame point, whereof you write, three or four days ago, being fo far from making any queftion of it, that he every day expected when a writ fhould come down. For at the creation of Prince Henry, the Lords of the council and Judges affured his Majefty of as much, as the precedents, mentioned in your letter, fpeak of. And fo I reft

Your Lordfhip's very loving friend

at command,

Newmarket, the 24th
of Novemb. 1620.

G. BUCKINGHAM.

Indorfed,

Shewing his Majefty is fatisfied with precedents, touching
the Prince's fummons to parliament.

To the Marquis of BUCKINGHAM.

My very good Lord,

YOUR Lordfhip may find, that in the number of patents, which we have reprefented to his Majefty, as like to be ftirred in by the Lower Houfe of Parliament, we have fet down three, which may concern fome of your Lordfhip's fpecial friends, which I account as mine own friends ; and fo fhewed myfelf, when they were in fuit. The one, that to Sir

(*) Harl. MSS. Vol. 7000.

R 3

Giles

Giles Mompesson, touching the inns; the second, to Mr. Christopher Villiers and Mr. Maule, touching the recognizances for ale-houses; the third, to Mr. Lieutenant of the Tower, touching the cask. These in duty could not be omitted, for that, specially the two first of them, are more rumoured, both by the vulgar, and by the gentlemen, yea, and by the Judges themselves, than any other patents at this day. Therefore I thought it appertained to the singular love and affection, which I bear you upon so many obligations, to wish and advise, that your Lordship, whom God hath made in all things so fit to be beloved, would put off the envy of these things, which I think in themselves bear no great fruit; and rather take the thanks for ceasing them, than the note for maintaining them. But, howsoever, let me know your mind, and your Lordship shall find I will go your way.

I cannot express, how much comfort I take in the choice his Majesty hath made of my Lord Chief Justice to be Lord Treasurer; not for his sake, nor for my sake, but for the King's sake; hoping, that now a number of counsels, which I have given for the establishment of his Majesty's estate, and have lain dead and buried deeper than this snow, may now spring up, and bear fruit; the rather, for that I persuade myself, he and I shall run one way. And yet I know well, that in this doubling world *cor una et via una* is rare in one man, but more rare between two. And therefore, if it please his Majesty, according to his prudent custom in such cases, to cast out, now at his coming down, some words, which may the better knit us in conjunction to do him service, I suppose it will be to no idle purpose.

And as an old truant in the commission of the treasury, let me put his Majesty in remembrance of three things now upon his entrance, which he is presently to go in hand with: the first, to make Ireland

to

to bear the charge thereof.: the second, to bring all, accounts to one purse in the Exchequer: the third, by all possible means to endeavour the taking off of the anticipations. There be a thousand things more; but these being his Majesty's last commands to the Commissioners of the Treasury, with such as in his Majesty's princely judgement shall occur, will do well to season his place.

> Your Lordship's most obliged friend,
>
> and faithful servant,

November 29, 1620.

> Fr. Verulam, *Canc.*

As soon as I had written this letter, I received your Lordship's letter, touching my Lord Chief Justice, which redoubled my comfort, to see how his Majesty's thoughts and mine, his poor servant's, and your Lordship's, meet.

I send inclosed names for the Speaker; and if his Majesty, or your Lordship, demand our opinion, which of them, my Lord Chief Justice will tell you. It were well it were dispatched; for else I will not dine with the Speaker; for his drink will not be laid in time enough.

I beseech your Lordship, care may be taken, that our general letter may be kept secret, whereof my Lord Chief Justice will tell you the reason.

To the K I N G.

It may please your most excellent Majesty,

ACCORDING to your commandment, we have heard once more the proctors of the Prerogative-Court, what they could say; and find no reason to alter, in any part, our former certificate. Thus much withall we think fit to note to your Majesty, that our former certificate, which we now ratify, is principally grounded upon a point in law, upon the statute of 21 Henry VIII, wherein we the Chancellor and Treasurer, for our own opinions, do conceive the law is clear; and your Sollicitor General *(d)* concurs.

Now whether your Majesty will be pleased to rest in our opinions, and so to pass the patents; or give us leave to assist ourselves with the opinion of some principal Judges now in town, whereby the law may be the better resolved, to avoid farther question hereafter; we leave it to your Majesty's royal pleasure. This we represent the rather, because we discern such a confidence in the proctors, and those upon whom they depend, as, it is not unlike, they will bring it to a legal question.

And so we humbly kiss your Majesty's hands, praying for your preservation.

Your Majesty's most humble
and obedient servants,

York-house, December
12, 1620.

FR. VERULAM, Canc.
HENRY MONTAGU,
ROBERT NAUNTON.

The LORD CHANCELLOR *and two* CHIEF JUSTICES *(e) to the Marquis of* BUCK-INGHAM.

Our very good Lord,

IT may please his Majesty to call to mind, that when we gave his Majesty our last account of

(d) Sir Thomas Coventry, who was made Attorney General, January 14, 162$\frac{0}{1}$.
(e) Sir Henry Montagu of the King's Bench, and Sir Henry Hobart of the Common Pleas.

parliament

parliament bufinefs in his prefence, we went over the grievances of the laft parliament in 7mo (f), with our opinion by way of probable conjecture, which of them are like to fall off, and which may perchance ftick and be renewed. And we did alfo then acquaint his Majefty, that we thought it no lefs fit to take into confideration grievances of like nature, which have fprung up fince the faid laft feffion, which are the more like to be called upon, by how much they are the more frefh, fignifying withall, that they were of two kinds ; fome proclamations and commiffions, and many patents ; which, neverthelefs, we did not trouble his Majefty withall in particular ; partly, for that we were not then fully prepared (as being a work of fome length,) and partly, for that we then defired and obtained leave of his Majefty to communicate them with the counciltable. But now fince, I, the Chancellor, received his Majefty's pleafure by Secretary Calvert, that we fhould firft prefent them to his Majefty with fome advice thereupon provifionally, and as we are capable, and thereupon know his Majefty's pleafure before they be brought to the table, which is the work of this difpatch.

And hereupon his Majefty may be likewife pleafed to call to mind, that we then faid, and do now alfo humbly make remonftance to his Majefty, that in this we do not fo much exprefs the fenfe of our own minds or judgements upon the particulars, as we do perfonate the Lower Houfe, and caft with ourfelves what is like to be ftirred there. And therefore if there be any thing, either in refpect of the matter, or the perfons, that ftands not fo well with his Majefty's good liking, that his Majefty would be gracioufly pleafed not to impute it unto us ; and withall

(f) that which began February 9, 1609; and was prorogued July 23, 1610.

3

to confider, that it is to this good end, that his Majefty may either remove fuch of them, as in his own princely judgement, or with the advice of his council, he fhall think fit to be removed; or be the better provided to carry through fuch of them, as he fhall think fit to be maintained, in cafe they fhould be moved; and fo the lefs furprifed.

Firft, therefore to begin with the patents, we find three forts of patents, and thofe fomewhat frequent, fince the feffion of 7 mo, which *in genere* we conceive may be moft fubject to exception of grievance; patents of old debts, patents of concealments, and patents of monopolies, and forfeitures for difpenfations of penal laws; together with fome other particulars, which fall not fo properly under any one head.

In thefe three heads, we do humbly advife feveral courfes to be taken; for the firft two, of old debts and concealments, for that they are in a fort legal, though there may be found out fome point in law to overthrow them; yet it would be a long bufinefs by courfe of law, and a matter unufual by act of council, to call them in. But that, that moves us chiefly, to avoid the queftioning them at the council-table, is, becaufe if they fhall be taken away by the King's act, it may let in upon him a flood of fuitors for recompence; whereas, if they be taken away at the fuit of the parliament, and a law thereupon made, it frees the King, and leaves him to give recompence only where he fhall be pleafed to intend grace. Wherefore we conceive the moft convenient way will be, if fome grave and difcreet gentleman of the country, fuch as have loft relation to the court, make, at fit times, fome modeft motion touching the fame; and that his Majefty would be gracioufly pleafed to permit fome law to pafs (for the time paft only, no ways touching his Majefty's regal power) to free the fubjects from the fame; and fo his Majefty, after due confultation, to give way unto it. For

For the third, we do humbly advife, that fuch of them, as his Majefty fhall give way to have called in, may be queftioned before the council-table, either as granted contrary to his Majefty's book of bounty, or found fince to have been abufed in the execution, or otherwife by experience difcovered to be burden-fome to the country. But herein we fhall add this farther humble advice, that it be not done as matter of preparation to a parliament; but that occafion be taken, partly updn revifing of the book of bounty, and partly upon the frefh examples in Sir Henry Yel-verton's cafe of abufe and furreption in obtaining of patents; and likewife, that it be but as a continuance in conformity of the council's former diligence and vi-gilancy, which hath already ftayed and revoked divers patents of like nature, whereof we are ready to fhew the examples. Thus, we conceive, his Majefty fhall keep his greatnefs, and fomewhat fhall be done in parlia-ment, and fomewhat out of parliament, as the na-ture of the fubject and bufinefs require.

We have fent his Majefty herewith a fchedule of the particulars of thefe three kinds; wherein, for the firft two, we have fet down all that we could at this time difcover: but in the latter, we have chofen out but fome, that are moft in fpeech, and do moft tend, either to the vexation of the common people, or the difcountenancing of our gentlemen and juftices, the one being the original, the other the reprefentative of the commons.

There being many more of like nature, but not of like weight, nor fo much rumoured, which, to take away now in a blaze, will give more fcandal, that fuch things were granted, than thanks, that they be now revoked.

And becaufe all things may appear to his Majefty in the true light, we have fet down, as well the fuitors as the grants, and not only thofe, in whofe names the patents were taken, but thofe, whom they concern, as far as comes to our knowledge. For

For proclamations and commiſſions, they are tender things; and we are willing to meddle with them ſparingly. For as for ſuch, as do but wait upon patents (wherein his Majeſty, as we conceived, gave ſome approbation to have them taken away,) it is better they fall away, by taking away the patent itſelf, than otherwiſe; for a proclamation cannot be revoked but by proclamation, which we avoid.

For thoſe commonwealth bills, which his Majeſty approved to be put in readineſs, and ſome other things, there will be time enough hereafter to give his Majeſty account, and amongſt them, of the extent of his Majeſty's pardon, which, if his ſubjects do their part, as we hope they will, we do wiſh may be more liberal than of later times, a pardon being the ancient remuneration in parliament.

Thus hoping his Majeſty, out of his gracious and accuſtomed benignity, will accept of our faithful endeavours, and ſupply the reſt by his own princely wiſdom and direction; and alſo humbly praying his Majeſty, that when he hath himſelf conſidered of our humble propoſitions, he will give us leave to impart them all, or as much as he ſhall think fit, to the Lords of his Council, for the better ſtrength of his ſervice, we conclude with our prayers for his Majeſty's happy preſervation, and always reſt &c.

Indorſed,

The Lord Chancellor and the two Chief Juſtices to the King, concerning parliament buſineſs.

To the LORD CHANCELLOR, *and the Lord* MANDEVILLE, *Lord Treaſurer of England* (*).

My honourable Lords,

HIS Majeſty is pleaſed, according to your Lordſhips certificate, to rely upon your judgements,

(*) Harl. MSS. Vol. 7000.

and

and hath made choice of Sir Robert Lloyd, Knight, to be Patentee and Mafter of the Office of ingroffing the Tranfcripts of all Wills and Inventories in the Prerogative-Courts, during his Highnefs's pleafure, and to be accountable unto his Majefty for fuch profits, as fhall arife out of the fame office. And his Majefty's farther pleafure is, that your Lordfhip forthwith proportion and fet down, as well a reafonable rate of fees for the fubject to pay for ingroffing the faid tranfcripts, as alfo fuch fees, as your Lordfhip fhall conceive fit to be allowed to the faid patentee for the charge of clerks and minifters for execution of the faid office. And to this effect his Majefty hath commanded me to fignify his pleafure to his Sollicitor General (g), to prepare a book for his Majefty's fignature. And fo I bid your Lordfhip heartily well to fare, and remain

Your Lordfhip's very loving friend,

Royfton, December
17, 1620.

G. BUCKINGHAM.

To the Marquis of BUCKINGHAM.

My very good Lord,

I WAS fo full of cold, as I could not attend his Majefty to-day. Yefterday I difpatched the proclamation with the council. There was a motion to have fharpened it; but better none, than over fharp at firft. I moved the council alfo for fupplying the committee for drawing of bills and fome other matters, in regard of my Lord Hobart's (h) ficknefs, who, I think, will hardly efcape : which, though it be happinefs for him, yet it is lofs for us.

(g) Sir Thomas Coventry.
(h), Lord Chief Juftice of the Common Pleas.

Mean

Mean while, as I propounded to the King, which he allowed well, I have broken the main of the parliament into queſtions and parts, which I ſend. It may be, it is an over-diligence; but ſtill methinks there is a middle thing between art and chance: I think they call it providence, or ſome ſuch thing, which good ſervants owe to their Sovereign, ſpecially in caſes of importance and ſtraits of occaſions. And thoſe huffing elections, and general licence of ſpeech, ought to make us the better provided. The way will be, if his Majeſty be pleaſed to peruſe theſe queſtions adviſedly, and give me leave to wait on him; and then refer it to ſome few of the council, a little to adviſe upon it. I ever reſt

Your Lordſhip's moſt obliged friend,

and faithful ſervant,

December 23, 1620.

Fr. Verulam, *Canc.*

To the Lord Chancellor (*).

My honourable Lord,

HIS Majeſty hath commanded me to ſignify his pleaſure unto your Lordſhip, that Sir Thomas Coventry, now his Sollicitor General, be forthwith made his Attorney General: and that your Lordſhip give order to the Clerk of the Crown to draw up a grant of the ſaid place unto him accordingly. And ſo I reſt

Your Lordſhip's faithful friend and ſervant,

Whitehall, 9th of
January, 1620.

G. Buckingham.

(*) Harl. MSS. Vol. 7000.

To

To the LORD CHANCELLOR (*).

My honourable Lord,

I HAVE been intreated to recommend unto your Lordſhip the diſtreſſed caſe of the Lady Martin, widow of Sir Richard Martin, deceaſed, who hath a cauſe to be heard before your Lordſhip in the Chancery, at your firſt ſitting in the next term, between her and one Archer, and others, upon an ancient ſtatute, due long ſince unto her huſband ; which cauſe, I am informed, hath received three verdicts for her in the common law, a decree in the Exchequer-Chamber, and a diſmiſſion before your Lordſhip : which I was the more willing to do, becauſe I have ſeen a letter of his Majeſty to the ſaid Sir Richard Martin, acknowledging the good ſervice, that he did him in this Kingdom, at the time of his Majeſty's being in Scotland. And therefore I deſire your Lordſhip, that you would give her a full and fair hearing of her cauſe, and a ſpeedy diſpatch thereof, her poverty being ſuch, that having nothing to live on but her huſband's debts, if her ſuit long depend, ſhe ſhall be inforced to loſe her cauſe for want of means to follow it : wherein I will acknowledge your Lordſhip's favour, and reſt

Your Lordſhip's faithful friend and ſervant,

Whitehall, the 13th of
January, 1620.

G. BUCKINGHAM.

(*) Harl. MSS. Vol. 7000.

To the LORD CHANCELLOR (*).

My honourable Lord,

HIS Majefty hath commanded me to fignify his pleafure unto you, that you give prefent order to the Clerk of the Crown to draw a bill to be figned by his Majefty for Robert Heath, late Recorder of London, to be his Majefty's Sollicitor General. So I reft

     Your Lordfhip's faithful friend and fervant,

Theobalds, 20th of
   January, 1620.   G. BUCKINGHAM.

To the KING (i).

May it pleafe your Majefty,

I THANK God I number days, both in thank-fulnefs to him, and in warning to myfelf. I fhould likewife number your Majefty's benefits, which, as, to take them in all kinds, they are without number; fo even in this kind of fteps and degrees of advance-ment, they are in greater number, than fcarcely any other of your fubjects can fay. For this is now the eighth time, that your Majefty hath raifed me.

You formed me of the learned council extraor-dinary, without patent or fee, a kind of *indivi-duum vagum*. You eftablifhed me, and brought me into ordinary. Soon after, you placed me Sol-licitor, where I ferved feven years. Then your Majefty made me your Attorney, or Procurator

(*) Harl. MSS. Vol. 7000.
(i) This feems to have been written by Lord St. Albans, juft after he was created a Vifcount by that title, January 27, 1620.

                           General;

General; then Privy Counsellor, while I was Attorney; a kind of miracle of your favour, that had not been in many ages: thence Keeper of your Seal; and, because that was a kind of planet, and not fixed, Chancellor: and, when your Majesty could raise me no higher, it was your grace to illustrate me with beams of honour, first making me Baron Verulam, and now Viscount St. Alban. So this is the eighth rise or reach, a diapason in music, even a good number, and accord for a close. And so I may, without superstition, be buried in St. Alban's habit or vestment.

Besides the number, the obligation is increased by three notes or marks: first, that they proceed from such a King; for honours from some Kings are but great chancels, or counters, set high; but from your Majesty, they are indeed dignities, by the co-operation of your grace. Secondly, in respect of the continuance of your Majesty's favour, which proceedeth, as the divine favour, from grace to grace. And, thirdly, these splendors of honour are like your freest patents, *absque aliquid inde reddendo*. Offices have burdens of cares and labours; but honours have no burden but thankfulness, which doth rather raise men's spirits, than *accable* them, or press them down.

Then I must say, *quid retribuam?* I have nothing of mine own. That, that God hath given me, I shall present unto your Majesty; which is care and diligence, and assiduous endeavour, and that, which is the chief, *cor unum et viam unam*; hoping, that your Majesty will do, as your superior doth; that is, finding my heart upright, you will bear with my other imperfections. And lastly, your Majesty shall have the best of my time, which, I assure myself, I shall conclude in your favour, and survive in your remembrance. And that is my prayer for myself. The rest shall be in prayers for your Majesty

S

To

To the LORD CHANCELLOR (*).

My noble Lord,

I HAVE shewed your letter of thanks to his Majesty, who saith there are too many thanks in it for so small a favour; which he holdeth too little to encourage so well a deserving servant. For myself, I shall ever rejoice at the manifestation of his Majesty's favour toward you, and will contribute all that is in me, to the increasing of his good opinion; ever resting

Your Lordship's faithful friend and servant,

G. BUCKINGHAM.

Speech of the Lord Viscount ST. ALBAN, *Lord Chancellor, to the parliament,* January 30, 1620.

My Lords and Masters,

YOU have heard the King's speech; and it makes me call to mind what Solomon saith, who was also a King: *The words of the wise are as nails and pins, driven in and fastened by the masters of assemblies.* The King is the master of this assembly; and though his words, in regard of the sweetness of them, do not prick; yet, in regard of the weight and wisdom of them, I know they pierce through and through; that is, both into your memories, and into your affections; and there I leave them.

As the King himself hath declared unto you the causes of the convoking of this parliament; so he hath commanded me to set before you the true insti-

tution

tution and use of a parliament, that thereby you may take your aim, and govern yourselves the better in parliament matters : for then are all things in best state, when they are preserved in their primitive institution ; for otherwise, ye know the principle of philosophy to be, that the corruption or degeneration of the best things is the worst.

The Kings of this realm have used to summon their parliaments or estates for three ends or purposes ; for advice, for assent, and for aid.

For advice, it is no doubt great surety for Kings to take advice and information from their parliament. It is advice, that proceedeth out of experience : it is not speculative or abstract. It is a well-tried advice, and that passeth many revenues, and hath Argus's eyes. It is an advice, that commonly is free from private and particular ends, which is the bane of counsel. For although some particular members of parliament may have their private ends ; yet one man sets another upright ; so that the resultate of their counsels is, for the most part, direct and sincere. But this advice is to be given with distinction of the subjects : they are to tender and offer their advice by bill or petition, as the case requires. But in those things, that are *Arcana Imperii*, and reserved points of sovereignty, as making of war or peace, or the like, there they are to apply their advice to that, which shall be communicated unto them by the King, without pressing farther within the vail, or reaching forth to the forbidden fruit of knowledge. In these things the rule holds, *tantum permissum quantum commissum.*

To the Marquis of BUCKINGHAM.

My very good Lord,

WITH due thanks for your laſt viſit, this day is a play-day for me. But I will wait on your Lordſhip, if it be neceſſary.

I do hear from divers of judgement, that to-morrow's conference *(k)* is like to paſs in a calm, as to the referrees *(l)*. Sir Lionel Cranfield, who hath been formerly the trumpet, ſaid yeſterday, that he did now incline to, Sir John Walter's opinion and motion, not to have the referrees meddled with otherwiſe, than to diſcount it from the King; and ſo not to look back, but to the future. And I do hear almoſt all men of judgement in the Houſe wiſh now that way. I woo no body : I do but liſten, and I have doubt only of Sir Fdward Coke, who, I wiſh, had ſome round *caveat* given him from the King; for your Lordſhip hath no great power with him : but I think a word from the King mates him.

If things be carried fair by the committees of the Lower Houſe, I am in ſome doubt, whether there will be occaſion for your Lordſhip to ſpeak to-mor-row; though, I confeſs, I incline to wiſh you did, chiefly becauſe you are fortunate in that kind; and, to be plain alſo, for our better countenance, when your Lordſhip, according to your noble propoſition,

(k) On Monday the 5th of March, 162⁰⁄₁, the Houſe of Lords received a meſſage from the Commons, deſiring a conference touching certain grievances, principally concerning Sir Giles Mompeſſon. See Journal of the Houſe of Lords.

(l) thoſe, to whom the King referred the petitions, to con-ſider, whether they were fit to be granted or no. This explana-tion of the word *referrees* I owe to a note in a MS. letter, written to the celebrated Mr. Joſeph Mead of Chriſt's College, Cam-bridge.

ſhall

fhall fhew more regard of the fraternity you have with great counfellors, than of the intereft of your natural brother.

Always, good my Lord, let us think of times out of parliament, as well as the prefent time in parliament, and let us not all be put *es pourpoint.* Fair and moderate courfes are ever beft in caufes of eftate; the rather, becaufe I wifh this parliament, by the fweet and united paffages thereof, may increafe the King's reputation with foreigners, who may make a far other judgement than we mean, of a beginning to queftion great counfellors and officers of the crown, by courts, or affemblies of eftates. But the reflection upon my particular in this makes me more fparing, than perhaps, as a counfellor, I ought to be.

God ever preferve and profper you.

Your Lordfhip's true fervant all and ever,

March 7, the day I re-
ceived the feal, 1620.   FR. ST. ALBAN, *Canc.*

To the KING (*m*).

It may pleafe your Majefty,

I RECEIVED your Majefty's letter about midnight: and becaufe it was ftronger than the ancient fummons of the Exchequer, which is, *ficut teipfum*

(*m*) The date of this letter is determined to be the 8th of March, 162⁹⁄₇, from the circumftance of its being mentioned to have been written on that Thurfday, on which the Houfe of Lords adjourned to the Saturday following. It appears from the Journal of that Houfe, that on the 8th of March, 1620, the faid Houfe, at which were prefent the Prince of Wales and Marquis of Buckingham, was adjourned to Saturday the 10th, on which day a conference of both Houfes was held relating to the complaint of that of the Commons againft Sir Giles Mompeffon. Of this conference the Lord Chancellor made report on Monday, March 12,

teipfum et omnia tua diligis; whereas this was *ficut me diligis*; I ufed all poffible care to effect your Majefty's good will and pleafure.

I fent early to the Prince, and to my Lord Treafurer; and we attended his Highnefs, foon after feven of the clock, at Whitehall, to avoid farther note. We agreed, that, if the meffage came, we would put the Lords into this way, that the anfwer fhould be, that we underftood they came, prepared both with examination and precedent; and we likewife defired to be alike prepared, that the conference might be with more fruit.

I did farther fpeak with my Lord of Canterbury, when I came to the Houfe, not letting him know any part of the bufinefs, that he would go on with a motion, which he had told me of the day before, that the Lords Houfe might not fit Wednefday and Friday, becaufe they were convocation-days; and fo was the former cuftom of parliament.

As good luck was, the Houfe read two bills, and had no other bufinefs at all: whereupon my Lord of Canterbury made his motion; and I adjourned the Houfe till Saturday. It was no fooner done, but came the meffage from the Lower Houfe. But the *confummatum eft* was paft, though I perceived a great willingnefs, in many of the Lords, to have recalled it, if it might have been.

to the Houfe of Lords, remarking, that " the inducement to this " conference was to clear the King's honour, touching grants " to Sir Giles, and the paffages in procuring the fame." After this report of the conference, the Lord Chamberlain, William Earl of Pembroke, complained to the Houfe, that *two great Lords*, meaning the Lord Chancellor and the Lord Treafurer, the Lord Vifcount Mandeville, had, in that conference, *fpake in their own defence, not being allowed to do fo when the committees were named.* Upon which both the Lords acknowledged their error, and begged pardon of the Houfe.

So

So with my best prayers for your Majesty's preservation, I rest

Your Majesty's most bounden

and most devoted servant,

Thursday, at eleven of our forenoon [March 8, 1620.]

FR. ST. ALBAN, *Canc.*

To the Marquis of B U C K I N G H A M (*o*).

My very good Lord,

YOUR Lordship spoke of purgatory. I am now in it; but my mind is in a calm; for my fortune is not my felicity. I know I have clean hands, and a clean heart; and, I hope, a clean house for friends or servants. But Job himself, or whosoever was the justest judge, by such hunting for matters against him, as hath been used against me, may for a time seem foul, especially in a time, when greatness is the mark, and accusation is the game. And if this be to be a Chancellor, I think, if the great seal lay upon Hounslow Heath, no body would take it up. But the King and your Lordship will, I hope, put an end to these my straits one way or other. And in troth that, which I fear most, is, left continual attendance and business, together with these cares, and want of time to do my weak body right this spring by diet and physic, will cast me down; and that it will be thought feigning, or fainting. But I hope in God I shall hold out. God prosper you.

(*o*) This letter seems to have been written soon after Lord St. Alban began to be accused of abuses in his office of Chancellor.

S 4

To

To the Chancellor of the Duchy, Sir HUMPHREY
MAY.

Good Mr. Chancellor,

THERE will come, upon Friday, before you a
patent *(p)* of his Majesty's for the separation
of the company of apothecaries from the company
of grocers, and their survey, and the erecting them
into a corporation of themselves under the survey of
the physicians. It is, as I conceive, a fair business
both for law and conveniency, and a work, which
the King made his own, and did, and, as I hear, doth
take much to heart. It is *in favorem vitæ*, where
the other part is *in favorem lucri*. You may perhaps
think me partial to apothecaries, that have been ever
puddering in physic all my life. But there is a
circumstance, that touches upon me but *post diem*,
for it is comprehended in the charge and sentence
passed upon me. It is true, that after I had put the seal
to the patent, the apothecaries *(q)* presented me with

(p) The patent for incorporating the apothecaries by themselves, by the appellation of *The Masters, Wardens, and Society of
the Art and Mystery of Apothecaries of London,* was dated December
6, 1617. They had been incorporated with the company of
grocers, April 9, 1606.

(q) His Lordship being charged by the House of Commons,
that he had received 100 l. of the *new company of apothecaries,
that stood against the grocers,* as likewise a taster of gold worth between 400 and 500 l. with a present of ambergrise, from *the
apothecaries that stood with the grocers,* and 200 l. of the grocers ;
he admits the several sums to have been received of the three
parties, but alledges, " that he considered those presents as no
" judicial business, but a concord of composition between the
" parties : and as he thought they had all three received good,
" and they were all common purses, he thought it the less matter
" to receive what they voluntarily presented ; for if he had taken
" it in the nature of a bribe, he knew it could not be concealed,
" because it must be put to the account of the three several
" companies."

an

an hundred pounds. It was no judicial affair. But howfoever, as it may not be defended, fo I would be glad it were not raked up more than needs. I doubt only the chair (r), becaufe I hear he ufeth names fharply ; and befides, it may be, he hath a tooth at me yet, which is not fallen out with age. But the beft is, as one faith, *fatis eft lapfos non erigere ; urgere verò jacentes, aut præcipitantes impellere, certè eft inhumanum.* Mr. Chancellor, if you will be nobly pleafed to grace me upon this occafion, by fhewing tendernefs of my name, and commiferation of my fortune, there is no man in that affembly, from whofe mouth I had rather it fhould come. I hope it will be no difhonour to you. It will oblige me much, and be a worthy fruit of our laft reintegration of friendfhip. I reft

Your faithful friend to do you fervice.

Memoranda of what the LORD CHANCELLOR *intended to deliver to the* KING, *April* 16, 1621 (s), *upon his firft accefs to his Majefty after his troubles.*

THAT howfoever it goeth with me, I think myfelf infinitely bound to his Majefty for admitting me to touch the hem of his garment ; and that, according to my faith, fo be it unto me.

The

(r) Sir Robert Philips was Chairman of the Committee of the Houfe of Commons for inquiring into the abufes of the courts of juftice. He was fon of Sir Edward Philips, Mafter of the Rolls, who died September 11, 1614, being fucceeded by Sir Julius Cæfar, to whom the King had given, January 16, 161⁴⁄₇, under the great feal, the reverfion of that poft.

(s) A committee of the Houfe of Commons had been appointed about the 12th of March, 162⁹⁄₀, to infpect the abufes of the courts of juftice, of which Sir Edward Sackville was named the Chairman, but by reafon of fome indifpofition, Sir Robert Philips

That I ought also humbly to thank his Majesty for that, in that excellent speech of his, which is printed, that

lips was chosen in his room. The first thing they fell upon was bribery and corruption, of which the Lord Chancellor was accused by Mr. Christopher Aubrey and Mr. Edward Egerton, who affirmed, that they had procured money to be given to his Lordship to promote their causes depending before him. This charge being corroborated by some circumstances, a report of it was made from the committee to the House, on Thursday the 15th of March; and a second, on the 17th, of other matters of the same nature charged upon his Lordship. The heads of the accusation having been drawn up, were presented by the Commons to the Lords, in a conference on Monday the 19th of the same month. The subject of this conference being reported, the next day, to the House of Lords by the Lord Treasurer, the Marquis of Buckingham presented to their Lordships a letter to them from the Lord Chancellor, dated that day. Upon this letter, answer was sent from the Lords to the Lord Chancellor, on the 20th, that they had received his letter, and intended to proceed in his cause, now before them, according to the rule of justice, desiring his Lordship to provide for his just defence. The next day, March 21, the Commons sent to the Lords a farther charge against the Lord Chancellor; and their Lordships, in the mean time, examined the complaints against him, and witnesses in the House, and appointed a select committee of themselves to take examinations likewise. Towards the latter end of March, the session was discontinued for some time, in hopes, as it was imagined, of softening the Lord Chancellor's fall: but upon the re-assembling of the parliament, more complaints being daily represented, on Wednesday, April 24, the Prince signified unto the Lords, that his Lordship had sent a submission, dated the 22d. Which the Lords having considered, and heard the collection of corruptions charged on him, and the proofs read, they sent a copy of the same, without the proofs, to him by Baron Denham and Mr. Attorney General, with this message, that his Lordship's confession was not fully set down by him; and that they had therefore sent him the particular charge, and expected his answer to it with all convenient expedition. To which he answered, that he would return their Lordships an answer with speed. On the 25th of April, the Lords considered of his said answer, and sent a second message by the same persons, that having received a doubtful answer to their message, sent him the day before, they now sent to him again, to know directly and presently, whether his Lordship would make his confession, or stand upon his defence. His answer returned by the same messengers was, that

he

that fpeech of fo great maturity, wherein the elements are fo well mingled, by kindling affection, by wafhing away afperfion, by eftablifhing of opinion, and yet giving way to opinion, I do find fome paffages, which I do conftrue to my advantage.

And laftly, that I have heard from my friends, that notwithftanding thefe waves of information, his Majefty mentions my name with grace and favour.

In the next place, I am to make an oblation of myfelf into his Majefty's hands, that, as, I wrote to him, I am as *clay in his hands*, his Majefty may make a veffel of honour or difhonour of me, as I find favour in his eyes ; and that I fubmit myfelf wholly to his grace and mercy, and to be governed both in my caufe and fortunes by his direction, knowing, that his heart is infcrutable for good. Only I may exprefs myfelf thus far, that my defire is, that the thread, or line, or my life, may be no longer than the thread, or line, of my fervice : I mean, that I may be of ufe to your Majefty in one kind or other.

Now for any farther fpeech, I would humbly pray his Majefty, that whatfoever the law of nature fhall teach me to fpeak for my own prefervation, your Majefty will underftand it to be in fuch fort, as I do neverthelefs depend wholly upon your will and pleafure. And under this fubmiffion, if your Majefty

he would make no manner of defence, but meant to acknowledge corruption, and to make a particular confeffion to every point, and after that an humble fubmiffion ; but humbly craved liberty, that where the charge was more full than he finds the truth of the fact, he may make declaration of the truth in fuch particulars, the charge being brief, and containing not all circumftances. The Lords fent the fame meffengers, to let him know, that they granted him time to do this till the Monday following ; when he fent his confeffion, and fubmiffion ; which being avowed by him to feveral Lords, fent to him, the Lords refolved, on the 2d of May, to proceed to fentence him the next morning, and fummoned him to attend ; which he excufing, on account of being confined to his bed by ficknefs, they gave judgement accordingly, on the 3d of May, 1621.

will

will gracioufly give me the hearing, I will open my heart unto you, both touching my fault, and fortune.

For the former of thefe, I fhall deal ingenuoufly with your Majefty, without feeking fig-leaves, or fubterfuges.

There be three degrees, or cafes, as I conceive, of gifts and rewards given to a Judge.

The firft is of bargain, contract, or promife of re-ward, *pendente lite.* And this is properly called *ve-nalis fententia,* or *baratria,* or *corruptelæ munerum.* And of this, my heart tells me, I am innocent; that I had no bribe or reward in my eye or thought, when I pronounced any fentence or order.

The fecond is a neglect in the Judge to inform himfelf, whether the caufe be fully at an end, or no, what time he receives the gift; but takes it up-on the credit of the party, that all is done; or other-wife omits to inquire.

And the third is, when it is received *fine fraude,* after the caufe ended; which, it feems by the opinion of the civilians, is no offence. Look into the cafe of fimony, &c.

Draught of another paper to the fame purpofe.

THERE be three degrees, or cafes, of bribery, charged, or fuppofed, in a Judge:

The firft, of bargain, or contract, for reward to pervert juftice.

The fecond, where the Judge conceives the caufe to be at an end, by the information of the party, or otherwife, and ufeth not fuch diligence, as he ought, to inquire of it. And the third, when the caufe is really ended, and it is *fine fraude,* without relation to any precedent promife.

Now

Now if I might fee the particulars of my charge, I fhould deal plainly with your Majefty, in whether of thefe degrees every particular cafe falls.

But for the firft of them, I take myfelf to be as as innocent, as any born upon St. Innocents day, in my heart.

For the fecond, I doubt in fome particulars I may be faulty.

And for the laft, I conceived it to be no fault; but therein I defire to be better informed, that I may be twice penitent, once for the fact, and again for the error. For I had rather be a briber, than a defender of bribes.

I muft likewife confefs to your Majefty, that at New-year's tides, and likewife at my firft coming in (which was, as it were, my wedding) I did not fo precifely, as perhaps I ought, examine, whether thofe, that prefented me, had caufes before me, yea or no.

And this is fimply all, that I can fay for the prefent, concerning my charge, until I may receive it more particularly. And all this while, I do not fly to that, as to fay, that thefe things are *vitia temporis*, and not *vitia hominis*.

For my fortune, *fumma fummorum* with me is, that I may not be made altogether unprofitable to do your Majefty's fervice, or honour. If your Majefty continue me as I am, I hope I fhall be a new man, and fhall reform things out of feeling, more than another can do out of example. If I caft part of my burden, I fhall be more ftrong and *delivré* to bear the reft. And, to tell your Majefty what my thoughts run upon, I think of writing a ftory of England, and of recompiling of your laws into a better digeft.

But to conclude, I moft humbly pray your Majefty's directions and advice. For as your Majefty hath ufed to give me the attribute of care of your bufinefs; fo I muft now caft the care of myfelf upon God and you.

Notes

(*t*) *Notes upon* Michael de la Pole's *Case.*

10 *Rich. 2.* THE offences were of three natures: 1. Deceits to the King.

2. Misgovernance in point of estate, whereby the ordinances, made by ten Commissioners for reformation of the state, were frustrated, and the city of Ghent, in foreign parts, lost.

3. And his setting the seal to pardons for murders, and other enormous crimes.

The judgement was imprisonment, fine, and ransom, and restitution to the King, but no disablement, nor making him uncapable, no degrading in honour mentioned in the judgement: but contrary-wise, in the clause, that restitution should be made and levied out of his lands and goods, it is expresly said, that because his honour of Earl was not taken from him, therefore his 20 l. *per annum* creation money should not be meddled with.

Observations upon Thorpe's *Case.*

24 *Edw. 3.* His offence was taking of money from five several persons, that were felons, for staying their process of exigent; for that it made him a kind of accessary of felony, and touched upon matter capital.

The judgement was the judgement of felony: but the proceeding had many things strong and new; first, the proceeding was by commission of *oyer* and *terminer*, and by jury; and not by parliament.

The judgement is recited to be given in the King's high and sovereign power.

(*t*) This paper was probably drawn up on occasion of the proceedings and judgement passed upon the Lord Viscount St. Alban by the House of Lords, May 3, 1621.

It

It is recited likewife, that the King, when he made him Chief Juftice, and increafed his wages, did *ore tenus* fay to him, in the prefence of his council, that now, if he bribed, he would hang him : unto which penance (for fo the record called it) he fubmitted himfelf. So it was a judgement by a contract.

His oath likewife, which was devifed fome few years before, which is very ftrict in words, that he fhall take no reward, neither before nor after, is chiefly infifted upon. And that, which is more to be obferved, there is a precife provifo, that the judgement and proceeding fhall not be drawn into example againft any, and fpecially not againft any, who have not taken the like oath : which the Lord Chancellor, Lord Treafurer, Mafter of the Wards, &c. take not, but only the Judges of both Benches, and Baron of the Exchequer.

The King pardoned him prefently after, doubting, as it feems, that the judgement was erroneous both in matter and form of proceeding ; brought it before the Lords of Parliament, who affirmed the judgement, and gave authority to the King in the like cafes, for the time to come, to call to him what Lords it pleafed him, and to adjudge them.

Notes upon Sir J o h n L e e's *Cafe, Steward of the King's Houfhold,*

44. *Edw.* 3. His offences were great oppreffions in ufurpation of authority, in attacking and imprifoning in the Tower, and other prifons, numbers of the King's fubjects, for caufes no ways appertaining to his jurifdiction ; and for difcharginging an appellant of felony without warrant, and for deceit of the King, and extortions.

His judgement was only imprifonment in the Tower, until he had made a fine and ranfom at the King's will ; and no more.

Notes

Notes upon Lord LATIMER's Case.

50 *Edw.* 3. HIS offences were very high and heinous, drawing upon high treason: as the extortious taking of victuals in Bretagne to a great value, without paying any thing; and for ransoming divers parishes there to the sum of 83,000 l. contrary to the articles of truce proclaimed by the King; for suffering his Deputies and Lieutenants in Bretagne to exact, upon the towns and countries there, divers sums of money, to the sum of 150,000 crowns; for sharing with Richard Lyons, in his deceit of the King; for inlarging, by his own authority, divers felons; and divers other exorbitant offences.

Notwithstanding all this, his judgement was only to be committed to the Marshalsea, and to make fine and ransom at the King's will.

But after, at the suit of the Commons, in regard of those horrible and treasonable offences, he was displaced from his office, and disabled to be of the King's Council; but his honours not touched, and he was presently bailed by some of the Lords, and suffered to go at large.

JOHN *Lord* NEVILLE's *Case.*

50 *Edw.* 3. HIS offences were the not supplying the full number of the soldiers in Bretagne, according to the allowance of the King's pay. And the second was for buying certain debts, due from the King, to his own lucre, and giving the parties small recompence, and specially in a case of the Lady Ravensholme.

And it was prayed by the Commons, that he might be put out of office about the King: but there was no judgement given upon that prayer, but only of restitution to the Lady, and a general clause of being punished according to his demerits.

3

To

To the Count GONDOMAR, *Ambassador from the court of Spain.*

Illuftriffime Domine Legate,

AMOREM illuftriffimæ Dominationis tuæ erga me, ejufque et fervorem et candorem, tam in profperis rebus, quam in adverfis, æquabili tenore conftantem perfpexi. Quo nomine tibi meritas et debitas gratias ago. Me verò jam vocat et ætas, et fortuna, atque etiam genius meus, cui adhuc fatis morofè fatisfeci, ut excedens è theatro rerum civilium literis me dedam, et ipfos actores inftruam, et pofteritati ferviam. Id mihi fortaffe honori erit, et degam tanquam in atriis vitæ melioris.

Deus illuftriffimam Dominationem tuam incolumem fervet et profperam.

Servus tuus,

Junii 6, 1621.

FR. ST. ALBAN.

To Count GONDOMAR (*u*).

Illuftriffime et excellentiffime Domine,

PERSPEXI et agnofco providentiam divinam, quod in tantâ folitudine mihi tanquam cœlitus fufcitaverit talem amicum, qui tantis implicatus negotiis, et in tantis temporis anguftiis, curam mei habuerit, idque pro me effecerit, quod alii amici mei aut non aufi fint tentare, aut obtinere non potuèrint. Atque illuftriffimæ Dominationi tuæ reddent fructum

(*u*) In the *Letters, Memoirs, &c. of the Lord Chancellor Bacon*, publifhed by Mr. Stephens, in 1736, p. 517, is a Spanifh letter to him from Count Gondomar, dated at London, June 14, 1621.

T   proprium

proprium et perpetuum mores tui tam generosi, et
erga omnia officia humanitatis et honoris propensi;
neque erit fortasse inter opera tua hoc minimum,
quod me, qui et aliquis fui apud vivos, neque om-
nino intermoriar apud posteros, ope et gratiâ tuâ
erexeris, confirmaris. Ego quid possum? Ero tan-
dem tuus, si minus usufructu, at saltem affectu,
voto. Sub cineribus fortunæ vivi erunt semper ignes
amoris. Te igitur humillimè saluto, tibi valedico,
omnia prospera exopto, gratitudinem testor, obser-
vantiam polliceor.

*Illustrissimo et excellentissimo Do. Do. Didaco Sarmienta
de Acuña, Comiti de Gondomar, Legato Regis Hispa-
niarum extraordinario in Angliâ.*

To the Marquis of BUCKINGHAM (w).

My very good Lord,

I HUMBLY thank your Lordship for the grace
and favour, which you did both to the message
and messenger, in bringing Mr. Meautys to kiss his
Majesty's hands, and to receive his pleasure. My
riches in my adversity hath been, that I have had a
good master, a good friend, and a good servant.

Perceiving, by Mr. Meautys, his Majesty's inclination, it shall be, as it hath ever used to be to me,
instead of a direction; and therefore I purpose to go
forthwith to Gorhambury, humbly thanking his
Majesty nevertheless, that he was graciously pleased
to have acquainted my Lords with my desire, if it
had stood me so much upon. But his Majesty knoweth

(w) This letter is reprinted here, because it differs, in some
respects, from that published in *Letters, Memoirs, Parliamentary
Affairs, State Papers, &c.* by Robert Stephens, Esq; p. 151. Edit.
London, 1736, 4to.

best

best the times and seasons ; and to his grace I submit myself, desiring his Majesty and your Lordship to take my letters from the Tower as written *de profundis*, and those I continue to write to be *ex aquis salsis*.

[June 22, 1621.]

Indorsed,

To Lord Buckingham, upon bringing Mr. Meautys to kiss the King's hands.

To the Marquis of B U C K I N G H A M.

My very good Lord,

I HAVE written, as I thought it decent in me to do, to his Majesty the letter I send inclosed. I have great faith, that your Lordship, now nobly and like yourself, will effect with his Majesty. In this the King is of himself, and it hath no relation to parliament. I have written also, as your Lordship advised me, only touching that point of means. I have lived hitherto upon the scraps of my former fortunes ; and I shall not be able to hold out longer. Therefore I hope your Lordship will now, according to the loving promises and hopes given, settle my poor fortunes, or rather my being. I am much fallen in love with a private life ; but yet I shall so spend my time, as shall not decay my abilities for use.

God preserve and prosper your Lordship.

[Sept. 5, 1621.]

To the P R I N C E.

May it please your Highness,

I CANNOT too oft acknowledge your Highness's favour in my troubles ; but acknowledgement now is but begging of new favour.   Yet even that is

not

not inconvenient ; for thankſgiving and petition go well together, even to God himſelf. My humble ſuit to your Highneſs, that I may be thought on for means to ſubſiſt ; and to that purpoſe, that your Highneſs will join with my noble friend to the King. That done, I ſhall ever be ready, either at God's call, or his Majeſty's, and as happy, to my thinking, as a man can be, that muſt leave to ſerve ſuch a King.

God preſerve and proſper your Highneſs.

On the back of the draughts of the three preceding letters were written the following memoranda.

Biſhops Wincheſter (*x*), Durham (*y*), London (*z*). Lord Duke (*a*), Lord Hunſdon.

Lord Chamberlain (*b*), to thank him for his kind remembrance by you ; and though in this private fortune I ſhall have uſe of few friends, yet I cannot but acknowledge the moderation and affection his Lordſhip ſhewed in my buſineſs, and deſire, that of thoſe few his Lordſhip will ſtill be one for my comfort, in whatſoever may croſs his way, for the furtherance of my private life and fortune.

Mr. John Murray. If there be any thing, that may concern me, that is fit for him to ſpeak, and me to know, that I may receive it by you.

Mr. Maxwell. That I am ſorry, that ſo ſoon as I came to know him, and to be beholding to him, I wanted power to be of uſe to him.

Lord of Kelly ; and to acquaint him with that part touching the confinement.

(*x*) Dr. Andrews.   (*y*) Dr. Richard Neile.
(*z*) Dr. George Mountain.   (*a*) Lenox.
(*b*) William, Earl of Pembroke.

To the K I N G.

It may pleafe your Majefty,

NOW that your Majefty hath paffed the recreation of your progrefs, there is neverthelefs one
kind of recreation, which, I know, remaineth with
your Majefty all the year; which is to do good, and
to exercife your clemency and beneficence. I fhall
never meafure my poor fervice by the merit, which
perhaps is fmall, but by the acceptation, which hath
been always favourably great. I have ferved your
Majefty now feventeen years; and fince my firft fervice (which was in the commiffion of the union,) I received from your Majefty never chiding or rebuke,
but always fweetnefs and thanks. Neither was I,
in thefe feventeen years, ever chargeable to your
Majefty, but got my means in an honourable fweat
of my labour, fave that of late your Majefty was
gracioufly pleafed to beftow upon me the penfion of
twelve hundred pounds for a few years. For in that
other poor prop of my eftate, which is the farming
of the petty writs, I improved your Majefty's revenue
by four hundred pounds the year. And likewife,
when I received the feal, I left both the Attorney's
place, which was a gainful place, and the Clerkfhip
of the Star-Chamber, which was Queen Elizabeth's
favour, and was worth twelve hundred pounds by
the year, which would have been a good *commendam*.
The honours, which your Majefty hath done me,
have put me above the means to get my living; and
the mifery I am fallen into hath put me below the
means to fubfift as I am. I hope my courfes fhall
be fuch, for this little end of my thread, which remaineth, as your Majefty, in doing me good, may
do good to many, both that live now, and fhall be
born hereafter. I have been the keeper of your feal,

　　　　　　　and

and now am your beadſman. Let your own royal heart, and my noble friend, ſpeak the reſt.

God preſerve and proſper your Majeſty.

Your Majeſty's faithful

poor ſervant and beadſman,

September 5, 1621.

FR. ST. ALBAN.

Cardinal Wolſey ſaid, that if he had pleaſed God as he pleaſed the King, he had not been ruined. My conſcience ſaith no ſuch thing; for I know not but in ſerving you, I have ſerved God in one. But it may be, if I had pleaſed God, as I had pleaſed you, it would have been better with me.

To the KING.

It may pleaſe your moſt excellent Majeſty,

I DO very humbly thank your Majeſty for your gracious remiſſion of my fine. I can now, I thank God and you, die, and make a will.

I deſire to do, for the little time God ſhall ſend me life, like the merchants of London, which, when they give over trade, lay out their money upon land. So, being freed from civil buſineſs, I lay forth my poor talent upon thoſe things, which may be perpetual, ſtill having relation to do you honour with thoſe powers I have left.

I have therefore choſen to write the reign of King Henry the VIIth, who was in a ſort your forerunner, and whoſe ſpirit, as well as his blood, is doubled upon your Majeſty.

I durſt not have preſumed to intreat your Majeſty to look over the book, and correct it, or at leaſt to
ſignify

fignify what you would have amended. But fince you are pleafed to fend for the book, I will hope for it.

[(*c*) God knoweth, whether ever I fhall fee you again; but I will pray for you to the laft gafp, refting]

The fame, your true beadfman,

October 8, 1621.

F R. S T. A L B A N.

Grant of pardon to the Vifcount S T. A L B A N, *under the privy feal* (*d*).

A SPECIAL pardon granted unto Francis, Vifcount St. Alban, for all felonies done and committed againft the common laws and ftatutes of this realm; and for all offences of præmunire; and for all mifprifions, riots, &c. with a reftitution of all his lands and goods forfeited by reafon of any the premifes; except out of the fame pardon all treafons, murders, rapes, inceft; and except alfo all fines, imprifonments, penalties, and forfeitures adjudged againft the faid Vifcount St. Alban by a fentence lately made in the parliament. Tefte Rege apud Weftm. 17 die Octob. anno Regni fuo 19.

Per lettre de privato figillo.

Dr. W I L L I A M S, *Bifhop of Lincoln elect, and Lord Keeper of the Great Seal, to the Vifcount* S T. A L B A N.

My very good Lord,

H AVING perufed a privy feal, containing a pardon for your Lordfhip, and thought ferioufly thereupon, I find, that the paffing of the

(*c*) This paffage has a line drawn over it.
(*d*) Cotton Library, Titus Book VII.

T 4

fame

fame (the affembly in parliament fo near approach-
ing(*e*)) cannot but be much prejudicial to the fervice
of the King, to the honour of my Lord of Buckingham, to that commiferation, which otherwife would
be had of your Lordfhip's prefent eftate, and efpecially to my judgement and fidelity. I have ever
affectionately loved your Lordfhip's many and moft
excelling good parts and endowments; nor had ever
caufe to difaffect your Lordfhip's perfon. So as
no refpect in the world, befide the former con-
fiderations, could have drawn me to add the leaft
affliction, or difcontentment, unto your Lordfhip's
prefent fortune. May it therefore pleafe your Lordfhip to fufpend the paffing of this pardon, until the
next affembly be over and diffolved; and I will be
then as ready to feal it, as your Lordfhip to accept
of it; and, in the mean time, undertake, that the
King and my Lord Admiral fhall interpret this fhort
delay, as a fervice and refpect iffuing wholly from
your Lordfhip; and reft, in all other offices whatfoever,

Your Lordfhip's faithful fervant,

JO. LINCOLN, *elect. Cuftos Sigilli,*

Weftminfter-College,
October 18, 1621.

*To the Right Honourable his very good Lord, the Lord
Vifcount St. Alban.*

(*e*) It met November 24, 1621; and was diffolved, February
8, 162½.

To the LORD KEEPER.

My very good Lord,

I KNOW the reasons muſt appear to your Lord-ſhip many and weighty, which ſhould move you to ſtop the King's grace, or to diſſuade it ; and ſome-what the more in reſpeƈt of my perſon, being, I hope, no unfit ſubjeƈt for noble dealing. The meſſage I received by Mr. Meautys did import inconvenience, in the form of the pardon ; your Lordſhip's laſt letter, in the time : for, as for the matter, it lay ſo fair for his Majeſty's and my Lord of Buckingham's own knowledge, as I conceive your Lordſhip doth not aim at that. My affliƈtion hath made me under-ſtand myſelf better, and not worſe ; yet loving ad-vice, I know, helps well. Therefore I ſend Mr. Meautys to your Lordſhip, that I might reap ſo much your fruit of your Lordſhip's profeſſed good affeƈtion, as to know in ſome more particular faſhion, what it is that your Lordſhip doubteth, or diſ-liketh (*f*) ; that I may the better endeavour your ſa-tisfaƈtion, or acquieſcence, if there be cauſe. So I reſt

Your Lordſhip's to do you ſervice,

Oƈtober 18, 1621.

FR. ST. ALBAN.

(*f*) The Lord Keeper, in a letter to the Marquis of Bucking-ham, dated Oƈtober 27, 1621, printed in the *Cabala*, p. 60. Edit. London, 1654, gives his reaſons, why he heſitated to ſeal that pardon.

Petition

Petition of the Lord Viscount St. Alban, *intended for the House of Lords.*

My right honourable very good Lords,

IN all humbleness, acknowledging your Lordships justice, I do now in like manner crave and implore your grace and compassion. I am old, weak, ruined, in want, a very subject of pity. My only suit to your Lordships is to shew me your noble favour towards the release of my confinement (so every confinement is,) and to me, I protest, worse than the Tower (g). There I could have had company, physicians, conference with my creditors and friends about my debts, and the necessities of my estate, helps for my studies and the writings I have in hand. Here I live upon the sword-point of a sharp air, indangered, if I go abroad, dulled, if stay within, solitary and comfortless without company, banished from all opportunities to treat with any to do myself good, and to help out any wrecks; and that, which is one of my greatest griefs, my wife, that hath been no partaker of my offending, must be partaker of this misery of my restraint.

May it please your Lordships therefore, since there is a time for justice, and a time for misery, to think with compassion upon that, which I have already suffered, which is not little; and to recommend this my humble, and, as I hope, modest, suit to his most excellent Majesty, the fountain of grace, of whose mer-

---

(g) He had been committed to the Tower in May, 1621, and discharged after two days confinement there, according to Camden, *Annales Regis Jacobi I.* p. 71. There is a letter of his Lordship to the Marquis of Buckingham, dated from the Tower, May 31, 1621, desiring his Lordship to procure his discharge that day.

cy,

cy, for fo much as concerns himfelf merely, I have already tafted, and likewife of his favour of this very kind, by fome fmall temporary difpenfations.

Herein your Lordfhips fhall do a work of charity and nobility : you fhall do me good; you fhall do my creditors good; and, it may be, you fhall do pofterity good, if out of the carcafe of dead and rotten greatnefs (as out of Samfon's lion) there may be honey gathered for the ufe of future times.

God blefs your perfons and counfels.

Your Lordfhips fupplicant and fervant,

FR. ST. ALBAN.

Indorfed,
Copy of the petition intended for the Houfe of Parliament.

To JOHN *Lord* DIGBY (*b*).

My very good Lord,

RECEIVING, by Mr. Johnfon, your loving falutations, it made me call to mind many of your Lordfhip's tokens, yea and pledges, of good and hearty affection in both my fortunes ; for which I fhall be ever yours. I pray, my Lord, if occafion ferve, give me your good word to the King, for the releafe of my confinement, which is to me a very ftrait kind of imprifonment. I am no Jefuit, nor no leper; but one, that ferved his Majefty thefe fixteen years, even from the commiffion of the union, till this laft parliament, and ever had many thanks of his Majefty, and was never chidden. This his Ma-

(*b*) Created fo in November, 1618, and in September, 1622, Earl of Briftol.

jefty,

jefty, I know, will remember at one time or other; for I am his man ftill.

God keep your Lordfhip.

Your Lordfhip's moft affectionate
to do you fervice,

Gorhambury, this laft
of December, 1621.

FR. ST. ALBAN.

To the Lord Vifcount St. ALBAN (*).

My honourable Lord,

I HAVE received your Lordfhip's letter, and have been long thinking upon it, and the longer, the lefs able to make anfwer unto it. Therefore if your Lordfhip will be pleafed to fend any underftanding man unto me, to whom I may, in difcourfe, open myfelf, I will, by that means, fo difcover my heart with all freedom, which were too long to do by letter, efpecially in this time of parliament bufinefs, that your Lordfhip fhall receive fatisfaction. In the mean time, I reft

Your Lordfhip's faithful fervant,

Royfton, December
16 [1621].

G. BUCKINGHAM.

To the Marquis of BUCKINGHAM.

My very good Lord,

T HE reafon, why I was fo defirous to have had conference with your Lordfhip at London, was indeed to fave you the trouble of writing : I mean, the reafon in the fecond place; for the chief was to fee your Lordfhip. But fince you are pleafed to give me the liberty to fend to your Lordfhip one, to whom you will deliver your mind, I take that in fo good part, as I think

(*) Harl. MSS. Vol. 7000.

my-

myfelf tied the more to ufe that liberty modeftly. Wherefore, if your Lordfhip will vouchfafe to fend to me one of your own (except I might have leave to come to London,) either Mr. Packer, my ancient friend, or Mr. Aylefbury (*i*), of whofe good affection towards me I have heard report; to me it fhall be indifferent. But if your Lordfhip will have one of my nomination, if I might prefume fo far, I would name, before all others, my Lord of Falkland. But becaufe perhaps it may coft him a journey, which I may not in good manners defire, I have thought of Sir Edward Sackville, Sir Robert Manfell, my brother, Mr. Sollicitor General (*k*), (who, though he be almoft a ftranger to me, yet, as my cafe now is, I had rather employ a man of good nature than a friend,) and Sir Arthur Ingram, notwithftanding he be great with my Lord Treafurer. Of thefe, if your Lordfhip fhall be pleafed to prick one, I hope well I fhall intreat him to attend your Lordfhip, and to be forry never a whit of the employment. Your Lordfhip may take your own time to fignify your will, in regard of the prefent bufinefs of parliament. But my time was confined, by due refpect, to write a prefent anfwer to a letter, which I conftrued to be a kind letter, and fuch as giveth me yet hope to fhew myfelf to your Lordfhip

Your Lordfhip's moft obliged friend,

and faithful fervant,

Fr. St. Alban.

Indorfed,

To the Lord of Buckingham, in anfwer to his of the 16th of December.

(*i*) Thomas Aylefbury, Efq; Secretary to the Marquis of Buckingham as Lord High-Admiral. He was created a Baronet in 1627. Lord Chancellor Clarendon married his daughter Frances.

(*k*) Sir Robert Heath, made Sollicitor in January 14, 162⁹⁄₀.

A Me-

A Memorial of Conference, when the Lord Viscount St. Alban *expected the Marquis of* Buckingham.

My Lord Marquis,

Inducement.] AFFLICTIONS are truly called trials; trials of a man's self, and trials of friends. For the first, I am not guilty to myself of any unworthiness, except perhaps too much softness in the beginning of my troubles. But since, I praise God, I have not lived like a drone, nor like a mal-content, nor like a man confused. But though the world hath taken her talent from me, yet God's talent I put to use.

For trial of friends, he cannot have many friends, that hath chosen to rely upon one. So that is in a small room, ending in yourself. My suit therefore to you is, that you would now, upon this vouch-safed conference, open yourself to me, whether I stand in your favour and affection, as I have done; and if there be an alteration, what is the cause; and, if none, what effects I may expect for the future of your friendship and favour, my state being not unknown to you.

Reasons of doubting.] The reasons, why I should doubt of your Lordship's coolness towards me, or falling from me, are either out of judgement and discourse, or out of experience, and somewhat that I find. My judgement telleth, that when a man is out of sight and out of use, it is a nobleness somewhat above this age to continue a constant friend: that some, that are thought to have your ear, or more, love me not, and may either disvalue me, or distaste your Lordship with me. Besides, your Lordship hath now so many, either new-purchased friends, or reconciled enemies, as there is scarce room for an old friend specially set

3   aside.

aſide. And laſtly, I may doubt, that that, for which I was fitteſt, ⬤ſich was to carry things *ſuavibus modis*, and not to briſtle, or undertake, or give venturous counſels, is out of faſhion and requeſt.

As for that, I find your Lordſhip knoweth, as well as I, what promiſes you made me, and iterated them back by meſſage, and from your mouth, conſiſting of three things : the pardon of the whole ſentence ; ſome help for my debts ; and an annual penſion, which your Lordſhip did ſet at 2000 l. as obtained, and 3000 l. in hope. Of theſe, being promiſes undeſired, as well as favours undeſerved, there is effected only the remiſſion of the fine, and the pardon now ſtayed. From me I know there hath proceeded nothing, that may cauſe the change. Theſe I lay before you, deſiring to know, what I may hope for ; for hopes are racks, and your Lordſhip, that would not condemn me to the Tower, I know will not condemn me to the rack.

The pardon ſtayed.] I have, though it be a thing trivial, and that at a coronation one might have it for five marks, and after a parliament for nothing, yet have great reaſon to deſire it, ſpecially being now ſtirred : chiefly, firſt, becauſe I have been ſo ſifted ; and now it is time there were an end. Secondly, becauſe I mean to live a retired life ; and ſo cannot be at hand to ſhake off any clamour.

For any offence the parliament ſhould take, it is rather honour, that in a thing, wherein the King is abſolute, yet he will not interpoſe in that, which the parliament hath handled ; and the King hath already reſtored judicature, after a long intermiſſion : but for matter of his grace, his Majeſty ſhall have reaſon to keep it intire.

I do not think any, except a Turk or Tartar, would wiſh to have another chop out of me. But the beſt is, it will be found there is a time for envy, and a time for pity ; and cold fragments will not

ſerve,

ferve, if the ftomach be on edge. For me, if they judge by that, which is paſt, they judge of the weather of this year by an almanack of the old year ; they rather repent of that they have done, and think they have but ferved the turns of a few.

Thomas Meautys, *Efq; (m)* to the Lord Vifcount St. Alban.

May it pleafe your Lordſhip,

A S foon as I came to London, I repaired to Sir Edward Sackville (*n*), whom I find very zealous, as I told your Lordſhip. I left him to do you ſervice, in any particular you ſhall command him, to my Lord Marquis (though it were with ſome adventure ;) and withall he imparted to me what advice he had given to my Lady this afternoon, upon his viſiting of her at York-houfe, when Mr. Packer alſo, as it fell out, was come, at the ſame time, to ſee my Lady, and ſeemed to concur with Sir Edward Sackville in the ſame ways ; which were, for my Lady to become a ſuitor to my Lady Buckingham (*o*), and my Lady Marchioneſs *(p)*, to work my Lord Marquis

(*m*) He had been Secretary to the Lord Viſcount St. Alban, while his Lordſhip had the great ſeal, and was afterwards Clerk of the Council, and knighted. He ſucceeded his patron in the manor of Gorhambury, which, after the death of Sir Thomas, came to his couſin and heir, Sir Thomas Meautys, who married Anne, daughter of Sir Nathaniel Bacon of Culford-Hall in Suffolk, Knight ; which Lady married a ſecond huſband, Sir Harbottle Grimſtone, Baronet, and Maſter of the Rolls ; who purchaſed the reverſion of Gorhambury from Sir Hercules Meautys, nephew of the ſecond Sir Thomas.

(*n*) afterwards Earl of Dorſet, well known for his duel, in 1613, with the Lord Kinlofs, in which the latter was killed.

(*o*) Mary, Counteſs of Buckingham, mother of the Marquis.

(p) Catharine, Marchioneſs of Buckingham, wife of the Marquis, and only daughter and heir of Francis, Earl of Rutland.

for obtaining of the King some bounty towards your Lordship; and in particular, that of the thousand pounds for the small writs. If I may speak my opinion to your Lordship, it is not amiss to begin any way, or with any particular, though but small game at first, only to set a rusty clock a-going, and then haply it may go right for a time, enough to bring on the rest of your Lordship's requests. Yet because your Lordship directed me to wish my Lady, from you, by no means, to act any thing, but only to open her mind, in discourse, unto friends, until she should receive your farther direction; it became not me to be too forward in putting it on too fast with Sir Edward; and my Lady was pleased to tell me since, that she hath written to your Lordship at large.

I inquired, even now, of Benbow, whether the proclamation for dissolving the parliament were coming forth. He tells me, he knows no more certainty of it, than that Mr. Secretary commanded him yesterday to be ready for dispatching of the writs, when he should be called for: but since then, he hears it sticks, and endures some qualms; but they speak it still aloud at court, that the King is resolved of it.

Benbow tells me likewise, that he hath attended, these two days, upon a committee of the Lords, with the book of the commission of peace; and that their work is to empty the commission in some counties by the score, and many of them parliament-men: which course sure helps to ring the passing-bell to the parliament.

Mr. Borough (q) tells me, he is at this present fain

(q) John Borough, educated in common law at Gray's Inn, Keeper of the Records in the Tower of London, Secretary to the Earl Marshal, in 1623 made Norroy; in July the year following knighted, and on the 23d of December, the same year, made Garter King at Arms in the place of Sir William Segar. He died October 21, 1643.

U   to to attend some service for the King ; but about Saturday he hopes to be at liberty to wait upon your Lordship. I humbly rest

Your Lordship's for ever to honour and serve,

January 3, 1621. T. MEAUTYS.

To the Right Honourable my most honoured Lord, the Lord Viscount St. Alban.

To the Lord Viscount St. Alban.

May it please your Lordship,

THIS afternoon my Lady found access to my Lord Marquis, procured for her by my Lord of Montgomery (r), and Sir Edward Sackville, who seemed to contend, which of them should shew most patience in waiting (which they did a whole afternoon) the opportunity to bring my Lord to his chamber, where my Lady attended him. But when he was come, she found time enough to speak at large : and though my Lord spake so loud, as that what passed was no secret to me and some others, that were within hearing ; yet, because my Lady told me she purposeth to write to your Lordship the whole passage, it becomes not me to anticipate, by these, any part of her Ladyship's relation.

I send your Lordship herewith the proclamation for dissolving the parliament ; wherein there is nothing forgotten, that we (s) have done amiss : but for most of those things, that we have well done, we must be fain, I see, to commend ourselves,

(r) Philip, afterwards Earl of Pembroke.
(s) Mr. Meautys was Member, in this Parliament, for the town of Cambridge.

I de-

I delivered your Lordſhip's to my Lord of Mont-gomery, and Mr. Matthew, who was even then come to York-houſe to viſit my Lady, when I received the letter ; and, as ſoon as he had read it, he ſaid, that he had rather your Lordſhip had ſent him a challenge ; and that it had been eaſier to anſwer, than ſo noble and kind a letter. He intends to ſee your Lordſhip ſome time this week ; and ſo doth Sir Edward Sackville, who is forward to make my Lady a way by the Prince, if your Lordſhip adviſe it.

There are packets newly come out of Spain : and the King, they ſay, ſeems well pleaſed with the contents ; wherein there is an abſolute promiſe, and undertaking, for reſtitution of the Palatinate ; the diſpenſation returned already from the Pope, and the match haſtened on their parts. My Lord Digby goes ſhortly ; and Mr. Matthew tells me, he means, before his going, to write by him to your Lordſhip.

The King goes not till Wedneſday, and the Prince certainly goes with him. My Lord Marquis, in perſon, chriſtens my Lord of Falkland's child to-morrow, at his houſe by Watford.

Mr. Murray (*t*) tells me, the King hath given your book (*u*) to my Lord Brooke (*w*), and injoined him to read it, recommending it much to him : and then my Lord Brooke is to return it to your Lordſhip ; and ſo it may go to the preſs, when your Lordſhip pleaſes, with ſuch amendments, as the King hath made, which I have ſeen, and are very few, and thoſe rather words, as *epidemic*, and *mild* inſtead of *debonnaire*, &c. Only that of perſons attainted, enabled to ſerve in parliament by a bare reverſal of their attainder, the King by all

(*t*) Thomas Murray, Tutor and Secretary to the Prince, made Provoſt of Eton-College, in the room of Sir Henry Savile, who died February 19, 162½. Mr. Murray died likewiſe, April 1, 1623.
(*u*) *The Hiſtory of the Reign of King Henry the Seventh.*
(*w*) Fulk Grevile.

means

means will have left out. I met with my Lord Brooke, and told him, that Mr. Murray had directed me to wait upon him for the book, when he had done with it. He desired to be spared this week, as being to him a week of much business; and the next week I should have it: and he ended in a compliment, that care should be taken, by all means, for good ink and paper to print it in; for that the book deserveth it.

I beg leave to kiss your Lordship's hands.

Your Lordship's in all humbleness

to honour and serve,

January 7, 1624.

T. MEAUTYS.

This proclamation is not yet sealed; and therefore your Lordship may please, as yet, to keep it in your own hands.

To the Lord Viscount ST. ALBAN.

My most honoured Lord,

I MET, even now, with a piece of news so unexpected, and yet so certainly true, as that, howsoever I had much ado, at first, to desire the relater to speak probably; yet now I dare send it your Lordship upon my credit. It is my Lord of Somerset's and his Lady's coming out of the Tower, on Saturday last (x), fetched forth by my Lord of Falkland, and without the usual degrees of confinement, at first to some one place (y); but absolute and free,

(x) January 6, 1624. *Camdeni Annales Regis Jacobi I. p. 77.*
(y) Camden, *ubi supra,* says, "that the Earl was ordered to "confine himself to the Lord Viscount Wallingford's house, or "neighbourhood."

to

so go where they please. I know not how peradventure this might occasion you to cast your thoughts, touching yourself, into some new mould, though not in the main, yet in something on the bye.

I beg leave to kiss your Lordship's hands.

Your Lordship's, in all humbleness,

for ever to honour and serve you,

T. MEAUTYS.

LODOWIC STUART, *Duke of Lenox, to the Lord Viscount* ST. ALBAN.

My Lord,

IT is not unknown to your Lordship, that, in respect I am now a married man, I have more reason than before to think of providing me some house in London, whereof I am yet destitute; and for that purpose, I have resolved to intreat your Lordship, that I may deal with you for York-house; wherein I will not offer any conditions to your loss. And, in respect I have understood, that the consideration of your Lady's wanting a house hath bred some difficulty in your Lordship to part with it, I will for that make offer unto your Lordship, and your Lady, to use the house in Canon-Row, late the Earl of Hertford's, being a very commodious and capable house, wherein I and my wife have absolute power; and whereof your Lordship shall have as long time, as you can challenge or desire of York-house. In this I do freelier deal with your Lordship, in respect I know you are well assured of my well-wishes to you in general; and that in this particular, though I have not been without thoughts of this house before your Lordship had it; yet I was willing to give way to your Lord-

U 3

ship's

ship's more preffing ufe thereof then. And as I do not doubt of your Lordfhip's endeavour to gratify me in this ; fo I fhall efteem it as an extraordinary courtefy, which I will ftudy to requite by all means.

So, with my beft wifhes to your Lordfhip, I reft

Your Lordfhip's moft loving friend,

LENOX.

In refpect my Lord of Buckingham was once defirous to have had this houfe, I would not deal for it till now, that he is otherwife provided.

Whitehall, the 29th
of January, 1621.

*To the Right Honourable my very good Lord, my Lord
Vifcount St. Alban.*

Anfwer of the Lord Vifcount of ST. ALBAN.

My very good Lord,

I AM forry to deny your Grace any thing ; but in this you will pardon me. York-houfe is the houfe, wherein my father died, and wherein I firft breathed ; and there will I yield my laft breath, if fo pleafe God, and the King will give me leave ; though I be now by fortune (as the old proverb is) like a bear in a monk's hood. At leaft no money, no value, fhall make me part with it. Befides, as I never denied it to my Lord Marquis, fo yet the difficulty I made was fo like a denial, as I owe unto my great love and refpect to his Lordfhip a denial to all my other friends ; among whom, in a very near place next his Lordfhip, I ever accounted of your Grace. So, not doubting, that
you

you will continue me in your former love and good
affection, I reft

Your Grace's, to do you humble fervice

affectionate, &c.

To the Marquis of B U C K I N G H A M.

My very good Lord,

AS my hopes, fince my misfortunes, have proceeded of your Lordfhip's mere motion, without any petition of mine; fo I leave the times and
the ways to the fame good mind of yours. True it
is, a fmall matter for my debts would do me more
good now, than double a twelvemonth hence. I
have loft fix thousand pounds by year, befides caps
and courtefies. But now a very moderate proportion would fuffice; for I ftill bear a little of the mind
of a Commiffioner of the Treafury, not to be over-
chargeable to his Majefty; and two things I may
affure your Lordfhip of : the one, that I fhall lead
fuch a courfe of life, as whatfoever the King doth for
me, fhall rather fort to his Majefty's and your Lordfhip's honour, than to envy : the other, that whatfoever men talk, I can play the good hufband, and the
King's bounty fhall not be loft. If your Lordfhip
think good, the Prince fhould come in to help, I
know his Highnefs wifheth me well; if you will let
me know when, and how, he may be ufed. But the
King is the fountain, who, I know, is good.

God profper you.

Your Lordfhip's moft bounden and faithful,

Gorhambury, January
30, 1621.

Fr. St. Alban.

To

To the Marquis of BUCKINGHAM.

My very good Lord,

YOUR Lordſhip dealeth honourably with me in giving me notice, that your Lordſhip is provided of an houſe (z), whereby you diſcontinue the treaty your Lordſhip had with me for York-houſe, although I ſhall make no uſe of this notice, as to deal with any other. For I was ever reſolved your Lordſhip ſhould have had it, or no man. But your Lordſhip doth yet more nobly, in aſſuring me, you never meant it with any the leaſt inconvenience to myſelf. May it pleaſe your Lordſhip likewiſe to be aſſured from me, that I ever deſired you ſhould have it, and do ſtill continue of the ſame mind.

I humbly pray your Lordſhip, to move his Majeſty to take commiſeration of my long impriſonment. When I was in the Tower, I was nearer help of phyſic; I could parly with my creditors; I could deal with friends about my buſineſs; I could have helps at hand for my writings and ſtudies, wherein I ſpend my time; all which here fail me. Good my Lord, deliver me out of this; me, who am his Majeſty's devout beadſman, and

> Your Lordſhip's moſt obliged friend,
>
> and faithful ſervant,

Gorhambury, this
3d of Feb. 1621.   FR. ST. ALBAN.

(z) Mr. Chamberlain, in a MS. letter to Sir Dudley Carleton, dated at London, January 19, 162½, mentions, that the Marquis of Buckingham had contracted with the Lord and Lady Wallingford, for *their houſe near Whitehall,* for ſome money.

JOHN

JOHN SELDEN, *Esq; to the Lord Viscount* ST. ALBAN.

My most honoured Lord,

AT your last going to Gorhambury, you were pleased to have speech with me about some passages of parliament; touching which, I conceived, by your Lordship, that I should have had farther direction by a gentleman, to whom you committed some care and consideration of your Lordship's intentions therein. I can only give this account of it, that never was any man more willing or ready to do your Lordship service, than myself; and in that you then spake of, I had been most forward to have done whatsoever I had been, by farther direction, used in. But I understood, that your Lordship's pleasure that way was changed. Since, my Lord, I was advised with, touching the judgements given in the late parliament. For them (if it please your Lordship to hear my weak judgement expressed freely to you) I conceive thus. First, that admitting it were no session, but only a *convention*, as the proclamation calls it; yet the judgements given in the Upper House (if no other reason be against them) are good; for they are given by the Lords, or the Upper House, by virtue of that ordinary authority, which they have as the supreme court of judicature; which is easily to be conceived, without any relation to the matter of session, which consists only in the passing of acts, or not passing them, with the royal assent. And though no session of the three states together be without such acts so passed; yet every part of the parliament severally did its own acts legally enough to continue, as the acts of other courts of justice are done. And why should any doubts be, but that a judgement out of the King's Bench, or Exchequer-Chamber, reversed there,

3   had

had been good, although no seffion? For there was truly a Parliament, truly an Upper Houfe (which exercifed by itfelf this power of judicature) although no feffion. Yet withall, my Lord, I doubt, it will fall out, upon fuller confideration, to be thought a feffion alfo. Were it not for the proclamation, I fhould be clearly of that mind; neither doth the claufe, in the act of fubfidy, hinder it. For that only prevented the determination of the feffion at that inftant; but did not prevent the being of a feffion, whenfoever the parliament fhould be diffolved. But becaufe that point was refolved in the proclamation, and alfo in the commiffion of diffolution on the 8th of February, I will reft fatisfied.

But there are alfo examples of former times, that may direct us in that point of the judgement, in regard there is ftore of judgements of parliament, efpecially under Edward I. and Edward II. in fuch conventions, as never had, for aught appears, any act paffed in them.

Next, my Lord, I conceive thus; that by reafon there is no record of thofe judgements, it may be juftly thought, that they are of no force. For thus it ftands. The Lower Houfe exhibited the declarations in paper; and the Lords, receiving them, proceeded to judgement verbally; and the notes of their judgements are taken by the clerk, in the journal only; which, as I think, is no record of itfelf; neither was it ever ufed as one. Now the record, that in former times was of the judgements and proceedings there, was in this form. The accufation was exhibited in parchment; and being fo received, and indorfed, was the firft record; and that remained filed among the bills of parliament, it being of itfelf as the bills in the King's Bench. Then out of this there was a formal judgement, with the accufation entered into that roll, or fecond record, which the clerk tranfcribes by ancient ufe, and fends into the Chancery. But

But in this cafe there are none of thefe : neither doth any thing feem to help to make a record of it, than only this, that the clerk may enter it, now after the parliament ; which, I doubt, he cannot. Becaufe, although in other courts the clerks enter all, and make their records after the term ; yet in this parliamentary proceeding it falls out, that the court being diffolved, the clerk cannot be faid to have fuch a relation to the parliament, which is not then at all in being, as the prothonotaries of the courts in Weftminfter have to their courts, which ftand only adjourned. Befides, there cannot be an example found, by which it may appear, that ever any record of the firft kind (where the tranfcript is into the Chancery) was made in parliament ; but only fitting the Houfe, and in their view. But this I offer to your Lordfhip's farther confideration, defiring your favourable cenfure of my fancy herein ; which, with whatfoever ability I may pretend to, fhall ever be defirous to ferve you, to whom I fhall perpetually own myfelf

Your Lordfhip's moft humble fervant,

From the Temple,
　February xiv.　　　　　　J. S E L D E N.
　CIↃDCXXI.

My Lord,

I F your Lordfhip have done with that *Mafcardus de Interpretatione Statutorum* (a), I fhall be glad, that you would give order, that I might ufe it. And for that of 12 *Hen.* 7, touching the grand council in the manufcript, I have fince feen a privy feal of the time of Henry 7. (without a year) directed to borrow for the King ; and in it there is a recital of a grand coun-

---

(a) *Alderani Mafcardi communes conclufiones utriufque juris ad generalem ftatutorum interpretationem accommodatæ :* printed at Ferrara, in 1608.

cil,

cil, which thought, that such a sum was fit to be levied; whereof the Lords gave 40,000 l. and the rest was to be gotten by privy seal upon loan. Doubtless, my Lord, this interprets that of the manuscript story.

*On the back of this letter are the following notes by the
Lord Viscount St. Alban.*

" The case of the judgement in parliament, upon
" a writ of error put by Just. Hu. (*b*).
" The case of no judgement entered in the Court
" of Augmentations, or Survey of first Fruits; which
" are dissolved, where there may be an entry after,
" out of a paper-book.
" *Mem.* All the acts of my proceeding were after
" the royal assent to the subsidy."

To Mr. TOBIE MATTHEW (*c*).

Good Mr. Matthew,

IN this solitude of friends, which is the base court. (*d*) of adversity, where almost no body will be seen stirring, I have often remembered a saying of my Lord Ambassador of Spain (*e*), *Amor sin fin no tiene fin* (*f*). This moveth me to make choice of his excellent Lordship for his noble succours towards not the aspiring, but the respiring of my fortunes.

I, that am a man of books, have observed his Lordship to have the magnanimity of his own nation,

(*b*) Hutton.
(*c*) This, and the following letter of March 5. 1611, to the Marquis of Buckingham, are inserted from the originals, much more complete and exact, than the copies of them printed in his works.
(*d*) *basse cour.*
(*e*) Count Gondomar, who returned to Spain about March, 1621.
(*f*) *Love without ends hath no end.*

and

and the cordiality of ours ; and, by this time, I think he hath the wit of both. Sure I am, that for myself I have found him, in both my fortunes, to esteem me so much above value, and to love me so much above possibility of deserving, or obliging, on my part, as if he were a friend reserved for such a time as this. I have known his Lordship likewise (while I stood in a stand where I might look about) a most faithful and respective friend to my Lord Marquis ; who, next the King and the Prince, was my raiser, and must be (he or none,) I do not say my restorer, but my reliever.

I have, as I made you acquainted at your being with me, a purpose to present my Lord Marquis with an offer of my house and lands here at Gorhambury ; a thing, which, as it is the best means I have now left to demonstrate my affection to his Lordship, so I hope it will be acceptable to him. This proposition I desire to put into no other hand but my Lord Ambassador's, as judging his hand to be the safest, the most honourable, and the most effectual for my good, if my Lord will be pleased to deal in it. And when I had thus resolved, I never sought, nor thought of any mean but yourself, being so private, faithful, and discreet a friend to us both. I desire you therefore, good Mr. Matthew, to acquaint my Lord Ambassador with this overture ; and both to use yourself, and desire at his Lordship's hands secrefy therein ; and withall to let his Lordship know, that in this business, whatsoever in particular you shall treat with him, I shall not fail, in all points, to make good and perform.

Commend my humble service to his Lordship. I ever rest

      Your most affectionate and assured friend,

Gorhambury, Feb.
  28, 1621.   Fr. St. Alban.

                              To

To the Marquis of BUCKINGHAM.

My very good Lord,

THOUGH I have returned anfwer to your Lordfhip's laft letter by the fame way, by which I received it; yet I humbly pray your Lordfhip to give me leave to add thefe few lines.

My Lord, as God above is witnefs, that I ever have loved and honoured your Lordfhip, as much, I think, as any fon of Adam can love or honour any fubject, and continue in as hearty and ftrong wifhes of felicity to be heaped and fixed upon you, as ever; fo, as low as I am, I had rather fojourn in a college in Cambridge, than recover a good fortune by any other but yourfelf. Marry, to recover yourfelf to me, if I have you not, or to eafe your Lordfhip in any thing, wherein your Lordfhip would not fo fully appear, or to be made participant of your favours in your own way, I would ufe any man, that were your Lordfhip's friend: and therefore, good my Lord, in that let me not be miftaken. Secondly, if in any of my former letters I have given your Lordfhip any diftafte by the ftyle of them, or any particular paffages, I humbly pray your Lordfhip's benign conftruction and pardon. For, I confefs, it is my fault, though it be fome happinefs to me withall, that I do moft times forget my adverfity. But I fhall never forget to be

Your Lordfhip's moft obliged friend,

and faithful fervant,

March 5, 1621.

FR. ST. ALBAN.

Fragments

Fragments of several kinds.

MY meaning was, if my Lord fhould obtain for me, by his noble mediation, in confideration of my fervices paft, and other refpects, to do that, for my relief, which I was fuitor for by my Lord's noble mediation, and whereof I was in good hope, to have prefented my Lord with Gorhambury in poffeffion, out of gratitude and love, for nothing.

My meaning was, if my Lord fhould prevail for me in my fuit to the King for reward of fervices, and relief of my poor eftate, to have prefented him with Gorhambury, out of gratitude and love, for nothing, except fome fatisfaction to my wife, for her intereft.

If my Lord like better to proceed by way of bargain, fo I find that I may but fubfift, I will deferve of his honour, and exprefs my love in a friendly pennyworth.

The third point to be added :

This as his work.] The more for kiffing the King's hands prefently.

The reafons, ftalling my debts.

Willingnefs in my friends to help me.

None will be fo bold as to opprefs me.

The pretence, that the King would give me direction, in what nature of writings to expend my time.

The letter to expect yet, and the manner of the delivery.

That my Lord do not impute it, if he hear I deal with others ; for he fhall better perceive the value, and I fhall make it good to his Lordfhip, being my ftate requireth fpeed.

To the Lord Viscount ST. ALBAN.

May it please your Lordship,

REMEMBRING, that the letter your Lordship put yesterday into my hand was locked up under two or three seals, it ran in my head, that it might be business of importance, and require haste : and not finding Mr. Matthew in town, nor any certainty of his return till Monday or Tuesday, I thought it became me to let your Lordship know it, that so I might receive your Lordship's pleasure (if need were) to send it by as safe a hand, as if it had three seals more.

My Lord, I saw Sir Arthur Ingram, who let fall somewhat, as if he could have been contented to have received a letter by me from your Lordship, with something in it like an acknowledgement to my Lord Treasurer (g), that by his means you had received a kind letter from my Lord Marquis. But, in the close, he came about, and fell rather to excuse what was left out of the letter, than to please himself much with what was within it. Only indeed he looked upon me, as if he did a little distrust my good meaning in it. But that is all one to me ; for I have been used to it, of late, from others, as well as from him. But persons apt to be suspicious may well be borne with ; for certainly they trouble themselves most, and lose most by it. For of such it is a hard question, whether those be fewest, whom they trust, or those, who trust them. But for him, and some others, I will end in a wish, that, as to your Lordship's service, they might prove but half so much honester, as they think themselves wiser, than other men.

(g) Lionel, Lord Cranfield, made Lord Treasurer in October, 1621.

It

It is doubtful, whether the King will come to-morrow, or not; for they fay he is full of pain in his feet.

My Lord Marquis came late to town laft night, and goeth back this evening: and Sir Edward Sackville watcheth an opportunity to fpeak with him before he go. However, he wifheth, that your Lordfhip would lofe no time in returning an anfwer, made all of fweet-meats, to my Lord Marquis's letter, which, he is confident, will be both tafted and digefted by him. And Sir Edward wifheth, that the other letter to my Lord Marquis, for prefenting your difcourfe of laws to his Majefty, might follow the firft. I humbly reft

Your Lordfhip's for ever truly

to honour and ferve you,

Martii 3, 1621.

THO. MEAUTYS.

To the Lord Vifcount ST. ALBAN.

May it pleafe your Lordfhip,

I HAD not failed to appear this night, upon your Lordfhip's fummons, but that my ftay till to-morrow, I knew, would mend my welcome, by bringing Mr. Matthew, who means to dine with your Lordfhip only, and fo to rebound back to London, by reafon my Lord Digby's journey calls for him on the fudden. Neither yet was this all, that ftayed me; for I hear fomewhat, that I like reafonably well; and yet I hope it will mend too; which is, that my Lord Marquis hath fent you a meffage by my Lord of Falkland (which is a far better hand than my Lord Treafurer's,) that gives you leave to come prefently to Highgate: and Sir Edward Sackville, fpeaking for

X

the

the other five miles, my Lord commended his care and zeal for your Lordſhip, but ſilenced him thus: " Let my Lord be ruled by me: it will be never " the worſe for him." But my Lord Marquis ſaying farther to him, " Sir Edward, however you play " a good friend's part for my Lord St. Alban; yet " I muſt tell you, I have not been well uſed by him." And Sir Edward deſiring of him to open himſelf in whatſoever he might take offence at; and withall, taking upon him to have known ſo much, from time to time, of your Lordſhip's heart, and endeavours towards his Lordſhip, as that he doubted not but he was able to clear any miſt, that had been caſt before his Lordſhip's eyes by your enemies; my Lord Marquis, by this time being ready to go to the Spaniſh Ambaſſador's to dinner, broke off with Sir Edward, and told him, that after dinner he would be back at Wallingford-houſe, and then he would tell Sir Edward more of his mind; with whom I have had newly conference at large, and traced out to him, as he deſired me, ſome particulars of that, which they call a treaty with my Lord Treaſurer about York-houſe, which Sir Edward Sackville knows how to put together, and make a ſmooth tale of it for your Lordſhip; and this night I ſhall know all from him, and to-morrow, by dinner, I ſhall not fail to attend your Lordſhip: till when, and ever, I reſt

Your Lordſhip's in all truth
to honour and ſerve you,

T. MEAUTYS.

Indorſed, *Received March 11.*

T.

To HENRY CARY, *Lord Viscount* FALKLAND (*h*).

My very good Lord, .

YOUR Lordship's letter was the beft letter I received this good while, except the laft kind letter from my Lord of Buckingham, which this confirmeth. It is the beft accident, one of them, amongft men, when they hap to be obliged to thofe, whom naturally and perfonally they love, as I ever did your Lordfhip; in troth not many between my Lord Marquis and yourfelf; fo that the fparks of my affection fhall ever reft quick, under the afhes of my fortune, to do you fervice; and wifhing to your fortune and family all good.

Your Lordfhip's moft affectionate,

and much obliged, &c.

I pray your Lordfhip to prefent my humble fervice and thanks to my Lord Marquis, to whom, when I have a little paufed, I purpofe to write; as likewife to his Majefty, for whofe health and happinefs, as his true beadfman, I moft frequently pray.

Indorfed,
March 11. *Copy of my anfwer to Lord Falkland.*

(*h*) appointed Lord Deputy of Ireland, September 8, 1622.

To

To the LORD TREASURER (*i*).

My very good Lord,

I HAVE received, by my noble friend, my Lord Vifcount Falkland, advertifement, as from my Lord Marquis, of three things ; the one, that upon his Lordfhip's motion to his Majefty, he is gracioufly pleafed to grant fome degree of releafe of my confinement. The fecond, that if I fhall gratify your Lordfhip, who, my Lord underftandeth, are defirous to treat with me about my houfe at London, with the fame, his Lordfhip will take it as well, as if it was done to himfelf. The third, that his Majefty hath referred unto your Lordfhip the confideration of the relief of my poor eftate. I have it alfo from other part, yet by fuch, as have taken it immediately from my Lord Marquis, that your Lordfhip hath done me to the King very good offices. My Lord, I am much bounden to you : wherefore if you fhall be pleafed to fend Sir Arthur Ingram, who formerly moved me in it for your Lordfhip, to treat farther with me, I fhall let your Lordfhip fee how affectionately I am defirous to pleafure your Lordfhip after my Lord of Buckingham.

So wifhing your Lordfhip's weighty affairs, for his Majefty's fervice, a happy return to his Majefty's contentment, and your honour, I reft

Your Lordfhip's very affectionate

to do you fervice,

Fr. St. Alban.

Indorfed,
March 12. To the Lord Treafurer.

(i) Lionel, Lord Cranfield.

To

To the LORD TREASURER.

My very good Lord,

THE honourable correfpondence, which your Lordfhip hath been pleafed to hold with my noble and conftant friend, my Lord Marquis, in furthering his Majefty's grace towards me, as well concerning my liberty, as the confideration of my poor eftate, hath very much obliged me to your Lordfhip, the more by how much the lefs likelihood there is, that I fhall be able to merit it at your Lordfhip's hands. Yet thus much I am glad of, that this courfe, your Lordfhip holds with me, doth carry this much upon itfelf, that the world fhall fee in this, amongft other things, that you have a great and noble heart.

For the particular bufinefs of York-houfe, Sir Arthur Ingram can bear me witnefs, that I was ready to leave the conditions to your Lordfhip's own making: but fince he tells me plainly, that your Lordfhip will by no means have to be fo, you will give me leave to refer it to Sir Arthur Ingram, who is fo much your Lordfhip's fervant, and no lefs faithful friend to me, and underftands values well, to fet a price between us.

For the reference his Majefty hath been gracioufly pleafed, at my Lord Marquis's fuit, to make unto your Lordfhip, touching the relief of my poor eftate (*k*), which my Lord of Falkland's letter hath fignified, warranting me likewife to addrefs myfelf to your Lordfhip touching the fame; I humbly pray your Lordfhip to give it difpatch, my age, health,

(*k*) The Lord Vifcount St. Alban, in a letter to the King, from Gorhambury, 20th of March, 162½, thanks his Majefty for *referring the confideration of his broken eftate to his good Lord, the Lord Treafurer.*

and

and fortunes, making time to me therein precious. Wherefore, if your Lordship (who knoweth best what the King may best do) have thought of any particular, I would desire to know from your good Lordship : otherwise I have fallen myself upon a particular, which I have related to Sir Arthur, and, I hope, will seem modest, for my help to live and subsist. As for somewhat towards the paying off my debts, which are now my chief care, and without charge of the King's coffers, I will not now trouble your Lordship ; but purposing to be at Chiswick, where I have taken a house, within this sevennight, I hope to wait upon your Lordship, and to gather some violets in your garden, and will then impart unto you, if I have thought of any thing of that nature for my good.

So I ever rest &c.

THOMAS MEAUTYS, *Esq; to the Lord Viscount* ST. ALBAN.

May it please your Lordship,

I HAVE been attending upon my Lord Marquis's minutes for the signing of the warrant. This day he purposed in earnest to have done it ; but it falls out untowardly, for the warrant was drawn, as your Lordship remembers, in haste at Gorhambury, and in as much haste delivered to Sir Edward Sackville, as soon as I alighted from my horse, who instantly put it into my Lord Marquis's hands, so that no copy could possibly be taken of it by me. Now his Lordship hath searched much for it, and is yet at a loss, which I knew not till six this evening: and because your Lordship drew it with caution, I dare not venture it upon my memory to carry level what your Lordship wrote, and therefore dispatched away this messenger, that so your Lordship, by a fresh post,

(for

(for this will hardly do it) may fend a warrant to your mind, ready drawn, to be here to-morrow by feven a clock, as Sir Arthur (*l*) tells me my Lord Marquis hath directed: for the King goes early to Hampton-Court, and will be here on Saturday.

Your books (*m*) are ready, and paffing well bound up. If your Lordfhip's letters to the King, Prince, and my Lord Marquis were ready, I think it were good to lofe no time in their delivery; for the printer's fingers itch to be felling.

My Lady hath feen the houfe at Chifwick, and may make a fhift to like it: only fhe means to come to your Lordfhip thither, and not to go firft: and therefore your Lordfhip may pleafe to make the more hafte, for the great Lords long to be in York-houfe.

Mr. Johnfon will be with your Lordfhip to-morrow; and then I fhall write the reft.

Your Lordfhip's in all humblenefs

and honour to ferve you.

To THOMAS MEAUTYS, *Efq.*

Good Mr. Meautys,

FOR the difference of the warrant, it is not material at the firft. But I may not ftir till I have it; and therefore I expect it to-morrow.

For my Lord of London's (*n*) ftay, there may be an error in my book (*o*); but I am fure there is none in me, fince the King had it three months by him, and allowed it: if there be any thing to be mended, it is better to be efpied now than hereafter.

(*l*) Ingram.　　　(*m*) *Hiftory of the Reign of King Henry VII.*
(*n*) Dr. George Mountain.
(*o*) His *Hiftory of the Reign of King Henry VII.*

X 4

I fend

I fend you the copies of the three letters, which you have; and, in mine own opinion, this demur, as you term it, in my Lord of London, maketh it more neceffary than before, that they were delivered, fpecially in regard they contain withall my thanks. It may be fignified they were fent before I knew of any ftay; and being but in thofe three hands, they are private enough. But this I leave merely at your difcretion, refting

> Your moft affectionate and affured friend,

March 21, 1621.

> FR. ST. ALBAN.

To *Mr.* TOBIE MATTHEW.

Good Mr. Matthew,

I DO make account, God willing, to be at Chifwick on Saturday; or, becaufe this weather is terrible to one, that hath kept much in, Monday. In my letter of thanks to my Lord Marquis, which is not yet delivered, but to be forthwith delivered, I have not forgotten to mention, that I have received fignification of his noble favour and affection, amongft other ways, from yourfelf, by name. If, upon your repair to the court (whereof I am right glad,) you have any fpeech with the Marquis of me, I pray place the alphabet (as you can do it right well) in a frame, to exprefs my love faithful and ardent towards him. And for York-houfe, that whether in a ftrait line, or a compafs line, I meant it his Lordfhip in the way, which I thought might pleafe him beft. I ever reft

> Your moft affectionate and affured friend,

March 21, 1621.

> FR. ST. ALBAN.
>
> Though

Though your journey to court be before your receit of this letter, yet it may ferve for another time.

To the QUEEN of BOHEMIA.

It may pleafe your Majefty,

I FIND in books (and books I dare alledge to your Majefty, in regard of your fingular ability to read and judge of them even above your fex) that it is accounted a great blifs for a man to have leifure with honour. That was never my fortune, nor is. For time was, I had honour without leifure ; and now I have leifure without honour. And I cannot fay fo neither altogether, confidering there remain with me the marks and ftamp of the King's, your father's, grace, though I go not for fo much in value, as I have done. But my defire is now to have leifure without loitering, and not to become an abbey-lubber, as the old proverb was, but to yield fome fruit of my private life. Having therefore written the reign of your Majefty's famous anceftor, King Henry the Seventh ; and it having paffed the file of his Majefty's judgement, and been gracioufly alfo accepted of the Prince, your brother, to whom it is dedicated, I could not forget my duty fo far to your excellent Majefty (to whom, for that I know and have heard, I have been at all times fo much bound, as you are ever prefent with me, both in affection and admiration) as not to make unto you, in all humblenefs, a prefent thereof, as now being not able to give you tribute of any fervice. If King Henry the Seventh were alive again, I hope verily he could not be fo angry with me for not flattering him, as well-pleafed in feeing himfelf fo truly defcribed in colours, that will laft, and be believed. I moft humbly pray your Majefty gracioufly to accept of my good will ; and fo, with all reverence,

reverence, kiss your hands, praying to God above, by his divine and most benign providence, to conduct your affairs to happy issue ; and resting

Your Majesty's most humble

and devoted servant,

April 20, 1622.

FR. ST. ALBAN.

Sir EDWARD SACKVILLE *to the Lord Viscount* ST. ALBAN.

My very honoured Lord,

LONGING to yield an account of my stewardship, and that I had not buried your talent in the ground, I waited yesterday the Marquis's pleasure, untill I found a fit opportunity to importune some return of his Lordship's resolution. The morning could not afford it ; for time only allowed leave to tell him, I would say something. In the afternoon I had amends for all. In the forenoon he laid the law, but in the afternoon he preached the gospel ; when, after some revivations of the old distaste concerning York-house, he most nobly opened his heart unto me, wherein I read that, which argued much good towards you. After which revelation, the book was again sealed up, and must, in his own time, only by himself be again manifested unto you. I have leave to remember some of the vision, and am not forbidden to write it. He vowed, not court-like, but constantly, to appear your friend so much, as if his Majesty should abandon the care of you, you should share his fortune with him. He pleased to tell me, how much he had been beholden to you ; how well he loved you ; how unkindly he took the denial of your house (for so he will needs understand it.) But the close, for all this,

2

was

was harmonious, since he protested he would seriously begin to study your ends, now that the world should see he had no ends on you. He is in hand with the work, and therefore will, by no means, accept of your offer; though, I can assure you, the tender hath much won upon him, and mellowed his heart towards you; and your genius directed you right, when you wrote that letter of denial unto the Duke *(p)*. The King saw it; and all the rest; which made him say unto the Marquis, you played an after-game well; and that now he had no reason to be much offended.

I have already talked of the revelation, and now am to speak in apocalyptical language, which I hope you will rightly comment; whereof, if you make difficulty, the bearer *(q)* can help you with the key of the cypher.

My Lord Falkland, by this time, hath shewed you London from Highgate. If York-house were gone, the town were your's; and all your straitest shackles cleared off, besides more comfort than the city-air only. The Marquis would be exceedingly glad the Treasurer had it. This I know; but this you must not know from me. Bargain with him presently, upon as good conditions as you can procure, so you have direct motion from the Marquis to let him have it. Seem not to dive into the secret of it; though you are purblind, if you see not through it. I have told Mr. Meautys, how I would wish your Lordship to make an end of it. From him, I beseech you, take it, and from me only the advice to perform it. If you part not speedily with it, you may defer the good, which is approaching near you, and disappointing other aims (which must either shortly receive content, or never,) perhaps anew yield matter of discontent, though you may be indeed

(p) of Lenox, of the 30th of January, 162¾.
(q) Probably Mr. Meautys.

as innocent as before. Make the Treasurer believe, that since the Marquis will by no means accept of it, and that you must part with it, you are more willing to pleasure him, than any body else, because you are given to understand my Lord Marquis so inclines; which inclination, if the Treasurer shortly send unto you about it, desire may be more clearly manifested, than as yet it hath been; since, as I remember, none hitherto hath told you *in terminis terminantibus*, that the Marquis desires you should gratify the Treasurer. I know that way the hare runs; and that my Lord Marquis longs untill Cranfield hath it; and so I wish too, for your good, yet would not it were absolutely passed, untill my Lord Marquis did send, or write, unto you, to let him have it; for then, his so disposing of it were but the next degree removed from the immediate acceptance of it, and your Lordship freed from doing it otherwise than to please him, and to comply with his own will and way.

I have no more to say, but that I am, and ever will be

Your Lordship's most affectionate friend,

and humble servant,

E. SACKVILLE.

Indorsed, *Received the 11th of May, 1622.*

To the LORD KEEPER, *Dr.* WILLIAMS, *Bishop of Lincoln.*

My very good Lord,

I UNDERSTAND, there is an extent prayed against me, and a surety of mine, by the executors of one Harrys, a goldsmith. The statute is

twelve

twelve years old, and falleth to an executor, or an executor of an executor, I know not whether. And it was fure a ftatute collected out of a fhop-debt, and much of it paid. I humbly pray your Lordfhip, according to juftice and equity, to ftay the extent, being likewife upon a double penalty, till I may better inform myfelf touching a matter fo long paft; and, if it be requifite, put in a bill, that the truth of the account appearing, fuch fatisfaction may be made, as fhall be fit. So I reft

Your Lordfhip's affectionate

to do you faithful fervice,

May 30, 1622.

Fr. St. Alban.

To the Marquis of B u c k i n g h a m (*w*).

My very good Lord,

I THOUGHT it appertained to my duty, both as a fubject, and as he, that took once the oath of a Counfellor, to make known to your Lordfhip an advertifement, which came to me this morning. A gentleman, a dear friend of mine, whom your Lord-fhip cannot but imagine, though I name him not, told me thus much, that fome Englifh priefts, that negotiated at Rome to facilitate the difpenfation, did their own bufinefs (that was his phrafe;) for they negotiated with the Pope to erect fome titulary Bi-fhops for England, that might ordain, and have other fpiritual faculties; faying withall moft honeftly, that he thought himfelf bound to impart this to fome Counfellor, both as a loyal fubject, and as a Catholic; for that he doubted it might be a caufe to crofs the graces and mercies, which the Catholics now enjoy, if it be not prevented: and he afked my advice,

whether

whether he fhould make it known to your Lordfhip, or to my Lord Keeper (r), when he came back to London. I commended his loyalty and difcretion, and wifhed him to addrefs himfelf to your Lordfhip, who might communicate it with my Lord Keeper, if you faw caufe, and that he repaired to your Lordfhip prefently, which he refolved to do. Neverthelefs, I did not think mine own particular duty acquitted, except I certified it alfo myfelf, borrowing fo much of private friendfhip in a caufe of ftate, as not to tell him I would do fo much.

Indorfed,

My letter to my Lord Marquis, touching the bufinefs of eftate advertifed by Mr. Matthew (s).

To the Lord Vifcount ST. ALBAN.

My moft honoured Lord,

I Come in thefe to your Lordfhip with the voice of thankfgiving, for the continuance of your accuftomed noble care of me and my good, which overtakes me, I find, whitherfoever I go. But for the prefent itfelf (whereof your Lordfhip writes,) whether or no it be better than that I was wont to bring your

---

(r) Dr. Williams, Bifhop of Lincoln.

(s) The date of this letter may be pretty nearly determined by one of the Lord Keeper to the Marquis of Buckingham, dated Auguft 23, 1622, and printed in the *Cabala*. The poftfcript to that letter is as follows : " The Spanifh Ambaffador " took the alarm very fpeedily of the titulary Roman Bifhop ; " and before my departure from his houfe at Iflington, whither " I went privately to him, did write both to Rome and Spain to " prevent it. But I am afraid, that Tobie will prove but an " apocryphal, and no canonical, intelligencer, acquainting the " ftate with this projeft for the Jefuits, rather than for Jefus's " fake."

Lordfhip,

Lordship, the end only can prove. For I have yet no more to shew for it, than good words, of which many times I brought your Lordship good store. But because *modicefideans* were not made to thrive in court, I mean to lose no time from assailing my Lord Marquis, for which purpose I am now hovering about New-hall (*t*), where his Lordship is expected (but not the King) this day, or to-morrow: which place, as your Lordship adviseth, may not be ill chosen for my business. For, if his Lordship be not very thick of hearing, sure New-hall will be heard to speak for me.

And now, my good Lord, if any thing make me diffident, or indeed almost indifferent, how it succeeds, it is this; that my sole ambition having ever been, and still is, to grow up only under your Lordship, it is become preposterous, even to my nature and habit, to think of prospering, or receiving any growth, either without, or besides your Lordship. And therefore let me claim of your Lordship to do me this right, as to believe that, which my heart says, or rather swears, to me, namely, that what addition soever, by God's good providence, comes at any time to my life or fortune, it is, in my account, but to enable me the more to serve your Lordship in both; at whose feet I shall ever humbly lay down all, that I have, or am, never to rise thence other than

> Your Lordship's in all duty
> and reverent affections,

September 11, 1622.

> T. MEAUTYS.

(*t*) In Essex.

To the Countefs of BUCKINGHAM (*u*), *mother to the Marquis of* BUCKINGHAM.

My very honourable good Lady,

YOUR Ladyfhip's late favour and noble ufage towards me were fuch, as I think your abfence a great part of my misfortunes. And the more I find my moft noble Lord, your fon, to increafe in favour towards me, the more, out of my love to him, I wifh he had often by him fo loving and wife a mother. For, if my Lord were never fo wife, as wife as Solomon ; yet, I find, that Solomon himfelf, in the end of his Proverbs, fets down a whole chapter of advices, that his mother taught him.

Madam, I can but receive your remembrance with affection, and ufe your name with honour, and intend you my beft fervice, if I be able, ever refting

Your Ladyfhip's humble

and affectionate fervant,

Bedford-houfe, this 29th
of October, 1622.

FR. ST. ALBAN.

(*u*) Mary, daughter of Anthony Beaumont, a younger fon of William Beaumont of Cole-Orton in Leicefterfhire. She was thrice married : 1. to Sir George Villiers, father of the Duke of Buckingham : 2. to Sir William Rayner : and 3. to Sir Thomas Compton, Knight of the Bath, a younger brother of William, Earl of Northampton. She was created Countefs of Buckingham, July 1, 1618; and died April 19, 1632.

To

To the Marquis of Buckingham.

My very good Lord,

I HAVE many things to thank your Lordſhip for, ſince I had the happineſs to ſee you; that your Lordſhip, before your going out of town, ſent my memorial to my Lord Treaſurer: that your Lordſhip offered, and received, and preſented my petition to the King, and procured me a reference: that your Lordſhip moved his Majeſty, and obtained for me acceſs to him, againſt his Majeſty comes next, which, in mine own opinion, is better than if it had been now, and will be a great comfort to me, though I ſhould die next day after: that your Lordſhip gave me ſo good Engliſh for my Latin book. My humble requeſt is, at this time, that becauſe my Lord Treaſurer keepeth yet his anſwer in ſuſpenſe (though by one, he uſeth to me, he ſpeaketh me fair,) that your Lordſhip would nick it with a word: for if he do me good, I doubt it may not be altogether of his own.

God ever proſper you.

Your Lordſhip's moſt bounden
and faithful ſervant,

4th of November, 1622.

Fr. St. Alban.

Memorial of Acceſs (w).

It may pleaſe your Majeſty,

I MAY now in a manner ſing, *nunc dimittis*, now I have ſeen you. Before methought I was ſcant

(w) This paper was written in Greek characters, ſoon after his acceſs to King James I. which had been promiſed him in a letter of the Marquis of Buckingham, from Newmarket, November 13, 1622.

in

in state of grace, but in a kind of utter darkness. And therefore, among other your mercies and favours, I do principally thank your Majesty for this admission of me to kiss your hands.

I may not forget also to thank your Majesty for your remission of my fine, for granting of my *quietus*, and general pardon; and your late recommendation of my debts; favours not small, specially to a servant out of sight, and out of use.

I beseech your Majesty to give me leave to tell you what had, in my misfortunes, sustained me. Aristotle says, *old men live by remembrance, young men by hope.* And so it is true, that young men live by hope, and fallen men by remembrance. Two remembrances have sustained me: the one, that since I had the prime vote in the Lower House, to be first Commissioner for the union, until the last assembly of parliament, I was chosen Messenger of both Houses, in the petitions of religion (which were my two first, and last services,) having past a number of services of importance, your Majesty never chid me; neither did ever any public service miscarry in my hands. This was the finishing act of my prosperity. The second was of my adversity, which, in few words, is this, that as my fault was not against your Majesty; so my fall was not your act; and therefore I hope I shall live and die in your favour.

I have this farther to say in the nature of an humble oblation; for things once dedicated and vowed cannot lose their character, nor be made common. I ever vowed myself to your service. Therefore,

First, if your Majesty do at any time think it fit, for your affairs, to employ me again publicly upon the stage, I shall so live and spend my time, as neither discontinuance shall disable me, nor adversity shall discourage me, nor any thing, that I shall do, give any scandal or envy upon me.

Secondly,

Secondly, if your Majesty shall not hold that fit; yet, if it shall please you at any time to ask my opinion, or require my propositions privately by my Lord Marquis, or any of your Counsellors, that is my friend, touching any commission or business; for, as Ovid said, *Est aliquid luce patente minus*; I shall be glad to be a labourer, or pioneer in your service.

Lastly, and chiefly, because your Majesty is an universal scholar, or rather master, and my pen (as I may * it, passed * *) gained upon the world, your Majesty would appoint me some task, or literary province, that I may serve you *calamo*, if not *consilio*.

I know, that I am censured of some conceit of mine ability, or worth: but, I pray your Majesty, impute it to desire *(possunt quia posse videntur.)* And again, I should do some wrong to your Majesty's school, if, in sixteen years access and near service, I should think I had learned, or laid in, nothing.

May it please your Majesty, I have borne your image in metal; and I shall keep it in my heart, while I live.

That his Majesty's business never miscarried in my hands, I do not impute to any extraordinary ability in myself; but to my freedom from particular, either friends, or ends, and my careful receit of his Majesty's directions, being, as I have formerly said to him, but as a bucket and cistern to that fountain; a bucket to draw forth, a cistern to preserve.

I may allude to the three petitions of the Litany, *Libera nos, Domine*; *parce mihi, Domine*; *et exaudi nos, Domine*. First, the first, I am persuaded, his Majesty had a mind to do it, and could not conveniently, in respect of his affairs. For the second, he had done it in my fine and pardon. For the third, I had likewise performed, in restoring to the light of his countenance.

There be mountebanks, as well in the civil body, as in the natural. I ever served his Majesty with modesty; no shouldering, no undertaking.

Y 2   Seneca

Seneca faith *Tam otii debet conftare ratio quam negotii.* So I make his Majefty oblation of both.

For envy, it is an almanack of the laft year; and, as a friend of mine faid, the parliament died penitent towards me.

Of my offences, far be it from me to fay, *dat veniam corvis; vexat cenfura Columbas :* But I will fay that I have good warrant for; *they were not the greateft offenders in Ifrael, upon whom the wall of Shilo fell.*

What the King beftowed upon me, will be farther feen, than upon Paul's fteeple.

My ftory is proud. I may thank your Majefty; for I heard him note of Taffo, that he could know which poem he made, when he was in good condition, and which when he was a beggar. I doubt he could make no fuch obfervation of me.

My Lord hath done many things to fhew his greatnefs. This of mine is one of them, that fhews his goodnefs.

I am like ground frefh. If I be left to myfelf, I will grow, and bear natural philofophy : but if the King will plow me up again, and fow me on, I hope to give him fome yield.

Kings do raife and pull down with reafon; but the greateft work is reafoning.

For my hap, I feek an *otium*, and, if it may be, a fat *otium*.

I am faid to have a feather in my head. I pray God fome are not wild in their head, that gird not well.

I am too old, and the feas are too long, for me to double the Cape of Good Hope.

Afhes are good for fomewhat; for lees, for falts. But I hope I am rather embers than afhes, having the heat of good affections, under the afhes of my fortunes.

Your Majefty hath power : I have faith. Therefore a miracle may be foon wrought.

I would

I would live to ftudy, and not ftudy to live; yet I am prepared for *date obolum Bellifario* ; and I that have borne a bag, can bear a wallet.

For my Pen:

If active,   1. The reconciling of laws.

        2. The difpofing of wards, and generally education of youth.

        3. Limiting the jurifdiction of courts, and prefcribing rules for every of them.

Reglement of Trade.

If contemplative,   1. Going on with the ftory of Henry the Eighth.

        2. General treatife of *de Legibus et Juftitiâ.*

        3. The Holy War.

For my Lord of Buckingham.

Thefe I rank high amongft his favours.

To the King of   *   *   *   that the goodnefs of his nature may ftrive with the goodnefs of his fortune.

He had but one fault, and that is, that you cannot mar him with any accumulating of honours upon him.

Now after this fun-fhine, and little dew, that fave war.

Whales will overturn your boat, or bark, or of Admiral, or other.

For the Prince.

Ever my chief patron.

The work of the father is creation ; of the fon redemption.

You would have drawn me out of the fire ; now out of the mire.

                                       To

To afk leave of the King to kifs the Prince's hands, if he be not now prefent.

Indorfed, *Mem. of accefs.*

To the Lord Vifcount St. Alban.

My moft honoured Lord,

SINCE my laft to your Lordfhip, I find, by Mr. Johnfon, that my Lord Treafurer is not twice in one mind, or Sir Arthur Ingram not twice in one tale. For Sir Arthur, contrary to his fpeech but yefterday with me, puts himfelf now, as it feems, in new hopes to prevail with my Lord Treafurer for your Lordfhip's good and advantage, by a propofition, fent by Mr. Johnfon, for the altering of your patent to a new mould, more fafe than the other, which he feemed to diffuade, as I wrote to your Lordfhip. I like my Lord Treafurer's heart to your Lordfhip, fo much every day worfe than other, efpecially for his coarfe ufage of your Lordfhip's name in his laft fpeech, as that I cannot imagine he means you any good. And therefore, good my Lord, what directions you fhall give herein to Sir Arthur Ingram, let them be as fafe ones, as you can think upon; and that your Lordfhip furrender not your old patent, till you have the new under feal, left my Lord Keeper fhould take toy, and ftop it there. And I know your Lordfhip cannot forget they have fuch a favage word among them, as *fleecing*. God in heaven blefs your Lordfhip from fuch hands and tongues; and then things will mend of themfelves.

Your Lordfhip's, in all humblenefs,

to honour and ferve you,

This Sunday morning.

T. MEAUTYS.

Indorfed, *25th of November* [1622].

To

To the Marquis of BUCKINGHAM.

My very good Lord,

I FIND my Lord Treafurer, after fo many days, and appointments, and fuch certain meffages and promifes, doth but mean to coax me (it is his own word of old) and to faw me afunder, and to do juft nothing upon his Majefty's gracious reference, nobly procured by your Lordfhip for this poor remnant. My Lord, let it be your own deed ; and, to ufe the prayers of the Litany, good Lord deliver me from this fervile dependance ; for I had rather beg and ftarve, than be fed at that door.

God ever profper your Lordfhip.

Your Lordfhip's moft bounden
and faithful fervant,

Bedford-houfe, this

FR. ST. ALBAN.

Indorfed,

To Buckingham, about Lord Treafurer Cranfield's ufing
of him.

Remembrances of the Lord Vifcount ST. ALBAN, *upon his going to the Lord Treafurer* (x).

My Lord,

FOR paft matters, they are memorial with me. I thank God I am fo far from thinking to re-trieve a fortune, as I did not mark where the game fell. I afcribe all to Providence. Your Lordfhip hath greatnefs ; and I hope you will line it with good-

(x) Thefe are written in Greek characters.

Y 4

nefs.

nefs. Of me you can have no ufe; but you may have honour by me, in ufing me well; for my fortune is much in your hands.

For Sir G. I heard by Sir Arthur *(y)*, you thought well of my dealing to him; for fo Ingram told me. But I doubt he reported fomewhat amifs of me, that procured that warrant; fince which he thinks he may bring me to his own conditions, never comes to me, flies from that he had agreed; fo to conclude with the letter upon even-terms.

For the King, I muft fubmit. Ingram told me there fhould be a favour in it, till I might fue to the King.

The fequeftration as much as a refumption; for if it be as in the King's hands, all will go back; fo it requires a farmer.

My penfion and that the rewards of my long fervice, and relief of my prefent means. In parliament he faid, he would not have me know what want meant.

LA. B. *(z)*.

OF York-houfe garden:
    Of New-hall:
Of my being with my Lord Treafurer:
Of my bufinefs.
It is well begun: I defire it may be your act.
It is nothing out of the King's purfe: it laid fair; a third part of the profit.
The King beftows honour upon reward, one honour upon alms and charity.
Time, I hope, will work this, or a better.
I know my Lord will not forfake me.

(y) Ingram.   *(z)* Lady Buckingham, mother of the Duke.

He

He can have but one mother. Friends wayfarers, fome to Waltham, fome to Ware, and where the ways part, farewell.

I do not defire to ftage myfelf, nor pretenfions; but for the comfort of a private life. Yet will I be ever at your and the King's call. Malcontent, or bufy-body, I fcorn to be.

Though my Lord fhall have no ufe of me, yet he fhall have honour by me.

For envy, the almanack of that year, is paft.

You may obferve laft parliament, though an high-aiming parliament, yet not a petition, not a clamour, not a motion, not a mention of me. Vifitations by all the noblemen about the town.

A little will make me happy: the debts I have paid.

I fhall honour my Lord with pen and words; and be ready to give him faithful and free counfel, as ready, as when I had the feal; and mine ever *fuavibus modis* for fafety, as well as for greatnefs.

The King and the Prince, I hear for certain, well-affected.

To dine with:

To go to New-hall.

To the Marquis of B U C K I N G H A M.

Excellent Lord,

I PERCEIVE this day, by Mr. Comptroller (*a*), that I live continually in your Lordfhip's remembrance, and noble purpofes concerning my fortunes, as well for the comfort of my eftate, as for countenancing me otherwife by his Majefty's employments and graces; for which I moft humbly kifs your

(*a*) Henry Cary, Vifcount Falkland.

hands,

bands, leaving the times to your good Lordfhip; which, confidering my age and wants, I affure myfelf, your Lordfhip will the fooner take into your care. And for my houfe at Gorhambury, I do infinitely defire your Lordfhip fhould have it; and howfoever I may treat, I will conclude with none, till I know your Lordfhip's farther pleafure, over refting

Your Lordfhip's moft obliged,

and faithful fervant,

Bedford-houfe, this 5th
of Feb. 1622 (*b*).

FR. ST. ALBAN.

To the Lord Vifcount ST. ALBAN.

My very good Lord,

I Have received, by this bearer, the privy feal for the furvey of coals, which I will lay afide, untill I fhall hear farther from my Lord Steward (*c*), and the reft of the Lords.

I am ready to do as much as your Lordfhip defireth, in keeping Mr. Cotton (*d*) off from the violence of thofe creditors: only himfelf is, as yet, wanting in fome particular directions.

I heartily thank your Lordfhip for your book; and all other fymbols of your love and affection,

(*b*) two days before the Marquis of Buckingham fet out privately, with the Prince, for Spain.   (*c*) Duke of Lenox.
(*d*) probably the furety of Lord Bacon, for the debt to Harris the goldfmith, mentioned in his Lordfhip's letter of May 30, 1622.

which

which I will endeavour, upon all opportunities, to deferve: and, in the mean time, do reft

Your Lordfhip's affured faithful

poor friend and fervant,

Jo, LINCOLN, C. S.

*To the Right Honourable his very good Lord, the Lord
Vifcount St. Alban.*

To the Marquis of BUCKINGHAM.

Excellent Lord,

THOUGH your Lordfhip's abfence (*f*) fall out in an ill time for myfelf; yet becaufe I hope in God this noble adventure will make your Lordfhip a rich return in honour, abroad and at home, and chiefly in the ineftimable treafure of the love and truft of that thrice-excellent Prince; I confefs I am fo glad of it, as I could not abftain from your Lordfhip's trouble in feeing it expreffed by thefe few and hafty lines.

I befeech your Lordfhip, of your noblenefs vouch-fafe to prefent my moft humble duty to his Highnefs, who, I hope, ere long will make me leave King Henry the Eighth, and fet me on work in relation of his Highnefs's adventures.

I very humbly kifs your Lordfhip's hands, refting ever

Your Lordfhip's moft obliged friend and fervant,

February 21, 1622.

(*f*) in Spain.

To

To the *Marquis* of BUCKINGHAM.

Excellent Lord,

UPON the repair of my Lord of Rochford unto your Lordship, whom I have ever known so fast and true a friend and servant unto you; and who knows likewise so much of my mind and affection towards your Lordship, I could not but kiss your Lordship's hands, by the duty of these few lines.

My Lord, I hope in God, that this your noble adventure will make you a rich return, especially in the inestimable treasure of the love and trust of that thrice-excellent Prince. And although to a man, that loves your Lordship so dearly, as I do, and knows somewhat of the world, it cannot be, but that in my thoughts there should arise many fears, or shadows of fears, concerning so rare an accident; yet nevertheless, I believe well, that this your Lordship's absence will rather be a glass unto you, to shew you many things, whereof you may make use hereafter, than otherwise any hurt or hazard to your fortunes, which God grant. For myself, I am but a man desolate till your return, and have taken a course accordingly. Vouchsafe, of your nobleness, to remember my most humble duty to his Highness. And so God, and his holy angels, guard you, both going and coming.

Indorsed, *March* 10, 1622.

To Sir FRANCIS COTTINGTON, *Secretary to the Prince.*

Good Mr. Secretary,

THOUGH I wrote so lately unto you, by my Lord Rochford; yet, upon the going of my Lord Vaughan *(g)*, the Prince's worthy and trusty servant, and my approved friend, and your so near ally, I could not but put this letter into his hand, commending myself and my fortunes unto you. You know the difference of obliging men in prosperity and adversity, as much as the sowing upon a pavement and upon a furrow new made. Myself for quiet, and the better to hold out, am retired to Grey's Inn *(h)*: for when my chief friends were gone so far off, it was time for me to go to a cell. God send us a good return of you all.

I ever rest &c.

My humble service to my Lord Marquis, to whom I have written twice. I would not cloy him. My service also to the Count Gondomar, and Lord of Bristol.

Indorsed,

To Mr. Secretary, Sir Francis Cottington, *March* 22, 1622.

(g) He was son and heir of Walter Vaughan, of Golden Grove, in Caermarthenshire, Esq; and was created Lord Vaughan in the year 1620. The Lord St. Alban, after he was delivered from his confinement in the Tower, was permitted to stay at Sir John Vaughan's house at Parson's Green, near Fulham.

(h) In a MS. letter of Mr. Chamberlain to Sir Dudley Carleton, dated at London, March 8, 162⅔, is the following passage: " The Lord of St. Alban is in his old remitter, and came to " lie in his old lodgings at Grey's Inn : which is the fulfilling " of a prophecy of one Locke, a familiar of his, of the same " house, that knew him *intus et in cute* ; who, seeing him go " thence in pomp, with the great seal before him, said to divers " of his friends, *we shall live to have him here again.*"

T

To the KING.

It may pleafe your Majefty,

NOW that my friend is abfent (for fo I may call him ftill, fince your Majefty, when I waited on you, told me, that fortune made no difference) your Majefty remaineth to me King, and mafter, and friend, and all. Your Beadfman therefore addreffeth himfelf to your Majefty for a cell to retire into. The particular I have expreffed to my very friend, Mr. Secretary Conway. This help, which cofts your Majefty nothing, may referve me to do your Majefty fervice, without being chargeable unto you: for I will never deny, but my defire to ferve your Majefty is of the nature of the heart, that will be *ultimum moriens* with me.

God preferve your Majefty, and fend you a good return of the treafure abroad, which paffeth all Indian fleets.

Your Majefty's moft humble

and devoted fervant,

March 25, 1623.

FR: ST. ALBAN.

Indorfed,

To the King touching the provoftfhip of Eton (i).

To Mr. Secretary CONWAY.

Good Mr. Secretary,

WHEN you did me the honour and favour to vifit me, you did not only in general terms exprefs your love unto me, but, as a real friend,

---

(i) Mr. Thomas Murray, the Provoft of that college, having been cut for the ftone, died April 1, 1623.

afked

afked me, whether I had any particular occafion, wherein I might make ufe of you? At that time I had none : now there is one fallen. It is, that Mr. Thomas Murray, Provoft of Eton (whom I love very well) is like to die. It were a pretty cell for my fortune. The college and fchool, I do not doubt, but I fhall make to flourifh. His Majefty, when I waited on him, took notice of my wants, and faid to me, that, as he was a King, he would have care of me. This is a thing fomebody would have; and cofts his Majefty nothing. I have written two or three words to his Majefty, which I would pray you to deliver. I have not expreffed this particular to his Majefty, but referred it to your relation. My moft noble friend, the Marquis, is now abfent. Next to him I could not think of a better addrefs than to yourfelf, as one likeft to put on his affection. I reft

Your Honour's very affectionate friend,

Grey's Inn, the 25th
of March, 1623.   FR. ST. ALBAN (*k*).

(*k*) To this letter Secretary Conway wrote an anfwer, acquainting the Lord Vifcount St. Alban, that the King could not value his Lordfhip fo little, or conceive, that he limited his defires fo low; in which, however, he fhould have been gratified, had not the King been engaged, by the Marquis of Buckingham, for Sir William Becher, his agent in France. See *Account of the Life of the Lord Bacon*, p. xxvi, prefixed to the edition of his *Letters, Memoirs, &c.* by Robert Stephens, Efq. The Duke of Buckingham himfelf likewife, after his return from Spain, in a letter to the Lord Vifcount St. Alban, dated at Hinchinbrook, October 27, 1623, expreffes his concern, that he could do his Lordfhip no fervice in that affair, " having engaged " myfelf, *fays he*, to Sir William Becher, before my going into " Spain; fo that I cannot free myfelf, unlefs there were means " to give him fatisfaction."

To Count GONDOMAR, *then in Spain.*

Illuftriffime Comes,

MULTA funt, quæ mihi animos addunt, et quandam alacritatem conciliant, ut Dominationem tuam illuftriffimam hoc tempore de meis fortunis compellam et deprecer. Primum, idque vel maximum, quod cum tam arêta regum noftrorum conjunêtio jam habeatur pro tranfaêtâ, inde et tu faêtus fis interceffor tanto potentior; et mihi nullus jam fubfit fcrupulus univerfas fortunas meas viro tanto, licet extero, debendi et acceptas referendi. Secundum, quod cum ea, quæ Dominatio tua illuftriffima de me promiffo tenus præfens impetraveras, neque ullam repulfam paffa fint, neque tamen ad exitum perduêta; videatur hoc innuere providentia divina, ut hoc opus me à calamitate eximendi planè tuum fit initio et fine. Tertium, quod ftellæ duæ, quæ mihi femper fuerunt propitiæ, major et minor, jam fplendent in urbe veftra, unde per radios auxiliares et benignos amoris erga me tui eum poffint nancifci influxum, qui me in aliquo non indigno priore fortuna gradu collocet. Quartum, quod perfpexi ex literis, quas ad amicum meum intimum Dominum Tobium Matthæum nuper fcripfifti, memoriam mei apud te vivere et vigere, neque tantâ negotiorum arduorum et fublimium mole, quanta Dom. tuæ incumbit, obrutam effe aut extinêtam. Poftremum accidit et illud, quod poftquam ex favore excellent. Domini Marchionis ad Regis mei confpeêtum et colloquium admiffus fuerim, videar mihi in ftatu gratiæ collocatus. Non me allocutus eft Rex ut criminofum, fed ut hominem tempeftate dejeêtum; et fimul conftantem meum et perpetuum in fermone fuo induftriæ et integritatis tenorem prolixè agnovit, cum infigni, ut videbatur, affeêtu : unde major mihi oboritur

fpes,

ſpes, manente ejus erga me gratiâ, et extinctâ omni ex diuturnitate invidiâ, labores illuſtr. Domin. tuæ pro me non incaſſum fore. Ipſe interim nec otio me dedi, nec rebus me importunè immiſcui, ſed in iis vivo, et ea tracto, quæ nec priores, quos geſſi, honores dedeceant, et poſteris memoriam nominis mei haud ingratam fortaſſe relinquent. Itaque ſpero me non indignam fore materiam, in quâ et potentiæ et amicitiæ tuæ vis elucescat et celebretur; ut non non minùs in privatâ hominis fortunâ potuiſſe videaris, quam in negotiis publicis. Deus illuſtriſſ. Dominationem tuam incolumem ſervet et felicitate cumulet.

Indorſed,

My Lord St. Alban's firſt letter to Gondomar, into Spain, March 28 1623.

To the Marquis of B U C K I N G H A M, *in Spain.*

Excellent Lord,

FINDING ſo truſty a meſſenger as Sir John Epſley, I thought it my duty to put theſe few lines into his hands. I thank God, that thoſe ſhadows, which either mine own melancholy, or my extreme love to your Lordſhip, did put into my mind concerning this voyage of the Prince and your Lordſhip, rather vaniſh and diminiſh, than otherwiſe. The groſs fear is paſt of the paſſage of France. I think you had the ring, which they write of, that, when the ſeal was turned to the palm of the hand, made men go inviſible. Neither do I hear of any novelty here worth the eſteeming.

There is a general opinion here, that your Lordſhip is like enough to return, and go again, before the Prince come : which opinion, whether the buſineſs lead you to do ſo, or no, doth no hurt ; for it keeps men in awe.

Z   I find,

I find, I thank God, some glimmering of the King's favour, which your Lordship's noble work of my access, no doubt, did chiefly cherish. I am much bound to Mr. Secretary Conway. It is wholly for your Lordship's sake; for I had no acquaintance with him in the world. By that I see of him, he is a man fit to serve a great King, and fit to be a friend and servant to your Lordship. Good my Lord, write two or three words to him, both of thanks, and a general recommendation of me unto him.

Vouchsafe, of your nobleness, to present my most humble duty to his Highness. We hear he is fresh in his person, and becomes this brave journey in all things. God provide all things for the best.

I ever rest &c.

Indorsed, *March* 30, 1623.

To Mr. Secretary CONWAY.

Good Mr. Secretary,

I AM much comforted by your last letter, wherein I find, that his Majesty, of his mere grace and goodness, vouchsafeth to have a care of me, a man out of sight, out of use; but yet his, as the Scripture saith, God knows those, that are his. In particular, I am very much bound to his Majesty (and I pray you, Sir, thank his Majesty most humbly for it,) that, notwithstanding the former designment of Sir William Becher *(1)*, his Majesty (as you write) is

(1) Sir William had not, however, that post; but, in lieu of it, the promise of 2500l. upon the fall of the first of the six clerks places, and was permitted to keep his clerkship of the council. MS. letter of Mr. Chamberlain to Sir Dudley Carleton, dated at London, July 24, 1624. The provostship was given to Sir Henry Wotton, who was instituted into it the 26th of

is not out of hope, in due time, to accommodate me of this cell, and to satisfy him otherwise. Many conditions, no doubt, may be as contenting to that gentleman, and his years may expect them. But there will hardly fall, especially in the spent hour-glass of my life, any thing so fit for me, being a retreat to a place of study so near London, and where (if I sell my house at Gorhambury, as I purpose to do, to put myself in some convenient plenty) I may be accommodate of a dwelling for summer time. And therefore, good Mr. Secretary, further this his Majesty's good intention, by all means, if the place fall.

For yourself, you have obliged me much. I will endeavour to deserve it: at least your nobleness is never lost ; and my noble friend, the Marquis, I know, will thank you for it.

I was looking of some short papers of mine touching usury (*m*), to grind the teeth of it, and yet make it grind to his Majesty's mill in good sort, without discontentment, or perturbation. If you think good, I will send it to his Majesty, as the fruit of my leisure. But yet I would not have it come from me, not for any tenderness in the thing, but because I know, in courts of Princes, it is usual, *non res, sed displicet auctor*. God keep your Honour &c.

Indorsed,

To Mr. Secretary Conway, touching the Provostship of Eton, March 31, 1623.

of that month, having purchased it by a surrender of a grant of the reversion of the Mastership of the Rolls, and of another office, which was fit to be turned into present money, which he then, and afterwards, much wanted [Life of him by Mr. Isaac Walton:] for when he went to the election at Eton, soon after his being made Provost, he was so ill provided, that the Fellows of the College were obliged to furnish his bare walls, and whatever else was wanting. MS. letter of Mr. Chamberlain, Aug. 7, 1624.

(*m*) In his works is published, *A Draught of an act against an usurious Shift of Gain, in delivering of Commodities, instead of Money.*

To Count GONDOMAR.

Illuftriffime Comes,

PRIMO loco, ut debeo, gratulor Dominationi tuæ illuftriffimæ novum honoris tui gradum per se sublimem, sed ex causâ, propter quam evectus es, haud parum nobilitatum.   Profectio Dom. Tobiæ Matthæi, qui mihi eft tanquam alter ego, ut Dominatio tua illuftriffima optimè novit, in illas partes, memoriam mihi renovat eximii tui erga me favoris, cum me pluries, paulo ante difceffum tuum, in campis, in urbe vifitares, et prolixè de voluntate tuâ erga fortunas meas pollicereris.   Quinetiam tam apud regem meum quam apud Marchionem de illis fedulo ageres, ut etiam promiffum ab illis de poftulatis meis obtinueris.   Quod fi illo tempore quis mihi genius aut vates in aurem infufurraffet et dixiffet, Mitte ifta in præfens.   Britannia eft regio paulo frigidior : differ rem donec Princeps Galliæ et Marchio Buckinghamiæ et Comes de Gondomar conveniunt in Hifpaniâ, ubi hujufmodi fructus clementius maturefcant : quin et viderit idem Dom. Tob. Matthæum, qui illic, quemadmodum nunc, inftabit, et negotium promovebit : fcilicet rififfem, sed fidem prorfus non adhibuiffem.   Quare, illuftriffime Comes, cum talia miracula edideris in fortunâ publicâ, etiam in fortunâ amici et fervi tui privatâ eniteat virtus tua.   Miraculum enim potentiæ et fidei proles eft.   Tu potentiam habes ; ego fide abundo, fi modo digna fit res, ad quam Dominatio tua illuftriffima manum falutarem porrigat.   Id tempus optimè demonftrabit.

Cum nuper ad Dominationem tuam illuftriffimam fcripferim, eo brevior fio.   Hoc tantum a te peto, ut etiam inter negotia, quæ feliciter adminiftras, confuetam digneris Dom. Matthæo libertatem proponendi et confulendi apud te ea, quæ in rem meam fore videbimus.   Deus

Deus illuſtriſſimam tuam Dominationem ſervet incolumem, ut enixè optat &c.

To the Earl of BRISTOL, *Ambaſſador in Spain.*

My very good Lord,

THOUGH I have written to your Lordſhip lately, yet I could not omit to put a letter into ſo good a hand as Mr. Matthew's, being one, that hath often made known unto me, how much I am beholden to your Lordſhip; and knoweth likewiſe in what eſtimation I have ever had your Lordſhip, not according to your fortunes, but according to your inward value. Therefore, not to hold your Lordſhip in this time of ſo great buſineſs, and where I have ſo good a mean as Mr. Matthew, who, if there be any thing that concerns my fortune, can better expreſs it than myſelf, I humbly commend myſelf, and my ſervice to your Lordſhip, reſting &c.

To Sir FRANCIS COTTINGTON, *Secretary to the* PRINCE.

Good Mr. Secretary,

THOUGH I think I have cloyed you with letters, yet had I written a thouſand before, I muſt add one more by the hands of Mr. Matthew, being as true a friend, as any you or I have; and one, that made me ſo happy, as to have the aſſurance of our friendſhip; which, if there be any ſtirring for my good, I pray practiſe in ſo good a conjunction as his. I ever reſt &c.

To

To Mr. Tobie Matthew.

Good Mr. Matthew,

BECAUSE Mr. Clarke is the first, that hath been sent since your departure, who gave me also the comfortable news, that he met you well, I could not but visit you with my letters, who have so often visited me with your kind conferences.

My health, I thank God, is better than when you left me; and, to my thinking, better than before my last sickness. This is all I need to write of myself to such a friend.

We hope well, and it is generally rather spoken, than believed, that his Highness will return very speedily. But they be not the best pieces in painting, that are dashed out in haste. I hope, if any thing want in the speed of time, it will be compensed in the fruit of time, that all may sort to the best.

I have written a few words, of duty and respect only, to my Lord Marquis, and Mr. Secretary. I pray you kiss the Count of Gondomar's hand.

God keep you.

Your most affectionate and assured friend,

May 2, 1623.

FR. ST. ALBAN.

To the Duke of Buckingham.

Excellent Lord,

I WRITE now only to congratulate with your Grace your new honour (*n*); which because I reckon to be no great matter to your fortune (though you

(*n*) the title of Duke, conferred on him May 18, 1623.

are

are the firſt Engliſh Duke, that hath been created ſince I was born) my compliment ſhall be the ſhorter. So having turned almoſt my hopes of your Grace's return, by July, into wiſhes, and not to them neither, if it ſhould be any hazard to your health, I reſt &c.

Vouchſafe, of your nobleneſs, to preſent my moſt humble duty to his Highneſs. Summer is a thirſty time ; and ſure I am, I ſhall infinitely thirſt to ſee his Highneſs's and your Grace's return.

Duke of Buckingham *to the Lord Viſcount* St. Alban.

My good Lord,

I HAVE received your hearty congratulation for the great honour, and gracious favour, which his Majeſty hath done me : and I do well believe, that no man is more glad of it than yourſelf.

Tobie Matthew is here ; but what with the journey, and what with the affliction he endures, to find, as he ſays, that reaſon prevails nothing with theſe people, he is grown extreme lean, and looks as ſharp as an eyas (o). Only he comforts himſelf with a conceit, that he is now gotten on the other ſide of the water, where the ſame reaſon, that is valuable in other parts of the world, is of no validity here ; but rather ſomething elſe, which yet he hath not found out.

I have let his Highneſs ſee the good expreſſions of your Lordſhip's care, and faithful affection to his perſon ; and ſhall ever be ready to do you, in all things, the beſt ſervice, that I can.

(o) A young hawk, juſt taken out of the neſt.

So

So wishing your Lordship much happiness, I rest

Your Lordship's faithful friend,

and humble servant,

Madrid, this 29th of
May, 1623, *st. vet.*

G. BUCKINGHAM.

To the Duke of BUCKINGHAM, *in Spain.*

Excellent Lord,

I HUMBLY thank your Grace for your letter of the 29th of May; and that your Grace doth believe, that no man is gladder of the increase of your honour and fortune, than I am; as, on the other part, no man should be more sorry, if it should in the least degree decline, nor more careful, if it should so much as labour. But of the first, I speak as of a thing, that is: but for the two latter, it is but a case put, which I hope I shall never see. And, to be plain with your Grace, I am not a little comforted to observe, that, although in common sense and experience, a man would have doubted, that some things might have sorted to your prejudice; yet in particulars we find nothing of it. For a man might reasonably have feared, that absence and discontinuance might have lessened his Majesty's favour: no such thing has followed. So likewise, that any, that might not wish you well, should have been bolder with you. But all is continued in good compass. Again, who might not have feared, that your Grace being there to manage, in great part, the most important business of Europe, so far from the King, and not strengthened with advice there, except that of the Prince himself, and thus to deal with so politic a state as Spain, you should be able to go through as you do? and yet nothing, as we hear, but for

your

your honour, and that you do your part.   Surely, my Lord, though your virtues be great, yet these things could not be, but that the blessing of God, which is over the King and the Prince, doth likewise descend upon you as a faithful servant; and you are the more to be thankful to God for it.

I humbly thank your Grace, that you make me live in his Highness's remembrance, whom I shall ever bear an heart to honour and serve.   And I much joy to hear of the great and fair reputation, which at all hands are given him.

For Mr. Matthew, I hope by this time he hath gathered up his crumbs; which importeth much, I assure your Grace, if his cure must be, either by finding better reason on that side the line, or by discovering, what is the motion, that moveth the wheels, that, if reason do not, we must all pray for his being in good point.   But in truth, my Lord, I am glad he is there; for I know his virtues, and particularly his devotion to your Lordship.

God return his Highness, and your Grace, unto us safe and sound, and according to your heart's desires.

To Mr. Tobie Matthew.

Good Mr. Matthew,

I HAVE received your letter of the 10th of June *(p)*, and am exceeding glad to hear you are in so good health.   For that, which may concern myself, I neither doubt of your judgement in choosing the fittest time, nor of your affection in taking the first time you shall find fit.   For the public business, I will not turn my hopes into wishes yet, since you write as you do; and I am very glad you are

(p) N. S.

there,

there, and, as I guess, you went in good time to his Lordship.

For your action of the case, it will fall to the ground; for I have not heard from the Duke, neither by letter, nor message, at this time.

God keep you, I rest always

Your most affectionate and faithful servant,

Grey's Inn, 17th of
June, 1623.

FR. ST. ALBAN.

I do hear, from Sir Robert Ker and others, how much beholden I am to you.

To Mr. TOBIE MATTHEW.

Good Mr. Matthew,

I THANK you for your letter of the 26th of June, and commend myself unto your friendship, knowing your word is good assurance, and thinking I cannot wish myself a better wish, than that your power may grow to your will.

Since you say the Prince hath not forgot his commandment, touching my History of Henry VIII, I may not forget my duty. But I find Sir Robert Cotton, who poured forth what he had, in my other work, somewhat dainty of his materials in this.

It is true, my labours are now most set to have those works, which I had formerly published, as that of *Advancement of Learning*, that of *Henry VII*, that of the *Essays*, being retractate, and made more perfect, well translated into Latin by the help of some good pens, which forsake me not. For these modern languages will, at one time or other, play the bankrupts with books: and since I have lost much time with this age, I would be glad, as God shall give me leave, to recover it with posterity.

2   For

For the effay of friendfhip, while I took your fpeech of it for a curfory requeft, I took my promife for a compliment. But fince you call for it, I fhall perform it (*q*).

I am much beholden to Mr. Gage for many expreffions of his love to me ; and his company, in itfelf very acceptable, is the more pleafing to me, becaufe it retaineth the memory of yourfelf.

This letter of yours, of the 26th, lay not fo long by you, but it hath been as fpeedily anfwered by me, fo as with Sir Francis Cottington I have had no fpeech fince the receit of it. Your former letters, which I received from Mr. Grieflcy, I had anfwered before, and put my letter into a good hand.

For the great bufinefs, God conduct it well. Mine own fortune hath taught me expectation.

God keep you.

Indorfed, *To Mr. Matthew, into Spain.*

To Mr. TOBIE MATTHEW.

Good Mr. Matthew,

I HAVE received your letter, fent by my Lord of Andover ; and, as I acknowledged your care, fo I cannot fit it with any thing, that I can think on for myfelf ; for fince Gondomar, who was my voluntary friend, is in no credit, neither with the Prince, nor with the Duke, I do not fee what may be done for me there ; except that, which Gondomar hath loft, you have found ; and then I am fure my cafe is amended : fo, as with a great deal of confidence, I commend myfelf to you, hoping, that you will do what in you lieth, to prepare the Prince and Duke to

(*q*) Among his *Effays*, publifhed in 4to, and dedicated to the Duke of Buckingham, is one upon *Friendfhip*.

think

think of me, upon their return. And if you have any relation to the Infanta, I doubt not but it shall be also to my use. God keep you.

Your most affectionate and assured friend, &c.

To the Duke of BUCKINGHAM.

Excellent Lord,

THOUGH I have formerly given your Grace thanks for your last letter, yet being much refreshed to hear things go so well, whereby we hope to see you here shortly, your errand done, and the Prince within the vail; I could not contain, but congratulate with your Lordship, seeing good fortune, that is God's blessing, still follow you. I hope I have still place in your love and favour; which if I have, for other place, it shall not trouble me. I ever rest

Your Grace's most obliged, and faithful servant.
July 22, 1623.

To the Duke of BUCKINGHAM.

Excellent Lord,

UPON Mr. Clarke's dispatch, in troth I was ill in health, as he might partly perceive. Therefore I wrote to my true friend, and your Grace's devoted servant, Mr. Matthew, to excuse me to your Grace for not writing. Since, I thank God, I am pretty well recovered; for I have lain at two wards, one against my disease, the other against my physicians, who are strange creatures.

My Lord, it rejoiceth me much, that I understand from Mr. Matthew, that I live in your Grace's remembrance;

membrance; and that I shall be the first man, that you will think on upon your return: which if your Grace perform, I hope God Almighty, who hath hitherto extraordinarily blessed you in this rocky business, will bless you the more for my sake. For I have had extraordinary tokens of his divine favour towards me, both in sickness and in health, prosperity and adversity.

Vouchsafe to present my most humble duty to his Highness, whose happy arrival will be a bright morning to all. I ever rest

Your Grace's most obliged

and faithful servant,

Grey's Inn, August 29,
1623.

Fr. St. Alban.

To Mr. Tobie Matthew.

Good Mr. Matthew,

I HAVE gotten a little health; I praise God for it. I have therefore now written to his Grace, that I formerly, upon Mr. Clarke's dispatch, desired you to excuse me for not writing, and taken knowledge, that I have understood from you, that I live in his Grace's remembrance; and that I shall be his first man, that he will have care of upon his return. And although your absence be to me as uncomfortable to my mind, as God may make it helpful to my fortunes; yet it is somwhat supplied by the love, freedom, and often visitations of Mr. Gage; so, as when I have him, I think I want you not altogether. God keep you.

Your most affectionate

and much obliged friend, &c.

Minutes

Minutes of a Letter to the Duke of BUCKINGHAM.

THAT I am exceeding glad his Grace is come home (*r*) with so fair a reputation of a sound protestant, and so constant for the King's honour a errand.

His Grace is now to consider, that his reputation will vanish like a dream, except now, upon his return, he do some remarkable act to fix it, and bind it in.

They have a good wise proverb in the country, whence he cometh, taken I think from a gentlewoman's sampler, *Qui en no da nudo, pierdo punto*, "he, that "tieth not a knot upon his thread, loseth his stitch."

Any particular I, that live in darkness, cannot propound. Let his Grace, who seeth clear, make his choice: but let some such thing be done, and then this reputation will stick by him ; and his Grace may afterwards be at the better liberty to take and leave off the future occasions, that shall present.

To the KING.

It may please your most excellent Majesty,

I SEND, in all humbleness, to your Majesty, the poor fruits of my leisure. This book (*s*) was the first thing, that ever I presented to your Majesty (*t*) ;

(*r*) The Prince and Duke arrived from Spain in London, October 6, 1623.

(*s*) *De Augmentis Scientiarum*, printed at London, 1623, in fol. The present to King James I, is in the royal library in the British Museum.

(*t*) *The two books of Sir Francis Bacon of the Proficiency and Advancement of Learning, Divine and Human:* printed at London, 1605, in 4to.

and

and it may be will be laft. For I had thought it fhould have *pofthuma proles*. But God hath otherwife difpofed for a while. It is a tranflation, but almoft inlarged to a new work. I had good helps for the language. I have been alfo mine own *index expurgatorius*, that it may be read in all places. For fince my end of putting it into Latin was to have it read every where, it had been an abfurd contradiction to free it in the language, and to pen it up in the matter. Your Majefty will vouchfafe gracioufly to receive thefe poor facrifices of him, that fhall ever defire to do you honour, while he breaths, and fulfilleth the reft in prayers.

Your Majefty's true beadfman,
and moft humble fervant, &c.

Todos duelos con pan fon buenos : itaque det veftra Majeftas obolum Bellifario.

To the PRINCE.

It may pleafe your excellent Highnefs,

I SEND your Highnefs, in all humblenefs, my book of *Advancement of Learning*, tranflated into Latin, but fo inlarged, as it may go for a new work. It is a book, I think, will live, and be a citizen of the world, as Englifh books are not. For Henry the Eighth, to deal truly with your Highnefs, I did fo defpair of my health this fummer, as I was glad to choofe fome fuch work, as I might compafs within days; fo far was I from entering into a work of length. Your Highnefs's return hath been my reftorative. When I fhall wait upon your Highnefs, I fhall give you a farther account. So I moft humbly kifs your Highnefs's hands, refting

Your Highnefs's moft devoted fervant.

I would

I would (as I wrote to the Duke in Spain) I could do your Highness's journey any honour with my pen. It began like a fable of the poets; but it deserveth all in a piece a worthy narration.

Conf. B u c. (*).

My Lord,

MY counsels bear not so high an elevation, as to have for their mark business of estate. That, which I level at, is your standing and greatness, which nevertheless I hold for a main pillar of the King's service.

For a parliament, I hold it then fit, when there have passed some more visible demonstrations of your power with the King, and your constancy in the way you are in: before not.

There are considerable, in this state, three sorts of men: the party of the Papists, which hate you; the party of the Protestants, including those they call Puritans, whose love is yet but green towards you; and particular great persons, which are most of them reconciled enemies, or discontented friends: and you must think there are a great many, that will magnify you, and make use of you for the breaking of the match, or putting the realm into a war; which after will return to their old bias.

For particulars, it is good to carry yourself fair; but neither to trust too far, nor to apply too much, but keep a good distance, and to play your own game, shewing yourself to have, as the bee hath, both of the honey, and of the sting.

The speech now abroad is, " My Lord of Buck-
" ingham's head is full of thoughts: he hath a great
" task; either he must break, or the match must
" break. He was wont to go the King's ways; but

(*) *Conference with Buckingham.*

" now

" now he goeth crofs his way, he will eafily lofe his
" way."

There is a point nice to be managed, yea, and tender to be fpoken of, which is your carriage between
the King and the Prince; fo that you may lofe no
manner of ground with the Prince; and yet the King
may not think himfelf the more folitary, nor that
you adore too much the fun-rifing. Though this
you may fet down, that the way to have the King
fure unto you is to keep great with the Prince.

Conf. with Bu. *December* 17, 1623.

YOU march bravely : but methinks you do not
draw up your troops.

You muft beware of thefe your pardons. If we
make men lefs in awe, and refpect you, *urina chiara
fa fico al medico.*

The points of the general advice.

If a war be proceeded in ; to treat a ftrait league
with France, under name of a renovation of the match
with France. Three fecret articles, the liberty of the
German nation, whereof there is a frefh precedent
of Henry the Second of France, that took it into
protection profperoufly, and to the arreft of the Emperor Charles's greatnefs. 2. The confervation of the
liberties of the Low-Countries for the United Provinces, and open trade into the Eaft and Weft Indies.

Offer of mine own fervice upon a commiffion into
France.

My Lord hath againft him thefe difadvantages ;
the catholic party ; the Spaniard ; the envy and fear
of particular great men ; the nice point of carrying
himfelf between the King and the Prince.

The knot, which is to be tied for his reputation,
muft either be advancing, or depreffing of perfons,
or putting by, or forwarding, of actions.

Conf. Bu ç. qu. *and old store,* January 2, 1625.

THERE is not an honester man in court than
Montgomery (*x*).

To have some opportunity, by the D.'s means, to
speak with the Prince in presence of the Duke.

To think, whether it be fit for me to speak with
the King, and to seek access before parliament; if
then.

The offer of my service to live a summer, as upon
mine own delight, at Paris, to settle a fast intelligence between France and us.

I have somewhat of the French: I love birds, as
the King doth, and have some childish mindedness,
wherein we shall consent.

To think of Belfast's sending over into Ireland.
Those, that find themselves obnoxious to parliament,
will do all they can, that those things, which are
likest to distaste the King, be first handled.

It is not to be forgotten, that as long as great men
were in question, as in my case, all things went sweet-
ly for the King. But the second meeting, when no
such thing was, the pack went higher.

Weeding time is not yet come. Cott. Car.
qu. of Car.

The battery will be chiefly laid on the Prince's
part, if they find any entry.

To be author of some counsel to the Prince, that
tasteth of religion and virtue, lest it be imputed, that
he entertains him only in pleasures, like a Pe. Ga.

The things remarkable for your Grace, to fix and
bind in the reputation, which you have gained,
must be either persons, or matters.

(*x*) Philip, Earl of Montgomery, afterwards of Pembroke.

The

The doubt the Prince is *mollis cera*, and formed *di ultima impressio*. Therefore good to have sure persons about him, or at least none dangerous.

For the pardons to proceed, it is a tender business. First, whatsoever useth to be done in parliament, is thankless. Then it is not good for his Grace. It will make men bolder with him. *Urina chiara fa fico al medico*. Lastly, remove the envy from others, it may beat upon my Lord himself, or the King.

Conf. B. *January* 2, 1623.

YOU have now tied a knot, as I wished you; *qui en no da nudo, pierde punto* (y); a jolly one, the parliament. Although I could have wished, that before a parliament, some remarkable thing had been done, whereby the world might have taken notice, that you stand the same in grace and power with the King. But there is time enough for that between this and parliament (z). And besides, the very prevailing for a parliament sheweth your power with the King.

You march bravely. Do you draw up your troops so well?

One of these days I shall turn my Lord Brooke, and say to you, *O brave Buckingham*.

I will commend you to all others, and censure you only to yourself.

You bowl well, if you do not horse the bowl an hand too much. You know the fine bowler is knee almost to ground in the delivery of the cast.

Nay, and the King will put a hook in the nostrils of Spain, and lay a foundation of greatness here to

(y) "He that tieth not a knot upon his thread, loseth his "stitch."

(z) It met February 19, 162⅘.

his

his children, in thefe weft parts. The call for me, it is book-learning. You know the King was wont to do me the honour, as to fay of me, *de minimis non curat lex :* if good for any thing, for great volumes, I cannot thread needles fo well.

The Chamberlain (*a*): for his perfon, not effectual; but fome dependances he hath, which are drawn with him. Befides, he can take no reputation from you.

Montgomery is an honeft man, and a good ob-ferver. Can you do nothing with Naunton (*b*)? Who would think now, that I name Naunton to my Lord of Buckingham? But I fpeak to you point-blank : no crooked end, either for myfelf, or for others turn.

The French treaty, befides alliance, is to have three fecret articles : the one, the protection of the liberty of Germany, and to avoid from it all forces thence, like to that, which was concluded between the Princes of Germany and Henry II (*c*), the laft King, except Henry IV, of value in France ; for the race of the Valois were *faitneants :* and, in the name of Germany, to conclude the Grifons and Valtoline. The fecond, the conferving the liberties of the Low Countries. The third, the free trade into all parts of both Eaft and Weft Indies. All thefe import no invafive hoftility, but only the uniting of the ftates of Europe againft the growing ambition of Spain. Neither do any of thefe touch upon the caufe of religion.

I am perfuaded, the hinge of the King's affairs, for his fafety and greatnefs, is now in Spain. I would the King had an abler inftrument.

Above all, you muft look to the fafety of Ireland, both becaufe it is moft dangerous for this ftate (for the difeafe will ever fall to the weakeft part ;) and be-

---

(*a*) William, Earl of Pembroke.

(*b*) Sir Robert Naunton, who had been Secretary of State, and was now Mafter of the court of Wards.

(*c*) This league firft arrefted the greatnefs of the Emperor, and cloiftered him. *Note of Lord Bacon.*

fides,

fides, this early declaration againſt Spain, which the Popiſh party call abrupt, and is your Grace's work, may be thought to be the danger of Ireland. It were good you called to you Belfaſt *(d)* and Grandifon *(e)*, and aſk their opinions, what is beſt to be done for the fafety of Ireland, either by increaſing the liſt of companies, and by contenting thoſe, that are in arrear, by paying ; or by altering any governor there ; or by having companies ready muſtered and trained here, towards the coaſt of Ireland ; or by having ſhipping in readineſs, &c. For this gown commiſſion, I like it well ; but it is but paper-ſhot for defence.

If the Papiſts be put in deſpair, it both endangereth Ireland, and maketh a greater difficulty in the treaty and alliance with France.

To think of a difference to be put between the Jefuits and other Prieſts and Papiſts, as to reduce, in ſome moderation, the baniſhment of the one, though not of the other : but to remember, that they were the reaſonableſt, as I take it, in the conſult ; and it may draw the blow of an aſſaſſin againſt Buckingham.

At leaſt, the going on with the parliament hath gained this, that the diſcourſe is ceaſed, " My Lord " of Buckingham hath a great taſk. His head is " full : either the match breaks, or his fortune " breaks. He has run his courſes with the ſtream of " the King's ways ; but now he goeth croſs-way, he " may ſoon loſe his own way."

If your Grace go not now conſtantly on for religion, and round dealing with Spain, men will either think they were miſtaken in you ; or that you are brought about ; or that your will is good, but you have no power.

(d) Arthur Chicheſter, Baron of Belfaſt, who had been made Lord Deputy of Ireland in 1604.

(e) Oliver St. John, Viſcount Grandifon, made Lord Deputy of Ireland in Auguſt, 1616.

Your

Your Grace hath a great party againſt you, and a good rough way. The Spaniards hate you : the Papiſts little better. In the opinion of the people, you are green, and not yet at a gage. Particulars are, for the moſt part, diſcontented friends, or reconciled enemies : and that nice dividing between the *ſol orient* and *occident.*

To the Duke of BUCKINGHAM.

Excellent Lord,

I DESIRE in this, which I now preſume to write to your Grace, to be underſtood, that my bow carrieth not ſo high, as to aim to adviſe touching any of the great affairs now on foot, and ſo to paſs it to his Majeſty through your hands ; though it be true, that my good affection towards his Majeſty and the Prince and the public is that, which will laſt die in me ; and though I think alſo his Majeſty would take it but well, if, having been that man I have been, my honeſt and loyal mind ſhould ſometimes feed upon thoſe thoughts. But my level is no farther, but to do the part of a true friend in adviſing yourſelf for your own greatneſs and ſafety ; although, even in this alſo, I aſſure myſelf I perform a good duty to the public ſervice, unto which I reckon your ſtanding and power to be a firm and ſound pillar of ſupport.

Firſt, therefore, my Lord, call to mind oft, and conſider duly, how infinitely your Grace is bound to God in this one point, which I find to be a moſt rare piece, and wherein, either of ancient or late times, there are few examples ; that is, that you are beloved ſo dearly, both by the King and the Prince. You are not as a Lerma, or an Olivares, and many others the like, who have inſinuated themſelves

felves into the favours of young Princes, during the
Kings, their fathers, time, againft the bent and inclination of the Kings: but contrary-wife, the King
himfelf hath knit the knot of truft and favour between
the Prince and your Grace, wherein you are not fo
much to take comfort in that you may feem to have
two lives in your own greatnefs, as in this, that
hereby you are enabled to be a noble inftrument for
the fervice, contentment, and heart's-eafe, both of
father and fon.   For where there is fo loving and indulgent a father, and fo refpective and obedient a
fon, and a faithful and worthy fervant, interefted in
both their favours upon all occafions, it cannot be
but a comfortable houfe.   This point your Grace is
principally to acknowledge and cherifh.

Next, that, which I fhould have placed firft, fave
that the laying open of God's benefits is a good preparation to religion and godlinefs, your Grace is to
maintain yourfelf firm and conftant in the way you
have begun; which is, in being and fhewing yourfelf
to be a true and found Proteftant.   This is your foul's
health.   This is that you owe to God above, for his
fingular favours: and this is that, which hath
brought you into the good opinion and good will of
the realm in general.   So that, as your cafe differeth
(as I faid) from the cafe of other favourites, in that
you have both King and Prince; fo in this, that you
have alfo now the hearts of the beft fubjects (for I do
not love the word *people,*) your cafe differeth from
your own, as it ftood before.   And becaufe I would
have your reputation in this point complete, let me
advife you, that the name of Puritans in a Papift's
mouth do not make you to withdraw your favour
from fuch, as are honeft and religious men; fo that
they be not fo turbulent and factious fpirits, or adverfe to the government of the church, though they
be traduced by that name.   For of this kind is the
greateft part of the body of the fubjects; and befides,

A a 4   (which

(which is not to be forgotten) it is safest for the King and his service, that such men have their dependance upon your Grace, who are intirely the King's, rather than upon any other subject.

For the Papists, it is not unknown to your Grace, that you are not, at this time, much in their books. But be you like yourself; and far be it from you, under a King and Prince of that clemency, to be inclined to rigour or persecution.

But three things must be looked unto : the first, that they be suppressed in any insolency, which may tend either to disquiet the civil estate, or scandalize our church in fact ; for otherwise, all their doctrine doth it in opinion. The second, that there be an end, or limit, of those graces, which shall be thought fit for them, and that there be not every day new demands hearkened to. The third, that for those cases and graces, which they have received, or shall receive, of the state, the thanks go the right way ; that is, to the King and Prince, and not to any foreigner. For this is certain, that if they acknowledge them from the state, they may perhaps sit down, when they are well. But if they have a dependance upon a foreigner, there will be no end of their growing desires and hopes. And in this point also, your Lordship's wisdom and moderation may do much good.

For the match with Spain, it is too great and dark a business for me to judge of. But as it hath relation to concern yourself, I will, as in the rest, deal freely with your Grace.

My Lord, you owe, in this matter, two debts to the King : the one, that, if in your conscience and judgement you be persuaded it be dangerous and prejudicial to him and his kingdoms, you deliver your soul, and in the freedom of a faithful counsellor, joined with the humbleness of a dutiful servant, you declare yourself accordingly, and shew your reasons. The other, that if the King in his high judgement,

or

or the Prince in his fettled affection, be refolved to have it go on; that then you move in their orb, as far as they fhall lay it upon you. But mean while, let me tell your Grace, that I am not of the general opinion abroad, that the match muft break, or elfe my Lord of Buckingham's fortune muft break. I am of another opinion; and yet perhaps it will be hard to make you believe it, becaufe both fides will perfuade you to the contrary. For they, that would not have it go on, will work upon that conceit, to make you oppofe it more ftrongly. They, that would have it go on, will do the fame, to make you take up betimes, and come about. But I having good affiance in your Grace's judgement, will tell you my reafons, why I thus think, and fo leave it. If the match fhould go on, and put cafe againft your counfel and opinion; doth any man think, that fo profound a King, and fo well feen in the fcience of reigning, and fo underftanding a Prince, will ever fuffer the whole fway of affairs and greatnefs to go that way? And, if not, who fhould be a fitter perfon to keep the balance even, than your Grace, whom the King and Prince know to be fo intirely their own, and have found fo nobly independent upon any other? Surely my opinion is, you are likely to be greater by counterpoife againft the Spanifh dependance, than you will by concurrence. And therefore, in God's name, do your duty faithfully and wifely; for behaving yourfelf well otherwife, as I know you will, your fortune is like to be well either way.

For that excellent Lady, whofe fortune is fo diftant from her merits and virtue, the Queen of Bohemia, your Grace being, as it were, the firft-born, or prime man of the King's creatures, muft in confequence owe the moft to his children and generations; whereof I know your noble heart hath far greater fenfe, than any man's words can infufe into you. And therefore whatfoever liveth within the compafs

of

of your duty, and of possibility, will no doubt spring from you out of that fountain.

It is open to every man's discourse, that there are but two ways for the restitution of the Palatinate, treaty and arms. It is good therefore to consider of the middle acts, which may make either of these ways desperate, to the end they may be avoided in that way, which shall be chosen. If no match, either this with Spain, or perhaps some other with Austria, no restitution by treaty. If the Dutch, either be ruined, or grow to a peace, of themselves, with Spain, no restitution by war.

But these things your Grace understandeth far better than myself. And, as I said before, the points of state I aim not at farther, than they may concern your Grace, to whom, while I live, and shall find it acceptable to you, I shall ever be ready to give the tribute of a true friend and servant, and shall always think my counsels given you happy, if you shall pardon them, when they are free ; and follow them, when they are good. God preserve and prosper you.

To the Duke of BUCKINGHAM (f).

Excellent Lord,

THERE is a suit, whereunto I may, as it were, claim kindred, and which may be of credit and profit unto me ; and it is an old arrear, which is called upon, from Sir Nicolas Bacon, my eldest brother. It may be worth to me perhaps two thousand pounds ; and yet I may deal kindly with my brother, and also reward liberally (as I mean to do) the officers of the Exchequer, which have brought it to light. Good my Lord obtain it of the King, and be earnest in it for me. It will acquit the King somewhat of his

(f) The Duke's answer to this letter, dated at Newmarket, the 28th of January, 1673, is printed in Lord Bacon's works.

promise,

promife, that he would have care of my wants ; for hitherto, fince my misfortunes, I have tafted of his Majefty's mercy, but not of his bounty. But your Lordfhip may be pleafed in this, to clear the coaft with my Lord Treafurer ; elfe there it will have a ftop. I am almoft at laft caft for means ; and yet it grieveth me moft, that at fuch a time as this, I fhould not be rather ferviceable to your Grace, than troublefome.

God preferve and profper your Grace.

Your Grace's moft obliged,

and faithful fervant,

This 23d of January, 1623.

FR. ST. ALBAN.

To the Earl of OXFORD (g).

My very good Lord,

LET me be an humble fuitor to your Lordfhip, for your noble favour. I would be glad to receive my writ this parliament (h), that I may not die in difhonour ; but by no means, except it fhould be with the love and confent of my Lords to re-admit me, if their Lordfhips vouchfafe to think me worthy of their company ; or if they think that, which I have fuffered now thefe three years, in lofs of place, in lofs of means, and in lofs of liberty for a great time, to be a fufficient expiation for my faults, whereby I may now feem in their eyes to be a fit fubject of their grace, as I have been before of their juftice. My good Lord, the good, which the commonwealth might reap of my fuffering, is already inned. Juftice

(g) Henry Vere, who died in 1625. He was Lord Great Chamberlain of England.

(h) that met February 19, 1623, and was prorogued May 29, 1624.

is

is done ; an example is made for reformation ; the authority of the House for judicature is established. There can be no farther use of my misery ; perhaps some little may be of my service ; for, I hope, I shall be found a man humbled as a Christian, though not dejected as a worldling. I have great opinion of your Lordship's power, and great hope, for many reasons, of your favour ; which, if I may obtain, I can say no more, but nobleness is ever requited in itself ; and God, whose special favour in my afflictions I have manifestly found to my comfort, will, I trust, be my pay-master of that, which cannot be requited by

Your Lordship's affectionate humble servant, &c.

Indorsed, *February* 2, 1623.

To Sir FRANCIS BARNHAM (*i*).

Good Cousin,

UPON a little searching, made touching the patents of the survey of coals, I find matter not only to accquit myself, but likewise to do myself much right.

Any reference to me, or any certificate of mine, I find not. Neither is it very likely I made any ; for that, when it came to the great seal, I stayed it. I did not only stay it, but brought it before the council-table, as not willing to pass it, except their Lordships allowed it. The Lords gave hearing to the business, I remember, two several days ; and in

---

(*i*) He appears to be a relation of his Lordship's Lady, who was daughter of Benedict Barnham, Esq; Alderman of the city of London. Sir Francis was appointed, by his Lordship, one of the executors of his last will.

the

the end difallowed it, and commended my care and circumfpection, and ordered, that it fhould continue ftayed; and fo it did all my time.

About a twelvemonth fince, my Lord Duke of Lenox, now deceafed (*k*), wrote to me to have the privy feal; which, though I refpected his Lordfhip much, I refufed to deliver to him, but was content to put it into the right hand; that is, to fend it to my Lord Keeper (*l*); giving knowledge how it had been ftayed. My Lord Keeper received it by mine own fervant, writeth back to me, acknowledging the receit, and adding, that he would lay it afide untill his Lordfhip heard farther from my Lord Steward (*m*), and the reft of the Lords. Whether this firft privy feal went to the great feal, or that it went about again, I know not: but all my part is, that I have related. I ever reft

Your faithful friend and coufin,

March 14, 1623.

FR. ST. ALBAN.

To the Duke of BUCKINGHAM.

My Lord,

I AM now full three years old in mifery; neither hath there been any thing done for me, whereby I might either die out of ignominy, or live out of want. But now, that your Grace (God's name be praifed for it) hath recovered your health, and are come to the court, and the parliament bufinefs hath alfo intermiffion; I firmly hope, your Grace will deal with his Majefty, that as I have tafted of

(*k*) He died fuddenly, February 12, 162$\frac{4}{5}$.
(*l*) See his letter to Lord St. Alban, of February 7, 1622.
(*m*) James, Marquis of Hamilton, who died March 2, 162$\frac{4}{5}$.

his

his mercy, I may also taste of his bounty. Your Grace, I know, for a business of a private man, cannot win yourself more honour; and I hope I shall yet live to do you service. For my fortune hath (I thank God) made no alteration in my mind, but to the better. I ever rest humbly

Your Grace's most obliged

and faithful servant,

FR. ST. ALBAN.

If I may know by two or three words from your Grace, that you will set in for me, I will propound somewhat that shall be modest, and leave it to your Grace, whether you will move his Majesty yourself, or recommend it by some of your Lordship's friends, that wish me well; [as my Lord of Arundel, or Secretary Conway, or Mr. James Maxwell (*n*).]

To the Duke of BUCKINGHAM.

Excellent Lord,

I UNDERSTAND, by Sir John Suckling, that he attended yesterday at Greenwich, hoping, according to your Grace's appointment, to have found you there, and to have received your Grace's pleasure touching my suit, but missed of you: and this day he sitteth upon the subsidy at Brentford, and shall not be at court this week: which causeth me to use these few lines to hear from your Grace, I hope, to my comfort; humbly praying pardon, if I num-

(*n*). The words included in brackets have a line drawn after them.

ber

ber, thus the days, and that misery should exceed modesty. I ever rest

Your Grace's most faithful

and obliged servant,

June 30, 1624.

Fr. St. Alban.

To Sir R I C H A R D W E S T O N, *Chancellor of the Exchequer.*

Mr. Chancellor,

THIS way, by Mr. Myn, besides a number of little difficulties it hath, amounteth to this, that I shall pay interest for mine own money. Besides, I must confess, I cannot bow my mind to be a suitor, much less a shifter, for that means, which I enjoy by his Majesty's grace and bounty. And therefore I am rather ashamed of that I have done, than minded to go forward. So that I leave it to yourself what you think fit to be done in your honour and my case, resting

Your very loving friend,

London, this 7th of
   July, 1624.

Fr. St. Alban.

To the Duke of B U C K I N G H A M.

Excellent Lord,

NOW that your Grace hath the King private, and at better leisure, the noise of soldiers, ambassadors, parliaments, a little ceasing, I hope you will remember your servant; for at so good a time,

time (*o*), and after so long a time, to forget him, were almost to forsake him. But, howsoever, I shall still remain

Your Grace's most obliged

and faithful servant,

Fr. St. Alban.

I am bold to put into my good friend, Sir Tobie Matthew's hand, a copy of my petition, which your Grace had sent to Sir John Suckling.

Indorsed, *August*, 1624.

To the Duke of Buckingham.

Excellent Lord,

I AM infinitely bound to your Grace for your late favours. I send your Grace a copy of your letter, signifying his Majesty's pleasure, and of the petition. The course, I take it, must be, to make a warrant for the execution of the same, by way of reference to Mr. Chancellor of the Exchequer, and Mr. Attorney (*p*). I most humbly pray your Grace likewise, to prostrate me at his Majesty's feet, with most humble thanks for the grant of my petition, whose sweet presence since I discontinued, methinks I am neither amongst the living, nor amongst the dead.

I cannot but likewise gratulate his Majesty on the extreme prosperous success of his business, since this time twelvemonth. I know I speak it in a dangerous

(*o*) This seems to refer to the anniversary thanksgiving-day for the King's delivery from the Gowry conspiracy, on the 5th of August, 1600.

(*p*) Sir Thomas Coventry.

time ;

time; becaufe the dye of the Low Countries is upon the throw. But yet that is all one. For if it fhould be a blow (which I hope in God it fhall not) yet it would have been ten times worfe, if former courfes had not been taken. But this is the raving of an hot ague.

God evermore blefs his Majefty's perfon and defigns, and likewife make your Grace a fpectacle of profperity, as you have hitherto been.

Your Grace's moft faithful,

and obliged, and by you revived fervant,

Grey's Inn, 9th of
  October, 1624.   Fr. St. Alban.

To the Chancellor of the Duchy (*q*)*, Sir* Humphrey
May.

Good Mr. Chancellor,

I Do approve very well your forbearance to move my fuits, in regard the Duke's return (*r*) is fo near at hand, which I thought would have been a longer matter; and I imagine there is a *gratiaſtitium* till he come. I do not, but you fhall find his Grace nobly difpofed. The laft time that you fpake with him about me, I remember you fent me word, he thanked you for being fo forward for me. Yet I could wifh, that you took fome occafion to fpeak with him, generally to my advantage, before you move to him any particular fuit; and to let me know how you find him.

My Lord Treafurer fent me a good anfwer touching my monies. I pray you continue to quick-

(*q*) This letter is indorfed, 1625.
(*r*) From Paris, whither the Duke of Buckingham went in May, 1625, to conduct the new Queen to England.

B b

en him, that the King may once clear with me. A fire of old wood needeth no blowing; but old men do. I ever reſt

> Yours to do you ſervice.

Conſultations in Parliament anno 1 Caroli Regis, *at Weſtminſter,* anno Domini 1625 (s). [*Found among Lord Bacon's papers.*]

THE conſultations now in parliament may be regulated into theſe four heads following.

1. The ſtate of the King in the conſtant revenue of his crown.

1. What it was; and how far the *introitus et exitus* there ordered. Vide my book of a medium for ten years before *primo Jacobi Regis.*

2. What now it is in clear revenue, either by

- Lands;
- Cuſtoms, and impoſitions;
- Caſualties.

Gifts of land, *ex more motu*, and no valuable conſideration. This may be revoked.

Grants of penſions, now 120,000 l. before but 18,000 l. Good times have reſumed them upon neceſſity.

Increaſe of houſehold, from 45,000 l. to 80,000 l.

(s) This parliament met on the 18th of June, and was diſſolved Auguſt 12, 1625.

The

The purveyors more, and the tables lefs furnifhed than formerly.

Fruitlefs ambaffages with larger allowance than formerly. To reducè them to the ordinary of the late Queen.

Treble increafe of the privy purfe. Double increafe of the treafury of the chamber and great wardrobe. In all, by not ufing the beft courfe of affignments, whereby the creditor is delayed in his payment, and the King furcharged in the price.

The exchequer-man making his beft profit from the King's wants.

3.
The means how it is abated by

Subfidies and fifteenths, fpent only in defence of the ftates, or aid of our allies.

Tonnage and poundage employed in guard of the feas. Loans rarely, and that employed entirely for the public. Impofition by prerogative, of old cuftom, rated eafily by the book of rates, if any, either limited to time or meafure.

1.
Formerly in taxes by parliament.

2.
The condition of the fubject in his freedom and fortune.

Cuftom

2. Now in
{
Cuftom inhanced by the new books of rates. Impofitions and monopolies multiplied; and this fettled to continue by grants.

Tonnage and poundage levied, though no act of parliament, nor the feas guarded. The times, the ways, and the perfons, that induced thefe.
}

3. The employment or wafte of treafure.
{

1. Public treafure is to be examined.
{
What fums have been granted for the defence of the ftate thefe laft three years.

How in particular fpent, and where.

By what advice, as by direction of
{
1. The council of war appointed by parliament.
2. By full order of the council.
3. By any other than thofe, and by whom.
}
}

2. The King's fubjects.
{
How many, and when transported, or employed, as to
{
1. The Palatinate.
2. Count Mansfield.
3. Land foldiers in the laft fleet.
}
}
}

The

The defign, where they were fent.

The council, that directed it.

The fuccefs of the action, and the return of the perfons in number, and the lofs.

4. Our own.

The number and quantity employed feverally.

The manner of imbarking thefe fhips, and what prejudice and difcouragement of trade.

The council, that directed fuch employments.

The feveral fucceffes, as at Argier, and Cadiz.

3. In fhips and munition of

5. Strangers, as prize.

6. Allies.

Hired by contract to ferve, and how ufed: or,

Taken as prize: if fo,

How then delivered and dealt withal in the courfe of juftice.

What fuccefs hath followed upon injuftice done them: as the arreft of our goods in France and Germany, whereby our goods are at a ftand for vent.

The

The number and true value of the goods.

The account made to his Majesty, or his officers, for it.

7. Enemies.

The dismissing and discharging of any of them and the goods, viz.

1. By whom the direction.

2. The pretence.

3. The value of the goods.

4. The place, whither they went.

Under this head will fall the complaint of Dover.

1. How formerly we stood.

A nation feared, renowned, victorious.

It made the Netherlands there a state, when it was none.

Recovered Henry IV. of France's kingdom, when he had nothing left but the town of Dieppe.

Conquered the invincible navy of Spain in 88.

Took towns in Portugal the year following, and marched 100 miles upon the firm land.

Fired, or brought away, the Spanish navy before Cadiz, and sacked the town.

Took the Spanish ships daily, and spoiled the Port-towns of the West-Indies, never losing but one ship during all the Spanish wars.

Reduced the ambition of that King for a fifth monarchy to so low an ebb, that in one

one year he paid 2500 millions of ducats for interest, so as after he was inforced to beg treaties of peace, in low terms, at the last Queen Regent's hands.

A carriage and readiness in the people to assist their sovereign in purse and person.

4. Honour of the King and state, which, as in all other, consists more *in famâ* than *vi*.

2. The cause of the good success then.

A wisdom and gravity of council, who ordered nothing but by public debate, and then assisted by the military professors either by land or sea, of the best repute, and such only employed.

3. In what condition.

4. Loss in reputation by the ill success

In the voyage of Algier.

In the Palatinate.

In the journey with Mansfield.

In this last to Cadiz (t).

Condition we now stand by

5. The reasons.

The unchearfulness we have either to adventure our purses or goods, occasioned by a distrust we have of the successes.

The want of the like courses and counsels, that were formerly used.

(u) In October, 1625.

B b 4

I could

I could wifh, that for every of thefe four heads, there were a particular committee to examine an apt report for the Houfes : and the Houfes, upon every report, to put itfelf into a committee of the whole affembly ; and, after a full and deliberate debate, to order a model, or form, for a conference with the Lords : and fo, together, humbly to prefent unto his Majefty a remonftrance of their labour ; offering withal a ferious confultation and debate amongft themfelves for the finding out the fitteft manner both for the defence of the ftate and our allies, reformation of the errors, and a conftant way to raife fuch fupplies of money and neceffaries, as may enable his Majefty to proceed chearfully, and I hope affuredly, in this his glorious action, not only for himfelf and the ftate, but for all that profefs the fame religion, and are alike to be overwhelmed in the ambition of the Spanifh monarchy.

To Sir ROBERT PYE.

Good Sir Robert Pye,

LET me intreat you to difpatch that warrant of a petty fum, that it may help to bear my charge of coming up (*x*) to London. The Duke, you know, loveth me, and my Lord Treafurer (*y*) ftandeth now towards me in very good affection and refpect (*z*). You, that are the third perfon in thefe bufineffes, I affure myfelf, will not be wanting ;

(*x*) From Gorhambury.

(*y*) Sir James Lord Ley, advanced from the poft of Lord Chief Juftice of the King's Bench, on the 20th of December 1624, to that of Lord Treafurer ; and created Earl of Marlborough on the 5th of February, 1625.

(*z*) His Lordfhip had not been always in that difpofition towards the Lord Vifcount St. Alban ; for the latter has, among the letters printed in his works, one to this Lord Treafurer, feverely expoftulating with him about his unkindnefs and injuftice.

for

for you have profeſſed and ſhewed, ever ſince I loſt the ſeal, your good will towards me. I reſt

Your affectionate and aſſured friend, &c.

Indorſed, *To Sir Robert Pye.* Gor. 1625.

To the Earl of DORSET (*a*).

My very good Lord,

THIS gentleman, the bearer hereof, Mr. Colles by name, is my neighbour. He is commended for a civil young man. I think he wanteth no metal, but he is peaceable. It was his hap to fall out with Mr. Matthew Francis, ſerjeant at arms, about a toy ; the one affirming, that a hare was fair killed, and the other foul. Words multiplied, and ſome blows paſſed on either ſide. But ſince the firſt falling out, the ſerjeant hath uſed towards him divers threats and affronts, and, which is a point of danger, ſent to him a letter of chalenge : but Mr. Colles, doubting the contents of the letter, refuſed to receive it. Motions have been made alſo of reconcilement, or of reference to ſome gentlemen of the country not partial: but the ſerjeant hath refuſed all, and now, at laſt, ſueth him in the Earl Marſhal's court. The gentleman ſaith, he diſtruſteth not his cauſe upon the hearing ; but would be glad to avoid reſtraint, or long and chargeable attendance. Let me therefore pray your good Lordſhip to move the noble Earl (*b*) in that kind, to carry a favourable hand towards him, ſuch as may ſtand

(*a*) Sir Edward Sackville ſucceeded to that title on the death of his brother Richard, March 28, 1624.
(*b*) Arundel, Earl Marſhal.

with juftice and the order of that court. I ever reft

Your Lordfhip's faithful friend and fervant.

Indorfed, *To E. Dorfet. Gor.* 1625.

Sir THOMAS COVENTRY, *Attorney General, to the Lord Vifcount* ST. ALBAN.

My very good Lord,

I Received from your Lordfhip two letters, the one of the 23d, the other of the 28th of this month. To the former, I do affure your Lordfhip I have not heard any thing of any fuits or motion, either touching the reverfion of your honours or the rent of your farm of petty writs; and, if I had heard any thing thereof, I would not have been unmindful of that caveat, which heretofore you gave in by former letters, nor flack to do you the beft fervice I might.

The debt of Sir Nicolas Bacon refteth as it did; for in the latter end of King James's time, it exhibited a *quo warranto* in the Exchequer, touching that liberty, againft St. Nicolas, which abated by his death; then another againft Sir Edmund, which by the demife of the King, and by reafon of the adjournment of the late term, hath had no farther proceeding, but that day is given to plead.

Concerning your other letter, I humbly thank your Lordfhip for your favourable and good wifhes to me; though I, knowing my own unaptnefs to fo great an employment (*c*), fhould be moft heartily glad, if his Majefty had, or yet would choofe, a man of more merit. But, if otherwife, humblenefs

(*4*) that of the great feal, of which Sir Thomas Coventry was three days after made Lord Keeper, on the 1ft of November 1625.

and fubmiffion becomes the fervant, and to ftand in
that ftation where his Majefty will have him. But
as for the requeft you make for your fervant, though
I proteft I am not yet engaged by promife to any;
becaufe I hold it too much boldnefs towards my
mafter, and difcourtefy towards my Lord Keeper (*d*),
to difpofe of places, while he had the feal: yet in
refpect I have fome fervants, and fome of my kindred, apt for the place you write of, and have been
already fo much importuned by noble perfons, when
I lately was with his Majefty at Salifbury, as it will
be hard for me to give them all denial; I am not
able to difcern, how I can accommodate your fervant;
though for your fake, and in refpect of the former
knowledge myfelf have had of the merit and worth
of the gentlemen, I fhould be moft ready and willing
to perform your defire, if it were in my power.
And fo, with remembrance of my fervice to your
Lordfhip, I remain

At your Lordfhip's commandment,

Kingfbury,
Oct. 29, 1625.

Tho. Coventry.

To the Right Honourable, and my very good Lord, the
Vifcount St. Alban.

To Mr. Roger Palmer.

Good Mr. Roger Palmer,

I THANK God, by means of the fweet air
of the country, I have obtained fome degree
of health. Sending to the court, I thought

(*c*) Bifhop Williams, who had refigned the great feal, on the
25th of October 1625, to Sir John Suckling, who brought his
Majefty's warrant to receive it, dated at Salifbury on the 23d of
that month.

3

I would

I would salute you: and I would be glad, in this solitary time and place, to hear a little from you how the world goeth, according to your friendly manner heretofore.

Fare ye well most heartily.

Your very affectionate and assured friend,

Gorhambury,
Oct. 29, 1625.

Fr. St. Alban.

To the Duke of Buckingham.

Excellent Lord,

I Could not but signify unto your Grace my rejoicing, that God hath sent your Grace a son and heir (e), and that you are fortunate as well in your house, as in the state of the kingdom. These blessings come from God, as I do not doubt but your Grace doth, with all thankfulness, acknowledge, vowing to him your service. Myself, I praise his divine Majesty, have gotten some step into health. My wants are great; but yet I want not a desire to do your Grace service; and I marvel, that your Grace should think to pull down the monarchy of Spain without my good help. Your Grace will give me leave to be merry, however the world goeth with me. I ever rest

Your Grace's most faithful,

and obliged servant, &c.

I wish your Grace a good new year.

(e) born November 17, 1625, and named Charles. Diary of the Life of Archbishop Laud, published by Mr. Wharton, p. 24. This son of the Duke died the 16th of March, 1625. Ibid. p. 40.

To

Good Mr. Chancellor,

I Did wonder what was become of you, and was very glad to hear you were come to court; which, methinks, as the times go, should miss you as well as I.

I send you another letter, which I wrote to you of an old date, to avoid repetition; and I continue my request then to you, to found the Duke of Buckingham's good affection towards me, before you do move him in the particular petition. Only the present occasion doth invite me to desire, that his Grace would procure me a pardon of the King of the whole sentence. My writ for parliament I have now had twice before the time, and that without any express restraint not to use it. It is true, that I shall not be able, in respect of my health, to attend in parliament; but yet I might make a proxy. Time hath turned envy to pity; and I have a long Cleansing week of five years expectation and more. Sir John Bennet hath his pardon; and my Lord of Somerset hath his pardon, and, they say, shall sit in parliament. My Lord of Suffolk cometh to parliament, though not to council. I hope I deserve not to be the only outcast.

God keep you. I ever rest

Your most affectionate friend,

to do you service.

I wish you a good new year.

Indorsed, *To the Chancellor of the Duchy.* Ger. 1625.

*To the Marquis d'*EFFIAT, *the French Ambaſſador.*

Monſ. l'Ambaſſadeur, mon fils,

VOUS ſcavez que le commencement eſt la moitié du fait. Voyla pourquoy je vous ay eſcrit ce petit mot de lettre, vous priant de vous ſouvenir de voſtre noble promeſſe de me ſmettre en la bonne grace de noſtre tres-excellente Royne, & m'en faire recevoir quelque gracieuſe demonſtration. Voſtre Excellence prendra auſſi, s'il vous plaiſt, quelque occaſion de preſcher un peu à mon advantage en l'oreille du Duc de Buckingham en general. Dieu vous ayt en ſa ſaincte garde.

Jan. 18, 1625.

Voſtre tres-affectionné

et tres-humble ſerviteur,

Fr. St. Alban,

The

The following letters, wanting both dates and cir-
cumstances to determine such dates, are placed here
together.

To KING JAMES I.

May it please your Majesty,

THINKING often, as I ought, of your Majesty's virtue and fortune, I do observe, not
without admiration, that those civil acts of sovereignty, which are of the greatest merit, and therefore of truest glory, are, by the providence of God,
manifestly put into your hands, as a chosen vessel to
receive from God, and an excellent instrument to
work amongst men the best and noblest things.
The highest degree of sovereign honour is to be
founder of a kingdom or estate; for, as in the acts
of God, the creation is more than the conservation;
and as, among men, the birth-day is accounted the
chiefest of the days of life; so, to found a kingdom,
is more worthy, than to augment, or to administer
the same. And this is an honour, that no man can
take from your Majesty, that the day of your
coming to the crown of England was as the birth-
day of the kingdom intire Britain.

The next degree of sovereign honour is the plantation of a country or territory, and the reduction
of a nation, from waste soil and barbarous manners,
to a civil population. And in this kind also your
Majesty hath made a fair and prosperous beginning
in your realm of Ireland.

The third eminent act of sovereignty is to be a
law-giver, whereof he speaketh,

> *Pace datâ terris, animum ad civilia vertit*
> *Jura suum, legesque tulit justissimus author.*

And

And another faith, " Ecquid eft, quod tam pro-
" priè dici poteft actum ejus, qui togatus in re-
" publicâ cum poteftate imperioque verfatur, quam
" lex. Quære acta Gracchi ; leges Semproniæ pro-
" ferentur : quære Syllæ, Corneliæ quid ? Cnei
" Pompeii tertius confulatus in quibus actis con-
" fiftit ? Nempe legibus. A Cæfare ipfo fi quæreres
" quidnam egiffet in urbe et toga.; leges multas fe
" refpondeat et præclaras tuliffe."

To the KING.

It may pleafe your Majefty,

A Full heart is like a full pen : it can hardly make
any diftinguifhed work. The more I look
upon my own weaknefs, the more I muft magnify
your favours ; and the more I behold your favours,
the more I muft confider mine own weaknefs. This
is my hope, that God, who hath moved your heart
to favour me, will write your fervice in my heart.
Two things I may promife; for, though they be not
mine own, yet they are furer than mine own, becaufe they are God's gifts ; that is, integrity and
induftry. And therefore, whenfoever I fhall make
my account to you, I fhall do it in thefe words,
ecce tibi lucrifeci, and not *ecce mihi lucrifeci*. And
for induftry, I fhall take to me, in this procuration,
not Martha's part, to be bufied in many things, but
Mary's part, which is to intend your fervice ; for the
lefs my abilities are, the more they ought to be contracted *ad unum*. For the prefent, I humbly pray
your Majefty to accept my moft humble thanks
and vows. as the forerunners of your fervice, which
I fhall always perform with a faithful heart.

Your Majefty's moft obedient fervant,

FR. BACON.

To

To the K I N G's *Most Excellent Majesty*

The humble petition of the Lord Verulam, *Viscount* St. Alban.

THAT whereas your fupplicant, for reward of full fixteen years fervice in the painfulleft places of your kingdom, (how acceptable or ufeful, he appealeth to your Majefty's gracious remembrance) had of your Majefty's gracious bounty two grants, both under the great feal of England; the one a penfion of 1200 l. the other a farm of the petty writs, about 600 l. *per annum* in value, which was long fince affigned to your fupplicant's wife's friends in truft for her maintenance: which two grants are now the fubftance of your fupplicant's and his wife's means, and the only remains of your Majefty's former favours, except his dignities, which, without means, are but burdens to his fortunes:

So it is, moft gracious Sovereign, that both thefe are now taken from him; the penfion ftopped, the leafe feized, the penfion being, at this prefent, in arrear 500 l. and at Michaelmafs 800 l. is ftopped, as he conceiveth, upon the general ftop of penfions; though he hopeth affuredly, that your Majefty, that looketh with the gracious eye of a King, and not the ftrict eye of an officer, will behold his cafe as efpecial, if not fingular. The latter was firft feized for fatisfaction of a private gentleman, your fupplicant unheard, and without any fhadow of a legal courfe. Since it hath been continued, in refpect of a debt to your Majefty for the arrear of rent upon the fame farm, amounting to 1500 l. But whereas your Majefty's farmers debtors for their rents, and other your debtors, have ufually favours, fometimes of ftallment, fometimes upon equity, if their farms decay, or at leaft when they are called upon, have days given,

C c

given, put in security, or the like; your supplicant was never so much as sent to, no warnings to provide, no days given, but put out of possession suddenly, by a private and peremptory warrant, without any spark of those favours used to the meanest subjects. So that now your supplicant having left little or no annual income, is in great extremity, having spread the remnant of his former fortunes in jewels and plate, and the like, upon his poor creditors, having scarce left bread to himself and family.

In tender consideration whereof, your supplicant, and overthrown servant, doth implore your Majesty's grace and goodness felt by so many, known to all, and whereof he cannot live to despair; first, in general, that your Majesty will not suffer him, upon whose arm your princely arm hath so often been, when you presided in counsel (so near he was) and who hath borne your image in metal, but more in his heart, utterly to perish; or, which is worse, to live, in his last days, in an abject and sordid condition. Next, in particular, that your Majesty would be graciously pleased to take present order to have the arrear of his pension paid, and likewise that for the future it may be settled, that he be not at courtesy, nor to beg at that door, which is like enough to be shut against him. Secondly, that the possession of his wife's lease may be restored to her; and this bit of arrear to your Majesty, that you will be pleased to remit it, according to your Majesty's gracious and pious promise, when you admitted him to you in the night of his troubles, which was, that you would not meddle with his estate, but to mend it. In the restoring the possession, you shall remove your hand of arms: in the remitting of the rent, you shall extend your hand of grace: and if he be not worthy of so much favour, as to have it released yet, that it may be respited for some good time, that he may make somewhat of that his father left him, and keep

him-

himfelf out of want, in fuch fort, that your fupplicant, that afpireth but to live to ftudy, be not put
to ftudy to live.　And he, according to his bounden
duty, fhall not intermit, as ever he hath done, to
pray to God for your Majefty's health and happinefs.

To the Marquis of B U C K I N G H A M.

My very good Lord,

I Hear yefterday was a day of very great honour
　to his Majefty, which I do congratulate. I hope
alfo his Majefty may reap honour out of my adverfity, as he hath done ftrength out of my profperity.
His Majefty knows beft his own ways; and for me
to defpair of him, were a fin not to be forgiven. I
thank God I have overcome the bitternefs of this
cup by Chriftian refolution; fo that worldly matters
are but mint and cumin.

God ever preferve you.

Indorfed, *To my Lord Buckingham after my troubles.*

To the Marquis of B U C K I N G H A M.

My very good Lord,

I Thought it my duty to take knowledge to his
　Majefty, from your Lordfhip, by the inclofed,
that, much to my comfort, I underftand his Majefty
doth not forget me nor forfake me, but hath a
gracious inclination to me, and taketh care of me;
and to thank his Majefty for the fame. I perceive,
by fome fpeech, that paffed between your Lordfhip
and Mr. Meautys, that fome wretched detractor
hath told you, that it were ftrange I fhould be in

debt;

debt; for that I could not but have received an hundred thousand pound gifts since I had the seal; which is an abominable falsehood. Such tales as these made St. James say, that the *tongue is a fire,* and *itself fired from Hell,* whither when these tongues shall return, they will *beg a drop of water to cool them.* I praise God for it, I never took peny for any benefice or ecclesiastical living; I never took peny for releasing any thing I stopped at the seal; I never took peny for any commission, or things of that nature; I never shared with any servant for any second or inferior profit. My offences I have myself recorded, wherein I studied, as a good confessant, guiltiness, and not excuse; and therefore I hope it leaves me fair to the King's grace, and will turn many men's hearts to me.

As for my debts, I shewed them your Lordship, when you saw the little house and the farm, besides a little wood or desert, which you saw not.

If these things were not true, although the joys of the penitent be sometimes more than the joys of the innocent, I could not be as I am.

God bless you, and reward you for your constant love to me. I rest, &c.

Draught of a Letter to the Marquis of BUCKING-HAM, *not sent (f).*

My Lord,

I Say to myself, that your Lordship hath forsaken me; and I think I am one of the last, that findeth it, and in nothing more, than that twice at London

(f) Among Lord Bacon's printed letters, is one without a date, in which he complains, as in this, that he *being twice now in London* the Marquis *did not vouchsafe to see him.*

your

your Lordſhip would not vouchſafe to ſee me, though the latter time I begged it of you.   If your Lordſhip lack any juſtification about York-houſe, good my Lord, think of it better; for I aſſure your Lordſhip, that motion to me was to me as a ſecond ſentence; for I conceived it ſentenced me to the loſs of that, which I thought was ſaved from the former ſentence, which is your love and favour.   But ſure it could not be that pelting matter, but the being out of ſight, out of uſe, and the ill offices done me, perhaps, by ſuch, as have your ear.   Thus I think, and thus I ſpeak; for I am far enough from any baſeneſs or detracting, but ſhall ever love and honour you, howſoever I be

Your forſaken friend and freed ſervant,

Fr. St. Alban.

To the Marquis of Buckingham.

My very good Lord,

IT is in vain to cure the accidents of a diſeaſe, except the cauſe be found, and removed. I know adverſity is apprehenſive; but I fear it is too true, that now I have loſt honour, power, profit, and liberty, I have, in the end, loſt that, which, to me, was more dear than all the reſt, which is my friend. A change there is apparent and great; and nothing is more ſure, than that nothing hath proceeded from and ſince my troubles, either towards your Lordſhip or towards the world, which hath made me unworthy of your undeſerved favours or undeſired promiſes. Good my Lord, deal ſo nobly with me, as to let me know, whether I ſtand upright in your favour, that either I may enjoy my wonted comfort, or ſee my griefs together; that I may the better order them;

C c 3   though,

though, if your Lordſhip ſhould never think more of me, yet your former favours ſhould bind me to be

Your Lordſhip's moſt obliged

and faithful ſervant,

FR. ST. ALBAN.

To the Marquis of BUCKINGHAM.

' **My very good Lord,**

THIS extreme winter hath turned, with me, a weakneſs of body into a ſtate, that I cannot call health, but rather ſickneſs, and that more dangerous than felt, as whereby I am not likely to be able to wait upon your Lordſhip, as I deſired, your Lordſhip being the perſon, of whom I promiſe myſelf more almoſt than of any other; and, again, to whom, in all loving affection, I deſire no leſs to approve myſelf a true friend and ſervant. My deſire to your Lordſhip is to admit this gentleman, my kinſman and approved friend, to explain to you my buſineſs, whereby to ſave further length of letter, or the trouble of your Lordſhip's writing back.

To Mr. TOBIE MATTHEW.

Good Mr. Matthew,

THE event of the buſineſs, whereof you write, is, it may be, for the beſt: for ſeeing my Lord, of himſelf, beginneth to come about, *quorſum* as yet? I could not in my heart ſuffer my Lord Digby to go hence without my thanks and acknow-

ledgements.

ledgements. I fend my Letter open, which I pray feal and deliver. Particulars I would not touch.

Your moft affectionate and affured friend,

Fr. St. Alban.

To Mr. Tobie Matthew.

Good Mr. Matthew,

WHEN you write by pieces, it fheweth your continual care; for a flufh of memory is not fo much; and I fhall be always, on my part, ready to watch for you, as you for me.

I will not fail, when I write to the Lord Marquis, to thank his Lordfhip for the meffage, and to name the nuntius. And, to tell you plainly, this care, they fpeak of, concerning my eftate, was more than I looked for at this time; and it is that, which pleafeth me beft. For my defires reach but to a fat *otium.* That is truth; and fo would I have all men think, except the greateft; for I know patents, *abfque aliquid inde reddendo*, are not fo eafily granted.

I pray my fervice to the Spanifh Ambaffador, and prefent him my humble thanks for his favour. I am much his fervant; and afhes may be good for fomewhat. I ever reft

Your moft affectionate and affured friend,

Fr. St. Alban.

I have fought for your little book, and cannot find it. I had it one day with me in my coach. But fure it is fafe; for I feldom lofe books or papers.

To the Lord Viscount ST. ALBAN.

Moſt honoured Lord,

I Have received your great and noble token and favour of the 9th of April, and can but return the humbleſt of my thanks for your Lordſhip's vouchſafing ſo to viſit this pooreſt and unworthieſt of your ſervants. It doth me good at heart, that, although I be not where I was in place, yet I am in the fortune of your Lordſhip's favour, if I may call that fortune, which I obſerve to be ſo unchangeable. I pray hard, that it may once come in my power to ſerve you for it; and who can tell, but that, as *fortis imaginatio generat caſum,* ſo ſtrange deſires may do as much? Sure I am, that mine are ever waiting on your Lordſhip; and wiſhing as much happineſs, as is due to your incomparable virtue, I humbly do your Lordſhip reverence.

> Your Lordſhip's moſt obliged,
>
>> and humble ſervant,
>>
>>> TOBIE MATTHEW.

POSTC. The moſt prodigious wit, that ever I knew of my nation, and of this ſide of the ſea, is of your Lordſhip's name, though he be known by another.

To the Lord Archbiſhop of YORK (g).

My very good Lord,

I Muſt uſe a better ſtyle, than mine own, in ſaying, *Amor tuus undequaque ſe oſtendit ex literis tuis*

(g) Dr. Tobie Matthew.

proximis,

proximis, for which I give your Grace many thanks, and so, with more confidence, continue my suit to your Lordship for a lease absolute for twenty one years of the house, being the number of years, which my father and my predecessors fulfilled in it. A good fine requires certainty of term; and I am well assured, that the charge I have expended, in reparations, amounting to 1000 marks at least already, is more than hath been laid out by the tenants, that have been in it since my remembrance, answerable to my particular circumstance, that I was born there, and am like to end my days there. Neither can I hold my hand, but, upon this encouragement, am like to be doing still, which tendeth to the improvement, in great measure, of the inheritance of your fee by superlapidations, if I may so call it, instead of dilapidations, wherewith otherwise it might be charged.

And whereas a state for life is a certainty, and not so well seen how it wears, a term of years makes me more depending upon you and your succession.

For the providing of your Lordship and your successors a house, it is part of the former covenant, wherein I desired not to be released.

So assuring myself of your grant and perfecting of this my suit; and assuring your Grace of my earnest desire and continual readiness to deserve well of you and yours chiefly, and likewise of the fee in any the causes or preeminences thereof, I commend your Grace to God's goodness, resting, &c.

☞ *The following letter being omitted in its proper place, between p. 44 and 45, is inserted from the original in the Advocate's library at Edinburgh.*

To the KING.

It may please your most excellent Majesty,

WE have, with all possible care and diligence, considered Cotton's *(h)* cause, the former and the latter, touching the book and the letter in the gilt

(h) The case of this gentleman will render the detail of it necessary for the illustration of this letter; and the circumstances of it, not known in our history, may be thought to deserve the reader's attention. He was a native of the West of England, and a recusant, against whom a proclamation was issued in June 1613, charging him with high treason against the King and State for having published a very scandalous and railing book against his Majesty, under the title of *Balaam's Ass*, which was dropt in the gallery at White-Hall. Just at the time of publishing this proclamation, he happened to cross the Thames, and enquiring of the watermen what news? they, not knowing him, told him of the proclamation. At landing, he muffled himself up in his cloke, to avoid being known; but had not gone many paces, when one Mr. Maine, a friend of his, meeting and discovering him, warned him of his danger; and being asked what he would advise him to do, recommended it to him to surrender himself; which he did to the Earl of Southampton. He denied himself to be the author of the libel: but his study being searched, among his papers were found many parts of the book, together with relics of those persons, who had been executed for the gunpowder treason, as one of Sir Everard Digby's fingers, a toe of Thomas Percy, some other part of Catesby or Rookewood, and a piece of one of Peter Lambert's ribs. He was kept prisoner in the Tower till March 161³, when the true author of the libel was discovered to be John Williams, a lawyer. The discovery was owing to this accident: a pursuivant in want of money, and desirous to get some by his employment, waited at the Spanish Ambassador's door, to see if he could light upon any prey. At last came out Mr. Williams, unknown to the pursuivant; but carrying.

gilt apple, and have advifedly perufed and weighed
all the examinations and collections, which were
formerly taken ; wherein we might attribute a good
deal of worthy induftry and watchful inquiry to my
Lord of Canterbury. We thought fit alfo to take
fome new examinations ; which was the caufe we
certified no fooner. Upon the whole matter, we
find the caufe of his imprifonment juft, and the
fufpicions and prefumptions many and great ; which
we little need to mention, becaufe your Majefty
did relate and inforce them to us in better perfection, than we can exprefs them. But, neverthelefs, the proofs feem to us to amount to this,
that it was poffible he fhould be the man ; and that

rying, in his conceit, the countenance of a prieft. The purfuivant, therefore, followed him to his inn, where Williams
having mounted his horfe, the purfuivant came to him, and
told him, that he muft fpeak a word or two with him. " Marry,
" with all my heart, *faid Williams :* what is your pleafure ?"
You muft light, anfwered the purfuivant ; *for you are a prieft.*
" A prieft ? *replied Williams :* I have a good warrant to the
" contrary ; for I have a wife and children." Being, however, obliged to difmount, the purfuivant fearched him ; and
in his pocket was found a bundle of papers fealed up ; which
the purfuivant going to open, Williams made fome refiftance,
pretending they were evidences of a gentleman, whofe law-bu-
fineffes he tranfacted. The purfuivant infifting upon opening
the papers, among them was found *Balaam's Afs,* with new an-
notations ; of which, upon examination, *Williams* confeffed himfelf to be the author. He was brought to the trial, and condemned at the King's Bench at Weftminfter the 3d of May 1619,
and executed at Charing-Crofs on the 5th. MS. letters of Mr.
Thomas Lorkin to Sir Thomas Puckering, Bart. dated at London,
June the 24th and 30th 1613, and March the 16th 161⅞, and
May the 4th and 5th 1619, among the Harleian MSS. Vol. 7002.
See likewife *Camdeni annales Regis Jacobi,* p. 43, 44. It is but
juftice to the memory of our great antiquary, Sir Robert Cotton,
Bart. to remark here a miftake of Dr. Thomas Smith in his
Life of Sir Robert, p. 25. prefixed to his catalogue of the Cot-
tonian library, where he has confounded the Cotton, mentioned
in the beginning of this note, with Sir Robert Cotton, and erroneoufly fuppofed, that the fufpicion of having written the libel
had fallen upon the latter.

it

it was probable likewife, he was the man: but no convicting proofs, that may fatisfy a jury of life and death, or that may make us take it upon our confcience, or to think it agreeable to your Majefty's honour (which, next our confcience to God, is the deareft thing to us on earth) to bring it upon the ftage: which, notwithftanding we, in all humblenefs, fubmit to your Majefty's better judgement. For his liberty, and the manner of his delivery (he having fo many notes of a dangerous man) we leave it to your princely wifdom. And fo, commending your Majefty to God's precious cuftody, we reft

Your Majefty's moft humble

and bounden fervants,

2e Jan. 1613.

FR. BACON.
H. MONTAGU.
H. YELVERTON.

INDEX.

INDEX.

INDEX.

I N D E X.

BARN-

DON-

INDEX.

INDEX.

the

MON-

INDEX.

INDEX.

INDEX.

FINIS.

CX 001 650 837

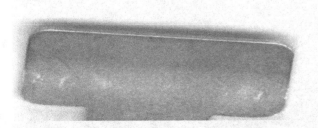

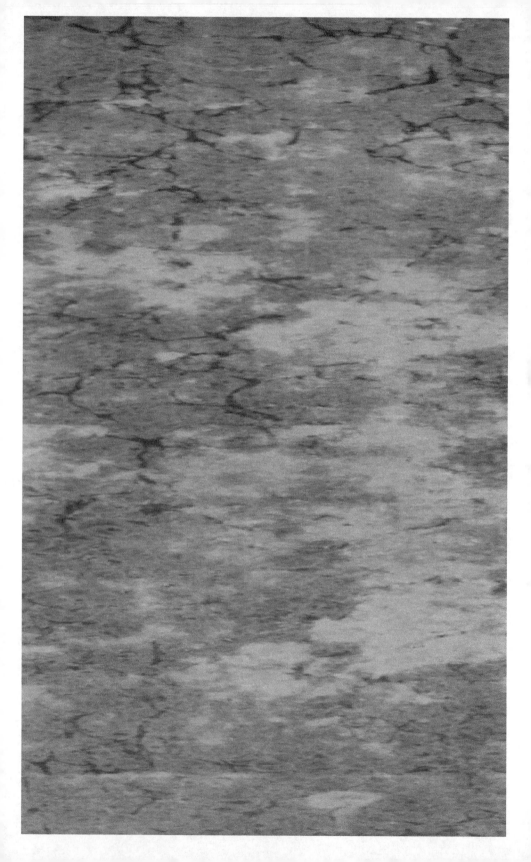

Check Out More Titles From HardPress Classics Series In
this collection we are offering thousands of classic and hard
to find books. This series spans a vast array of subjects – so
you are bound to find something of interest to enjoy reading
and learning about.

Subjects:
Architecture
Art
Biography & Autobiography
Body, Mind &Spirit
Children & Young Adult
Dramas
Education
Fiction
History
Language Arts & Disciplines
Law
Literary Collections
Music
Poetry
Psychology
Science
…and many more.

Visit us at www.hardpress.net